Ike's Spies

Eisenhower and the Espionage Establishment

Also by Stephen E. Ambrose

Halleck: Lincoln's Chief of Staff (1962)

Upton and the Army (1964)

Duty, Honor, Country: A History of West Point (1966)

Eisenhower and Berlin, 1945: The Decision to Halt at the Elbe (1967)

The Supreme Commander:
The War Years of General Dwight D. Eisenhower (1970)

Crazy Horse and Custer: The Parallel Lives of Two American Warriors
(1975)

Pegasus Bridge: June 6, 1944 (1985)

Nixon, Vol. 1: The Education of a Politician, 1913–1962 (1987)

Nixon, Vol. 2: The Triumph of a Politician, 1962–1972 (1989)

Eisenhower: Soldier and President (1990)

Nixon, Vol. 3: Ruin and Recovery, 1973–1990 (1991)

*Band of Brothers: E Company, 506th Regiment, 101st Airborne from
Normandy to Hitler's Eagle's Nest* (1992)

D-Day: June 6, 1944—The Climactic Battle of World War II (1994)

*Undaunted Courage: Meriwether Lewis, Thomas Jefferson, and the Opening
of the American West* (1996)

*Citizen Soldiers: The U.S. Army from the Normandy Beaches to the Bulge to
the Surrender of Germany—June 7, 1944–May 7, 1945* (1997)

Americans at War (1997)

The Victors: Eisenhower and His Boys: The Men of World War II (1998)

Comrades: Brothers, Fathers, Heroes, Sons, Pals (1999)

*Nothing Like It in the World: The Men Who Built the Transcontinental
Railroad, 1863–1869* (2000)

The Wild Blue: The Men and Boys Who Flew the B-24s Over Germany
(2001)

To America: Personal Reflections of an Historian (2002)

This Vast Land: A Young Man's Journal of the Lewis and Clark Expedition
(2003)

Ike's Spies

*Eisenhower and the
Espionage Establishment*

Stephen E. Ambrose

with Richard H. Immerman

Research Associate

Anchor Books
A Division of Random House, Inc.
New York

FIRST ANCHOR BOOKS EDITION, JANUARY 2012

The Cataloging-in-Publication Data is on file at the
Library of Congress.

Anchor ISBN: 978-0-307-94660-7

www.anchorbooks.com

Printed in the United States of America
10 9 8 7 6 5 4 3 2

For William B. Hesseltine, 1902-1964
and
T. Harry Williams, 1909-1979
great teachers, both

Preface

Between World War I and World War II, the U.S. Government did almost no spying on anyone. Spying was not a gentleman's profession, it was thought, and anyway an isolationist America had no need for spies. Harry Truman reverted to this position immediately after World War II.

But during the war, the United States was forced to use spies. The success of the British Secret Service had impressed Dwight Eisenhower. As Supreme Commander of the Allied Forces in Europe, Ike was the beneficiary of information obtained by the cream of British society, academia, and the arts. He was also at the center of a successful deception program that fooled the Germans time after time, while simultaneously he commanded a series of covert operations that played a crucial role in the final victory.

So, when Eisenhower became President, he encouraged the growth of the CIA, which under his direction and orders grew in size, expanding the scope of its activities and becoming one of America's chief weapons in the Cold War. It helped to overthrow governments in the Middle East and Latin America, tried to do so in Central and Eastern Europe, flew spy flights over the Soviet Union and other countries, and hatched assassination plots against foreign leaders. To its critics, it was a rogue elephant, totally out of control; to its defenders, it was a vital instrument in the fight to keep the Free World free. To Ike, it was necessary.

1981

Contents

Part One

WORLD WAR II
1942-45

CHAPTER ONE

Churchill Introduces Ike to the ULTRA Secret

LATE JUNE, 1942. One of those beginning-of-summer days in Britain when it seems that twilight will last forever. At Chequers, the Prime Minister's official weekend retreat, the butler informs Winston Churchill that the car with the American general in it has just arrived. Churchill goes to the front door to personally greet his overnight guest. The Prime Minister watches as the general emerges from his car and reaches for his bags.

STUDYING THE OFFICER, Churchill may well have thought of how little he knew about this man to whom he was about to tell so much. Churchill had seen him in action at high-level staff conferences, knew that he was thorough, well-prepared, thoughtful, and respected by his peers. Churchill had also been told that he was immensely popular with his associates, who called him "Ike" as a mark of their affection.

Churchill realized that this Ike had Chief of Staff George C. Marshall's unlimited confidence, so much so that Marshall had just made General Dwight D. Eisenhower the commander of the American military forces in Great Britain. Marshall had indicated that he felt there was no job too big for Ike. Churchill had also been impressed when told that Eisenhower had spent five years writing speeches for Marshall's predecessor, General Douglas MacArthur, whose standards for clarity of expression and thought in written English were nearly as high as Churchill's own.

Most of all, Churchill realized that the Supreme Commander for the Anglo-American counteroffensive against Hitler would have to be an American. That was inevitably one of the prices Britain would have to pay to keep America from turning her back on the European war and concentrating instead on Japan. Knowing that President Franklin Roosevelt stood almost in awe of General Marshall, and would certainly not buck him on a purely military assignment, and knowing Marshall's attitude toward Eisenhower, Churchill realized that this general walking toward him, suitcase in one hand, briefcase in the other, would be in command of the first Anglo-American amphibious assault since the French and Indian War.

Churchill had called Ike to him because the time had come to introduce the future Supreme Commander to the wizard war, that silent backstage battle between the British intelligentsia and the German intelligentsia that was as critical as it was unknown. This big, hearty, raw-boned, grinning Yank was a professional soldier, fifty-two years old, with nearly thirty years of active duty, but he knew almost nothing about codes or code breaking, about new weapons, or about spies, counterspies, covert actions, or any other aspect of the dark arts. His ignorance came about because the U. S. Army and the nation it defended had virtually no intelligence arm. In 1929, Secretary of War Henry L. Stimson had abolished the small code-breaking apparatus of the Army on the grounds that "gentlemen don't read each other's mail." The intelligence branch of the Army was so small, unimportant, in fact despised, that it was widely assumed that no officer of ability ever went into it.

The man approaching the front door at Chequers was truly an innocent abroad. Waiting for him with a cigar in one hand, some documents in the other, and a smile on his face, was Churchill, who delighted in the task of introducing this naïve Yank to the labyrinth of the British Secret Service. Over in the New World they might be saying that Britain was finished, that her day was done, and Churchill knew painfully well that the British could never by themselves produce the guns or divisions in sufficient number to overcome the Germans, but—by God!—in this war of brains, the British were the best in the world, and Churchill was justifiably proud of that fact.

Ike put down his bags and in his warm, friendly, casual American fashion stuck out his hand. Churchill shook hands heartily, meanwhile looking Ike up and down. As Eisenhower removed his hat, two features stood out—his full grin, and his large, prominent forehead. Both the grin and the bald pate seemed as wide, broad, and sunny as the Kansas prairie.

He had no middle-aged sag, either under his eyes or around his belly. Instead, he had the broad shoulders and powerful build of a star athlete (which he had been), and he carried himself lightly, almost catlike. His hands were large, his handshake firm. He looked Churchill right in the eye, not trying to avoid either his gaze or his first questions. Overall, he gave the impression of straightforwardness, strength, boundless energy, and great determination. Churchill liked him at once.

For his part, Ike was meeting Churchill privately for the first time. Churchill had the appearance and manners of a British aristocrat, while Ike was only a year or two away from having been an obscure colonel in a minuscule army. Despite the difference in their backgrounds, prestige, power, and reputation, Ike was not awestruck. He was curious about this great man who had rallied the British people to stand alone for a year against Hitler and his Nazis, and he was anxious to get along with Churchill. Together with Roosevelt, Stalin, and Hitler, the Prime Minister was one of the four best-known and most powerful men in the world. Everyone in America had seen his picture, cigar clamped between his teeth, standing over the ruins of bombed-out London, holding his first two fingers apart, high in the air, in the V-for-Victory signal. Plump, almost cherubic in the face, he could resemble a bulldog when he was determined to have his way (which was nearly all the time). His face would become a violent red when he was angry or crossed. He too had boundless energy and had therefore stuck his finger into every pie in Britain, most of all the war of wits with the Germans, which excited his imagination and limitless curiosity.

Through cocktails, through dinner, through the brandy, coffee, and more brandy, on into the early hours of the morning, Ike listened enthralled as the P.M. briefed him on the secret war. He explained radar, its shortcomings and its promise, how it was being used in the Battle of Britain, what the British hoped it could do in the future. Churchill fairly glowed as he described the Battle of the Beams. German night-bombers were finding their targets over blacked-out London by flying along radio beams sent by transmitters located on the French coast. Crossbeams, sent from another spot on the coast, intersected the beam over the target, letting the German bombers know the precise moment to drop their bombs. A young British scientist, R. V. Jones, had figured out how the system worked, which gave the British an opportunity to jam the signals, or misdirect the Germans, or mislead them into dropping their bombs over open countryside.[1]

With a chuckle, Churchill described some of the wilder ideas British scientists had produced, such as suspending time bombs by parachute in the path of approaching German bomber formations, or the search for "death rays" for both humans and engines. An idea Churchill liked and intended to follow up was to take masses of seaweed, mix them with huge quantities of dry ice, and thereby create an unsinkable aircraft carrier that could be towed up and down the coast of Europe.

Ike was never tempted to laugh, however absurd some ideas seemed, because he knew that it was this same Churchill who had, in 1914, found private funds to support the research for and development of a new weapon of war that all the generals laughed at. That weapon became the tank, and in 1917 Ike had been one of the first officers of the U. S. Army to recognize its potential. He took command of the "Tank Corps" and trained it at Gettysburg, Pennsylvania. In late 1918, within a week of his receiving orders to take his unit to France to enter the battle, the armistice came. Ike had therefore never held a combat command, but his appreciation of the tank—and his respect for Churchill for his key role in its creation—remained undiminished.

Churchill told Ike of some of the fears his scientists had with respect to what the Germans were developing in the way of new weapons. The German Navy was making rapid progress with its diesel submarines, while the Luftwaffe was thought to be experimenting with some sort of jet-propelled aircraft. Rocket research was also going forward. It was thought that the Germans might have an operational pilotless aircraft, or even a true rocket, within a year or two. Another innovation was a bomb with eyes—the Germans were experimenting with a ballistic bomb which would be steered from the launching aircraft on the receipt of pictures "televised" back by the bomb.

More cheerful news was that German atomic research seemed to be misdirected. Churchill and Roosevelt, meanwhile, had agreed to pool their resources, and British physicists—along with some of the best European physicists, who had fled Hitler's Europe to work at their specialties—were now participating fully in the Manhattan Project in America.

As for spies, Churchill was pleased to report that the British had managed to maintain contact with the Polish and French secret services through MI-6 of the British Secret Service, headed by Brigadier Stewart Menzies. The Special Operations Executive (SOE), a branch of Menzies' Secret Service, was establishing contacts with the French underground forces. Best of all, Menzies believed that the British had managed to identify and then either execute or "turn" every German spy in the United Kingdom, which if true meant that the British Secret Service controlled every piece of information the Germans received from their spies. There was rich potential in such a situation.

(Churchill would not have been quite so pleased with MI-6 if he had known that the Germans had done the same to his MI-6 agents in Holland. The British had parachuted sabotage agents into that country, but the Germans had caught the first one and forced him to send back suitable messages to London. The Germans then knew where subsequent agents were to be dropped, as MI-6 sent radio messages to their agents to be ready for them. The Nazis captured every one of them, at the same time sending messages back to London that led MI-6 to believe that the agents were at large and operating a successful campaign.[2])

Finally, triumphantly, Churchill turned to what he called ULTRA. Before explaining the term, however, he rather dramatically made Ike swear that he would never expose himself to capture during the remainder of the war, which meant explicitly that he was never to go into a war zone or fly over one. Everyone who knew about ULTRA had to make that promise, Churchill explained, because this was the most valuable secret of the war, and the Germans had their own ways of making captured men talk.

ULTRA, Churchill then declared, was the term the British used for their systematic breaking of the German code. By itself, difficult though the feat may have been (and was, in fact), breaking an enemy's code was not a decisive factor, primarily because the enemy changed his code at regular intervals, and when he did, the code breakers had to start all over at point zero. But in this case, a delighted Churchill declared, the Germans believed they had an absolutely safe encoding machine, which was called Enigma. It consisted of two machines somewhat like electric typewriters, which were attached to three rotating drums, which in turn were interconnected by an intricate set of electric wires. An operator would type a plain text on one typewriter; the drums would rotate according to a predetermined setting, and the other typewriter would rap out the encoded message, which was then sent over the airwaves. At the receiving end, all the operator needed to do was put the machine on the proper setting, feed in the encoded message, and take out the plain text.

The Germans believed the system to be foolproof because even if the enemy had an Enigma machine, it would do him no good without the settings. The possible variations were numbered in the tens of thousands and a code breaker would go crazy before cracking even one of them. Enigma could produce an almost infinite number of cipher alphabets merely by changing the keying procedure.

But the British *had* broken the system, and the Germans did not know it, which gave the British a major asset in the Battle of Britain and the Battle of the Atlantic. The way in which the British had earned this asset was in itself a fascinating story, involving spies, double-agents, traitors, and the cream of British universities.[3]

The French and the Poles had both made contributions to ULTRA. A Polish Jew who had worked on an Enigma machine in Berlin managed to contact MI-6; the British arranged to get him from Warsaw to London to direct the building of a duplicate. The French had obtained earlier, commercial models of the Enigma machine, which they made available to MI-6. With these examples before them, the British proceeded to construct a strange contraption, eight feet by eight feet, called "the Bomb," which was installed at Hut Three, a Nissen hut under the trees at a wretched estate named Bletchley Park. The Bomb, as described by its chief engineer, Harold Keen, was not a computer, and "there was no other machine like it. It was unique, built especially for this purpose. Neither was it a complex tabulating machine, which was sometimes used in cryptanalysis. What it did was to match the electrical circuits of Enigma. Its secret was in the internal wiring of Enigma's rotors, which 'the Bomb' sought to imitate."[4]

Bletchley Park, or BP as it inevitably came to be called, soon had an overflow of British intelligentsia. Nissen huts covered the grounds. They were staffed by German-language experts, military technicians, and code breakers, with a heavy emphasis on mathematicians, which meant a high number of eccentrics and "absent-minded" professors.

"There was an amazing spirit at the place," Alfred Friendly, who was there, later wrote. "Morale was high because everyone knew the fantastically successful results of our daily-and-nightly endeavours. It was one place in the military where there was no sense of futility, or useless work or of nonsense. Had he served there, Heller would have had no material for *Catch 22*."[5] William Filby, a Britisher who served through the war at BP, later scoffed at the idea of a vacation or even a short leave. "You couldn't wait to get back in the morning to see what had happened overnight," he said in an interview. "It was like your baby—you never wanted to leave it."[6] At BP, in brief, there was a tremendous feeling of excitement and contribution. Churchill conveyed some of that feeling to Eisenhower in his description of the place and its work.

Breaking the Enigma secrets open had been a brilliant team effort, but there were problems. The codes needed to be broken on a continuous basis, as the Germans were consistently changing the key. The new settings had to be found before each new code could be mastered. As the war went along the thousands of men and women working at BP got better at it, but in the early years they were baffled more often than not. ULTRA was not an important factor in the August–September 1940 Battle of Britain; even by October, BP, after straining every resource of human intelligence and endurance, could break only one message in three in time to act on the information. With the decoded messages, as R. V. Jones pointed out, "I was able to tell the Duty Air Commodore at Fighter Command the exact place of the German bomber attack, the time of the first bomb to within ten minutes or so, the expected ground speed of the bombers, their line of approach to within 100 yards, and their height to within two to three hundred metres. Could any air defence system ask for more?"

And yet, the bombers still got through. Jones complained that "reading the Enigma signals was just like reading tomorrow's paper today." As an extreme example, he recorded that the British knew of the German invasion plans for the island of Crete at least three weeks in advance, and still could not stop the enemy. In part this was because of British military weakness, in part because they dared make only the most limited use of their ULTRA-derived information.[7]

Ronald Lewin, author of *Ultra Goes to War*, the first detailed examination of the use of ULTRA in the campaigns of World War II, writes, "It was impossible to risk disclosing its intelligence to those in actual contact with the enemy, or liable to capture for other reasons, even though the knowledge might improve their chance of success or survival."[8] So it was at Crete.

An inability to take advantage of the information, or an inability to use it for fear of revealing its source, put definite limits on what ULTRA could contribute. Another limitation was distribution, getting the right information to the right man at the right time, and without tipping their hand. Only the very highest-ranking officers in the British service knew about ULTRA. It was the best-kept secret of the war, a secret that lasted for almost a full generation after the Nazi surrender.

Then, in 1974, Group Captain F. W. Winterbotham revealed *The Ultra Secret* in a book by that name.* Winterbotham was the officer who brought the ULTRA intercepts directly to Churchill, who delighted in reading Hitler's messages. Because Winterbotham was so close to the Prime Minister throughout the war, his memoirs were filled with inside stories that made an exciting tale even more appealing.

In the mid-1970s *The Ultra Secret* came as a surprise to the public, as well as to most World War II scholars. Its immediate reception was one of puzzlement by the public, anger by the scholars (they would have to rewrite their books). Why, the public wondered, if the Allies listened in on everything the Germans said to each other over the radio, did it take so long to win the war? And why was the victory so costly?

Churchill's initial reactions to ULTRA were similar. In 1941 and throughout 1942, for example, he kept reading Rommel's messages from Africa, messages in which Rommel complained that his gasoline had not arrived, nor his spare parts, nor his reinforcements, nor his new tanks, nor his communications equipment. Because Churchill knew that Rommel was short on everything, he could not understand why his Middle East commanders hesitated to attack,

---

* He did so "to the mortification of those of us who had kept our oath of secrecy," according to one insider.[9]

and one by one he sacked them. Thanks to ULTRA, Churchill knew what the generals knew, and it made the generals furious and apprehensive because it invited criticism by Churchill, who was always at his happiest when he was dressing down a general.

But although Churchill called ULTRA an oracle (which it was when it worked) and the key to victory (which it could be if the right lock were found), it could provide only intelligence, not a strategy or the power to enforce one. General Bernard Law Montgomery pointed out to Churchill time and time again the obvious fact that knowing about Rommel's supply shortages did not solve the British supply problems.

The Germans never caught on to the ULTRA operation, however. They used Enigma to the last day of the war. So the question persists: Why did the Allies not win sooner, at less cost? An American football analogy may help the perspective here. Suppose you were coaching against a National Football League team, and your intelligence system was so good that you knew not only the height, weight, speed, and characteristics of every opponent (all gathered from open sources, mainly films) but you also knew every one of your opponent's plays. Even better, suppose you managed to hook up a radio transmitter in the quarterback's helmet, while each of your players had receivers in their helmets. Your information about the enemy's strength and intentions would then be perfect, as would your system of getting that information into the right hands in time to act on it.

But if your team consisted of eleven out-of-shape office workers who had never played together and who were all smaller and slower than their opposite numbers, all that perfect information would do you no good. The professional team would still score on every play.

Code breaking could work both ways, of course, since the Allies also used the radio. Patrick Beesly, who worked in the Naval Intelligence Division of the Admiralty, points out in his excellent work *Very Special Intelligence* that "no service in any of the belligerent powers during the Second World War succeeded in keeping every cipher it used secure." Before Winterbotham broke the ULTRA secret, the ups and downs in the crucial Battle of the Atlantic were inexplicable. German sinkings of Allied merchant vessels would rise dramatically one month, then fall off sharply while Allied sinkings of German submarines went up. The explanation lay with the thousands of men and women, in Germany and England, who toiled night and day to break the other side's code. Success at this tremendously difficult and demanding task was immediately translated into ships sunk at sea. The ups and downs came as one side or the other changed its code, or broke the code the enemy was using that month.

The British won the Battle of the Atlantic partly because the Royal Navy was good, partly because of American reinforcements, but mainly because Churchill's code breakers were better than Hitler's. To a lesser extent this was also true on land, although some of Rommel's victories in North Africa came about because his people had broken the British code and were reading the radio traffic. Beesly points out, "While each nation accepted the fact that its own cryptanalysts could read at least some of their enemy's ciphers, they were curiously blind to the fact that they themselves were being subjected to exactly the same form of eavesdropping."[10]

Curious, too, was the fact that some Americans had to be sold on the value of ULTRA. Ike fairly beamed as Churchill brought him in on the secret, but others were to be dubious at best, especially Eisenhower's deputy, General Mark Clark. Shortly after Eisenhower's visit to Chequers, Winterbotham went to Eisenhower's headquarters in London to brief Clark. Accompanying him was the legendary Menzies, head of MI-6, "to lend a bit of weight to the proceedings." Eisenhower introduced Clark and three members of his intelligence staff, then excused himself since he already knew about ULTRA. It is a measure of the tightness of security around ULTRA that this visit by Winterbotham and Menzies did not get entered into Eisenhower's official office log, which makes it a unique event.

Winterbotham recorded what happened: "Mark Clark was restless from the start. I explained not only what the source was, but in an endeavour to catch Mark Clark's interest gave some pertinent examples of what it could do. I had intended to follow this with an explanation of how the information would reach him, and the security regulations which accompanied its use. But Mark Clark didn't appear to believe the first part, and after a quarter of an hour he excused himself and his officers on the grounds that he had something else to do."[11]

Patton was equally cavalier. When Winterbotham sought to

brief him in Algiers, Patton cut him short, saying, "You know, young man, I think you had better tell all this to my Intelligence staff, I don't go much on this sort of thing myself. You see I just like fighting."[12]

Ike was not so foolish. He saw at once the value of ULTRA, both immediate and potential, just as he responded to everything Churchill had told him. One of the reasons Ike had won Marshall's confidence was his openness to new ideas, new techniques, new approaches to old problems. Marshall liked to say that Ike was broad-based, not narrow or traditional. Churchill and Eisenhower were neither scientists nor engineers, but they both loved gadgets, inventions, technology, especially when the new devices could help them win a war.

As Ike drove back to London after his evening at Chequers, he reflected on how lucky the United States was to have the British for allies. What an inheritance to fall into! Churchill, for his part, looked forward to working with this American general, who did not seem so stuck in the mud, so resistant to scientific and technological change, as his British generals. Together, they would make a fine team.

CHAPTER TWO

Preparing the TORCH

DAWN, SEPTEMBER 15, 1942. A group of Flying Fortresses is about to take off from an Army Air Force field near Washington, D.C. Their destination is Prestwick, Scotland, where the big bombers will be thrown into the battle raging over Europe's skies. A tall passenger called McGowan, in a U. S. Army uniform and wearing the insignia of a lieutenant colonel, ducks under the wing of one of the planes and scrambles aboard. He sighs with relief—sure he hasn't been seen.

MCGOWAN WAS RELIEVED because he was not the man he seemed to be. He had nothing to do with the highly publicized air war that his plane was about to join. His uniform was fake, his name was false, his instructions were secret. Those instructions had come directly from the President himself, after a secret meeting at Hyde Park. Franklin Roosevelt's last words to McGowan were, "Don't tell anybody in the State Department about this. That place is a sieve!" The disguise came about because Army Chief of Staff George C. Marshall believed "nobody ever pays any attention to a lieutenant colonel." McGowan's secrecy was a result of an order from the Commander of the European Theater of Operations, U. S. Army, Lieutenant General Dwight David Eisenhower.[1]

"McGowan's" real name was Robert Murphy. He had been a State Department employee for twenty years, but was now on special assignment, reporting directly to the President. His mission was to brief Eisenhower on the political and military situation in French North Africa, and on OSS activities in the area. Murphy thought all the secrecy stuff rather silly and was not inclined to take it seriously until the morning of September 16, when his plane touched down at Prestwick. Murphy got out to stretch while the plane was being refueled for the flight to London and heard a familiar voice call out, "Why, Bob! What are you doing here?" It was an old friend from the Foreign Service, Don Coster. Eisenhower's chief security officer, Colonel Julius Holmes, had Coster arrested almost before he finished speaking. As Murphy gaped, Coster was hustled off by two burly policemen.

At noon, Murphy landed at a military airfield near London. There he was picked up in an unmarked car driven by Lieutenant Kay Summersby, Eisenhower's personal driver. They went by a circuitous route around the outskirts of London until they arrived in midafternoon at Ike's private retreat, Telegraph Cottage.

The first of Ike's spies had come to report. Over the next twenty years, Eisenhower would hear hundreds of secret reports from dozens of spies, but none ever surpassed Murphy's in excitement, if only because his was the first. And the first thing Ike wanted to know from Murphy was, "Who is your boss?"[2]

Murphy really did not know. Although his paycheck came from the Department of State, he was under direct orders from the President to avoid all contact with Secretary of State Cordell Hull or any other member of the department hierarchy. In Algiers, Murphy directed the activities of a few dozen oss agents, but he did not work for or take orders from the oss. He was the principal American official in North Africa, which was soon a theater of war under Eisenhower's command, but he had no connection with Ike's headquarters. The lines of authority were badly blurred, even nonexistent. In his initial encounter with the world of spies, therefore, Eisenhower had to face problems that would persist for the next two decades and beyond: To whom does the spy report? Who gives him orders? Who decides where and when covert operations will take place? In short, who is in charge?

IT WAS NOT a new problem to Eisenhower, because he had been involved since 1941 in the attempts to create clear-cut lines of authority for America's first intelligence-gathering and covert-operations agency. On July 11, 1941, Roosevelt, acting at Prime Minister Winston Churchill's suggestion, had created a new office, the Coordinator of Information (COI) under William Donovan, who had insisted on a military title and had been granted the rank of colonel. FDR's directive to Donovan had given him a wide scope, and the President's fondness for Donovan and his interest in the secret war had led him to give virtually unlimited funds to the COI.

The arrangement upset the military, where the chain of command is sacrosanct even in peacetime. With a worldwide war going on, the Joint Chiefs of Staff wanted to ensure that all activities carried on by Americans anywhere were controlled by them. Donovan, a free-wheeling type who hated restraint of any kind, resisted. Eisenhower became involved four months after Pearl Harbor, when he urged his boss, General Marshall, to advise the President to make the COI directly responsible to the JCS. But the Army did not want to sully its reputation by having its officers engage in spying or subversive actions, so Ike recommended that such work in foreign countries "should be conducted by individuals occupying a civilian rather than a military status." Despite their status, Ike recommended that they "should be subject to the higher control of the Joint Chiefs of Staff."[3]

Marshall accepted Eisenhower's proposal, which remained in effect until June 1942. Meanwhile, there was a furious bureaucratic struggle going on for control of intelligence and covert operations between the Army, the Navy, the State Department, the White House, and various other agencies and departments, all of whom could see that however restricted COI was at the time, its growth potential was unlimited. But in wartime, the military usually gets what it wants, and so it was here. In June 1942, Roosevelt changed the name of COI to Office of Strategic Services, put Donovan at its head, and placed OSS directly under the JCS in the chain of command.[4]

Donovan still hoped that he could operate independently, as FDR had intended that he should, but Eisenhower had not spent a lifetime in the Army without learning the crucial importance of flow charts and lines of authority. After he became commander of the European Theater of Operations and was placed at the head of the invasion force for North Africa (code named TORCH), Ike moved to bring Donovan under his authority. On September 10, a week before Murphy's arrival in London, he got what he wanted. The JCS informed Donovan that his activities in England, Europe, and North Africa were all subject to the supervision and direction of General Eisenhower, including such matters as paying bribe money, propaganda radio broadcasts, equipment to be supplied to guerrilla groups, distribution of leaflets, and the collection and dissemination of intelligence.[5]

That directive put Donovan where Eisenhower wanted him, but what of Murphy? He did not belong to the OSS, although FDR had casually placed OSS agents in North Africa under his authority. Eisenhower would not have anyone in his theater of operations who was not under his command. Both as soldier and later as President, Ike was a self-confessed fanatic on the subject of unity of command, perhaps because he came to command so late in life (he was fifty-two years old when he took over at ETO, his first real command). "As I am responsible for the success of the operations I feel that it is essential that final authority in all matters in that theater rest in me."[6]* Further, it was important that the Allies present the French with "a clean cut and single authority."[7] Roosevelt then made Murphy a "political adviser," responsible directly to Ike.

WITH MURPHY'S STATUS SETTLED, Ike was ready to listen to his report. The two men went out onto the lawn of Telegraph Cottage. They sat down under some pine trees, facing the fifth green of the neighboring golf course. Hedges protected them from curious eyes. Ike listened with what his aide, Harry Butcher, described as "horrified intentness" as Murphy spent the afternoon telling his long and complex story. Murphy, Butcher said, "talked more like an American businessman canvassing the ins and outs of a prospective merger than either a diplomat or a soldier."[9]

Murphy's story was full of plots and intrigues, proposed assassinations, possible coups, secret contacts with the enemy, the whole tangled mess of French politics under the German occupation, and bureaucratic in-fighting among various American agencies as well as between American and British groups maneuvering for power. The military operation Eisenhower was about to launch added to the complications. The United States, along with the British, was

---

* Eisenhower's insistence on control of his own theater was nicely illustrated in November 1942 when movie producer Darryl Zanuck arrived in Algiers to make a movie about the invasion. He acted as if he could go where he wanted, when he wanted, filming whatever he wished. Ike told his subordinate, General Mark Clark, to tell Zanuck "that he will obey my orders as long as he is in this theater, or I will have him out of here so fast he won't know what's happening to him. I am not going to have a bunch of free-lancers dashing around here and flouting established authority. Please tell him this in no uncertain terms."[8]

going to invade a neutral nation in a surprise attack without provocation and without a declaration of war. Murphy's job was to arrange for the active cooperation of the armed forces of the nation being attacked!

On the face of it, this was an absurd situation. It came about as a result of the inglorious surrender of the French Army to Germany in 1940, and the armistice that followed. Hitler had allowed the French to retain administrative control over the southern part of France and over the French colonies, the most important of which was Algeria. The capital of "independent" France was in Vichy; the head of government was the aging hero of World War I, Marshal Henri Pétain. Vichy was collaborationist, but that did not necessarily mean that it was unpopular, especially with the hierarchy in the French Army and in the colonies. Many French leaders in civil service, in business, in the military, and in the Church welcomed a semi-fascist government that emphasized work, discipline, and law and order.

But French political life did not come to an end just because the Germans occupied Paris and Marshal Pétain ruled from Vichy. There were right-wing plotters who hated Pétain, not because of his politics, but because of his supine groveling under the German heel. Democrats and socialists also plotted against the government, while the Communists were beginning to form underground organizations that could someday participate in subversive actions. In the colonies, a few high-ranking officers were casting about for some form of support from the United States or Britain as a preliminary to their breaking free of Vichy. In London, meanwhile, an obscure French general had denounced Pétain as a traitor and claimed that he—Charles de Gaulle—was the true head of the true government of the real France. Most of the French soldiers who had escaped to Britain had rallied to the Gaullist cause. In the French colonies, meanwhile, the native populations were seeking opportunities to exploit France's weakness to win their own independence, and they too looked to the United States for help. Finally, Pétain's highest-ranking military officer, Admiral Jean Darlan, had hinted to the Americans that if they came in force to North Africa, he would be ready to throw in with them.

Marshal Pétain, in short, did not enjoy full and enthusiastic support. No polls were taken, but it is doubtful that even one in ten Frenchmen would have expressed loyalty to Vichy. It was precisely this unpopularity that had made Vichy territory the first objective of the first Allied offensive of World War II. Churchill and Roosevelt had selected North Africa as the target, against the vigorous objections of Generals Marshall and Eisenhower, who wanted to invade France itself, primarily because the politicians needed a sure victory in the initial battle. This was partly for domestic political reasons, but it also served a purpose Churchill and the British thought was essential—"blooding" the green American troops. Far better to make them into veterans by fighting the underequipped, divided, unmotivated, demoralized French in Algeria than by fighting crack Wehrmacht panzer divisions in Normandy or Flanders.

With luck, there might be no fighting at all, or only a few token exchanges of gunfire. The Allies wanted transit rights in Algeria and Tunisia in order to trap General Erwin Rommel's Afrika Korps in a two-front battle, with General Bernard Montgomery's British Eighth Army attacking Rommel's panzers from the east while Ike's troops hit him from the west. But although the Allies wanted French cooperation, they were unwilling to take the French into their confidence. It was assumed among the Allies that no Frenchman could keep a secret, and surprise was essential to success in TORCH.

Murphy told Eisenhower that, despite these and other difficulties, he hoped to obtain full French cooperation once the invasion began. As a career State Department official stationed in North Africa, Murphy, in 1941, had worked out an economic accord (the Murphy-Weygand Accord) between the United States and Vichy. Under the terms, the United States sent food, clothing, and other supplies to North Africa for distribution to the native population. Murphy sent twelve agents to different locations in the French colonies to check on the distribution of the supplies in order to make certain none were diverted to German use. Murphy's "twelve disciples" were the first American spies in the area, or anywhere else, for that matter, at least on a systematic basis. As Ray Cline, former Deputy Director of the CIA, has written of Murphy's disciples, "For the first time . . . Americans listed as diplomatic officials found themselves competing for scraps of information in the cafes and casinos with foreign diplomats and assorted spies of all countries."[10]

Although there were almost no supplies to distribute, Murphy's disciples were able to make valuable reports on French military dispositions and strength in North Africa, and to make a start on the job of organizing underground groups for subversive operations. Murphy, meanwhile, had attempted to induce General Maxime Weygand, Vichy's chief officer in French North Africa, to throw in on the Allied side. Unfortunately for Murphy and for the Allies, Weygand showed interest. It was unfortunate because the Germans had broken the State Department's code and were reading Murphy's messages reporting on Weygand's growing defiance of the Germans; indeed, Murphy's telegrams were regularly circulated in Berlin. As a result, in November 1941, Hitler forced Pétain to retire Weygand.[11]

The Weygand connection broken, Murphy established contact with a small group of French conspirators of the far right. A conservative Catholic, Murphy was, in de Gaulle's words, "skillful and determined, long familiar with the best society and apparently inclined to believe that France consisted of the people he dined with in town."[12]

Those he dined with included a vegetable-oil magnate, Jacques Lemaigre Dubreuil, leader of a group called "The Five." As described in one secret OSS report, Dubreuil was "a big businessman" and one of the founders and "Minister of Finance" of the secret anti-communist movement known as *La Cagoule*." This movement was supported by French rightists who, according to another OSS report, were "politically the equivalent of any group of stockbrokers in an exclusive Long Island Club." But according to a third OSS source, the Ku Klux Klan would have been a more fitting analogy. The Cagoulards (literally "hooded men") had staged an almost successful coup against the Republic in 1937, with General Henri Giraud as one of the leaders, along with some of the biggest bankers in France. The OSS agents also noted that Dubreuil and his friends had "rendered valuable services" to Franco during the Spanish Civil War.

In early 1942, this leading collaborationist came to Murphy with the improbable story that his record was "deceptive, that he was actually a courageous, patriotic Frenchman who hates the Germans and Italians with an intelligent implacability and favors the Allies." Dubreuil told Murphy that "he had arranged a carefully concocted police record of himself which indicated that he had been a pro-Nazi collaborator long before the war, and that he had

placed this false record in files available to the Germans." Therefore the Germans trusted him, which explained why he was allowed
to travel freely throughout the French Empire and Europe.

It might be thought that anyone who could believe such a tale
could believe anything, but Murphy was convinced.* He set about
to cooperate with Dubreuil in overthrowing the authority of Vichy
in North Africa while simultaneously preventing de Gaulle and the
Free French from seizing power (Dubreuil and Murphy had come
to a quick agreement about the need to keep the supposedly radical
Free French isolated). Dubreuil and a friend of his, General
Charles Mast, chief of staff to the Army corps commander in Algiers, convinced Murphy that the French Army in North Africa
was ready to support the Allies if only General Giraud could be
brought over to Algiers from France.[14]

Murphy's dealings with Dubreuil were only one of many secret
contacts the oss had managed to establish with French dissidents.
Ike listened carefully as Murphy described some of the activities of
his chief assistant, U. S. Marine Colonel William A. Eddy. Eddy
was one of those oss characters so beloved by Donovan—a scholar
with a taste for intrigue and adventure, a war hero with an appreciation of clandestine and unorthodox methods. Eddy was the head
of the oss mission in Tangier, what the CIA would later call Chief
of Station. Born in Syria of missionary parents, he was the only intelligence officer in the U.S. armed forces who spoke Arabic. He
was a professor of English at the American University in Cairo, a
published scholar, and a college president (Hobart)—no ordinary
officer. When he first met General George S. Patton, one of Ike's
chief lieutenants in TORCH, Eddy had worn all his campaign rib-
bons and medals from World War I. Noticing the five rows of rib-
bons and Eddy's empty sleeve, Patton burst out, "The son-of-a-
bitch has really been shot at, hasn't he!"[15]

After persuading the British to give oss a free hand in North
Africa, Eddy set out to help win the war. His first plot was a scheme
to replace the pro-Vichy Arab prime minister in Tunis with an
Arab leader who was pro-Ally. In March 1942, Donovan made
$50,000 available to use as a bribe, if necessary. Murphy vetoed

---

* And remained so. After the war, Murphy wrote, "Dubreuil, his charming
wife and two fine children, all anti-Nazi and eager for the French to resume combat, were a source of inspiration and comfort to me."[18]

the idea. He had assured the French that the United States was not disposed "to meddle with the native populations" and insisted that the United States would never interfere with relations between France and the native peoples of Africa. Murphy confessed that he was "shocked" by Eddy's plot. "Nothing," he declared, "would have enraged our French colleagues more than this kind of monkey business."[16]

Dubreuil was delighted with Murphy's attitude, and with Murphy's willingness to support his requests for arms and money. He hoped to arm dissident elements in North Africa and then establish a pro-Allied provisional government there, secretly supported by the United States with Dubreuil as the power behind the throne. Eddy and Murphy both backed this wild scheme and sent a detailed list of the necessary arms that would have to be shipped to North Africa. Donovan turned them down cold. They pleaded. Donovan said no again. Eddy then dispatched the first of thousands of priority messages that oss and cia station chiefs would send to headquarters over the next twenty years. Eddy said a German invasion of North Africa was imminent (which was not true) and declared, "If Murphy and I cannot be trusted with a few million francs in an emergency then I should be called back and someone who can be trusted sent." In Washington, one oss official scrawled on the message, "The war may be won or lost by our response to Colonel Eddy." Such nonsense did not sway the Joint Chiefs, who quickly vetoed the project.[17]

Murphy did not need to tell Eisenhower about three other activities Eddy had begun, because Ike had been involved in them. The first and most important was straightforward intelligence gathering. In the middle of August 1942, Eddy had obtained a report on French military dispositions from General Mast and other sources. Eddy's intelligence gave Ike the first clear picture of what he might expect to encounter on the North African shores. In a pessimistic cable to Marshall, Eisenhower summed up Eddy's information: There were fourteen French divisions in North Africa, poorly equipped. If they acted as a unit they would be strong enough to "so delay and hamper operations that the real object of the expedition could not be achieved, namely the seizing [of] control of the north shore of Africa before . . . the Axis." Despite his extensive contacts with the French officer corps, or perhaps because of them, Eddy was realistic. He warned Ike to expect resistance in

Oran and Casablanca, while the French in Algiers should be friendly.

In summing it up, Eisenhower told Marshall that chances of getting ashore successfully were good, but the chances for overall success, especially the early capture of Tunis, were "considerably less than 50 per cent."[18]

Eisenhower's gloom put the spotlight on the oss. The Germans, potentially, outnumbered the Allies at the critical spot because German access to airfields in Sicily gave them a great advantage in the race for Tunis that would ensue the moment TORCH was launched. Eisenhower's great advantage was surprise, plus—if Eddy and Murphy could arrange it—French cooperation. The oss was responsible for arranging for the cooperation or, where that was impossible, subversive actions that would paralyze the French Army. North Africa was the testing ground for oss, as Donovan and his subordinates knew all too well. oss had excluded the British soe from the area, claiming that it could do the job itself. Kermit Roosevelt, in his official (and until 1978 secret) history of the oss, written in 1946, said that "success in North Africa was important, both in Washington for the future of the agency, and in the field as a demonstration to the theater commanders of its potentialities in support of the more orthodox forms of warfare."[19]

This "do or die" attitude had led to some desperate proposals, as Ike already knew. On September 11, 1942, the jcs had accepted some of Eddy's ideas for covert actions, subject to Ike's approval. Immediately, Ike had to deal with the first of many assassination plots. Eddy proposed to murder key Gestapo officers in North Africa when the landings began. Eisenhower refused to take the idea seriously and squashed it. He also squashed a plan of Eddy's to stir up a Moslem revolt against the French, partly for political reasons, mainly because Eddy wanted 80,000 rifles to arm the Arabs, an impossible demand.[20]

Just a day or two before Murphy's arrival in London, Eisenhower had another contact with Eddy. The British soe complained to him that Eddy had indulged in "unauthorized body-snatching." He had, it seemed, kidnaped two hydrographers from Morocco, one a tugboat captain, the other the chief pilot at Port Lyautey. The kidnaping, the soe charged, might tip off the Germans as to the site of the landings. Always sensitive to hints that the Americans were amateurs at making war, Eisenhower was furious. He demanded to know why the OSS had taken such action without his approval. Investigation revealed that Patton had asked Eddy to provide him with the hydrographers, but Patton had failed to inform Ike.[21]

Marshall pointed out in a message to Eisenhower that the kidnaping would "rivet attention" on the Port Lyautey area. Ike replied, "I have not repeat not been consulted by OSS or any other authority. My orders to OSS representatives have been to do nothing in that area without my approval and that nothing unusual is to take place there."[22] Back in August, and many times thereafter, Ike had insisted that the OSS clear all operations with him. In this, its first major test, OSS had shown that it was independently minded and felt free to act first and explain later.

Murphy was a great talker, Eisenhower a great listener. As Murphy spun his tale and Ike concentrated on what he was saying, the sun started to set. Lights began to blink on in Telegraph Cottage in the long end-of-summer British twilight. It grew chilly. Murphy and Eisenhower went inside for dinner in front of a bright coal fire. Harry Butcher had driven the other guests to the site, waiting until dark so that the location of Telegraph Cottage would remain secret. Butcher pulled all the drapes, a near disaster in a room full of cigar-smoking diplomats and army officers, plus Ike, who ordinarily smoked a pack of Camels after dinner (four packs in a day).

It was a gathering of Very Important Persons. The supreme commander for Operation TORCH was the host. His deputy, General Mark Clark, was there, along with his chief of staff, General Walter Bedell Smith, and Colonel Julius Holmes from the newly established Civil Affairs Section. Three American civilians were present: Ambassador (to the Court of St. James') John Winant, Presidential Adviser W. Averell Harriman, and Foreign Service official Freeman Matthews. Ike's political adviser from the British, Hal Mack, was also there, along with Brigadier Eric Mockler-Ferryman of the British Army. Mockler-Ferryman was head of the TORCH G-2 (intelligence) section. Butcher served, he wrote, as "kibitzer, water boy, cigarette girl, and flunky."[23]

After dinner, Murphy began by explaining the attitude of the French Army. He said the Allies should not expect to find an enthusiastic welcome, if only because most French officers "cherished their oath of fidelity to Marshal Pétain." Murphy said he had talked freely with a number of French officers about the possibilities of an Allied invasion of North Africa. They were anxious for it to happen, but they feared the Allies would come in insufficient force and leave it to the French to do the rest. Ike quickly reassured Murphy on the last point; indeed, he overdid it. He told Murphy to tell his French friends there would be 150,000 troops in the initial landings, with a rapid buildup to 500,000. Murphy said the French "would be greatly encouraged by the size of the expedition," as they were when he told them. Later, however, the French officers were bitter, because the actual figures were 100,000 and 250,000.[24]

Murphy wanted to tell Dubreuil and his other French friends the date of the attack, so that they could be fully prepared. Ike shook his head decisively. Under no circumstances would he let the French in on the secret. Murphy pointed out that it would be difficult to arrange for effective collaboration if the Allies did not take the French into their confidence, but Eisenhower was adamant. If the French knew on Monday, the Germans would know on Tuesday and have troops in Algiers by Wednesday. Ike told Murphy to tell the French that the contemplated date of the invasion was February 1943.

Who was Murphy to tell this story to? The question was crucial, the options many. Whatever Frenchman or group Murphy chose to deal with would have the inside track to power in North Africa. He could go to Admiral Darlan, via his son in Algiers— Darlan was commander in chief of French armed forces and had already shown a keen interest in involving himself in such an operation. But Darlan was known to be violently anti-British, so Murphy had not followed up his overtures.* Or Murphy could approach General Alphonse Juin, in command of the French North African land and air forces, with his headquarters in Algiers. A tough patriot, a man of great integrity and spirit, and an out-

---

* As early as April 14, 1942, Murphy had reported that he had talked at length with Admiral Darlan's son Alain and Admiral Fenard. Murphy said they expected and would welcome an Allied victory, and that they were anxious to throw in on the Allied side at the right moment. "I was greatly encouraged by their apparent eagerness, sincerity, and desire for Franco-American collaboration," Murphy wrote.[25]

standing soldier, Juin would have been the perfect collaborator. But Murphy had not reached out to him, nor any of the other leaders of the French armed forces.

There still remained a number of options, chief of which was working with de Gaulle's Free French, who were anxious to take control in North Africa. The British, hating Darlan and not trusting Juin, were ready to bring de Gaulle in on the operation; Churchill had said that the Free French movement was "the core of French resistance and the flame of French honour."[26] But Roosevelt neither liked nor trusted de Gaulle, who had denounced FDR for maintaining diplomatic relations with Vichy. Besides, there were few Gaullists in Algeria at this time, or so Murphy reported. De Gaulle had charged French officers who stayed at their posts after Pétain signed the armistice with treason; such officers could hardly be expected to welcome de Gaulle as their leader.

That brought it down to Dubreuil on the civil side, and Generals Mast and Giraud on the military side. Murphy had maintained and expanded his contacts with Dubreuil and The Five, who were building an underground army in Algiers under the command of Henri d'Astier de la Vigerie, who has been described by historian Arthur Funk as "a character from the Italian Renaissance, a brilliant, persuasive charmer, fascinated with intrigue, at heart a royalist, who exercised an almost hypnotic influence on the young men he led."[27] D'Astier's "army" was a new organization a few hundred strong known as the Chantiers de la Jeunesse. Murphy, repeating what he had heard from d'Astier, said the group was well organized and capable of decisive action on D-Day. When TORCH began, the Chantiers de la Jeunesse would take possession of such key points as the radio stations in Algiers, the police stations, and military headquarters. Then if all went well the Americans could walk into the city unopposed.

With regard to the regular French Army, Murphy's contact was General Mast, chief of staff to the corps commander in Algiers. Mast, a friend of Dubreuil's, told Murphy that General Giraud was the key to success. Murphy explained to Ike and the others at Telegraph Cottage that Giraud, a one-legged hero of World War I, had escaped from a German prison camp in 1941 and was in hiding in the South of France.

(As Murphy talked and the others listened intently, Ambassador Winant signaled to Butcher with his big Corona cigar—he had heard a noise outside the window. Butcher took his flashlight and investigated. He found only the sergeant on patrol duty, who had stubbed his toe in marching around the cottage.)

Murphy said that Mast had told him that Giraud might be willing to come out of France to lead Operation TORCH, and that if he did come, Giraud would rally the French Army to his cause. On the face of it, that was highly improbable. Giraud had participated in the attempted Cagoulard coup of 1937, had no place in the hierarchy of the French Army, no popular following, no organization, no social imagination, no program, and no administrative abilities. But Murphy insisted that his sources were correct. Giraud was the man.

Murphy was aware of one possible difficulty. Giraud, Mast said, would insist on having the supreme command of all Allied forces fighting in North Africa. Ike scowled, his face reddened, as it always did when he was angry. He would never hand over his command to an unknown Frenchman, even if he had the authority to do so and thought it a good idea, which he most emphatically did not. Ike told Murphy to tell Mast to tell Giraud that the Allies could not place a half million of their fighting men under a French commander.

With that, the meeting broke up, Butcher driving the guests home. At breakfast the next morning, Ike and Murphy talked again, about civil affairs, about the need to bring in food and other supplies for the native population, and so on. Over coffee, Murphy suggested that Ike secretly send a high-ranking officer to Algeria, possibly by submarine, so that he could confer with Murphy's French Army friends about fifth-column activities at strategic points, such as seizure of airfields, the designation of coast artillery to be silenced by the French conspirators from the rear, and signals to the convoys by lights as to whether or not opposition should be expected. Ike mused that if such an officer were captured, it would be a tip-off to the enemy. Still, the idea of a surreptitious landing by submarine of an American general on the French North African coast appealed to him and he promised to think it over. Murphy then left, to be driven by Butcher to a nearby British airfield where a waiting plane carried him to Prestwick, whence he got on a TWA Stratoliner bound for Washington. After reporting to the President, he flew across the Atlantic again, back to Algiers.[28]

Two days after Murphy left London, Eisenhower reported to

Marshall on his reactions to his first spy. "I was very much impressed by Mr. Murphy. We had an afternoon and evening conference on the most secretive basis possible, and I believe much good was accomplished by his trip to this country."[29]

CHAPTER THREE

Lighting the TORCH

DAWN, SATURDAY, OCTOBER 17, 1942. A month after Murphy's departure. Eisenhower arrives at his office at 20 Grosvenor Square, in the middle of London, within walking distance of Hyde Park and 10 Downing Street. So completely have the Americans taken over Grosvenor Square that Londoners call it "Eisenhowerplatz." Ike picks up a series of messages that had come in overnight from Murphy, reads them, and immediately telephones Clark.

"Come up," Ike tells him. "Come up right away."

EISENHOWER'S CHIEF OF STAFF, Bedell Smith, was already there. When Clark joined them, the three American generals began a lively discussion of Murphy's messages.

Murphy had two requests. The first was to send a senior American general, accompanied by a small staff, to a secret rendezvous on the North African coast, near Cherchel. They were to land on a lonely beach about seventy-five miles west of Algiers. At the home of a close friend of Henri d'Astier's, who was the head of the underground resistance movement called the Chantiers de la Jeunesse and a member of Dubreuil's group, the American team would be met by French General Charles Mast, who had insisted on the meeting. Mast had convinced Murphy that if the Americans took him into their confidence, and if they brought General Giraud in on the conspiracy as commander in chief of the French and Allied forces, he could arrange a peaceful reception for TORCH. Clark took one look at the message from Murphy and blurted out, "When do I go?"

From the point of view of a professional intelligence service, it was obviously a terrible idea. If Clark were to be captured, the Vichy authorities in Algeria would certainly turn him over to the Germans. Clark, Ike's deputy, knew everything about TORCH. But to ignore Mast's request, or to send a low-ranking subordinate, could—according to Murphy, Ike's chief spy—jeopardize the whole operation. So Ike grinned as Clark asked when he could leave and replied, "Probably right away." It was already the morning of October 17 and Mast had scheduled the meeting for the evening of October 20.[1] Harry Butcher, who saw him later in the day, said "Clark was as happy as a boy with a new knife."

In another message, Murphy reported that Mast remained unhappy with the idea of Giraud serving under Ike and proposed instead that Ike retain command of the American troops while Giraud became supreme commander. The French knew the terrain, Giraud outranked Eisenhower, and with Giraud in command the Allies could enter Algiers without firing a shot, Mast claimed.

A third message from Murphy said that Admiral Darlan had again conveyed to Murphy his willingness to cooperate with the Allies. Murphy had good reason to believe Darlan meant it, as the word came from the admiral's son, with whom Murphy had been in contact for over a year. Murphy said he had raised with Mast the possibility of bringing Darlan in on the conspiracy with Giraud, Dubreuil, and The Five, but Mast would have none of it. He denounced Darlan as a skunk, a traitor, an opportunist, and a man without a following. "The Army is loyal to General Giraud," Mast declared, "and it will follow him, not Darlan. The Navy will fall in line with the Army."[2]

Murphy wanted a directive on Darlan. So did Eisenhower. Whatever Mast said of him, Darlan was the man in command of the entire Vichy military establishment, including the North African Army and Navy, while Mast was a one-star general who commanded nothing—he was only chief of staff to an officer who was not part of the conspiracy. Moreover, even the uninformed and naïve Americans at Grosvenor Square had to wonder if French military discipline had so far collapsed that the army was ready to ignore its established hierarchy to follow the lead of a man, Giraud, who had no official position at all. But Mast insisted that it was so, and Murphy believed Mast. Still, one could not ignore Darlan.

Eisenhower mused that sooner or later the Allies would have to pick between Darlan and Giraud as "our chief collaborator," but he hoped that it would be possible to "secure the advantages accruing to us" if both men would cooperate. These were, however, not military matters, but political and foreign policy problems. Ike needed authoritative direction from his bosses, one of whom was the Prime Minister.

It being the weekend, Churchill was at his country home, Chequers. Clark got through on the phone to Churchill's personal chief of staff, General Sir Hastings Ismay. "We've got a hot message here," Clark said.

"How hot?" Ismay asked.

"Well, it's too hot for the telephone."

Ismay gave the phone to Churchill, who growled, "What do you have? This phone is secret."

Clark handed the phone over to Ike, who said the message was too important to talk about over the telephone. Churchill growled again—he hated having his weekend interrupted. Would Ike come to Chequers to talk about it? There was not enough time, Eisenhower replied.

"Damn!" said Churchill. Then, formally: "Very well. Should I come back to London?"

"Yes, sir."

"All right, I'll meet you at Number Ten late this afternoon."[3]

When Eisenhower and Clark arrived at the Prime Minister's residence, Clark recorded, "There was about as dazzling an array of Britain's diplomatic, military and naval brains as I had yet seen." Clement Attlee was there, along with Lord Louis Mountbatten, Admiral of the Fleet Sir Dudley Pound, Field Marshal Alan Brooke, and Foreign Secretary Anthony Eden, plus Churchill. It was, in short, the British Government and its top military establishment, answering an impromptu summons from an American lieutenant general and his two-star deputy. One might have thought that such an august group would brush aside the details about a highly romantic secret rendezvous with obscure French officers off the African coast in order to concentrate on the deadly serious subject of whether or not to deal with Darlan. It was not to be.

Like Clark and Ike, Churchill was keen for high adventure. Clark said the P.M. "was as enthusiastic as a boy with a new electric train." Consequently, the meeting concentrated on trivia,

Churchill advising Clark on what clothes to wear, how much bribe money to take, how to carry the money, and so on. Churchill got Admiral Pound to agree that the Royal Navy could have a submarine waiting that night in Gibraltar for Clark. "The entire resources of the British Commonwealth are at your disposal," he said solemnly to Clark, shaking hands gravely.[4]

There was one brief discussion about command problems. Ike said he proposed to have Clark tell Mast that eventually military command in North Africa could pass to a French officer, but that Ike would retain the right to decide when the switch could be made. To soften the blow to Giraud's ego at losing the top military command, Ike said he would place Giraud at the head of the government of French North Africa (Eisenhower did not need to say that his power to do so was based solely on the right of conquest). Perhaps Darlan would accept a position in a Giraud government as commander in chief of the North African armed forces. Churchill rather casually agreed to these proposals, then turned back to the more exciting subject of Clark's mission.[5] For the first time, but not the last, Eisenhower learned that where the dark arts are concerned, heads of government are sometimes more interested in cloak-and-dagger covert operations than in sophisticated political and military analysis. To echo Butcher and Clark, secrecy brought out the little boy in nearly all of them.

After some weather delays, Clark got off at 6:30 A.M. on October 19, wearing a lieutenant colonel's insignia, flying in a B-17 whose pilot, Major Paul Tibbets, was generally regarded as the best flyer in the U. S. Army Air Forces (Tibbets was Ike's personal pilot for much of the war; in 1945 he was the pilot of the B-29 that dropped the first atomic bomb on Hiroshima). Eisenhower went to Scotland to inspect a field exercise, which would help pass the time as he worried about Clark.

Two days later, Ike received a message from Gibraltar. Clark's submarine had arrived too late for the rendezvous of October 20 and would have to lay offshore all through the day, submerged, and hope to spot the correct signal light that night. It put Ike in a "state of jitters." Thinking aloud in Harry Butcher's presence, he said that if there were treachery, Clark and his party might go ashore never to return, but if the conference led to French cooperation, the whole operation was virtually assured of success. If it did not work, Ike concluded, "we will have one hell of a fight on our hands." On

October 22, Butcher recorded in his diary, "Ike greatly concerned about Clark. A further message from 'Colonel McGowan' [Murphy] had indicated the meeting would take place tonight."

By October 24 there was still no word from Clark. Eisenhower kept himself as busy as he could, but it did little good. Finally he shut up the office at Grosvenor Square and announced that he was going to drive out to Telegraph Cottage that night. He was not sure of the way, had never driven in England before, and had no driver's license, but he started the car and zoomed off. "When last seen," Butcher reported, "he was going down the middle of the road, veering a little bit to the right and a bit uncertain."[6]

At midnight, the phone rang. One of Eisenhower's aides reported that a message had come in from Gibraltar, from General Clark. His meeting with Mast had been broken up by French police. Clark and the American group had been forced to hide in an "empty, repeat empty, wine cellar." There was one other misadventure. In getting into the rubber boat for his trip back to the submarine, Clark had lost his pants and the gold coins he had taken with him. He had taken off his pants and rolled them up, hoping to keep them dry. But he was safe in Gibraltar and would be in London later that day. Butcher, using the metaphor once more, said Ike was "as pleased as a boy" and eager to hear all about Clark's adventure.

Tom Sawyer and Huck Finn could not have enjoyed telling or listening to a tale more than Clark and Ike did this one. Clark described his flight to Gibraltar, the submarine trip to the rendezvous point, the long submerged wait through the day after he missed the first appointment, practice drills at dusk getting into the canvas boats that took them to shore (the British commando who showed them how to do it fell on his fanny, to everyone's vast amusement), and finally the coming of total darkness, the blinking signal light, and the trip ashore.

Mast was there, along with some of his staff officers, accompanied by Murphy. They started talking at 10 P.M. and kept at it through the night. Shortly after dawn, the police arrived—Arabs had reported footprints in the sand. Mast and the other French officers fled through the windows and disappeared into the brush along the beach. Clark and the Americans hid in the wine cellar. Murphy, his aide, and the Frenchman who owned the house stayed to meet the police. They broke out some brandy, sang songs, and acted very jovial, while Murphy identified himself as the American consul in Algiers and hinted that a little party was going on. The girls were upstairs, he said, and he hoped the French police would not embarrass him. Ike gave out one of his big hearty laughs when he heard that one.

Anyway, Clark went on, the police finally left and the Americans dashed pell-mell down to the beach, where they had an awful time trying to launch the flimsy canvas boat against a heavy surf. It was in this process that Clark lost his pants and his money. But he made it, got back on the submarine, returned to Gibraltar, and flew back to London with Major Tibbets that afternoon. There were many other details—Butcher, who was present when Clark reported to Ike, filled eight single-spaced typewritten pages in his diary with Clark's escapades—but the fact that mattered was that Clark had established secret contact with the French.[7]

A great risk had been successfully run. Clark was a hero. Like Ike, Churchill had to hear the whole story, minute by minute. Later, Eisenhower took Clark to Buckingham Palace to meet King George, who said to Clark, "I know all about you. You're the one who took that fabulous trip."[8]

What were the practical results? In his memoirs, Eisenhower's praise was slight at best. "This expedition was valuable in gathering more details of information," he wrote. "These did not compel any material change in our planned operation."[9] In fact, nothing new had been learned, either about French military dispositions or political possibilities. Mast's staff officers gave Clark's staff a mass of information on the placement of shore batteries around Algiers, troop locations and strength, roads, checkpoints, and so on. The information was accurate, but it was not new—Colonel Eddy's OSS agents had already informed Ike's headquarters on all these points. The best that could be said about Clark's information was that it confirmed earlier OSS intelligence.

In other areas, the Murphy-Mast meeting was even less helpful. Mast wanted to know the date of the invasion, so that he could make the necessary preparations to work together with Henri d'Astiers' young men in the Chantiers de la Jeunesse to take possession of the key points in Algiers the night of the attack. But Ike had strictly forbidden Clark to divulge the date (which had been set for November 8; indeed, on the very day of the Mast-Clark conference, General George S. Patton's combat-loaded forces had embarked from Norfolk, Virginia, target Casablanca). Clark, therefore, was vague about dates—sometime in February, he hinted, the assault would come. He was specific about the overwhelming force involved—there would be half a million troops, plus two thousand planes and a battle fleet from the U. S. Navy. "Mast was pretty impressed," Clark recorded, as well he might have been.

The deception did not end there. Clark said it would be entirely an American operation, when in fact more than half the total military strength of TORCH was British. (It was assumed, on the basis of Murphy's and Eddy's reports, that the French in North Africa were so Anglophobic that they would resist a British landing while welcoming an American force.) Finally, Clark tried to reassure Mast about the command arrangements by saying that at some point in the future Giraud could have the supreme command.

For his part, Mast was not above a little deception. He continued to insist that French officers in Algeria would rally to the name Giraud, that they were seething with desire to strike out against the hated Germans and would seize the first opportunity to do so. But what would happen, Clark asked, if for some reason it was impossible to get Giraud out of France? Mast replied, "I will assume command." It was a preposterous claim for a one-star chief of staff to make, and Clark asked the obvious follow-up question: "But will the troops rally to you?" Mast insisted that they would. What about General Juin, head of the French Army in North Africa? Mast was emphatic—he and his friends would take care of Juin.

How? Through d'Astier's underground army of young men. This led Mast to make a request for two thousand Bren guns for the Chantiers de la Jeunesse. Clark might have picked up the hint here that Mast did not have the force he claimed to have, but instead Clark indulged in his own little deception, telling Mast that there would be no problem about getting the Brens. And so it went —bluff, subterfuge, and deception were the hallmarks of the clandestine meeting between Clark and Mast.[10]

How completely the potential collaborators misunderstood each other was shown immediately afterward. Murphy's first act was to provide Dubreuil with a complete briefing on the meeting. Dubreuil then flew to France to meet with Giraud. He returned to Algiers the next day with a letter from Giraud, demanding an agreement in writing that he, Giraud, would be placed in charge of the "Interallied Command" forty-eight hours after the attack began, plus an assurance that an invasion of France proper would be launched shortly thereafter.[11] Ike snorted at these obviously impossible requests.

On October 28, Mast indicated to Murphy that Giraud would not be coming out of France for a month or more. Much alarmed at the prospect of losing his chief actor, Murphy requested from Ike permission to tell Mast that the attack was imminent. Eisenhower reluctantly agreed. Murphy then told Mast that the Americans would arrive "early in November." Mast, much agitated, charged Murphy with political blackmail, said it was simply impossible, and complained loudly about the lack of confidence. But eventually he got the word to Giraud, who responded that he could not possibly come to North Africa before November 20.

At this, Murphy went into a panic. He sent a message to Roosevelt, asking the President to postpone the expedition for two weeks. In justification, he concluded, "I am convinced that the invasion of North Africa without favorable French High Command will be a catastrophe."

So, on the very eve of the invasion, at the first critical moment in his career as supreme commander, Eisenhower was being advised by his chief spy to call off his attack and reschedule it for two weeks later, or else face catastrophe. Ike's reaction was to laugh. The intricate movement of vast fleets, coming from both England and the United States, as Murphy himself later wrote, could not be delayed by even one day without upsetting "the meticulous plans which had been meshed into one master plan by hundreds of staff officers of all branches of the armed forces of both Allied powers."[12] Ike wired Marshall, "Recent messages from McGowan indicate that he has a case of jitters." In one message, Murphy had urged simultaneous attacks in Norway and western France. It was all ridiculous, but Ike was charitable: "I don't mean to say that I blame McGowan," he told Marshall. "He has a most delicate position and a stupendous job and one that is well calculated to develop a bit of hysteria as the critical hour approaches."[13]

By this time, November 7, Ike had transferred his headquarters to Gibraltar. Arrangements had finally been made with Giraud, who was spirited out of France in a submarine, then transferred to a flying boat and taken to Gibraltar, where on the night of the invasion he met Ike. Giraud's first words were a demand for command of the operation. He ordered a plane made ready to fly him to Algiers, enumerated the staff positions he wanted filled, and demanded that communications facilities be made available to him.

Ike ignored the demands. What we want, he said, is for you to make a broadcast to the French Army. Giraud flatly refused—he would not participate in TORCH except as supreme commander. Ike promised him "the governorship, virtually the kingship, of North Africa," with unlimited funds to build an army and an air force, but Giraud kept saying *non*. He must have the command.

That is preposterous, Ike insisted. Very well, Giraud responded, he would stand aside, the French Army would fight, and the Allies would not even get ashore. With that, the seven-hour meeting ended. A disgruntled, exhausted, furious Eisenhower went off to the radio room to see if he could get any news from the invasion forces.[14]

What he got in the way of news was confused. One thing stood out—the Germans had no inkling of what was happening. Over 150 Allied ships had passed through the Straits of Gibraltar that day, a fact well known to the Germans, thanks to their Spanish friends, but the Gestapo and German military intelligence were convinced that the convoy's destination was Malta. The basis for that judgment was the number of stories in the British press about "poor, suffering, brave Malta" and the need to resupply the island, stories that were planted to achieve that exact effect. Hitler's intelligence service, in other words, was no good to him at all. While 110,000 Allied troops went ashore in North Africa, seven squadrons of Sicily-based Luftwaffe fruitlessly circled the Mediterranean opposite Cape Bon, waiting to bomb the "Malta-bound" convoy.[15]

Ike knew that the Germans were deceived, thanks to ULTRA, which provided proof through the Germans' own words that they were fooled. The radio traffic between Sicily and Italy showed no indication of any special alert, much less a movement of troops to Tunisia. This negative information was heartening.[16]

And the French? Only the event itself could tell if Mast would be able to bring the army around, even without Giraud, or if Henri d'Astier's young men could take control of Algiers, even without their Bren guns, or if Darlan and Juin would cooperate. The least Ike needed was to "find divided councils among the French, which should prevent them offering really effective resistance."[17] He was attacking in sufficient force to ensure success, but any delay imposed by French resistance might prove disastrous to his real objective, which was to get control of Tunisia before the Germans could get there from Sicily. Much depended on how well Murphy, Eddy, and the oss had done their jobs; even more depended, according to Murphy's best intelligence, on whether or not Giraud would cooperate. And his parting words to Ike had been, "Giraud will be a spectator in this affair."[18]

CHAPTER FOUR

Who Murdered
the Admiral?

NOVEMBER 9, 1942, the day after Operation TORCH started. A tired Supreme Commander dictates a letter to Bedell Smith, still in London: "It isn't this operation that's wearing me down—it's the petty intrigue and the necessity of dealing with little, selfish, conceited worms that call themselves men. All of these Frogs have a single thought—'ME.'"[1]

Later that day, from his office deep inside the Rock of Gibraltar, Ike wires Marshall, "I find myself getting absolutely furious with these stupid Frogs."[2]

STRONG STATEMENTS, especially coming from Eisenhower, who often expressed himself in blunt terms in conversation but usually was circumspect in his correspondence. He had reason for his passionate outburst. When the invasion began, Giraud and Darlan continued to jockey for position and refused to commit themselves to the Allied side, Colonel Eddy's attempted coup at Oran failed, Henri d'Astier's pro-Allied young men lost control of Algiers to the French Army, and, worst of all, fighting raged between Frenchmen and Americans at all three landing sites: Algiers, Oran, and Casablanca.

The Germans, meanwhile, although caught by surprise, were reacting with energy and efficiency, which only made Eisenhower more enraged at the French. ULTRA intercepts on the night of the invasion had shown that the Germans were sleeping, so Ike could take comfort in knowing that security for TORCH had been successful. But the next day ULTRA intercepts told Ike that Field Marshal Albert Kesselring, in Italy, was rushing men and supplies into

Tunis and that Hitler had ordered the occupation of southern France. Forty-eight hours before the first Germans set foot in Tunis, Ike knew they were coming, in what strength, and how, but he could do nothing about it because his troops were tied down fighting the French. He had lost the strategic objective of the campaign before the campaign was even under way, and he knew it. Thus his tremendous rage, which grew in intensity with each passing hour. He was angry at Darlan, Juin, and Giraud for putting their "individual fortunes and opportunities" ahead of the Allied cause. "Right this minute," he wrote Smith, "they should all be making it impossible for Admiral Esteva to permit the Germans into Tunisia. He apparently has the equivalent of three divisions down there and, without the slightest trouble, could cut the throat of every German and Italian in the area and get away with it." He confessed that "a situation such as this creates in me so much fury that I sometimes wish I could do a little throat-cutting myself!"[3]

Ike meant it as a tiny joke, but joke or not, the subject of assassination kept coming up in conversations between the Allied leaders on Gibraltar. Giraud continued to say *non* to every proposal Ike made, and for the first twenty-four hours of the operation Ike assumed that Giraud was the only man who could get the French Army to stop fighting the Allies. Admiral Andrew Brown Cunningham, Eisenhower's naval commander, suggested that they put Giraud in a cell and then make an announcement in his name. Butcher recorded that "all felt something had to be done . . . even a little airplane accident." The Governor of Gibraltar told Ike that "he had a good body disposal squad if needed."[4]

By the morning of the second day, Giraud began to sense the hostility and to realize that Ike was never going to turn over command to him. To everyone's delight, he announced that he was ready to lead the French Army and agreed to fly to Algiers. He did so on November 10—and nothing happened. No one paid any attention. All of Mast's promises to Murphy about the effect of Giraud's announcement, and all of Murphy's promises to Ike, turned out to be false. Not one French soldier rallied behind Giraud.

In Algiers, meanwhile, there was a terrible mess. On the night of the invasion, Henri d'Astier's Chantiers de la Jeunesse had taken Juin and Darlan prisoner,* seized the radio station and police

* The admiral was in Algiers because his secret service had tipped him off that the invasion was imminent.

headquarters, and generally managed to get temporary control of the city, although not of the naval batteries or the harbor. But their arms were woefully out of date—none of the guns the OSS and Clark had promised had been delivered—and they acted without proper coordination or leadership. Worst of all, they struck too soon. Expecting the Americans at dawn, they seized control during the middle of the night. They could not hold it against the overwhelming force of the regular French Army in Algiers. By dawn, Juin had regained control.

General Mast, meanwhile, was out of touch, on the outskirts of Algiers, at a beach where he expected the Americans to land. But the landings were miles from the city and hours later than Mast expected them. The result of all these errors was that, instead of the Americans walking into a city already controlled by Mast and d'Astier's underground army, they met stiff French resistance.[5]

In Morocco, too, the attempt to arrange a peaceful reception had been botched and the French were resisting. Vichy police arrested a pro-Allied French general, and General Auguste Nogues, in command in Casablanca, ordered all-out resistance. In Oran, Eddy's OSS organization had been unable to take control, but the Allies arrived in such overwhelming force that they quickly overcame the French forces there. Ike was not especially worried about Casablanca, either, because Patton was in command at that site and it would not be long before he forced a French surrender. Even in Algiers, on November 10, Juin ordered his troops to cease fire. At all three sites, in short, Eisenhower's men had arrived in sufficient strength to overwhelm the French. The trouble was that the French in Tunisia were allowing the Germans to come into Tunis and none of the French officers in Algiers would issue orders to resist.

When a message came into Gibraltar from Murphy, saying that Darlan would talk to Eisenhower but to no one else, most especially not Giraud, "Ike spluttered." Butcher reported that he swore, "What I need around here is a damn good assassin!"[6] Admiral Cunningham laughed, then reminded Ike that Churchill had told him, "Kiss Darlan's stern if you have to, but get the French Navy." The French fleet was then in Toulon and it was thought that if Darlan ordered it to join the Allies, the fleet would do so. Ike decided to send Clark to Algiers to see what could be done about bringing Darlan over to the Allied side.

In selecting Clark, Eisenhower was indulging an old friendship, because certainly Clark's first visit to Algeria had not been of any benefit to the Allies. Nevertheless, Ike continued to think highly of Clark, and even found cause for praise. In a letter to Marshall on November 10, Eisenhower said that Clark's secret trip "had been immensely important to us in finding out exactly what was the majority sentiment in North Africa and in preparing the way for effective U.S.-French collaboration." The exact opposite was the truth —Clark's visit had failed to discover the crucial fact that Giraud's name was of no consequence in North Africa, and there was no U.S.-French collaboration.[7] Still Ike recommended Clark's promotion to lieutenant general. He also remained loyal to Murphy, despite Murphy's embarrassing failures.

Ike's instructions to Clark, which served as the basis for the famous Darlan Deal, were straightforward and entirely in accord with the directions Ike had received from his superiors, Churchill and Roosevelt. Eisenhower said that the Allies had not come to North Africa to stir up "the tribes" or to replace any Vichy officials. It would be business as usual, and Darlan could be in charge, if only he would order the French forces in Tunisia to resist the German landings there. "I don't see why these Frenchmen, that are jockeying for personal power, do not see these things and move with speed," Ike told Clark. He had become so cynical about Darlan, Juin, and Giraud that he added, "Give them some money if it will help."[8]

Mark Clark flew to Algiers, where he quickly confirmed a deal that Murphy had already made with Darlan. It gave Darlan the title of High Commissioner in French North Africa. In return, Darlan promised to order Admiral Esteva in Tunis to resist. At Murphy's insistence, backed up by Eisenhower, Darlan also had to agree to make Giraud the commander in chief of French forces in North Africa, which showed a rather astonishing loyalty to Giraud in view of his ineffectiveness. On November 13, Eisenhower and Cunningham flew to Algiers, where Ike took possession of his new headquarters, in the Hotel St. Georges, and summoned Darlan and Giraud to a meeting, where they examined and discussed the details of the deal.

Eisenhower was in a position to say no, to call it off, but he never considered such a possibility. His chief political adviser and spy, Robert Murphy, previously so forward and dogmatic in his recommendations, now threw up his hands and said, "The whole matter has now become a military one. You will have to give the final answer."[9] Ike never hesitated. All Murphy's previous reporting had emphasized the importance of maintaining order in Algeria, and Murphy and Clark had both insisted that only the established Vichy officials could do that. Like American southern politicians dealing with blacks, they argued that only French colonial officers knew how to "handle" the Arabs. Ike himself had warned Clark not to create any dissension among the Arab tribes "or encourage them to break away from existing methods of control."[10]

At 2 P.M., November 13, Eisenhower and Darlan signed the agreement, which gave Darlan civil control of French North Africa. Thus, in its first offensive of the war, the United States committed itself to supporting and upholding a Nazi collaborator who was a notoriously anti-Semitic fascist. The United States had sent a large military force to North Africa, but for the Jews and Arabs of Algiers, nothing had changed. They still could not attend public schools, practice professions, vote, or otherwise exercise civil or political rights.

There was an immediate outburst of protest against the Darlan Deal, from liberals in England and America, led by Edward R. Murrow, the CBS radio newsman based in London and one of the most respected commentators in the United States. Murrow demanded to know what the hell was going on. Were we fighting Nazis or sleeping with them? Didn't Eisenhower and his bosses realize that we could lose this war in winning it? Was Eisenhower himself a fascist?

Much of the intense reaction resulted from naïveté. As Arthur Funk has pointed out, "Many Americans were still, in 1942, wallowing comfortably in a Wilsonian delusion that wars are fought to preserve the world for those on the side of right."[11] Another factor contributing to the storm was the reaction of Churchill and Roosevelt. Those worthies acted as if they had never heard the name Darlan before and were astonished that General Eisenhower had taken such liberties in political matters. In fact, both had approved the Darlan Deal weeks earlier, in principle if not specific detail, when Darlan first approached Murphy. Both heads of government had given Murphy, Clark, and Eisenhower full authority to deal with anyone who could deliver the goods, whether it was Mast, Juin, Giraud, or Darlan. And both Churchill and Roosevelt had insisted from the start that the invading force should do nothing to upset local government. But neither man would come to Eisenhower's defense, which encouraged the press and radio to mount a campaign demanding that the deal be called off.

Eisenhower began to realize how far out he had stuck his neck. He had made a political blunder or—more correctly—was being made the victim of one. He had no power base of his own, he was unknown, he had won no great victories, he was expendable. At a critical moment in his career, his head was on the block.

Ike defended himself in a series of brilliantly written and argued messages to the Combined Chiefs of Staff, Roosevelt, and Churchill. (To Churchill: "Please be assured that I have too often listened to your sage advice to be completely handcuffed and blindfolded by all of the slickers with which this part of the world is so thickly populated.")[12] His principal justification was military expediency; as Funk notes, this turned Clausewitz on his head by "insisting that military achievement be sought at the expense of diplomatic disaster."[13] Another of Ike's justifications was to put the blame on his intelligence service (although he never blamed Murphy); to the Combined Chiefs he declared, "The actual state of existing sentiment here does not repeat not agree even remotely with some of our prior calculations."[14]

The military case was indeed a strong one, but it would have been much stronger if Ike had immediately captured Tunisia and if the French fleet had rallied to Darlan. Because neither happened, it was hard to see exactly what benefits the Allies had received from dealing with Darlan.*

Making matters worse, one of the chief radio stations broadcasting from North Africa to the Allied world, Radio Maroc, had fallen into the hands of some of Colonel Donovan's oss agents. These agents, according to Ike's younger brother Milton, were "idealistic New Dealers." They broadcast critical news stories on the Darlan Deal, stories that emphasized the point that the coming of the Allies had made no difference in day-to-day life, as Vichy officials continued to run a fascist state in North Africa.[15]

---

* Darlan did order Admiral Esteva to use the fleet to resist, but the French Army in Tunisia, under General Georges Barre, had withdrawn into the mountains, refusing either to fight the Germans or to follow Vichy orders to collaborate with them. The Germans were already arriving. Esteva decided to do nothing. The main French fleet, meanwhile, at Toulon, had scuttled itself rather than sail to join the Allies or be taken over by the Germans.

At this point, Roosevelt must have been tempted to fire Eisenhower, repudiate the Darlan Deal, put a soldier like Juin or Giraud in Darlan's place, and make a fresh start on creating an intelligence establishment for the United States. Churchill had fired a string of generals in Egypt and now looked like a genius for having done so, as Montgomery had just won the Battle of El Alamein. But FDR did have a sense of fair play and he knew perfectly well that, in dealing with Darlan, Ike had stayed well within his orders.

In addition, three men, representing three levels of the American Government, came to Ike's defense. One was a senior official and elder statesman, Secretary of War Henry L. Stimson. Another was the Chief of Staff of the Army, General George C. Marshall. The third was a young, up-and-coming bureaucrat, formerly assistant to Henry Wallace in the Department of Agriculture, currently Elmer Davis' number two man in the Office of War Information, Milton Eisenhower. What these three men, so far apart in age and experience, had in common was the President's trust. FDR had a long and deep relationship with all three men and he believed what they told him, and in Roosevelt's administration—as in all others —personal relationships were often crucial.

Secretary Stimson barged into the White House and flatly told Roosevelt that he, as President, absolutely had to speak out in Eisenhower's defense. Marshall too insisted that Roosevelt had to defend Ike. Marshall also tried to get the press to soften its criticism. At a press conference, he pointed out that the Americans suffered 1,800 killed in action in taking North Africa, although planning estimates had been that the losses would be around 18,000. Marshall claimed that the figures showed the Darlan Deal had saved 16,200 American lives.* Marshall told Roosevelt that criticism of Ike played into the hands of the British, who would demand Ike's replacement by a British general, and American leadership of an Allied expedition would have such a black eye that there would be great difficulty getting an American into such an exalted position again. Marshall thought that Eisenhower, if successful, would put the United States into a position of world prestige beyond anything Roosevelt had ever imagined.[16]

Roosevelt was impressed by Marshall's arguments. He called in

---

* Putting it the other way around, Murphy's and Clark's failure to coordinate with the French had cost 1,800 American lives.

Milton and asked a series of questions about Ike's politics. Reassured that Eisenhower was comfortably in the middle of the American road and certainly no fascist, FDR then asked Milton to draft a presidential statement accepting the Darlan Deal but emphasizing that it was temporary in nature and undertaken only for military expediency. Milton did as directed, brought back the draft for Roosevelt's approval, and then watched "with some pain as FDR added the word 'temporary' about six more times, which plus my four made ten times the word was used."[17]

The most immediate result of Roosevelt's statement was a note from Darlan to Clark. The tiny admiral was hurt. Mustering what dignity he could, he declared, "Information coming from various parts tends to give credit to the opinion that I am but a lemon which the Americans will drop after it is crushed."[18] Roosevelt, meanwhile, had sent Milton Eisenhower over to North Africa to take control of Radio Maroc (which he quickly did) and to do what he could to bolster Ike's reputation (which he tried but without much luck). Milton met with Darlan, who used the same analogy with him, saying, "I know I am but a lemon which you intend to use and then toss aside."[19] Murphy records that Milton, furious that some newspaper and radio commentators were still calling his brother a fascist, said that "unless drastic action were taken immediately, the General's career might be irreparably damaged. 'Heads must roll, Murphy!' he exclaimed. 'Heads must roll!' "[20]

Despite Milton's best efforts, and despite Roosevelt's and Churchill's endorsement, the Darlan Deal continued to stink. Pro-Allied French officers who had conspired with Murphy and Eddy were either in hiding or in jail, while the Vichy officials who had caused so much American bloodshed remained in power. Ike tried to put pressure on Darlan to liberalize his administration, asking that he at least give back to the Jews the rights of citizenship, but Darlan moved slowly. He told Ike progress would be difficult "because of the anti-Semitism of the Arabs," which may have been the first and only time during the French occupation of Algeria that the French took Arab sentiment into account.[21] Like Diem in Saigon in the early sixties, Darlan in Algiers in late 1942 had become an acute embarrassment for the Americans.

For Ike, it was terribly frustrating. He wanted to be fighting Germans in Tunisia, not up to his neck in politics in Algiers. Nor did he enjoy being a target of criticism. "I have been called a Fascist and almost a Hitlerite," he complained to his son John, then a cadet at West Point. Ike told his son that it was in fact his most earnest conviction that "no other war in history has so definitely lined up the forces of arbitrary oppression and dictatorship against those of human rights and individual liberty."[22] To his British political adviser, Harold Macmillan, he confessed, "I can't understand why these long-haired, starry-eyed guys keep gunning for me. I'm no reactionary. Christ on the mountain! I'm as idealistic as Hell."[23]

It was true, however, that only American and British arms— commanded by Eisenhower—kept Darlan in power. The admiral had no political base, no support. The Germans had occupied all of France, ending whatever pretensions Vichy had as an independent, legitimate government. Vichy officials in North Africa, led by Darlan, stood revealed as opportunists who would collaborate with whatever side seemed to be winning the war. It was an inherently unstable, dangerous situation.

Especially for Darlan, who had an impressive list of enemies. The Germans wanted him dead because he had double-crossed them. Marshal Pétain and his gang at Vichy felt the same way. De Gaulle and the Free French needed to remove Darlan in order to make way for a new regime in Algiers. The British had always hated Darlan and now held him responsible for the fact that the French fleet was at the bottom of Toulon Harbor instead of sailing beside the Allied navies. The Americans, terribly embarrassed by the Darlan Deal, were anxiously looking for a way out.

Dubreuil and Henri d'Astier, meanwhile, were dismayed at the way things had turned out. They had expected Murphy and Ike to put Giraud in command, and they had been confident they could control the politically innocent Giraud. Having hoped to become the real authorities in North Africa, Dubreuil found himself completely excluded from Darlan's government while d'Astier was chief of police for Algiers only.

In sum, potential assassins were lining up to get at Darlan. Algiers murmured with intrigue. Darlan was aware of the activity; at one point in mid-December he told Murphy, "You know, there are four plots in existence to assassinate me."[24]

One of those plots involved men who were directly or indirectly associated with the oss. Colonel Edmond Taylor of the oss, a Chicago journalist before the war, headed a small group of American officials attached to the Anglo-American Psychological Warfare Branch (PWB), which was in theory a staff section of Eisenhower's headquarters. But OSS station chiefs, like their CIA successors, were inclined to independent action based on their own perception of the situation. Ike's policy was clear—to cooperate with Darlan—but Taylor and his PWB officers rejected it. The PWB became a haven for American critics of the Darlan Deal, and Taylor sought out anti-Vichy Frenchmen to assure them that not all Americans had abandoned them. PWB officers also acted on their own to arrest, without warrants, in the best "Chicago gangster style," fascist politicians and pro-Nazi journalists. The French authorities protested vigorously, and Eisenhower later remarked that the PWB had given him more trouble than all the Germans in Africa.[25]

PWB became a rallying point for anti-Darlan Frenchmen, which gave Taylor an excellent listening post on attempted coups or assassinations. In mid-December, Taylor told Murphy that his information was that Henri d'Astier was involved in a conspiracy to replace Darlan with the Comte de Paris as head of a new French provisional government, with Dubreuil as finance minister. Taylor's informants noted that the Comte de Paris had recently arrived in Algiers, and said that d'Astier might well try an armed coup d'etat. Murphy, according to Taylor, was unconcerned; in fact, Murphy had played a role in persuading Darlan to appoint d'Astier as chief of police in Algiers, which put d'Astier in the perfect position to execute a plot.[26]

D'Astier's young men of the Chantiers de la Jeunesse were meanwhile seeking an opportunity to strike a blow. They had been humiliated on the night of the invasion, when the regular French Army had disarmed them as if they were children. They burned for revenge. They were political innocents, representing every point of view, from Communist sympathizers to royalists supporting the Comte de Paris, but they were united in their fervent patriotism and their hatred of Darlan, who had sullied the honor of France.

Many of these youths had joined the Corps Franc d'Afrique, a new commando unit formed under the direction of OSS Arab specialist and Harvard anthropologist Major Carleton Coon. One such recruit was Roger Rosfelder, and he provides a good example of how d'Astier could confuse and manipulate his youngsters. An impetuous eighteen years of age, Rosfelder was ready to act, not think. D'Astier told him that, after Darlan's removal, the Comte de

Paris would become King of France, and that he would then call on de Gaulle to form a government. Rosfelder objected, said he was no royalist, but finally agreed to help remove Darlan. His attitude, he later declared, was: "First of all, there is a traitor to be executed and that is the important thing. The political calculations are beyond me."

In Rosfelder's account, which he wrote in 1972, he stated that "Mario Faivre and I propose some projects for Darlan's execution. My plan is finally retained. . . . [It was to] form a barrage with two cars; Darlan's car is stopped. I approach and empty my Sten at him. I abandon the Sten (I am covered by another gun) and regain the Boulevard where another car takes me to the Special Detachment of the Corps Franc where I have several witnesses who will recognize that I had spent the day with them."

Fortunately for Rosfelder, older heads decided against his indulging his passion for a blaze of machine-gun fire and vetoed his plan. The Abbé Cordier, d'Astier's associate, told Rosfelder that Bonnier de la Chapelle had been selected to execute Darlan, directly and alone, in the Summer Palace in Algiers.* On December 23, Rosfelder took Bonnier to meet Abbé Cordier at the Church of St. Augustine. The priest heard Bonnier's confession, gave him absolution, and then and there, in the confessional, turned over Henri d'Astier's two dueling pistols.

The following day, Christmas Eve, Rosfelder, Faivre, and Henri d'Astier's son Jean drove Bonnier to the Summer Palace. As Bonnier—dressed all in black—got out of the car (with a new pistol belonging to Faivre, as the dueling pistols did not work), he gave Rosfelder his identity papers and a photo of himself. "You will give them back to me afterward," he said. "If not, you will burn them!" Bonnier was convinced, Rosfelder recorded, that there was no risk. Both d'Astier, the chief of police, and Abbé Cordier, his priest, had told him, "Don't worry, everything is accounted for."[27] After all, when one has the chief of police's own pistols, one has a certain confidence.

At 2 P.M., Christmas Eve, Bonnier strolled into the Summer

---

* According to Michael R. D. Foot, *SOE in France* (a British official history, published in 1966), "members of d'Astier's Algiers group had drawn lots for which of them should have the honour of killing the admiral," but French sources do not support his statement. Mario Faivre supports Rosfelder in his own confession, *Nous avons tue l'Admiral Darlan* (Paris, 1976).

Palace. No one challenged him. The usual guards seemed to be missing; it was quiet in the palace. Bonnier knew his way around and placed himself in a waiting room outside Darlan's study. About 3 P.M. Darlan returned from lunch. As the admiral approached his study, Bonnier stepped forward and fired two shots from his .25-caliber revolver at point-blank range. Darlan died almost immediately. When his aide, Commandant Hourcade, rushed forward, Bonnier shot him in the leg, but then Darlan's chauffeur managed to knock Bonnier down and disarm him. He was hustled off to police headquarters.[28]

AS THESE EVENTS TRANSPIRED, Eisenhower was not even in Algeria, but at the front lines in Tunisia. For the preceding two weeks he had been trying to get an offensive started for Tunis, but heavy rains, cold weather, and poor roads had frustrated his attempts. The mud made movement impossible, and local intelligence—the Arab natives—said the rains would be worse in January and February. General Kenneth Anderson, commanding the British First Army, which was to lead the drive on Tunis, starting off on Christmas Eve, told Ike that the offensive could not begin before March. It was "a bitter disappointment" to Eisenhower.

Equally frustrating was the status of the French North African Army. As a result of the Darlan Deal, General Juin and his forces had taken their place beside the Allies on the battlefront. The British held the positions in the north, facing Tunis; the Americans were at the southern end of the line; the French held the hilly area in the center. The problem was that Juin refused to take orders from Anderson. Anderson wanted Ike to talk to Juin, which Ike agreed to do. On Christmas Eve the two men met at a farmhouse that was serving as headquarters for the British V Corps. They had just sat down for dinner when Ike was summoned to the telephone.

Clark was calling from Algiers. He told Ike there was big trouble and he should return immediately. Clark, according to Butcher, put his message "in terms so guarded that Ike suspected, but wasn't sure, that Darlan had been shot."[29] Within the hour, Eisenhower, Butcher, a staff officer, and their driver had piled into Ike's armored Cadillac and were off. They drove all through the night and most of Christmas Day, stopping only to get fuel and for breakfast at the command post in Constantine, where the news of Darlan's assassination was confirmed. They lunched from emergency rations along the road and reached Algiers around 6 P.M. on Christmas Day. "Ike's comment while en route home from the east," Butcher recorded, "was that Darlan's death ended one problem, but no doubt created many more."[30]

Upon arrival at the Hotel St. Georges, Eisenhower's first act was to write a sympathy note to Mrs. Darlan. Then he had his staff brief him on events. Next he sent word to the "Imperial Council" (the top Vichy officials in North Africa) that he wanted Giraud elected to replace Darlan, which was immediately done. Giraud then held a drumhead trial, found Bonnier guilty, and much to Bonnier's surprise ordered a firing squad to shoot him. No attempt had been made to force Bonnier to reveal who his fellow conspirators were. Because Bonnier had been assured that only a pretense would be made of executing him, he displayed impressive courage and calmness in front of the firing squad.[31] The execution was real, however; it was carried out during a German air raid on December 27, at a moment when antiaircraft fire drowned out the sound of the firing squad's guns.[32]

The reason for the lack of an investigation, according to Rosfelder, was plain. The authorities, Rosfelder noted, "showed an evident willingness to minimize the whole affair." For this phenomenon, Rosfelder said, "there is only one explanation: five or six political or patriotic groups had Darlan in their sights and each one believed for quite some time that it was 'his' plot that had succeeded." Indeed, the police superintendent "had even pushed his obligingness to the point of burning all our files . . . still another who believed in the success of 'his' plot!"[33]

It was indeed true that few men ever had more enemies than Darlan, which opened the way to wild speculation in the world press about who was behind Bonnier. The Germans said the British Secret Service did it in order to forestall American influence in North Africa. Nazi radio stations claimed that Darlan's last words were, "Now the British have succeeded in reaching their goal." From Italy, Radio Rome declared that the conspirators were "French de Gaullists in the pay of the British intelligence service."[34] The Spanish press blamed Vichy. The New York *Times* said Bonnier was an Italian.[35]

Colonel Eddy, meanwhile, dispersed the oss agents working with Corps Franc d'Afrique for fear they would be implicated.

Eddy sent Major Carleton Coon, who was in charge of the unit Bonnier belonged to, off to Tunisia before he could be accused of collusion in the murder.[36]

At the same time, Ike was trying to manipulate the French so that all Frenchmen outside of Vichy could join together to fight the Nazis, which meant in the first instance a rapprochement between Giraud and de Gaulle. De Gaulle wanted to come to North Africa, and Ike tried to convince Giraud to allow him to do so. But on December 27, Giraud told Ike that de Gaulle should wait until the political and military situation in North Africa had become more settled.[37] Eisenhower agreed to wait, and on December 28 he wired Churchill, "I believe that Giraud will serve as the medium through which the desired rapprochement can soon be effected if the matter is not pressed too precipitately."[38]

The next evening, December 29, a highly agitated oss officer rushed into PWB headquarters to announce breathlessly, "They've arrested all our friends!"[39] Algiers was in an uproar as squads of Vichy police descended on their victims at their homes, handcuffed them, and whisked them out of the city. One rumor had it that only Gaullists were being arrested; another held that it was Dubreuil and his gang. Twelve men were arrested; four were police officers, and two or three were said to have helped the Americans land.

Charles Collingwood of CBS interviewed Giraud, who told him that the conspirators who had murdered Darlan also intended to assassinate Giraud and Murphy. Giraud said the arrested men were being held in preventive arrest and would not be executed. "We have arrested people who helped the Americans to land and those who helped the Germans," Giraud told Collingwood, "as well as those police who knew of the plot against Darlan but did not tell their superiors. I am following the French thesis that it is better to prevent than to punish."

Collingwood asked about the policemen who had been arrested. "They knew that Darlan was going to be murdered and did not warn their superiors. I did not want to start that again. I only carried out the arrests when I knew beyond doubt that there were to be other assassinations."[40]

The oss had different explanations of what happened and why. One agent reported that Dubreuil and the Cagoulards had attempted a royalist coup d'etat.[41] Agent Taylor believed that all those arrested were Gaullists who had supported the American landings. He protested through "every bureaucratic channel, political and military, formal and informal, in a vain attempt to make Eisenhower realize the catastrophic effect on world opinion if we tolerated this vindictive Vichy counteroffensive against the underground allies who had risked their lives in our common cause a few weeks earlier."

But Ike refused to act. Taylor went to Murphy. Surely Murphy would not allow the very men he had conspired with in October to be arrested on the pretext that they had designs on his life? To Taylor's amazement, Murphy gave the same reply Ike had used: he could not interfere in an internal French matter. Taylor's bitter conclusion was, "Darlan had been our son-of-a-bitch, and Giraud was now, and whoever was against an officially approved son-of-a-bitch must ipso facto be against us."

Taylor turned his PWB headquarters at the Hotel de Cornouailles into a sanctuary for Frenchmen being hunted by the Algiers police. One of the refugees was the head of that police force, but Henri d'Astier had learned that his own police agents were looking for him, supposedly with orders to shoot on sight. Taylor gave d'Astier a PWB jeep to take him to the cathedral for mass. Two weeks later d'Astier was arrested.[42]

Giraud had thrown a wide net, as he had indicated to Collingwood, arresting men of all political persuasions and backgrounds. By so doing, he implicated everybody in Darlan's murder, which may very well have been his objective, as it is probable that he himself did not know who the successful conspirators were, but assumed it could have been any one of a half-dozen groups.[43]

Within a year, after de Gaulle and Giraud had achieved their rapprochement, they joined hands to make Bonnier into a hero. On the first anniversary of his execution, according to the Associated Press, "a group of about 50 persons, the majority of whom fill official positions under the orders of Generals Giraud and de Gaulle, celebrated the anniversary of the death of Fernand Eugene Bonnier de la Chapelle, who assassinated Admiral Darlan, by placing a wreath on his tomb and observing a minute of silence."

That incredible scene was followed up a week later by an incredible act—the Algerian Court of Appeals, under de Gaulle's control, annulled the sentence against Bonnier, citing as its reason "documents found which showed conclusively that Admiral Darlan had been acting against the interests of France and that Bonnier's act had been accomplished in the interests of the liberation of France."

Bonnier's crime disappeared from the record. As a consequence, so did that of any of his accomplices and the case was closed. Shortly thereafter, Henri d'Astier and his associates were released; the day he got out of jail, d'Astier received the Croix de Guerre with palms from Giraud, and the following day the Medal of the Resistance from de Gaulle. Two days later de Gaulle named him a member of the Consultative Assembly.[44]

Because of these actions, and because de Gaulle benefited so immediately and decisively from Darlan's removal, most commentators have pointed to him as the ultimate source of the conspiracy. But although both Giraud and de Gaulle were delighted to have Darlan out of the way and made no effort to hide their pleasure, they were not necessarily in on the plot, either together or as individuals. Rosfelder's confession, published thirty years after the event, and confirmed by much other evidence gathered in that time,[45] raises many questions about the ultimate conspirators. Certainly Abbé Cordier was at the heart of it, and he worked for d'Astier, who worked for Dubreuil. And beyond Dubreuil? Another Frenchman? Or perhaps an American?

The ultimate source of authority in North Africa was Franklin Roosevelt. He put it bluntly when he cabled Churchill on January 2, 1943, "I feel very strongly that, in view of the fact in North Africa we have a military occupation, our commanding general has complete control of all affairs, both civil and military. Our French friends must not be permitted to forget this for a moment. If these local officials will not cooperate, they will have to be replaced."[46]

Robert Murphy was the President's personal representative in North Africa, as well as head of an OSS organization that included Major Coon's Corps Franc, of which Bonnier was a member, and Taylor's PWB, which had close contacts with d'Astier. Further, Murphy was a close friend of Dubreuil and had made a strong commitment to Giraud, while he detested de Gaulle (as did Roosevelt). The question arises, was Murphy a part of the conspiracy? Was Darlan's murder the first assassination for the American secret service? Was Ike himself in on the plot? Does that explain the rather curious circumstance that at the moment the murder was committed the commanding general of all Allied operations in

North Africa was at a corps headquarters on a farm more than a day's drive from Algiers?

At the time, in 1942, few Americans would have believed it possible for their government to be involved in such dastardly work; a generation later, however, millions of Americans would take it for granted that if there was foul play and the predecessor of the CIA was in the area, and if the Americans benefited from the foul play, then the OSS must have been involved. These questions also persist because of Murphy's continued association with Dubreuil, whose hopes to become finance minister and the real power in a Giraud government (or prime minister under the Comte de Paris) disappeared when Giraud and de Gaulle got together in January 1943. De Gaulle despised Dubreuil as a collaborator. When de Gaulle emerged in the spring of 1943 as the head of government in Algiers, Dubreuil fled to Spain, where he joined a number of his old associates from the Cagoule.[47] In 1944, following the liberation of France, Dubreuil slipped across the border. He was promptly arrested by French police on charges of having "negotiated with a foreign power."[48]

Murphy used his position as Ike's chief political adviser to persuade the French to drop the charges against Dubreuil and held a party in Paris in celebration of Dubreuil's freedom.[49] After the war, Murphy refused to discuss his loyalty to Dubreuil or events surrounding the murder of Darlan,* but in his memoirs he made the astonishing statement that "the motive for the assassination of Darlan still remains a mystery."[50] In 1947, Dubreuil was tried for treason but acquitted; on July 12, 1955, he was shot to death by unknown assailants for unknown reasons on the doorstep of his Casablanca home.[51]

Murphy's loyalty to Dubreuil aside, the fact that the Americans benefited so directly from Darlan's death makes them at least suspect. Clark, in his memoirs, published in 1950, added to the suspicion because he expressed such delight over the assassination. "Admiral Darlan's death was, to me, an act of Providence. It is too bad that he went that way, but, strategically speaking, his removal from the scene was like the lancing of a troublesome boil. He had served

---

* At least with this author, who asked on a number of occasions in the 1960s. Carleton Coon also refused three separate requests for an interview made in 1979.

his purpose, and his death solved what could have been the very difficult problem of what to do with him in the future. Darlan was a political investment forced upon us by circumstances, but we made a sensational profit in lives and time through using him."[52]

That almost sounds like a confession, but despite Clark's carelessly chosen words, and despite speculation linking Murphy with the conspirators, there is no direct evidence connecting Eisenhower, his chief subordinates, or the OSS with the murder of Darlan. Eisenhower's attitude was best expressed by his reaction to Roosevelt's message saying that if the French leaders would not cooperate "they will have to be replaced." Ike was terribly upset, according to Butcher. He said that without the good will of the French Army, the Americans would have to take on the "man-wasting" job of providing civil administration for Algeria and guarding the lines of communication through North Africa. Instead of active assistance from the French, Ike said he feared there would be "passive resistance à la Ghandi, or possibly resumption of French fighting Americans 'pour l'honneur.' "

If FDR insisted on dictating to the French to the point that it brought on French resistance, Butcher noted, "Ike said he would of course carry out the order, but would then ask to be relieved, which would no doubt mean reversion to the rank of lieutenant colonel, and retirement."[53] Ike had come to admire Darlan and appreciate his cooperative spirit. He did not put the finger on the man.

Neither did Murphy or the OSS, if only because they did not have to do so. Anyone living in Algiers in December 1942 would have had to have been deaf and blind not to know that there were numerous plots to kill the little admiral. The analogy that fits is Saigon in 1963, where the CIA did not have to lift a hand against Diem but simply stood aside and let the South Vietnamese themselves do the killing. As Rosfelder makes so abundantly clear, in Algiers there were plenty of Frenchmen on the prowl for Darlan. And as de Gaulle's and Giraud's actions after the event indicate, there were many highly placed Frenchmen who were delighted to have the admiral out of the way, so much so that they made a hero out of the murderer.

CHAPTER FIVE

Ike and ULTRA
in Africa, Sicily, and Italy

FEBRUARY, 1942. A fox brought to bay by a pack of hounds is a fearful sight, snarling, snapping, turning left, right, backward, never resting, always alert. The fox is the dreaded Erwin Rommel and his famous Afrika Korps; the hounds are Montgomery's Eighth Army, pursuing from the east, the American II Corps (General Lloyd Fredendall) closing in from the west, the French from the northwest, and the British First Army (General Kenneth Anderson) covering the northern escape route.

ROMMEL had just retreated across half of North Africa, following his defeat by the British at El Alamein in November 1942. When he reached the Mareth Line, a prepared defensive position, partly underground, along the Tunisian-Libyan border, Rommel turned on the British, who recoiled, then settled down to await reinforcements. The chase across Africa had been exhilarating, but to close in on the "Desert Fox" in his den was another matter altogether. Monty gave Rommel time to catch his breath and plan his next move.

The American II Corps was to Rommel's west and north, stretched out along the eastern dorsal of the Atlas Mountains. The front line was too long for the Americans to hold in strength, but neither Fredendall nor Eisenhower were overly worried. Intelligence indicated that any German attack would come from north of the II Corps line at Fondouk, which was a British and French responsibility.

According to Ike's intelligence reports, Rommel was fully occupied by Monty, so General Jürgen von Arnim, who commanded the German forces in Tunis, would lead the offensive. Ike's G-2 (intelligence) officer at Allied Force Headquarters (AFHQ) was British Brigadier Eric E. Mockler-Ferryman. He reported that all available information indicated that von Arnim was going to draw on Rommel's Africa Korps for reinforcements, then attack through a pass at Fondouk, with the aim of scattering the French, then turning north, driving to the coast, to isolate Anderson's First Army.[1]

Eisenhower did not fully accept Mockler-Ferryman's judgment, but he did not have sufficient self-confidence to overrule his G-2. He was worried enough to go to the front to oversee preparations to meet von Arnim's attack. On February 13–14 he made an all-night tour of the front. He was disturbed by what he saw. The American troops were complacent, green, and unblooded. They had not received intensive training in the United States, as they were the first divisions to go to England in 1942. In November they had shipped out for North Africa, where operations were just active enough to prevent training but not enough to provide real battlefield experience. Officers and men alike showed the lack of training.[2]

Ike was also upset at the disposition of the 1st Armored Division, which had been split into two parts, Combat Command A and Combat Command B (CCA and CCB), and was therefore incapable of operating as a unit. General Anderson had insisted upon keeping CCB near Fondouk to help the British meet the expected attack from von Arnim; CCA was to the south, near Faïd Pass.

General Paul Robinett commanded CCB, and on the night of February 13–14 he insistently told Ike that he was sure Mockler-Ferryman's information was wrong. Robinett said he did not expect an attack at Fondouk because he had sent patrols all the way across the eastern dorsal without encountering any enemy buildup. Further, air reconnaissance had failed to reveal any preparations for an attack. Robinett said he had reported this intelligence to his superiors, Generals Fredendall and Anderson, but they did not believe him. Ike said he did, and promised to change the dispositions the next day.[3]

After his talk with Robinett, Ike drove south for a couple of hours, then paid a visit to CCA. Everything there seemed to be in order. Just after midnight he went for a walk into the desert. The moon shone. Looking eastward, he could just make out the gap in the black mountain mass that was Faïd Pass. Nothing moved.

Shaking off the mood of the desert, Eisenhower returned to CCA headquarters and then drove toward Tebessa, Fredendall's headquarters. He arrived three hours later, around 5:30 A.M. The Germans, he learned to his astonishment from a radio message, had attacked CCA, coming through Faïd Pass at 4:00 A.M. Reports indicated, however, that it was only a limited attack, probably designed to draw off strength from the northern end of the line. CCA said it could hold on with no difficulty. Climbing into his Cadillac, Eisenhower drove on toward his advance command post at Constantine. Along the way he stopped to visit the famous Roman ruins at Timgad and did not reach Constantine until the middle of the afternoon, St. Valentine's Day.[4]

The news he received when he got to his headquarters was bad. The attack out of Faïd Pass was much bigger and more aggressive than CCA had thought at first. The Germans had destroyed an American tank battalion, overrun a battalion of artillery, isolated two large segments of American troops, and driven CCA out of its position. Nevertheless, General Anderson continued to insist that Mockler-Ferryman's intelligence was correct and that the main attack would come at Fondouk. He refused to release Robinett's CCB to join CCA in the defense. Ike tried to speed a flow of reinforcements to CCA, but his main strategic reserve, the U. S. 9th Infantry Division, was unable to move with any dispatch because it had no organic truck transportation. As a result, outnumbered and inexperienced American troops had to take on German veterans led by Erwin Rommel himself. The result was one of the worst American defeats of the war. CCA lost ninety-eight tanks, fifty-seven half-tracks, and twenty-nine artillery pieces. It had practically been destroyed—half an armored division gone![5]

Fortunately for Ike, the German command setup was almost as muddled as the Allied one. Rommel and von Arnim operated independently. Von Arnim wanted to confine himself to limited attacks against Fondouk. Rommel was after much bigger results—he wanted to break through the mountains at Kasserine Pass, capture the great Allied supply base at Le Kef, then possibly drive on to Algiers itself. He wanted to turn a tactical advantage into a strategic triumph, destroying the II Corps, isolating the First Army, and thus reversing the entire position in North Africa. If all went well, he could accomplish his objectives before Monty was ready to attack the Mareth Line.[6]

Von Arnim was a vain, ambitious man who refused to cooperate in Rommel's bold (but wildly impractical) plan. Higher headquarters (Kesselring) had ordered him to give his best panzer division, the 10th, to Rommel for the original attack, but von Arnim had stalled and it was not committed on February 14. Ironically, this turned out to benefit Rommel, because the location of the 10th Panzer was, according to Mockler-Ferryman, the key piece of information. As long as those tankers were facing CCB at Fondouk, that was where Mockler-Ferryman insisted that the attack would come.

Over the next two days Rommel pressed his initial advantage. On February 20 the 10th Panzer, finally released to his command, moved into Kasserine Pass. It was too late. American reinforcements had arrived. The German offensive stalled.

That same day, February 20, Ike asked the British Chief of the Imperial General Staff, Alan Brooke, to replace Mockler-Ferryman "with an officer who has a broader insight into German mentality and method."[7] It was the only time in his three-year career as Allied Commander in Chief that Eisenhower asked the British to relieve one of their officers on his staff. In a cable to Marshall the next day, Ike explained that "due to faulty G-2 estimates" Anderson had not become convinced "until too late that the attack through Faïd was really the main effort."

Then, in guarded language, he added, "I am provoked that there was such reliance placed upon particular types of intelligence that general instructions were considered inapplicable. In this connection and for your eyes only, I have asked for the relief of my G-2. He is British and the head of that section must be a British officer because of the network of special signal establishments he operates, but Brooke has agreed to make available a man in Great Britain who is tops in this regard."[8] The man was General Kenneth Strong. He stayed with Ike through the remainder of the war and the two officers established a close and effective relationship. Mockler-Ferryman returned to London to head the Special Operations Executive (SOE), which controlled sabotage and underground efforts in occupied France.

But what, meanwhile, was the origin of Mockler-Ferryman's

terrible mistake at Kasserine Pass? It was ULTRA. An entry of February 20 in Butcher's previously unpublished diary provides some of the details: "An explanation of the defeat, as seen by Ike, lies in a misinterpretation of radio messages we regularly intercept from the enemy. This source is known as 'Ultra.' It happens that our G.2 Brigadier Mockler-Ferryman, relies heavily upon this source. It has frequently disclosed excellent information as to the intentions of the Axis. However, the interpretation placed by G.2 on the messages dealing with the place of attack—an attack that has been expected for several days—led Mockler-Ferryman to believe that a feint would be made where the attack actually occurred . . . and that the real and heavy attack would come in the north."[9]

What Butcher did not know was that Rommel's initial attack was as much a surprise to von Arnim and his superiors as it was to Mockler-Ferryman. Rommel, not for the first time, had disobeyed orders.[10]

On March 14, after Rommel had been driven back both at Kasserine and then at the Mareth Line (and had consequently left Africa), Ike wrote Brooke again about Mockler-Ferryman. He said that his G-2's performance, up to Kasserine, had been outstanding, pointing out specifically that "his forecast of the extent of French opposition proved in the event to be more accurate than that of any other authority." Ike wanted Mockler-Ferryman's relief to be "without prejudice." Then he added, "In his successor, I now look for a little more inquisitiveness and greater attention to checking and cross-checking reports from various sources."[11]

The Battle of Kasserine Pass has often been pointed to as the contest where the American Army of World War II came of age. Green troops became veterans; new commanders gained badly needed combat experience; over-cocky Americans learned what a tough opponent they were up against. The man who learned the most was the commander himself, Dwight Eisenhower, and one of the most important lessons he learned was that no one source of information, no matter how sensational, is ever by itself sufficient. Mockler-Ferryman had been so confident of ULTRA's insight and trustworthiness that he had neglected other, more traditional sources. As Butcher noted in his diary, "Ike insists we need a G.2 who is never satisfied with his information, who procures it with spies, reconnaissance, and any means available."[12]

In the aftermath of Kasserine, Ike also learned from interrogation of German prisoners that the enemy was "easily and constantly" breaking the low-level codes used by the 1st Armored Division. He decided that the Germans were probably as enamored with this information as Mockler-Ferryman, and that he could take advantage of them. He told Patton, "We should obviously but clumsily change the code at frequent intervals, so that the Hun will not suspect a plant, but never enough so that it will be impossible for him to break them quickly. As long as nothing is hurt the orders given in this way should be faithfully executed (unimportant patrols, etc.). But when the time comes for real surprise, use an erroneous order in order to support your other measures of deception. This effort should not be difficult to make—and it might work!"[13] The innocent American was learning quickly.

DESPITE ITS RELATIVE FAILURE at Kasserine Pass, ULTRA was Ike's single most effective spy throughout the war. It proved itself in every campaign from 1943 onward, beginning with Operation HUSKY, the invasion of Sicily, Ike's second amphibious assault. Well before HUSKY was launched in July 1943, thanks to ULTRA, Eisenhower had a complete picture of the enemy's order of battle on Sicily and in Italy. Equally valuable, ULTRA allowed him to penetrate the German mind and judge how successful Allied deception measures had been.

The major attempt at deception for HUSKY showed the British Secret Service at the top of its form. In an imaginative subterfuge, the British managed to convince the Germans that Eisenhower's troops would land either on Sardinia or in Greece, rather than Sicily. This sophisticated deception scheme was potentially decisive, because the Germans had more than enough troops scattered throughout Italy and the Mediterranean to reinforce Sicily sufficiently to produce another Gallipoli.

The story is well known—it was superbly told by Ewen Montagu in his 1954 book, *The Man Who Never Was*—and needs only a brief summary here. A British Secret Service team searched the London morgues to find a suitable body—they needed a once fairly healthy, fairly young, and completely unknown man. Once found, they used odds and ends to give him an identity, a biography, a history. He became "Captain (acting Major) William Martin, 09560,

Royal Marines." His pockets and his briefcase were stuffed with documents, matches, loose change, love letters, a bill or two, a bank statement, a photo of "mom," all prepared with exquisite care to prove that Major Martin was authentic.

Major Martin was a courier. His briefcase was attached to his wrist by handcuffs. In it were various travel orders and other documents, some labeled "Most Secret." The planted material consisted of two private letters, one from the vice chief of staff to General Harold Alexander, the overall ground commander in the Mediterranean, under Ike, and the other from Lord Louis Mountbatten to Admiral Cunningham. Each letter hinted that the next operations would strike at Sardinia and Greece.

At dawn, April 30, 1943, Major Martin was dumped overboard from a British submarine off Huelva on the Spanish coast. (At the last minute in London, there had been an anxious discussion about what would happen if the tide failed to sweep him to shore. Churchill gave his verdict: "You will have to get him back and give him another swim.") The Spanish picked him up, opened the briefcase, gave the documents to a German intelligence agent (who photographed them and sent the film on to Berlin), replaced the documents in the briefcase, then gave it to the British vice-consul in Huelva. Major Martin was interred and his documents returned to London in the freshly sealed briefcase.

Had the Germans taken the bait? ULTRA showed that they had. From the War Cabinet Office to Churchill, then in Washington, the signal flashed, "Martin swallowed rod, line and sinker by the right people and from best information they look like acting on it." The phrase "best information" meant ULTRA.[14] Between early May and July 10, the date of the invasion, ULTRA provided mounting evidence of the successful deception, primarily through order of battle information, the area in which ULTRA was always at its strongest and most reliable. ULTRA reported that the Germans had moved the 1st Panzer Division from France to Greece, that they had moved units from Russia into Greece, that reinforcements from Germany were sent into Sardinia, and so on. In May, the Luftwaffe had had 415 aircraft in Sicily with 125 in Greece; by July there were 305 in Greece and only 290 in Sicily.[15]

ULTRA was precise about the opposition Ike's forces would face on Sicily. Field Marshal Kesselring gave Berlin a complete run-down on his dispositions. He had the Hermann Göring Panzer Division on Sicily, along with the German 15th Panzer Division and some Italian troops (who were without transportation and badly equipped). Part of the 15th Panzer was in Palermo, on the north coast; the remainder, along with the Hermann Göring Panzer Division, was in the center of the island, ready to move in any direction. This was priceless information, as was Ike's knowledge that via ULTRA he would be able to listen in on the German reaction to the landings.[16]

The initial assault went according to plan. On the morning of D-Day, from his advance headquarters on Malta, Eisenhower sent a cable to the Combined Chiefs: "Fragmentary information obtained mostly from intercept of messages indicates that leading waves of British 5th, 51st and Canadian Divisions are ashore and advancing."[17] ULTRA, in other words, was giving him not only the German reaction—which was slow and confused—but was also his best source on the immediate tactical dispositions of his own troops. The following day, July 11, was the critical one in the campaign, as German armor from the Hermann Göring Division counterattacked against American forces at Gela. ULTRA had provided an alert, and the Americans were ready with a combination of superb naval gunfire, artillery, infantry action, and tanks. The Germans were repulsed with heavy loss.[18]

The operation in Sicily did reveal ULTRA's inescapable limitations. The Allies dared not act on ULTRA information that stood alone—i.e., there had to be some explanation other than a code break as to how they found out this or that, or the Germans would realize what had happened and change their code. Churchill and Menzies insisted that those "in the know" had to promise never to use ULTRA information until it was possible to point to some other source.

For example, parachutists, under the command of General James Gavin, dropped onto Sicily on the eve of the invasion, could not be told that the Hermann Göring Division was in their drop zone for fear of revealing the ULTRA secret. The men were not told they would encounter German tanks. They were also *not* given antitank weapons. They were told that there were some German "technicians" in the area and "nothing more." In 1979, General Gavin commented, "From the viewpoint of protecting Ultra, I think that this was the proper course for the high command to take, *provided* they equipped us with adequate antitank weapons."[19]

IF THE SECURITY OF ULTRA was a first objective, the question arises, how was ULTRA information relayed to the field commanders safely and swiftly? The British had worked out a system of Special Liaison Units (SLUs) to speed the intercepted messages from Bletchley Park (BP), where the decoding and translating took place, to Churchill and the generals. In 1943 the United States began to create its own SLUs. The result was a huge success and an extraordinary achievement, showing Americans at their best.

The Army's selection process was superb. It managed to locate precisely the two dozen or so officers who were perfect for the job. They had to be young and healthy, because the SLUs worked long, taxing hours on intricate problems and because the SLUs had to be junior officers, usually captains or majors, so that they would not attract attention by their rank. They had to be diplomatic enough not to offend the senior generals to whom they reported, but firm enough to make sure the generals heard what they had to say (not always as easy as it might seem, especially when Patton or Clark were the recipients). Men who are absolutely trustworthy, mentally quick, tireless, and self-effacing (they knew there would be no battlefield promotions for them in this war, nor any opportunity to lead men into combat) are few in number—but America had enough of them, and the Army found them. To a man, they did an outstanding job during the war; to a man, they kept their trust, not one of them ever revealing the ULTRA secret or his part in the war.* It may not be too much of an exaggeration to say that the ULTRA system, from BP to the SLUs, was a triumph of the Western democracies nearly on a par with the creation of the atomic bomb.

TELFORD TAYLOR headed the American SLU effort. His later career, as was true of all the SLUs, was marked by success after suc-

---

* In an interview in 1979, former SLU Stuyvesant Wainwright II agreed that it was remarkable that the secret was kept so long. He explained, "Don't forget we all signed the British Secrecy Act. Have you ever seen one? It practically says your testicles will be cut off and you'll spend the rest of your life in the local clink if you open your mouth, that you would practically disappear in a Stalinist camp in Northern Siberia if anything came out about ULTRA. . . . It never occurred to me to discuss it until thirty years later. I never discussed it with my wife. She always wanted to know what I had done and I never told her."

cess. Taylor was the prosecutor at the Nuremberg War Crimes Trials and later a distinguished author and professor of law at Columbia University. His young men, selected for brains and ability rather than rank or background, included William Bundy, who became Assistant Secretary of State; Alfred Friendly, who became managing editor of the Washington *Post;* John Oakes, who became an editor of the New York *Times;* Langdon van Norden, a businessman who became chairman of the Metropolitan Opera Association; Curt Zimansky, a noted philologist; Yorke Allen, of the Rockefeller Brothers Fund; Stuyvesant Wainwright II, four-term congressman; Lewis Powell, Associate Justice of the U. S. Supreme Court; Josiah Macy, vice president of Pan American Airways; and Adolph Rosengarten, who was a little older than the others but still had a successful postwar career, first as a director of the Fidelity Philadelphia Trust Company, then—in 1975, at age seventy—earning his Ph.D. in history from the University of Pennsylvania. Clearly the SLUs were outstanding junior officers.[20]

The SLUs served in a new Army organization, Special Branch of the Military Intelligence Service. In defining their responsibilities, General Marshall insisted, without any question of misinterpretation, that these officers were in a special category and that the generals in command must allow them (no matter how young or unmilitary) the necessary scope and authority.

Marshall gave his SLUs more latitude, and demanded of them a great deal more, than their British counterparts. In the British system, the SLUs were only glorified messengers who handed on the complete ULTRA intercepts to their superiors. Under the system that Marshall and Taylor created, the American SLUs synthesized, summarized, and interpreted the intercepts. As Marshall put it, "Their primary responsibility will be to evaluate Ultra intelligence, present it in usable form to the Commanding officer, assist in fusing Ultra with intelligence derived from other sources, and give advice in connection with making operational use of Ultra intelligence in such fashion that the security of the source is not endangered."[21] As Lewin notes, "This directive was so comprehensive and permissive that it allowed and indeed encouraged the representative to think of himself as a kind of private intelligence center."[22] As the SLUs were, in fact, for in the field each had his own tent, van, or trailer as an office—under continuous guard—in which his safe contained ULTRA papers plus a great deal more information.

To train these men, Taylor first of all sent them to BP, where they saw 10,000 of the most valuable people in the British Empire at work. They were deeply impressed. The exposure of the SLUs to the inner workings of BP meant that they understood the magnitude and significance of what ULTRA offered in a way that few field commanders could.

In addition, Taylor carefully indoctrinated the SLUs in all aspects of intelligence gathering, which gave them a perspective that was crucial to their effectiveness. The temptation to rely completely on ULTRA was always there, but usually spurned. In 1978, Rosengarten wrote, "I am bold to say that Ultra was *primus inter pares,* some of the time but not all of the time, among the sources of information which were available to our section. These were principally prisoners, civilians who crossed the line, air photography, and low level deciphering."[23]

Rosengarten's point was made over and over again by the American SLUs. After the war, Taylor had each of his men answer a long questionnaire about their experiences. In his summary of these reports, Taylor noted that "the need for careful study of all sources of intelligence was stressed by most of the representatives." Everything that the commanding general's G-2 section knew, the SLU knew, because he made it his business to read all papers passing through the G-2 situation room. This enabled him to fuse ULTRA with other intelligence.

One SLU wrote, "It is most easy for the Ultra representative to allow himself to become isolated from the mainstream of the intelligence section, so that he loses awareness of what other sources are producing. Another facile error, induced by inertia, is to permit Ultra to become a substitute for analysis and evaluation of other intelligence. The two easy errors, isolation from other sources and the conviction that Ultra will provide all needed intelligence, are indeed the Scylla and Charybdis of the representative. Ultra must be looked on as one of a number of sources; it must not be taken as a neatly packaged replacement for tedious work with other evidence."[24]

Another point Taylor stressed in his final report was that ULTRA's "normal function was to enable the SLU and his recipients to select the correct information from the huge mass of P/W, agent, reconnaissance, and photographic reports. Ultra was the guide and the censor to conclusions arrived at by means of other intelligence; at the same time the latter was a secure vehicle by which Ultra could be disseminated under cover."[25]

As will be seen, the system Taylor created worked well. Time and again his SLUs were able to get crucial information to their commanders in time for decisive action. Most SLUs had a daily briefing for the general; some held two briefings; all had round-the-clock access to the general if they had an intercept that called for immediate action. It was Anglo-American cooperation at its most highly developed—recall that all decoding and translating was done by British at BP—and as the Germans can testify, it was remarkably effective. As Lewin concludes, "After the Americans first became fully involved in Ultra they entered into an enormous inheritance which they did not squander."[26]

IF THE SLUS WERE THE PICK of America's young men, Donovan's OSS agents were supposed to be almost as good. But in Sicily, and then during the invasion of Italy in September 1943, the OSS was of no help to Ike, unless it was to provide some comic relief.

Colonel Donovan claimed that the OSS had proved itself in North Africa and that it should therefore be given a free hand in Sicily and Italy. He nearly got it, although Ike was able to stop one or two harebrained schemes before they got started. In late June, for example, Donovan wanted to send an OSS team to Sicily for sabotage operations, but when Eisenhower learned of the plan he vetoed it, on the obvious grounds that sending in agents at so late a date would alert German coastal defenses.

Donovan ran a far more serious risk on D-Day for HUSKY when he went ashore with Patton's troops to direct the efforts of his ten-man OSS unit for Sicily. How it happened is a mystery, except that Donovan somehow managed to do it without Ike finding out. It was a bit of madness, obviously, for a man who knew all about ULTRA, the atomic bomb, the British Secret Service organization for France, not to mention the OSS secrets, to put himself in a position where he might be captured. Anthony Cave Brown, the British journalist, comments, "This rash behavior on the part of senior OSS officials was one of the root causes of the intense suspicion with which the British secret services were now coming to regard their American comrades-in-arms."[27]

It was probably inevitable that the American Government's secret agencies, initially the OSS and then the CIA, would find occasion to work in close cooperation with another secret organization that also had nearly unlimited funds, the Mafia. It happened first in 1943 during the Sicilian campaign. Assistant New York District Attorney Murray Gurfein, at that time attached to the Office of Naval Intelligence (ONI), later an OSS colonel in Europe, and eventually a federal judge in New York, made a deal with Mafia chief "Lucky" Luciano. Luciano was in prison for crimes concerning prostitution. The deal was that if the Mafia in Sicily cooperated with the OSS there to provide information, the ONI would get him out of prison. Although no concrete evidence has been produced to indicate that the Mafia turned over intelligence of any value, on the day World War II ended in Europe, ONI sent a petition for executive clemency for Luciano to Governor Thomas E. Dewey of New York. The petition said Luciano had "cooperated with high military authorities" and had rendered "a definite service to the war effort." Dewey approved the appeal and Luciano was let out of prison and deported from the United States.[28]

As the Mafia connection indicated, the Americans had a tremendous potential advantage in carrying out spying in Italy—millions of Americans were from Italy or second-generation immigrants with close personal ties to the old country. Speaking the language perfectly, knowing the country and its ways thoroughly, the Italian-Americans were ideal agents. Donovan had gone deep into the military to find volunteers; the leader of his Sicily unit was Max Corvo, a U. S. Army private of Sicilian descent. Corvo in turn recruited twelve Sicilian-Americans and two young lawyers to become recruiters and organizers. One OSS man who helped train the larger group remembered them as "tough little boys from New York and Chicago, with a few live hoods mixed in. . . . Their one desire was to get over to the old country and start throwing knives." One or two had been recruited directly from the ranks of Murder, Inc., and the Philadelphia "Purple Gang."[29] They did not, unfortunately, meet expectations. Although Corvo's group did recruit on Sicily, they were unable to find a sufficient number of Sicilians who, in the words of one OSS wit, were willing "to take a shot at their relatives."[30]

OSS had all the problems of a new organization, compounded by the fact that it had more agents and more money to spend than it could use effectively. The result was its own private war, often either at odds with the aims of the real war or a duplication of effort. During the invasion of Italy, OSS agents dashed off on missions without the knowledge or approval of Eisenhower's headquarters. It was the only time in the war that Ike allowed this to happen—during the Normandy landings nine months later nothing went on that he had not personally approved—and it appears to have been a result of Donovan's enthusiasm plus FDR's strong backing of Donovan.

The absence of communication between OSS and the regular forces was the cause of an absurd mix-up on D-Day at Salerno. A "MacGregor unit" (OSS code name for a sabotage team), consisting of Peter Tompkins, John Shahhen, and Marcello Girosi, commandeered a high-speed British motorboat. They had a wild plot to reach the Italian Naval Command, there to force the Italian admirals to turn their fleet over to the Allies. What they did not know was that the secret surrender negotiations with the Italians, which had been going on for some weeks, had already made arrangements for turning over the fleet, which was indeed sailing at that moment to surrender to the British at Malta.

Elsewhere the ninety-man OSS detachment for Italy, commanded by Colonel Donald Downes, did some good service. Wading ashore on D-Day, the agents managed to exploit the early confusion in order to infiltrate through enemy lines, make contact with resistance groups, and recruit spies. An occasional piece of helpful information came out of this effort.[31]

Before much could be accomplished, however, Donovan came onto the scene to reorganize the unit. He had Downes join him on a typical Donovan expedition—a jaunt to the Isle of Capri, just across the bay from Naples, which was still held by the Germans. On the way over, Donovan told Downes that Colonel Eddy had taken ill and would be replaced in Algiers by a West Point colonel. Another colonel, Ellery Huntington, Jr., a Wall Street lawyer and former Yale quarterback, would take Downes' place as head of the OSS detachment in Italy. Downes would stay in the country, but only as chief of counterintelligence. Finally, Donovan said that in the future the OSS would have to follow the President's political line, which in Italy meant that the OSS could work only with or recruit Italians who pledged their loyalty to the King, Victor Emmanuel.

All this was rather too much for the idealistic Downes, who told Donovan point-blank that he would not serve under Huntington, "a good-natured incompetent" who had been a key fund raiser for Donovan in 1932 when Donovan ran for governor of New York. As to the political directive, he asked Donovan, "How could we betray all the Italian democrats, almost to a man rabidly anti-House of Savoy, by insisting that they swear allegiance to the ridiculous little king who had saddled them with fascism and thumped for Mussolini until military defeat was inevitable?"

They arrived at Capri, where a MacGregor team was plotting a new daredevil operation to rescue an Italian scientist from German-occupied Italy. Capri was peaceful. "Elegant ladies in sun suits and big hats strolled about followed by their little dogs and gigolos. The smart hotels were open and at cafe tables the indolent conversation of the idle rich was to be heard." To Downes' amazement, Donovan announced that his first objective was to visit the villa of Mona Williams, wife of a prominent New York utilities magnate who had made the second largest contribution to Donovan's 1932 campaign. Donovan explained that he had promised to protect her magnificent resort home from being "ruined by a lot of British enlisted personnel." He told Downes to get on it. Downes replied curtly, "I don't want to fight a war protecting Mrs. Williams' pleasure dome." That night, Donovan ordered Downes to get out of Italy and stay out.[32]

The contrast between Taylor's SLUs and Donovan's OSS could scarcely have been greater. The one was professional, serious, efficient, dedicated, and self-effacing, while the other was amateur, comic, unproductive, and self-serving.

THE ITALIAN CAMPAIGN WAS, for the Allies, the most frustrating of the war. Hopes were high and expenditures of men and equipment were heavy, but results were slim. In August, three weeks before the invasion, ULTRA revealed that Hitler had decided to pull out of southern and central Italy. He wanted Kesselring to bring his divisions north and put them under Rommel, who had taken over command in northern Italy. As this plan seemed to make good strategic sense, and because the Italians were negotiating secretly with Ike's chief of staff, Bedell Smith, and his G-2, Ken

Strong, to pull a double-cross on the Germans, Eisenhower expected a relatively unopposed landing at Salerno. What he got was some of the toughest fighting of the war, and another lesson in the perils of undue reliance on ULTRA.

It is widely believed that Hitler kept a tight control on the various Wehrmacht battlefields, retaining for himself the right to make not only strategic but also tactical decisions. That may have been generally true on the Russian front, but elsewhere the German generals seem to have been able to use their own judgment and even flaunt Hitler's direct orders. If it worked, they got away with it. For Kesselring, in Italy, it worked.

Kesselring did not like Rommel and liked even less the prospect of turning his troops over to Rommel's command. Further, Kesselring believed that Rome could be successfully defended. He therefore delayed and obstructed the movement of his troops northward, so that when the attack came on September 9 he still had the bulk of his forces south of Rome. Against Hitler's better judgment and contrary to his orders, Kesselring decided to launch an all-out counterattack against the Allied beachhead at Salerno. ULTRA revealed only a little of Kesselring's movements, mainly because the Germans had relatively secure telephone lines in Italy and thus did not need to use the radio.[33]

ULTRA could provide only an insight into the enemy's plans, intentions, and capabilities. It could not provide fighting men, tanks, planes, ships, or aggressive generals. At Salerno, Mark Clark had expected a cakewalk. Instead, his troops were under terrific pressure from the Germans in what was one of the most dangerous moments of the entire war for the Allied armies in Europe. An army of two corps, with four divisions, was on the verge of annihilation. Ike received a message from Clark that indicated that Clark was about to put his headquarters on board ship. It made Ike almost frantic. He told Butcher that the headquarters should leave last, that Clark ought to show the spirit of a naval captain and if necessary go down with his ship. Like the Russians at Stalingrad, he should stand and fight.

Fortunately, Clark stayed, rescued by the Allied naval and air forces. Eisenhower put every bomber in the Mediterranean to work pounding the German forces at Salerno, and brought in the British Navy to bombard the German positions with their big naval guns.[34] Meanwhile, Monty's Eighth Army was coming up from the toe of

Italy after an unopposed crossing from Sicily to Italy over the Straits of Messina, a crossing supported by an all-out artillery barrage that was comic-opera stuff. The only casualty was an escaped lion from the Reggio zoo.[35] Kesselring reluctantly decided that his attempt to throw the Allies back into the sea had failed, and he signaled Hitler—ULTRA picked it up—that he was withdrawing to a line just north of Naples. Hitler approved—he was much impressed by Kesselring's resistance to date—and Eisenhower breathed a sigh of relief.

In the campaign in Italy that followed, ULTRA continued to provide the Allied commanders with high-grade information. Why, then, did the campaign go so badly? The major reason was the Germans themselves, who fought skillfully and fanatically in mountainous terrain ideally suited to their defensive genius. Another factor of considerable importance was that the Allied divisions were being steadily withdrawn from the Mediterranean to go to England to prepare for the 1944 invasion of France. A third factor was incompetent Allied, especially American, generalship.

Nowhere did this incompetence show more clearly than in the Anzio landings of January 1944. Briefly, the idea was to get an American corps behind Kesselring's lines in order to cut his communications with Rome and thus force him to retreat to northern Italy. Churchill said he wanted to hurl a wildcat ashore; what he got instead, he later complained, was a stranded whale. The Americans sat at Anzio while the Germans pounded them day after day, week after week. In the end, far from forcing Kesselring to pull back, the troops at Anzio had to be rescued by Allied forces coming up from the south.

Who was to blame? Mark Clark pointed to ULTRA. He said that his forces would have moved inland on the first day, thus effectively cutting Kesselring's supply line, but ULTRA information indicated that the Germans were moving major units into the region and that therefore his men had to dig in to await the assault. This claim has made various British writers furious, and rightly so. Lewin shows conclusively that the ULTRA information was absolutely sound, that it did indicate a German buildup against the beachhead, but that it also showed that it would take two or three days for the Germans to get to the scene. Meanwhile, Clark's men sat and the campaign was lost before it got started.[36]

By then, Ike had left the Mediterranean. Roosevelt had selected him to be the Supreme Commander, Allied Expeditionary Forces —one of the most coveted commands in the history of warfare. In England, he would have available to him for the cross-Channel attack the resources of the two great democracies, including thousands of war planes and ships and millions of fighting men.

By no means the least of the resources under his command were the secret ones, which had been built with such skill and patience by the British (and later the Americans) for the moment when the democracies would hurl their armed might across the Channel. These secret resources included guerrilla forces in France, sabotage units, British and American spies, turned German spies in Britain, ULTRA, and countless deception devices. Success in OVERLORD would depend not only on how well Ike used his ships, planes, and fighting men, but also on how well he managed his secret forces.

CHAPTER SIX

The Secret Side
of OVERLORD

JANUARY 15, 1944. Eisenhower's task is staggering. Forces under his command have to transport 176,000 fighting men, covered by thousands of airplanes, carried in thousands of ships, across the English Channel onto the coast of France in one day, without letting the Germans know in advance where or when this mighty host will make its assault. Because of another requirement, that of making the Germans believe that the attack will come at some point other than the actual site, the already difficult assignment is nearly impossible.

IT PUTS TOO GRAND A FACE ON IT to say that the future of Western civilization was at stake, but that is not far wrong. OVERLORD was a tremendous gamble. Britain and America were putting everything they could into it in a display of unity of purpose not seen before or since in either country. The bet was that the whole of this effort could be concentrated on one operation, and that the operation would be decisive. Failure in OVERLORD would mean the loss of the bet, and the size of the bet was stupendous, a fortune in men and matériel carefully built up by the British and Americans over the past two years.

Eisenhower and Hitler both knew what was at stake. In one of his first messages to the Combined Chiefs in his capacity as Supreme Commander, Allied Expeditionary Force, Eisenhower declared, "This operation marks the crisis of the European war. Every obstacle must be overcome, every inconvenience suffered and every risk run to ensure that our blow is decisive. We cannot afford to fail."[1]

At about the same time, Hitler was saying, "The destruction of the enemy's landing attempt means more than a purely local decision on the Western Front. It is the sole decisive factor in the whole conduct of the war."[2]

EVERY COMMANDER hopes to surprise his enemy, but in Ike's case surprise was crucial, because he was on the offensive with forces that were numerically woefully inferior. Ike's one great material advantage was Allied air superiority. On the ground, the Germans had fifty-nine divisions in France, while the initial Allied assault would be only seven divisions strong. By no means were those German divisions contemptible garrison troops—they were armed with the latest weapons, including tanks, and their morale was high. Many were veterans of the Eastern front. The Allies therefore needed to do better than simply surprise the enemy—they had to induce Hitler to move the best of his units, especially the panzer divisions, away from the invasion site, and keep them away.

To accomplish this seemingly impossible objective, Ike was fortunate to have working for him the best spies in the world, the men and women of the British Secret Service. While the American factories produced landing craft to carry the troops across the Channel, the British intelligentsia completely fooled the Germans as to where those landing craft would come ashore. British brains and American brawn made OVERLORD a smashing success. How it was done makes a remarkable story.

IT BEGAN, for Ike, with his arrival in London late on January 15, 1944, to assume command of the Supreme Headquarters, Allied Expeditionary Force (SHAEF). On Marshall's orders, he had left the Mediterranean two weeks earlier and taken a short vacation with his wife, Mamie, at White Sulphur Springs, West Virginia. His movements had been kept secret from the press and public, and a heavy security blanket had been laid on for his arrival in London. When he got there, fortunately, a London pea-souper took care of security. Two men had to lead the way for Ike's car and they got lost in the distance between curb, car, and the front door of 20 Grosvenor Square.[3]

Eisenhower had returned to his old headquarters of the summer of 1942. Only the most senior government and military officials in Britain knew that he was there, and it was nearly a week before a public announcement was made. But almost as soon as he arrived, a German spy, code name Tate, managed to send a radio report to his controller in Hamburg that the new supreme commander had taken up his duties in London. It was an intelligence coup of the first magnitude.[4]

Tate received his information from General Stewart Menzies, head of the British Secret Service. A few days later Menzies explained to Eisenhower why it was that the Abwehr, the intelligence arm of the German General Staff, was told of his arrival and new command when the information was kept secret from the British and American people. Ike listened, incredulous, as Menzies outlined for him the activities of the London Controlling Section and the workings of the Double-Cross System.

Section BI-A, the counterespionage arm of MI-5, the British internal security agency, had located every German spy in the British Isles. Each had been evaluated by Sir John Masterman, former university don and avid cricketer, who served during the war as head of BI-A. If Masterman thought the man unsuitable for any reason, he was either executed or imprisoned. The rest were "turned," that is, made into double-agents. They continued to report by radio to the Abwehr, but only under the direct supervision of their controllers, who were BI-A agents. The queries the spies received from Berlin, along with ULTRA intercepts, provided a constant feedback and check on how well the Double-Cross System was functioning. As Masterman later claimed, correctly, "For the greater part of the war we did much more than practise a large-scale deception through double agents: by means of the double-agent system we *actively ran and controlled the German espionage system in this country.*"[5]

Tate was only one of more than a dozen double-agents under Masterman's control, but he was typical enough. He had landed by parachute in September 1940, been picked up almost immediately, broke down under interrogation, and agreed to work for the British (his alternative was a firing squad). He transmitted and received messages to and from Hamburg from October 1940 until the day the Allies overran Hamburg in May 1945. The Abwehr sent him large sums of money (he kept demanding more) and awarded him the Iron Cross, First and Second Class. Meanwhile he merged with the British public, working as a newspaper photographer, and even managed to get himself on the voting rolls, which in 1945 gave him an opportunity of voting for or against Mr. Churchill. Regrettably, Masterman would not allow him to exercise that privilege.

Menzies told Ike that from the moment the Double-Cross System came into being, the British had decided to aim it exclusively toward that moment when the Allies returned to France. In the dark days of 1940, control of German spies and ULTRA were the two most precious possessions the British held, and they did not intend to squander them for short-term gains. Displaying impressive patience, the British had not used the spies for purposes of deceiving the Germans, only controlling what information they got. Even more impressive, the BI-A risked providing the Abwehr with authentic information via the spies, information that would not otherwise have been available to the enemy. The London Controlling Section (LCS), a branch of the Joint Planning Staff (of the British Chiefs of Staff), was responsible for the devising and coordinating strategic cover and deceptions schemes. It made the decision as to what information to give to the Germans.

It was a complex game. What the British told the Germans through the turned agents had to be authentic, new, and interesting, but either relatively unimportant or something that the Germans were bound to discover in any case. The idea was to make the agent trustworthy and valuable in the eyes of the Germans, so that when the supreme moment came, on D-Day, the agents could be used to deceive the enemy into thinking the attack was coming someplace other than the actual site. As Masterman wrote in 1972, in his book *The Double-Cross System,* "We always expected that at some one moment all the agents would be recklessly and gladly blown sky high in carrying out the grand deception, and that this one great coup would both repay us many times over for all the efforts of the previous years and bring our work to an end."[6]

Double-agents, even triple-agents, are as old as war itself, but never before had all the spies in one country been turned. Ike grinned as Menzies sketched out to him some of the possibilities for deception, and nodded his understanding as Menzies explained that the supersecurity surrounding Ike's movements the past couple of weeks, and Tate's message to his controller in Hamburg on Ike's appointment to the supreme command and his arrival in London, were an integral, although small, part of the scheme. Masterman wanted Berlin to think that Tate had high-level contacts inside SHAEF itself, and giving Hamburg a scoop on Eisenhower's appearance in London was exactly the kind of information the British liked to give the Germans. It was exciting news, it made Tate (and his controller) look good, it gave the Germans something to gossip about, but it was, in the end, of no real military value.

So, when Eisenhower took up his post, he got not only the British Army, Navy, and Air Force to help him accomplish his objective, but the use of every German spy in Britain.

THE QUESTION WAS, how to use this invaluable asset to deceive the Germans. Before this query could be answered, the Allies had first of all to decide where and when and in what strength they were going to land, what other means of deception were available to them, and how these means could be used.

The whole plan had to be internally consistent, a unified and believable operation. The Allies could hardly hope to make the Germans believe that the assault was not coming in 1944—all the world knew that it was—or that it would come ashore far from the actual site, because it was a relatively simple matter for German intelligence to figure out the maximum distance at which fighter airplane cover could be supplied, and thus define the limits of possible invasion sites. Further, the Germans had good military sense and, for a variety of fairly obvious reasons, they knew that the attack would come somewhere between the Cotentin Peninsula and Dunkirk.

Ike had long ago selected Normandy as the site. Back in 1942, before the decision to invade North Africa had been made, Eisenhower had been planning a cross-Channel attack for 1943. At that time he chose Normandy as the target for numerous reasons—the proximity of the port of Cherbourg for unloading purposes, the narrowness of the Cotentin Peninsula, the nature of the terrain, and the access to the major road network at Caen—but the major factor had been surprise. For all Normandy's advantages, the Pas de Calais had even more. It seemed the obvious target—it was close to Antwerp, Europe's best port, and closer to Germany and to the British home base, and inland the terrain was good—but precisely because it was so obvious, the Germans had their strongest defenses there. That eliminated the Pas de Calais as a target, as far as Ike was concerned, a decision that remained in force when he took command of the cross-Channel operation again in January 1944.

The aim of OVERLORD was to get ashore and stay. Once a solid beachhead was established, the war was as good as won because American productivity would overwhelm the Germans. But landing craft, always short because they were so badly needed in the Pacific as well as in the Atlantic Theater, were sufficient to lift only five divisions to France on D-Day. The follow-up capacity was also limited, painfully so.

To get ashore, Ike absolutely had to fool the Germans into believing that he was landing somewhere other than Normandy; to stay ashore, he needed to fool them into believing that OVERLORD was a feint. Otherwise, the Germans would draw on their nearly ten-to-one manpower and armored superiority in France to mount a counterattack of such proportions as surely to drive the Allies back into the sea whence they came. The air forces could help keep the Germans away from Normandy by blowing up bridges and railroad facilities, but by themselves the Allied planes could not keep panzer divisions immobilized. Only a successful deception could do that.

Fooling the Germans would not be easy—the Germans themselves were experts at deception. At the beginning of 1942 they had mounted one of the more elaborate and successful operations of World War II, Operation Kreml. Its objective was to make the Russians think that the main German offensive for 1942 would take place on the Moscow front, not at Stalingrad. As Earl Ziemke writes, Kreml "was a paper operation, an out-and-out deception, but it had the substance to make it a masterpiece of that highly speculative form of military art." To make it appear real, the German High Command did not inform division commanders and their staffs that it was a phony, depending on the skill of Soviet intelligence officers to pick up hints and find the pieces to fit together into a picture. They used false radio traffic to manufacture dummy armies that supposedly threatened Moscow.

The Germans were successful, probably even more successful than they themselves realized, in an operation that in most of its essentials was similar to FORTITUDE (code name for the OVERLORD deception plan). In fact, Kreml was exactly like FORTITUDE in one especially crucial aspect—both aimed to make the enemy believe the attack would come at the most logical spot. That is, in the spring of 1942, Moscow was a more sensible target than Stalingrad, just as in 1944 the Pas de Calais was a more sensible target than Normandy.[7]

The Pas de Calais was the obvious choice for the false target for Normandy because the Germans were already inclined to believe that it would be the landing site. The task was to reinforce that belief, strengthen it, harden it until it became a dogma with both Hitler and the German General Staff. Geography reinforced Ike's choice of Normandy, with the Pas de Calais as the feint, because Hitler would not keep troops in Normandy following major landings at the Pas de Calais for fear of their being cut off from Germany. But he might be persuaded to keep troops in the Pas de Calais after a landing in Normandy, for they would still be between the Allied forces and Germany.

The execution of FORTITUDE involved thousands of men and women in dozens of distinct tasks and roles. FORTITUDE included dummy armies, fake radio traffic, false spy reports, and elaborate security precautions. It was a joint venture, with British and American officers working together in complete harmony. In terms of the time, resources, and energy devoted to it, FORTITUDE was unique in the history of warfare—never before had any commander gone to such lengths or expense to deceive his enemy.

The British and American governments had given Ike tremendous resources to draw upon. This vast force needed a single guiding head. Someone had to give it direction; someone had to take all the information gathered, make sense of it, and impose order on it; someone had to maintain a grip on all the various acts of subterfuge going on at once; someone had to decide; someone had to take the responsibility.

It all came down to Eisenhower. This put enormous pressure on him, pressure that increased geometrically with each passing day. "Ike looks worn and tired," Butcher noted on May 12. "The strain is telling on him. He looks older now than at any time since I have been with him."[8]

Under the weight of his responsibilities, the number of cigarettes he smoked went up, to an average of eighty Camels daily while his hours of sleep went down, to an average of not much more than four hours per night. But Ike could take it.

He enjoyed attacking the problems posed by FORTITUDE. "I like all this," he scribbled along the margin of one set of proposals for deception.[9] Obviously he did not himself initiate the specific programs, but he had to approve them all, make sure they were coordinated, and order the time of execution.

General Harold R. Bull, head of the Operations Division (G-3) at SHAEF, exercised day-to-day control of the deception plan. He worked closely with the LCS and its American counterpart, the Joint Security Control (JSC). LCS and JSC were the organizations responsible to Ike's bosses, the Combined Chiefs, for devising and coordinating strategic cover and deception schemes. The one they came up with for OVERLORD was complex, wide-ranging, and dangerously ambitious.

Operation FORTITUDE, as Ike approved it, was designed to make the Germans think that the invasion would begin with an attack on southern Norway, launched from Scottish ports in mid-July, with the main assault coming later against the Pas de Calais. The attack on Norway would be the responsibility of a nonexistent British "Fourth Army," while the wholly imaginary First United States Army Group (FUSAG) would make the landings at the Pas de Calais. There were other elements to FORTITUDE, designed to pose threats to the Biscay coast and the Marseilles region, to keep Hitler worried about possible landings in the Balkans, and in general to distract German attention away from Normandy, but Norway and the Pas de Calais were the big operations.

FORTITUDE built on German preconceptions. Field Marshal Gerd von Rundstedt, commanding German forces in the West, agreed with Hitler that the invasion would come "across the narrower part of the Channel," for such obvious reasons as shorter distance, which would reduce ships' and planes' transit time, closeness to the Ruhr and the Rhine, the heart of the German industrial system, and because the V-1 missile-launching sites were located near the Pas de Calais. Rundstedt felt that the Allies might make diversionary landings elsewhere, but the Pas de Calais was the certain site of the main attack.[10]

To get the Germans to look north, toward Norway, instead of south, toward Normandy, for the diversionary attack, the Allies had first of all to convince their enemies that they had sufficient strength to carry out such a diversion. The task was doubly difficult because of Ike's acute shortage of landing craft—it was touch and go as to whether there would be enough lift capacity to carry five divisions ashore at Normandy alone. Ike had been forced to put the target date for OVERLORD back from early May to early June, in order to have another month's production of landing craft on hand for the assault, and the Combined Chiefs had been forced to cancel a simultaneous landing in the South of France because there were no landing craft available. Ike, in short, had neither the men nor the landing craft to make a diversion.

To make the Germans believe the opposite, the Allies had to create fictitious divisions, on a grand scale. This was done chiefly by radio signals. There is a delicious irony here. The Germans thought that with Enigma they had the best encoding machine for radio signals in the world. They also believed that they were the best in intercepting and decoding the enemies' signals. They were right about both conceits, but drew the wrong conclusions. As much as any other factor, these two beliefs caused the German defeat.

The British Fourth Army, scheduled to invade Norway in mid-July, existed only on the airwaves, but that did not mean that its creation was a simple matter of sending out a few random messages. The Allies had to fill the air with an exact duplicate of the real wireless traffic that accompanied the assembly of an army, some of it in cipher, some in the clear. Colonel R. M. MacLeod was in command of the operation. He was told in his briefing, "The Germans are damn good at interception and radio-location. They'll have your headquarters pinpointed with a maximum error of five miles. And it won't take them more than a few hours to do so. What is more they'll be able to identify the grade of the headquarters—whether army, divisions, corps, or what not—from the nature of the traffic and the sets being used."[11]

Twenty overage officers were involved at army headquarters in Edinburgh Castle; fake corps and division headquarters were scattered across Scotland. Through the spring of 1944, they exchanged messages: "80 Div. requests 1800 pairs of crampons, 1800 pairs of ski bindings . . ." "2 Corps Car Company requires handbooks on engine functioning in low temperatures and high altitudes." "7 Corps requests the promised demonstrators in the Bilgeri method of climbing rock faces . . ."[12]

Other elements in the deception involved planting stories in Scottish newspapers, such as reports on "4th Army football matches," or BBC programs like "a day with the 7th Corps in the field." German spies in Scotland, operating under the close supervision of their British controllers, sent messages to Hamburg and Berlin about the heavy train traffic, new division patches seen on the streets, and rumors among the troops about going to Norway. Wooden twin-engined "bombers" appeared on Scottish airfields. British commandos made a series of raids on the coast of Norway, designed to look like preinvasion tactics.[13]

ULTRA provided feedback, letting the Allies know what the Germans swallowed and what they rejected. It showed that Hitler had taken the bait. He not only kept his garrison troops in Norway, he reinforced them. By late spring, he had thirteen army divisions stationed there, along with 90,000 naval and 60,000 air personnel, including one panzer division.[14] This was more than double the force Germany needed in Norway for occupation duties. It was a major triumph for the Allies—a maximum return on a minuscule investment.

The other main part of FORTITUDE, creating FUSAG to threaten the Pas de Calais, was even more elaborate. It included radio traffic for an army group, dummy landing craft inadequately camouflaged, fields packed with papier-maché tanks (jeeps dragging chains drove around to create dust and tracks), and the full use of the Double-Cross System. The spies reported intense activity—construction, troop movements, an increase in the volume of train traffic across the Midlands, and the like—all the activities that would have taken place in fact if the Pas de Calais were the target. Everything the spies said had to match what the radio signals were revealing to the Germans, with the emphasis on hard fact. As Masterman wrote, "Speculations, guesses, or leakages, would have little or no effect on the German military mind, for the German staff officer would make his own appreciations and his own guesses from the facts put before him. What he would require would be the location and identification of formations, units, headquarters, assembly areas and the like."[15]

At Dover, across from the Pas de Calais, the British built a phony oil dock. They used film and theater stagehands. The King inspected it. Eisenhower gave a speech to the "construction" workers at a dinner party held at the White Cliffs Hotel in Dover. The mayor made satisfied remarks about the "opening of a new installation" in town. The RAF maintained constant fighter patrols; German reconnaissance aircraft were permitted to fly overhead, but only after they had been forced to 33,000 feet, where their cameras would not be able to pick out any defects in the dock. Dover resembled an enormous film lot.

The capstone to FORTITUDE was Ike's selection of General George S. Patton to command FUSAG. The Germans thought Patton the best commander the Allies had (Patton agreed) and expected him to lead the assault. Eisenhower thought Patton an excellent commander for certain specific situations, most of all in the pursuit of a retreating enemy, but not the man for OVERLORD, which required a breadth of vision and an ability to get along with the British (especially Montgomery) that Patton did not possess. Ike's plan was to use Patton after the Allies broke out of the Normandy beachhead. At that time Patton would take command of the U. S. Third Army for the drive through France.*

Until then, Eisenhower used Patton's reputation and visibility to strengthen FORTITUDE. Once again, the Germans knew of Patton's arrival in England before a public announcement was made, thanks to agents Tate and Garbo. Later, Patton attended a play in London, went to a few bars, attended a party at the Savoy Hotel, and in other ways got his name in the paper. FUSAG radio signals also told the Germans of his comings and goings, meanwhile showing that he had taken a firm grip on his new command.

These fictitious armies mixed real and notional divisions, corps and armies. The FUSAG order of battle included the U. S. Third Army, which was real but still in the United States, the British Fourth Army, which was notional, and the Canadian First Army, which was real and scheduled to go ashore in Normandy on D-Day. There were, in addition, fifty follow-up divisions (organized as the U. S. Fourteenth Army, which was notional) in the United

---

* Ike's analysis of Patton, as expressed to Marshall, is worth quoting at length: "Many generals constantly think of battle in terms of first, concentration, supply, maintenance, replacement, and second, after all the above is arranged, a *conservative* advance. This type of person is necessary because he prevents one from courting disaster. But occasions arise when one has to remember that under particular conditions, boldness is ten times as important as numbers. Patton's strength is that he thinks only in terms of attack as long as there is a single battalion that can keep advancing. Moreover, the man has a native shrewdness that operates in such a way that his troops always seem to have ammunition and sufficient food no matter where they are. Personally, I doubt that I would ever consider Patton for an army group commander or for any higher position, but as an army commander under a man who is sound and solid, and who has sense enough to use Patton's good qualities without becoming blinded by his love of showmanship and histrionics, he should do as fine a job as he did in Sicily."[16]

States awaiting shipment to the Pas de Calais after FUSAG established its beachhead. Many of the divisions in the Fourteenth Army were real and were assigned to Bradley's U. S. First Army. Thus the actual order of battle had the main weight of Allied forces in the west, southwest, and Midlands of Britain, while the notional one showed the main weight in Scotland, the east, and the southeast.[17]

RELATIONS WITH THE PRESS were an important part of keeping OVERLORD secret. A year earlier, when preparations for the invasion of Sicily were under way, Ike had worried that newspaper speculation about the next Allied offensive might tip off the Germans. He hit upon a unique method to prevent such speculation. Calling together all the correspondents accredited to his headquarters, he told them he thought of them as quasi-members of his staff, explained that he did not want them doing speculative stories on the next target, and concluded with an announcement that Sicily would be it. He asked them not even to discuss it among themselves and added that many senior officers in his own headquarters did not know what they did. One reporter told Butcher, "My God, I'm afraid to take a drink." No one talked.[18]

Eisenhower did not go so far as to tell correspondents the FORTITUDE-OVERLORD secret, but he did tell them that he thought of them as quasi-staff officers and instructed his unit commanders to cooperate with the press in every way possible. In a general order, he said that war correspondents "should be allowed to talk freely with officers and enlisted personnel and to see the machinery of war in operation in order to visualize and transmit to the public the conditions under which the men from their countries are waging war against the enemy."[19] But any mention of possible operations, or movement of units, or their location, was strictly censored. FORTITUDE was too precious, too complex, to allow mention of a division or corps by an unsuspecting reporter to ruin it.

The German press was much more tightly censored by Herr Goebbels' Propaganda Ministry, so the Allies could not get much information from French or German newspapers. But with ULTRA, they had an even better insight into German dispositions. ULTRA feedback was supplemented by air reconnaissance, spies reporting from France, POW interrogation (much was learned about the German Army by bugging the prison cells of German generals captured in Tunis, Sicily, and Italy), and other traditional methods of collecting raw information. General Kenneth Strong, Eisenhower's

G-2, had a staff of well over a thousand working for him, sifting, analyzing, cross-checking, and collating the information received and reducing it to manageable proportions. To give some idea of the scope of the intelligence network Strong had under his command, he recorded that in general a "take" of two hundred reports "would give me one sentence for my report to General Eisenhower."[20]

Strong was an affable, hearty sort of fellow, usually smiling, always optimistic, plain-spoken—a man much like Ike—and the two generals got on famously. Strong gives a good picture of Eisenhower's methods in dealing with intelligence: "I discovered that the best way to deal with him was to be completely frank, no matter what national considerations or other controversial factors were involved in any issue. . . . I learned that Eisenhower had an immense talent for listening to oral explanations and distilling their essence. . . . Only on a few occasions, when it was essential that something should appear on the record, did I produce a written Intelligence appreciation for Eisenhower. He much preferred oral reporting, as this gave him an opportunity to question uncertainties and to probe below the surface of the apparent points at issue. I found that a visit to him was worth a pile of memoranda, especially as he was so often looking far ahead of current events. He never insisted on seeing the raw Intelligence on which judgments were based, as I am told that Churchill always did."[21]

Through the spring of 1944, Strong's reports were decidedly encouraging. From ULTRA and other sources it was clear that the Germans had overestimated Allied ground strength by a factor of two, and that they believed Ike had four times more landing craft than was actually the case. At one particularly memorable session, Strong showed Ike a German map of the British order of battle, captured in Italy, which showed how completely the enemy was swallowing FORTITUDE and the notional Fourth Army. A recognition booklet, distributed to German field officers, picked up by an agent in France, included full-color drawings of the imaginary divisional shoulder patches.[22] By June 1, German intelligence counted a total of nearly eighty-nine Allied divisions in Great Britain, when in fact there were forty-seven.[23]

VON RUNDSTEDT and his principal subordinate, Rommel, were badly mistaken about the Allied order of battle. Eisenhower, thanks to ULTRA and other sources, knew the German order of battle almost as well as Rundstedt and Rommel did. And ULTRA not only told Eisenhower where the Germans were, and in what strength, but it also allowed him to eavesdrop on the debate between Rommel and Rundstedt over how to meet the attack. To oversimplify, Rundstedt wanted to keep his best panzer units well back from the coast, make sure the invasion was the real thing and not a feint, and then, and only then, counterattack in great strength. Rommel thought differently. As Strong put it in his estimate of May 5, "Rommel has now learnt that once a lodgement area has been firmly established Allied superiority in aircraft, tanks and artillery makes the elimination of such an area impossible. He will therefore strike hard and immediately at the forces facing him." To do so, Rommel wanted all his fighting units well forward, right on the beaches.[24]

Fortunately, ULTRA showed that Rommel and Rundstedt were in agreement over the most likely invasion site—the Pas de Calais. Rommel had two armies in his Army Group B, the Seventh and the Fifteenth. The best-equipped and most mobile units were the eighteen divisions in the Fifteenth Army, which included the crack 116th Panzer Division and other armored formations. Rommel had concentrated the Fifteenth Army in and around the Pas de Calais, while the Seventh Army covered the French coast from the mouth of the Seine River to Brest, which of course included Normandy.

ULTRA also revealed that the Germans estimated that Eisenhower had sufficient landing craft to bring twenty divisions ashore in the first wave. Partly because they credited him with so much strength, partly because it seemed to make such good military sense, the Germans also believed that the real invasion would be proceeded by diversionary attacks. Strong's staff had worked up precise tables on the ability of the Germans to move reinforcements into Normandy. The conclusion was that if the Germans correctly gauged OVERLORD as the main assault, they could concentrate—by D-Day plus twenty-five—some thirty-one divisions in the Normandy area, including nine panzer divisions. If that happened, the Allies would be overwhelmed. Ike could not match that rate of buildup; if he could, he would not be able to supply the men with enough ammunition, gasoline, and food to fight with, because of insufficient unloading capacity at the artificial ports. In short, if FORTITUDE did not work, if the Germans pulled their Fifteenth

Army away from the Pas de Calais and hurled it against Normandy, OVERLORD would fail.[25]

In May, the Joint Intelligence Committee of the British War Cabinet began putting together weekly summaries of "German Appreciation of Allied Intentions in the West," a one- or two-page overview of where, when, and in what strength the Germans expected the attack. These documents were stamped "Top Secret" and were circulated on a very limited basis—only fifty copies were made. In 1979, the National Archives of the United States made these summaries available to scholars for the first time. Reading them today, in a dusty cubbyhole in the Archives Building on Constitution Avenue in Washington, one is struck by the high drama and tremendous stakes involved, but even more by two facts: how completely the Germans were fooled, and how thoroughly the Allies knew not only the German order of battle, but also German plans and intentions.

The summaries came in week after week with exactly the report Eisenhower wanted to read. FORTITUDE was an edifice built so delicately, precisely, and intricately that the removal of just one supporting column would bring the whole thing crashing down. On May 29, with D-Day less than a week away, the appreciation included a chilling sentence: "The recent trend of movement of German land forces towards the Cherbourg area tends to support the view that the Le Havre-Cherbourg area is regarded as a likely, and perhaps even the main, point of assault."[26]

Had there been a slip somewhere? Had the Germans somehow penetrated FORTITUDE? There was no way to know, unless there was a lucky ULTRA intercept, but meanwhile Ike's chief air officer wanted to call off the scheduled paratrooper and glider landings on the grounds that the Germans had somehow learned the secret and would be waiting to slaughter the young men dropping into Normandy from the skies. This request caused Ike his most anxious moments in the entire war. The Allies were taking a tremendous risk and security for OVERLORD was absolutely crucial.

IN FACT, Eisenhower had spent more of his own preinvasion time and energy on security than he did on deception. It was more important for the Germans *not* to know that Normandy was the site than it was for them to think that the Pas de Calais was it. Ike's single greatest advantage over Rommel and von Rundstedt was that he knew where and when the battle would be fought, while his opponents had to guess. To keep them guessing, Eisenhower would and did go to any length to keep the secret of OVERLORD secure.

"The success or failure of coming operations depends upon whether the enemy can obtain advance information of an accurate nature," Eisenhower declared in a memorandum he sent around to all his commanders.[27] To keep that advance information from the Germans, Eisenhower had to make some hard requests of the British Government. The tremendous activity going on in the British Isles, the heavy concentration of troops, the constant coming and going of aircraft—all were potential sources of security leaks. This was especially true on the coastal areas, where the training exercises could provide much information to an enemy observer.

Eisenhower asked Churchill to move all civilians out of the coastal areas for fear there might be an undiscovered spy among them. Churchill said no—he could not go so far in upsetting people's lives. British General Frederick Morgan of Ike's staff said it was all politics, and growled, "If we fail, there won't be any more politics."

Still the government would not act. Then, in late March, Montgomery said he wanted the civilians kicked out of his training areas, and Ike sent an eloquent plea to the War Cabinet. He warned that it "would go hard with our consciences if we were to feel, in later years, that by neglecting any security precaution we had compromised the success of these vital operations or needlessly squandered men's lives." Churchill gave in. The civilians were put out and kept out until months after D-Day.[28]

In April, Eisenhower again forced the War Cabinet to take an unwelcome step. He proposed nothing short of a full stoppage of privileged diplomatic communications from the United Kingdom. Churchill was reluctant to apply so drastic a measure, but Eisenhower was insistent. "I feel bound to say frankly that I regard this source of leakage as the gravest risk to the security of our operations and to the lives of our sailors, soldiers and airmen." He said he knew a diplomatic ban would make great difficulties for the British Government, and he also realized that the War Cabinet would have to take all the blame attached to the action. Still, he said, "I cannot conceal my opinion that these difficulties are far outweighed by the greater issues which are at stake."

On April 17 the War Cabinet ruled that foreign diplomatic representatives would not be permitted to send or receive uncensored messages, and couriers of such staffs would not be allowed to leave the United Kingdom. These restrictions did not apply to the Americans or the Russians. All the Allied governments and their representatives in the United Kingdom protested, and de Gaulle broke off negotiations with SHAEF over the command and employment of the French underground.*

Churchill was understandably agitated, therefore, when Eisenhower told him that he wanted to continue the ban after D-Day. Ike feared that if it were lifted the Germans would realize that OVERLORD was the real thing and FORTITUDE would be compromised. Anthony Eden, Foreign Secretary in the War Cabinet, spoke for Churchill when he expressed shock at the request. He said that all the Allied governments expected the ban to be lifted as soon as the invasion was announced, and that if it were not, their anger at the British for imposing it would be all the greater. He asked Ike to agree to lifting the ban on D-Day plus one or two.

Eisenhower said that would not do. If the ban were lifted Hitler would "deduce the fact that from that moment he is safe in concentrating his forces to repel the assault we have made." Churchill responded by saying he could not agree to an indefinite diplomatic ban because of the great inconveniences and frictions which it caused. He proposed that it be continued until D-Day plus seven. Ike said that was still not good enough, and in the end he had his way. The ban continued until D-Day plus thirteen.[29]

With the British Government cooperating so admirably, Eisenhower could not do less. His orders on security to his commanders and their units were clear, direct, and stern. He told all units to maintain the highest standard of individual security and to mete out the severest possible disciplinary action in cases of violations. He was as good as his word.

In April, General Henry Miller, chief supply officer of the Ninth Air Force and a West Point classmate of Ike's, went to a cocktail party at Claridge's Hotel. He began talking freely, complaining about his difficulties in getting supplies but adding that his problems would end after D-Day, which he declared would begin

---

* Imposing the ban gave Hitler a useful clue as to the timing of OVERLORD. He remarked in late April that "the English have taken measures that they can sustain for only six to eight weeks."

before June 15. When challenged on the date, he offered to take bets. Ike learned of the indiscretion the next morning and acted immediately. He ordered Miller reduced to his permanent rank of colonel and sent him back to the States—the ultimate disgrace for a career soldier. Miller protested his innocence. Ike wrote back, "Dear Henry, I know of nothing that causes me more real distress than to be faced with the necessity of sitting as a judge in cases involving military offenses by officers of character and of good record, particularly when they are old and warm friends." But his decision stood.[30]

There was another flap in May when Ike learned that a U. S. Navy officer got drunk at a party and revealed details of impending operations, including areas, lift, strength, and dates. Ike confessed to Marshall, "I get so angry at the occurrence of such needless and additional hazards that I could cheerfully shoot the offender myself. This following so closely upon the Miller case is almost enough to give one the shakes." The officer was sent back to the States.[31]

Despite all precautions, there were more than 2.5 million men under Ike's command, and thus, inevitably, there were scares. One came in late March when documents relating to OVERLORD, including information on strength, places, equipment, and the tentative target date, were discovered loosely wrapped in the Chicago post office. A dozen postmen had seen some or all of the documents. The package was intended for the War Department in Washington but had been addressed to a girl in Chicago. What made it especially frightening was the fact that the sergeant who had put the wrong address on the package, Richard E. Tymm, was of German extraction. He underwent a thorough grilling; it turned out that he was not a spy, just careless. He had been daydreaming about home when he addressed the package and wrote his sister's address on it. No wonder Ike was getting the shakes and talking about cheerfully cutting a few throats himself.[32]

Security for OVERLORD included keeping the Germans from discovering the various new devices on which the Allies were counting for success, such as artificial harbors and swimming tanks. If the Germans learned about Mulberry (code name for concrete platforms to be floated across to Normandy, then sunk to create an artificial port), they would know that the Allies were coming across an open beach, not directly at a port city. ULTRA and the

Double-Cross System combined to tell Eisenhower that the Germans were unsuspecting; there was nothing about the artificial ports on German radio, and the spy masters in Berlin were not asking their spies in England for any information about Mulberry.[33]

These devices were but small aspects of the larger scene. World War II, as the phrase has it, was fought in large part on the drawing boards. All the nations involved were striving frantically to make technological breakthroughs. By far the most important of these was the development of the atomic bomb. In the United States the Manhattan Project, under General Leslie Groves, was making rapid progress toward its objective, but Groves and several of the leading scientists on the project were worried about the possibility of the Germans using radioactive poisons against the OVERLORD forces. Groves told Marshall there was a remote chance of it happening, and Marshall sent Arthur Peterson of the Manhattan Project to London to see Ike and explain the danger to him. Peterson emphasized the need for secrecy so strongly, however, there was little Ike could do to meet the possible threat. He did not brief his senior commanders, but he did have the medical channels informed about symptoms.[34]

IN MID-MAY, Eisenhower ordered the concentration of the assault force near the invasion ports in southern England. The enormous heaps of supplies that had been gathered and stored throughout the United Kingdom then began the final move, carried by unending convoys to the south, filling all available warehouses, overflowing into camouflaged fields. Hundreds of thousands of men meanwhile traveled to tented areas in the southern counties. They were completely sealed off from the rest of the world, with barbed-wire fences stretching around their camps, keeping all the troops in and all civilians out. Some two thousand Counter Intelligence Corps men guarded the area. Camouflage was everywhere, for this was the most tempting and profitable military target in Europe, and the Germans were known to be on the verge of making their V weapons operational.

Within the encampment, the men received their final briefings. For the first time they learned they were going to Normandy. They pored over foam-rubber models of the beaches, examined photographs, were made familiar with landmarks, were assured of overwhelming naval and air support, and finally given the overall picture, the broad outline of OVERLORD. Ike's men were set to go. "The mighty host," he later wrote, "was tense as a coiled spring, ready for the moment when its energy should be released and it would vault the English Channel."[35]

Everything had been done that could be done. Would the Germans be surprised? The question could not be answered. The last-minute signs could not have been worse. At the end of May the mighty Panzer Lehr Armored Division showed up in Normandy, along with the 21st Panzer Division, which moved from Brittany to Caen, exactly to the site where the British Second Army would be landing. Even more alarming, ULTRA revealed that the German 91st Divison, specialists in fighting paratroopers, and the German 6th Parachute Regiment had moved on May 29 into exactly the areas where the American 82d and 101st Airborne Divisions were to land the night before D-Day. Finally, the German 352d Division, veterans of the Russian front, had moved forward from St. Lô, at the base of the neck of the Cotentin Peninsula, to the coast, taking up a position overlooking Omaha Beach, where the U. S. First Army was going to land.[36]

These movements gave everyone the jitters. They caused Ike's air commander, Leigh-Mallory, to urge Eisenhower to call off the landings of the 82d and 101st for fear they would be destroyed. As Ike later wrote, "It would be difficult to conceive of a more soul-racking problem."[37]

He quickly got one. SHAEF had prepared for everything, except the weather. On June 4, a storm roared in from the northwest. Waves and wind were much too high to attempt a landing. Suddenly, the SHAEF weatherman became the most important intelligence officer of all.

CHAPTER SEVEN

D-Day
and the French
Resistance

JUNE 4, 1944. Group Captain J. M. Stagg of the RAF must provide Ike with the final piece of information he needs to launch OVERLORD—one that no one could control or keep secret. What will the weather be like on D-Day?

TO HELP HIM answer that crucial question, Stagg had six different weather services (American and British land, sea, and air) feeding him information. On the morning of June 4, to his dismay, he had six distinct weather predictions to pick from.

The Germans, too, had their problems in predicting the weather. Stagg explained their predicament in his book *Forecast for Overlord:* "Deprived of weather reports from the British Isles and the ocean areas to the west and north, German forecasters could be kept in ignorance of the development and movement of weather systems over an area which is always important for forecasting throughout north-western and central Europe—in ignorance, except in so far as the Germans organized their own reports from their own reconnaissance aircraft or submarines, and they were known to go to great lengths to do this."[1]

Stagg was the beneficiary of the German effort, because ULTRA picked up the weather reports from German submarines and helped him fill in his charts. He made up his own prediction, one that drew upon all the others but was uniquely his. Despite the intense storm on June 4, Stagg predicted a break in the weather for June 6. Ike trusted his source. He decided to take the risk and go.

THE INVASION WAS UNDER WAY. At 1 A.M. on June 6, 1944, German agent Garbo sent to the Abwehr the most sought-after secret of the war—where and when the invasion was coming. Garbo reported that OVERLORD was on the way, named some of the divisions involved, indicated when they had left Portsmouth, and predicted that they would come ashore in Normandy at dawn.

The report had to be deciphered, read, evaluated, reenciphered, and transmitted to Berlin. There it was deciphered, typed up, and sent to army headquarters, then on to Hitler. The whole process was reversed to get orders out to the German forces on the French coast. The word did not arrive in time to do any good. By the time the Germans got it, they could see 6,000 planes overhead, 5,000 ships off the coast, the first wave of troops coming ashore.

But it surely raised their opinion of Garbo.[2]

At dawn, June 6, Eisenhower's mighty host crossed the Channel successfully, hurled itself against the Normandy beaches, and established a beachhead. Paratrooper losses, although heavy, did not approach the 70 percent mark that Leigh-Mallory had predicted. There were many anxious moments along Omaha Beach, where the U. S. 1st Division faced the German 352d Division, but by nightfall of June 6, the Americans were there to stay. The British and Canadian forces also generally achieved their D-Day objectives.

The foul weather had been a positive help to the Allies because the Germans believed the weather was so bad that no invasion could be launched. In fact, due to the weather they canceled the customary air and sea reconnaissance missions that would have warned them of the approaching fleet. A war game at Rennes, attended by a number of army and divisional commanders from the Normandy area, went off on schedule. And Rommel, after studying the weather reports, had gone on leave!

Not one submarine, not one small boat, not one airplane, not one radar set, not one German, anywhere, detected the launching of the largest force of warships in history, or the passage of that fleet—covered by the largest force of airplanes ever assembled—across the Channel. As General Walter Warlimont, deputy chief of operations at German Supreme Headquarters, recorded, on the eve of OVERLORD the leaders of the Wehrmacht "had not the slightest idea that the decisive event of the war was upon them."[3]

ONE ASPECT of Eisenhower's decision to go on June 6 that is seldom mentioned was his fear that if he postponed OVERLORD until the next suitable date (June 16), FORTITUDE might well be compromised. Tens of thousands of Allied soldiers had been told that Normandy was the site; to keep them sealed off from the outside world for two weeks seemed impossible. Further, German air reconnaissance was sure to discover the immense buildup of forces around Portsmouth and southern England. Already Rommel seemed to be reinforcing Normandy and the Cotentin Peninsula. OVERLORD almost had to go on June 6, if it were to go at all.

BY DAWN OF JUNE 7, OVERLORD had achieved its first crucial goal, to get ashore. Now began the second test: Had FORTITUDE convinced the Germans that Normandy was a feint? Rommel and Rundstedt greatly outnumbered Ike on the Continent. If they operated at full tilt, rushing reinforcements into Normandy with maximum speed, they still had plenty of time and opportunity to drive the Allies into the sea. Because the Germans could move by truck, tank, or railroad, while the Allied forces had to journey to the battlefield via ship and landing craft, the advantage was with the Germans. Ike had three weapons to keep the enemy away from the battlefield while he steadily brought in more units from Britain.

One was air superiority. From dawn to dusk, Allied airmen bombed and shot up every enemy column, whether on the roads or on the rails, that was spotted trying to move into Normandy. Eisenhower's second weapon was the French underground, working in close coordination with SHAEF, against targets designated by Ike, to harass the German columns, blow bridges, create roadblocks, and in countless other ways slow the rate of German movement.

Ike's third weapon in the battle of the buildup was the cheapest, in terms of men and matériel, and the most successful in terms of keeping German troops away from the battle area. It was a continuation of FORTITUDE, this time with one of the most brazen operations of the war.

On D-Day plus three, June 9, Garbo sent a message to his spy master with a request that it be submitted urgently to the German High Command. "The present operation, though a large-scale assault, is diversionary in character," Garbo stated flatly. "Its object is to establish a strong bridgehead in order to draw the maximum of our reserves into the area of the assault and to retain them there so as to leave another area exposed where the enemy could then attack with some prospect of success."

Citing the Allied order of battle, Garbo said that Eisenhower had committed only a small portion of his seventy-five divisions (Ike's actual total was fifty). He pointed out that no FUSAG unit had taken part in the Normandy attack, nor was Patton there. Further, "The constant aerial bombardment which the sector of the Pas de Calais has been undergoing and the disposition of the enemy forces would indicate the imminence of the assault in this region which offers the shortest route to the final objective of the Anglo-American illusions: Berlin."[4]

Within half a day, Garbo's message was in Hitler's hands. On the basis of it, the Führer made a momentous decision. Rundstedt had wanted to commit his best division, the 1st SS Panzer Division, together with the 116th Panzer Division, to the battle in Normandy, where Rommel desperately needed reinforcements. They had started for Caen, but now Hitler ordered the armored units back to the Pas de Calais to help the Fifteenth Army defend against the main invasion. He also awarded an Iron Cross, Second Class, to Garbo.[5]

The Double-Cross System orchestra was now playing at full volume, with every instrument involved. The Germans had great confidence not only in Garbo but in all their spies. Whenever troops of real formations reached France, they were always troops who had been identified and reported on by the agents. As a consequence of finding the reports to be accurate, the Germans naturally believed the reports which concerned the imaginary troops supposedly still stationed in England, poised to hit the Pas de Calais. It was relatively easy to convince the Germans that the real divisions that were coming into Normandy had been shifted from FUSAG to Normandy because of the Allies' unexpected difficulties in breaking out of the beachhead.

The deception went on. On June 13, an agent warned that another attack would take place in two or three days around Dieppe or Abbeville, near the Pas de Calais. Another agent reported that airborne divisions (wholly fictitious) would drop around Amiens, halfway between Paris and the Pas de Calais.

In late June, agent Tate reported. Masterman had convinced the Germans that he was a man with a genius for making friends in high places—he was the spy who reported Eisenhower's arrival in London in January—so the Abwehr was not surprised when Tate claimed to have obtained the railway schedule for moving the FUSAG forces from their concentration areas to the embarkation ports, thus reinforcing from a new angle the imminence of the threat to the Pas de Calais. Tate's report was considered so important by one Abwehr officer that he gave it as his opinion that it could "even decide the outcome of the war." He was not far wrong.

FORTITUDE had remarkable durability. As Masterman notes, "In German eyes, the threat to the Pas de Calais was as great and dangerous in July as it had been in May. In fact, and beyond the wildest hopes of those responsible, the threat held until the autumn."[6]

One of Ike's greatest pleasures during the first two months of the campaign was to read the weekly intelligence summaries (or, more often, hear Strong's oral report) on "German appreciation of Allied intentions in the West," the principle source being ULTRA. Each summary was brief and to the point.

The summary of June 19 read, "The Germans still believe the Allies capable of launching another amphibious operation. The Pas de Calais remains an expected area for attack. Fears of landings in Norway have been maintained. Enemy naval and ground forces have remained unaltered since D-Day."

On July 10: "So far the enemy's fear of large scale landings between the Seine and the Pas de Calais has not diminished. The second half of July is given as the probable time for this operation." Not so good was the report that "German fears of a landing in Southern Norway continue to diminish."

By July 24, Ike had almost thirty divisions in Normandy and had by then won the battle of the buildup. On that date, the summary was again welcome reading: "The Germans have identified in Normandy some units that they believe to have been part of the army held in readiness for a second major landing between the Seine and the Franco-Belgian frontier. But there has been no considerable transfer of German forces from the Pas de Calais, which remains strongly garrisoned." The summary did note that one division was moving out of the Pas de Calais, and another from Belgium, both presumably headed for the battle area in Normandy.

The next summary, on July 31, noted that the two divisions had shown up in Normandy "and the last remaining armoured division

North of the Seine has now arrived in the battle area. It is likely that these movements have been forced on the enemy by the increasing urgency of battle requirements despite his fears of an Allied landing north of the Seine. Though the enemy now regards such a landing as rather less imminent, these fears still remain."[7]

By August 3, when Patton came onto the Continent with his U. S. Third Army, most German officers realized that Normandy was the real thing. By then, of course, it was too late. The Germans had kept hundreds of their best tanks and thousands of their finest fighting men (a total of fifteen divisions) out of this crucial battle of the war in order to meet a threat that was always imaginary. Equally remarkable, as Masterman noted, was "that no single case was compromised by the grand deception for OVERLORD, but that, on the contrary, those agents who took a leading part in it were more highly regarded by the Germans after it than before."[8]

On October 25, 1944, Colonel John Bevan, the Controlling Officer of Deception and Masterman's boss, wrote his immediate superior, "When the history of this war is written, I believe it will be found that the German High Command was, largely through the medium of BI-A channels, induced to make faulty dispositions, in particular during the vital post-OVERLORD D-Day period."[9] It was British understatement on a grand scale. To paraphrase Churchill, never had so many been immobilized by so few.

FORTITUDE and the Double-Cross System held the Fifteenth Army in place at the Pas de Calais, but the Germans had other formations in France to draw upon in the battle of the buildup. Again, the role of the air forces in immobilizing these troops cannot be overemphasized, but that story is not part of the secret side of OVERLORD. An equally important role was played by the French underground, and that story *is* a part of any account of Eisenhower and the intelligence community, for it was in this area that the OSS made its contribution to a successful OVERLORD.

"Ah, those first OSS arrivals in London! How well I remember them," wrote the British humorist Malcolm Muggeridge, "arriving like *jeune filles en fleur* straight from a finishing school, all fresh and innocent, to start work in our frowsty old intelligence brothel. All too soon they were ravished and corrupted, becoming indistinguishable from seasoned pros who had been in the game for a quarter century or more."[10]

Donovan insisted that the OSS had to have a major role in OVERLORD, one at least equal to that of its British counterpart, Special Operations Executive (SOE), which had been controlling all Allied relations with the French Resistance since 1941. In Donovan's view, SOE did not think or act on a big enough scale. Its operations were geared to a spy here, a clandestine radio operator there, or sporadic contact with underground cells, all reflecting the time when the British were fighting the war alone, on a shoestring. But by 1944, things were different—the Allies could draw on the seemingly unlimited production of the United States. Donovan wanted to do much more, beginning with a program of supplying arms on a large scale to the Maquis.

The British disagreed. They wanted to limit the amount of supplies sent to France because of their belief that rival resistance groups would use the weapons to fight each other instead of the Germans, and that after liberation the Communists would use the arms to take political power. Donovan ignored the threat. He had Communists in the OSS and was sure he knew how to control them —besides, they were fighting Germans, were they not? In place of small, secret, self-contained cells directed from London by radio, Donovan wanted nothing less than a French Army, albeit on paramilitary lines, with the French sharing leadership equally with Americans and Englishmen on the spot. To hell with the political consequences—he wanted as many well-armed Frenchmen as possible taking part in the national uprising against the Nazis.[11]

So, in the spring of 1944, Donovan advocated a substantial increase in the quantity of arms, ammunition, and other supplies sent to France in order to increase participation in the Maquis and to assure maximum military effectiveness of the Resistance on D-Day.

Again the British, more accustomed to fighting the Germans with brains than with brawn, were hesitant. Compounding that problem, the British had a monopoly on relations with the Maquis through SOE, and those few supplies that were air-dropped to the French came from the British. Ike tried to explain to Frenchmen who complained about American stinginess that the supplies the British were dropping had come from America in the first place, but it made little impression.

After D-Day, when the Maquis began to prove its worth, Eisenhower—acting at Donovan's request—greatly increased the rate of supply, using as many as three hundred bombers on one operation to parachute supplies to the French. Donovan gleefully reported to Marshall, "It is now possible to publicize our aid to the French Resistance and thus to cultivate for the U.S. the good will of the French people."[12]

As the supply controversy indicates, there was profound mistrust between the Allies. Some Anglophobic Frenchmen, including de Gaulle, suspected that the British were trying to reestablish the old English kingdom of Aquitaine in France. Others charged that the British were willing to "fight to the last Frenchman."

The British, for their part, continued to fear that communism would take over when the Germans left France and they were irritated at Donovan's bull-in-the-china-shop methods and his lack of political sophistication. The Americans just wanted to kill Germans, as quickly and efficiently as possible. Under the circumstances, the British would not trust the French; the OSS would not trust the British; the French would not trust anyone.

How then to use the potential of the Maquis? The answer was a brilliant compromise, a remarkable international secret service plan code-named JEDBURGH (the name came from the training quarters at Jedburgh on the Jed River in Scotland). The JED teams, as they were called, were three-man groups—one Frenchman, one Englishman, one American. Starting on D-Day, the JEDS were to parachute in uniform to areas known to have heavy concentrations of Maquis, where they would act as liaison with the underground, arm and train the guerrilla forces, and coordinate activity with SHAEF. Altogether, between D-Day and the liberation of France, 91 JED teams were parachuted into France.[13]

Initially, control of the JEDS was supposed to remain with the two secret services, SOE and OSS. But Ike was hardly the man to allow an activity so closely connected to OVERLORD to go on under someone else's command. On March 23, 1944, he assumed control of all secret service activity connected with OVERLORD. The joint special operations unit formed by OSS and SOE was divorced entirely from its parent organizations and renamed Special Force Headquarters, reporting directly to SHAEF.[14] This naturally displeased de Gaulle (who had set up his own government, the French Committee of National Liberation, in Algiers) because the Maquis was, he felt, his army—but he could not supply it, did not command it, and could only barely communicate with it as the radio contacts were controlled by SHAEF.

Ike had not lived through the night of November 8–9, 1942, arguing with Giraud for nothing. He was keenly sensitive to de Gaulle's complaint and, as will be seen, he was much more willing to meet de Gaulle's demands—and thus get de Gaulle's cooperation—than any other highly placed Anglo-American leader. He went to great lengths to keep de Gaulle's people in Algiers informed, to ask their opinion, to coordinate activity with them.

Such coordination became impossible, however, after the imposing of the diplomatic ban, because de Gaulle said he would be damned if he would use the British cipher to communicate with his military leaders in London. If the French could not use their own cipher, they would not talk to Ike or anyone else.

An additional problem was that both Churchill and FDR mistrusted the French so completely that they insisted Eisenhower *not* tell any Frenchman the date or place of the attack. The complex story of how these problems were worked out takes a volume in itself to describe fully; suffice it to say here that Ike spent much of his preinvasion time on relations with the French without ever achieving a satisfactory resolution.[15] His main accomplishment was to convince de Gaulle that he was honest, intelligent, and a sincere friend of France.

Through the spring of 1944 the JEDs went through their training, under SHAEF supervision, while the staff at Special Force Headquarters pored over charts, maps, railroad schedules, and timetables to select targets in France for the Maquis to hit on D-Day and in the follow-up period.

The British official history of SOE outlines the role SHAEF assigned to the Maquis: "A preliminary increase in the tempo of sabotage, with particular attention to fighter aircraft and enemy morale; attacks on local hq, simple road and telephone wrecking, removal of German explosive from mined bridges likely to be useful to the allies, and more and more sabotage as the air battle reached its climax; and then, simultaneously with the seaborne assault, an all-out attack on roads, railways and telephones, and the harassing of occupation troops wherever they could be found by any available means." All this had to be coordinated with FORTITUDE—i.e., the sabotage activities had to be spread out evenly over all possible landing sites, with the emphasis on the Pas de Calais.[16]

The JEDs had some ingenious techniques to work with. Julian Huxley, the zoologist, developed a cyclonite plastic explosive that could be manufactured by the thousands and that looked to be cattle droppings. They were powerful enough to burst a rubber tire. The idea was for the Maquis to spread them in the path of panzer columns trying to make their way to Normandy. The JEDs learned how to disrupt German communications systems in such a way that the Germans could not find the breaks—one such technique was to drive a thumbtack into a signals cable. All across France, in the days following June 6, signposts were turned to point in the wrong direction, causing terrible confusion among the Wehrmacht. A cube or two of sugar in the gas tank could immobilize a Tiger Royal tank.

JED agents in the north of France managed to sabotage more than a hundred factories producing war materials for the Germans. The favorite technique was simplicity itself: A JED, or more likely a Frenchman of the Maquis speaking for him, would approach the manager of a factory requesting that he allow the sabotage of certain machines, and threatening Allied bombing of the plant if he did not agree. Most agreed, if only to prevent the destruction of the entire plant. Those who did not were amazed at how quickly and accurately the JEDs could call in air strikes on their factories.[17]

THE VAST MAJORITY of regular army officers are disdainful of irregular forces, for in their view the guerrilla warriors are without order, control, discipline, or clearly defined purpose. But Ike was not an ordinary professional soldier, and from the moment he took up the reins of command for OVERLORD he counted on the Maquis for a significant contribution to victory, most of all in the areas of interrupting communications and slowing the flow of German reinforcements to Normandy. In short, the Maquis would be one of his chief weapons in the battle of the buildup, nearly as important as FORTITUDE.

In late April, Eisenhower made one of his most basic decisions on the Maquis and OVERLORD. Special Forces Headquarters had planned to keep the Resistance in the South of France out of action on D-Day. The idea was to turn the Maquis loose only after the Allied landings at Marseilles (code name ANVIL), which was scheduled for mid-August. Headquarters feared that if they rose up in June, the Germans would identify them and probably eliminate most of them before ANVIL. In that case, the French Resistance would not be able to do for ANVIL what it was counted on to do for OVERLORD.

On April 18, however, Eisenhower decided to overrule Special Forces. He sent a cable to the Supreme Commander, Mediterranean, General Henry Wilson, saying that because OVERLORD had the top priority, and because "it is unlikely that Resistance forces in south France could be restrained from rising when OVERLORD is launched," he had decided to have SHAEF take operational control of the Resistance in the South of France and make it an integral part of the whole JED setup. The objective, Ike ordered on May 21, would be to "delay the movement of enemy forces to the lodgement area," and to "harass such enemy lines of communications as pass through the South of France." Special Forces then worked up long, detailed, extensive charts on exactly what bridges, railroad crossings, and other key points the supreme commander wanted destroyed.[18]

The results, all across France, were tremendous and spectacular. The BBC broadcast the famous "personal messages" that set off the Maquis and started a vast army in motion. On the night of June 5–6 alone, the Maquis successfully attacked 950 of the 1,050 railroad targets it had been given.[19]

Sensational as that achievement was, there was even better to follow. All across France that night, JED teams landed from the air, made contact with the local Maquis leaders, and went into action. On D-Day plus one, a German SS armored division equipped with the latest and best German tanks started out from Toulouse toward Normandy. Its progress was excruciatingly, infuriatingly slow. All the bridges over the Loire River were down, some destroyed by air, some by the Maquis.

The 2d SS Panzer Division had its own bridging train, and much experience with the broad Russian rivers in how to use it, so the downed bridges held it up for only a few hours. What really slowed it down was the incessant guerrilla activity. The division's gasoline dumps were blown before it even got started. There was only a single open railway line running north, of almost no help to the tankers because one stick of dynamite could derail the whole train. So they marched, and at every appropriate spot along the way, the Maquis sprayed the column with machine-gun and mortar fire. That action caused the panzers to halt in their tracks. Then the

JED teams could put in a call to the Allied air forces, and Ike's pilots would give the Germans a good pounding. The British official history records that the Maquis "left the Germans so thoroughly mauled that when they did eventually crawl into their lagers close to the fighting line, heaving a sigh of relief that at last they would have real soldiers to deal with and not these damned terrorists, their fighting quality was much below what it had been when they started."[20]

When Rommel persuaded Hitler to send the 2d SS Panzer Division to Normandy, he expected it to arrive on D-Day plus three. It actually arrived, after passing through its ordeal of fire, on D-Day plus seventeen. One more panzer division at Omaha Beach on June 9 or 10 might well have made the difference, so it may be said with truth that in this operation alone the Maquis made an invaluable contribution to the Allied victory. Of course, not all German columns moving toward Normandy were so badly hit, but SHAEF estimated that the overall action of the Resistance resulted in an average delay of two days on all German units attempting to move to the battle.[21]

The French paid heavily for their own liberation. If regular soldiers do not like fighting with guerrillas, they like even less having to fight against them. The Germans, in any event, had fallen into the habit of behaving like absolute beasts in France. Consequently, the revenge they reaped for Maquis actions was terrible. The worst and most famous case was Oradour-sur-Glane, where in retaliation for sniper fire that had killed a popular company commander, the Germans rounded up the entire population in the village square. The women and children were sent into the church; the men were shot down where they stood; the Germans then set fire to the church. Armed SS guards stood around it to make certain nobody got out alive. About seven hundred were killed.[22]

The Maquis not only harassed the German columns headed toward Normandy; the French also provided the SHAEF forces with priceless information on German troop movements in general, on the strength of various units, their equipment, their leaders, their weaknesses. When, in August, the Germans began their retreat from Normandy, the Maquis ambushed the retreating columns, attacked isolated groups, and protected bridges from destruction.

The OSS official history declared, "The most significant discovery was the enormous importance of French resistance as a source of accurate tactical intelligence. The Maquis role in this respect had originally been contemplated as incidental, but it proved to be a major contribution. Just before the break-through at St. Lô, for example, the Maquis gave the Americans excellent coverage of German artillery placements, tank units, troops dispositions and the condition of strategic bridges."[23]

Was the Maquis worth five divisions to Ike? Ten? Twenty? It was and is impossible to make an exact estimate. Ike used the word "invaluable" on numerous occasions in his postwar praise of the Resistance forces. He also frequently pointed to the most intangible but perhaps most valuable contribution of those forces: "Not least in importance," Eisenhower declared in his official report, "they had, by their ceaseless harassing activities, surrounded the Germans with a terrible atmosphere of danger and hatred which ate into the confidence of the leaders and the courage of the soldiers."[24]

Nor did Eisenhower wait until after the war to show his appreciation. On June 15, when the campaign was less than ten days old, he greatly increased the rate of supply drops to the Maquis throughout France. "These extra sorties are being given," he explained, "in order to further assist the resistance movement which at the moment is giving unexpected results." An especially big drop came on June 25, when 180 bombers of the U. S. Eighth Air Force delivered three hundred tons of supplies to guerrillas in four separate areas in southern France. A Resistance leader signaled London, "The Maquis' thanks to the U. S. Air Force for a damned good show! When is the next?" The next came on Bastille Day and was also a great success.[25]

Until June 17, the Resistance received its missions (and thus in practice its orders) from Special Forces, a part of SHAEF. De Gaulle found this fact distressing. He insisted that French troops had to be commanded by French generals, and he had already declared that all those who took part in the national uprising against the enemy would be considered part of the French Army and entitled to all the rights and privileges of regular soldiers. Ike, anxious to please de Gaulle as a necessary part of maintaining coordination with the Resistance, had seen the point long before the invasion, but Churchill and Roosevelt would not give him permission to put the Resistance under a French general.

By mid-June, however, they had come to see that their mistrust of de Gaulle was misplaced, and they allowed Ike to appoint General Pierre Joseph Koenig the head of the French Forces of the Interior, as the Maquis was now called officially. A week later, Ike announced that Koenig had the same status of any Allied commander serving under SHAEF.[26] The humiliation and shame of the occupation, 1940–44, was finally over. The French had once again taken their place alongside their British and American friends to drive the Boche from their soil.

When Special Force Headquarters disbanded in 1945, Eisenhower wrote a personal letter of appreciation. He said no final assessment of the operational value of the Resistance had yet been made, but "I consider that the disruption of enemy rail communications, the harassing of German road moves and the continual and increasing strain placed on the German war economy and internal security services throughout occupied Europe by the organized forces of resistance, played a very considerable part in our complete and final victory."

Ike added his own "great admiration for the brave and often spectacular exploits" of the Resistance and the JED teams. Finally, he put the effort into perspective: "In no previous war, and in no other theater during this war, have resistance forces been so closely harnessed to the main military effort."[27]

THE AMERICANS were also getting better in the spy game. Two young SLUs, Stuyvesant Wainwright II and John Oakes, captured the first German stay-behind agent, a Frenchman whose code name was Frutos. They knew Frutos was in Cherbourg because they had monitered his trial-run messages back to Germany, sent before American troops overran the port city. Frutos' assignment was to send the Germans information on troop units coming into France, ships in port, and so on. From one of the practice messages, Wainwright and Oakes knew Frutos had a girl friend. As soon as the Americans entered Cherbourg, they found her. She talked. They picked up Frutos, turned him into a double-agent, and used him exactly as the British used their agents in the Double-Cross System. That is, Frutos was allowed to send on accurate information about matters the Germans already knew, while feeding them false information on key points, designed to support FORTITUDE.[28]

Frutos was only the first of many stay-behinds picked up by

both the British and the Americans. Most were found thanks to ULTRA. To the end, the Germans never suspected a thing.

The American SLUs found themselves gaining prestige in the eyes of their commanders during the battle of the buildup. Earlier, before D-Day, Wainwright said that General Bradley and his staff "were very, very skeptical" of the ULTRA information. They just could not believe any intelligence officer could be that good. But once the battle was joined, "SLU breaks were such that you could find out practically where small units were moving, and, Christ, you just had to believe. Because going through Normandy . . . you'd get a message that 110th headquarters was at a certain place, and by God it was there. This you had to believe."

Wainwright's biggest problem was providing a cover story for his source. Most of the intelligence officers he dealt with did not know about ULTRA; they were naturally curious as to where Wainwright was getting all his fabulous information. "Nine out of ten times we made it up out of whole cloth. The cover story was picked out of the air." For example, when asked how he knew that the 106th Panzer Division would be moving into the line that night, Wainwright replied that he was running a spy who overheard a conversation at a local bar between two German officers.

That spy was fictitious, but the story rang true because in fact the SLUs had "a helluva lot of confidential funds. . . . They could run agents on their own. Hire agents. I did that. My boss was very keen on that. He used to call these agents midgets. He'd say, 'Wainwright, how many midgets are you running?' "[29]

BY JULY 1944 the Allies had won the battle of the buildup. A handful of men in the British Secret Service, spearheaded by Masterman, along with thousands of Frenchmen and Frenchwomen of all ages, aided in no small measure by the SLUs and ULTRA, had imposed just enough delay on the Germans to make the victory by the British and American troops possible. It was a damn close-run thing, as Wellington is reported to have said about Waterloo, but if the margin was slim, it was sufficient.

CHAPTER EIGHT

The Battle of Mortain—
ULTRA'S Greatest Triumph

MID-JULY 1944. Cherbourg has been captured, the damage to the port repaired. On July 19 the first supply ships start unloading. The Americans have landed a total of 770,000 troops in Normandy. They have suffered 73,000 casualties, which are more than compensated for by reserve divisions in England (including the 82d and 101st Airborne, which have been withdrawn from the Continent for refitting) waiting their chance to cross over and join the battle.

The British and Canadians have landed 591,000 troops, suffered 49,000 casualties, and also have reserve forces waiting to cross. The Germans, meanwhile, continue to hold the Fifteenth Army at the Pas de Calais, despite the overwhelming Allied commitment to Normandy, because they still overestimate Ike's total force. The Wehrmacht has taken 116,863 casualties. In Normandy, the Germans have twenty-six divisions, many of them understrength, facing thirty-four Allied divisions.[1]

ALL GERMAN ATTEMPTS to drive the Allies off the Continent had failed miserably, partly because of poor generalship—they committed their reserves piecemeal, feeding them into the battle as soon as they arrived at the front—and partly because of ULTRA. Whenever the Germans did try to assemble forces for a major counterattack, ULTRA passed the word to Allied artillery, airmen, and naval forces, who together unleashed a horrendous bombardment on the assembly center.

Still, the Wehrmacht on the defensive remained a formidable

foe. Winterbotham went to Normandy to see Bradley and check on the operation of the SLU system. Bradley thanked him and all those involved in ULTRA's performance: "Never did I expect to get such concise information about my opponents," he said, then added, "The only trouble is that there seems to be too many of them."[2]

So, although he was in control of most of Normandy and was the winner in the battle of the buildup, as July drew to a close Ike was close to despair. Flying bombs were falling on London. Monty's attempts to take Caen had failed, despite the massive application of air power. Bradley's progress in the hedgerow country was agonizingly slow. After seven weeks of fighting, the deepest Allied penetrations were some thirty miles inland, on a front of only eighty miles. There was hardly enough room to maneuver or to bring in the reserves waiting in England. The Germans were fighting savagely, taking advantage of every piece of cover and laying mines with extraordinary skill.

The Wehrmacht was, however, stretched thin, too thin to keep up the fight much longer. ULTRA revealed that Hitler was ordering his generals to stay put, which indicated that they were asking him for permission to retreat.[3] Fortunately for the Allies, Hitler decided that Rundstedt was a defeatist and replaced him with General Guenther von Kluge.

Even better, Rommel was wounded on July 17 when an Allied fighter strafed the staff car in which he was riding. He was then implicated in the July 20 plot against Hitler and eventually committed suicide to avoid the shame of a trial. Von Kluge assumed Rommel's duties in addition to his other responsibilities, but Hitler did not trust Kluge either and therefore insisted on maintaining a tight personal control over his battle plans and actions. That situation forced the Germans to use the radio extensively, which was ideal for ULTRA.

Nevertheless, the Germans, in their fixed positions, with their panzers dug in, utilizing every fold of ground, most especially the famous hedgerows of Normandy, could not be dislodged. If the Allies could ever break through, they could use their air and transport superiority to launch a war of maneuver that would crush the Germans in France. The trick was to break through. In a sense the situation of 1940 had been reversed, with the Germans in the role of the immobile French at the Maginot Line and the Allies ready to begin a blitzkrieg of their own, if only they could crack the shell.

Bradley had a plan to force a breakout. It called for the massive use of air power in a manner that resembled a 1916-type offensive, with the bombers substituting for artillery to blast a hole through the German line. The big difference between Bradley's plan, code name COBRA, and a World War I offensive was the relative thinness of the German line in 1944, coupled with the presence of American tanks to exploit the hole blasted in the line.

COBRA began on July 25. The tremendous bombardment left the Germans in a dazed condition. At the same time the Canadians, on the left, began a drive toward Falaise, which gained little ground but did pin down the panzers facing Montgomery. Meanwhile, General "Lightning Joe" Collins, a veteran of Guadalcanal, led his U. S. VII Corps to St. Lô, through the German lines, and broke out into the open countryside of France.

The Germans, finally, abandoned their *idée fixe* that the main landings would come at the Pas de Calais. Kluge obtained Hitler's permission to transfer two divisions from the Fifteenth Army to Normandy. Hitler told Kluge to "keep his eyes riveted to the front and on the enemy without ever looking backward."[4] ULTRA picked up that signal, to Ike's great delight, because it told him the Germans were doing exactly what he hoped they would do—stand in Normandy and take a beating there. What Eisenhower most feared was that the Germans would retire to the line of the Seine River, or perhaps all the way back to the Franco-German border, there to take up prepared defensive positions.

But with Hitler in charge, there was no danger of a German retreat. Ike counted on what he called Hitler's "conqueror's mentality." He believed that Hitler, like most aggressive leaders, could not bring himself to give up land he had conquered. Throughout the war, Eisenhower took it for granted that his enemies would stand and fight, no matter how precarious their situation or how bad their position, rather than retreat to shorter, more easily defended lines. It was a leap into the mind of the man directing the battle from the other side of the hill, the kind of intelligence that comes from study and observation over a period of time, as well as from a study of history, rather than as the result of an intercepted radio message or a spy's report.[5]

Collins' breakthrough opened the way for a flow of reinforcements from England to France led by Patton. The situation was the culmination of a soldier's dreams. Eisenhower had armored units loose in the enemy rear and they could go in any direction he wanted them to go. Patton might be sent east, toward Paris, or northeast, toward the German rear at Caen, or south into central France, or west into Brittany.

As Ike told Marshall on August 2, he now had a golden opportunity not only to defeat the German Army but to destroy it. Patton sent one corps into Brittany to get possession of the ports there; the other three corps of his Third Army sped southward from Avranches, with the ultimate intention of swinging around the exposed German left flank and encircling Kluge's Seventh Army. The Third Army's food, fuel, ammunition and other supplies had to come through the narrow bottleneck at Avranches.

At this moment, Hitler decided to counterattack. He ordered an offensive along the Mortain-Avranches axis on through to the coast. It was a brilliant strategic move that promised, if successful, to isolate Patton and possibly even drive the Allies back into the sea.

It was a gamble, and Hitler signaled to Kluge, "The decision in the Battle of France depends on the success of the Avranches attack. You have a unique opportunity, which will never return, to drive into an extremely exposed enemy area and thereby to change the situation completely."[6]

To succeed, Hitler needed to convince Kluge that the plan would work. In this he failed. Hitler wanted to delay the counterattack until an imposing force of panzers had been gathered opposite Mortain, so that the blow, when it came, would be a strategic and not just a tactical one. But Kluge attacked five days ahead of schedule, precisely because he thought the best that could be attained would be minor changes in the front line, not a strategic turnaround. Furthermore, Kluge could not afford to pull more of his tanks off Monty's front; he had already brought down to Normandy most of the armor in the Fifteenth Army, and in any case the combination of Allied air forces guided by ULTRA and the French Resistance made movement of units into Normandy too costly and time-consuming to be worth the effort.

The other element Hitler counted on for success was surprise. Here he was on much better ground, because the Allies were predisposed to believe that the Germans were fighting with their backs to the wall, thinking only about an orderly retreat to the Franco-German border, incapable of even contemplating, much less launching, a major counterattack. His plan was so bold, Hitler believed, that the Allies would never suspect it until too late. But thanks to ULTRA, Eisenhower and Bradley were able to fight a classic defensive battle, a textbook example of how to meet and throw back an armored attack.

The story began on August 3, when ULTRA picked up a Hitler-to-Kluge signal that read, "The armoured divisions which have up to now been employed on that front must be released and moved complete to the left wing. The enemy's armoured forces [Patton's Third Army] which have pressed forward to the east, south-east and south will be annihilated by an attack which these armoured formations—numbering at least four—will make, and contact will be restored with the west coast of the Contentin at Avranches—or north of that—without regard to the enemy penetrations in Brittany."[7]

Everyone involved in the process of decoding, translating, interpreting, and disseminating ULTRA material realized immediately the import of this message. The SLUs got it to Eisenhower and SHAEF within the hour, while Winterbotham personally rang up Churchill with the intercept.

Ike's deputy, Air Chief Marshal Sir Arthur Tedder, as Winterbotham relates, "took the rather unprecedented step of ringing me up and, as he put it, 'in view of the extreme importance of Hitler's signal,' asking if I would be quite certain that it was not a bluff. Again he said that the substance was of such importance that Eisenhower didn't want to take any chances. I phoned Hut 3 [in Bletchley Park] to make quite sure that the original German version was in Hitler's own distinctive style and language. They told me we had no reason to doubt it on any score, and the signal had without doubt come from Fuehrer headquarters. Tedder was satisfied."[8]

So were Eisenhower and Bradley. They agreed at once to keep Patton driving forward, even sending more units through the narrow opening between Mortain and the coast while holding at Mortain with only one infantry division, the 30th, and two others in reserve.

The three Americans had all been outstanding athletes (Bradley in baseball, Patton in polo, Ike in football); all were West Pointers; they had been friends for nearly thirty years. Patton was the oldest, Bradley the youngest. Bradley had served under Patton's command in Sicily; now Patton was under Bradley; it was a measure of their closeness that Ike never heard a word of complaint from either man about the relationship.

Patton and Bradley seemed to be exact opposites. Patton was a great actor, deliberately portraying the role of the ruthless soldier, swashbuckling, profane, insensitive. His frown was enough to scare a man half to death, his shouts were legendary. Bradley was quiet, self-effacing, never raised his voice, was considerate of his men, and shunned any hint of role-playing. Where Patton loved uniforms, with pearl-handled pistols sticking out on his hips, Bradley wore a simple Eisenhower jacket and plain pants.

But both men had much in common too, beginning with a belief in Ike and a willingness to trust him, no matter what. In addition, each man had dark, deep-set, penetrating eyes that missed nothing; a grim, determined, square chin; a broad, hard-set mouth; and a face that displayed singleness of purpose. The United States could well be proud of this trio of generals.

Eisenhower was with Bradley at his headquarters when Bradley made the decision to hold at Mortain. Ike approved his plan, Tedder recalled, "there and then. He told Bradley that if the Germans should temporarily break through from Mortain to Avranches and thus cut off Patton's thrust, we could give the advance forces two thousand tons of supply per day by air."[9]

How could the American leaders take such a risk, knowing that Hitler intended to attack with four armored divisions in the initial assault? Partly because air power could supply Patton and protect his flanks, more because of ULTRA. They were confident that the oracle of Bletchley Park would give sufficient advance warning of where, when, and in what strength the attack would come for them to prepare for it. What they were really depending on was that Hitler would try to control the battle and thus fill the air with radio signals.

By August 6, Kluge had three armored divisions ready at their jump-off points. Although well-camouflaged, for reasons that were inexplicable to the Germans, they were taking a terrific air and naval gun bombardment. In contrast to the usual daily personnel losses of about 3 percent for units in combat, the casualty reports for August 6 in the divisions scheduled for the attack reached heights of 40 percent.[10]

The Germans had to attack or fall back. Right after midnight, the engines of two hundred assault tanks roared into life and the Battle of Mortain was on. By daylight, the 2d ss Panzer Division had overrun Mortain. There was no significant American opposition. The Germans assumed they had achieved complete surprise and gleefully began to drive beyond Mortain toward Avranches.

As they did so, and as the light strengthened, American artillery shells began to drop all around them, setting vehicles afire, kicking up dust, raising hell generally, forcing the panzers to seek cover, throw up camouflage, and dig in. On the flanks, the 1st ss Panzer Division and the 2d Panzer Division were going through similar experiences. The attack had come to a halt almost before it got started.

What had happened was that elements of the U. S. 30th Division had stayed on Hill 317, immediately east of Mortain, while other elements had thrown up road blocks that funneled the German tanks in predetermined and selected directions. Bradley had also set up artillery batteries on each flank. With daylight, the men on Hill 317, enjoying unexcelled observation, called the artillery fire right down on the Germans' heads.[11]

Simultaneously, British rocket-firing Hurricane and Typhoon fighter airplanes swooped down on the enemy, firing rocket after rocket into the massed tanks. They were soon joined by American Lightnings, Thunderbolts, and Mustangs from General Pete Quesada's 9th Tactical Air Command. Thirty years later, Quesada still recalled that triumphant attack. He told Lewin, "You know, Brad and I never used to talk together about our ULTRA signals. We just took it for granted that each of us knew what was in them. But I can still see that moment when we stood with those signals in our hands, and grinned, and said, 'We've got them.' "[12]

Hitler promised Kluge extensive air cover. He said that every Luftwaffe plane in France would be thrown into the battle. But not one—not one—appeared in the sky over Mortain that August 7. Where were they? Mostly shot up. Thanks to ULTRA, the Allies were able to engage them the moment they got off the ground from their airfields around Paris. Only a few got out of sight of their airfields; none reached Mortain.[13]

On the afternoon of August 7, Kluge sent a gloomy report to Hitler's headquarters. He had lost fully half his tanks, he said, and was still losing them. The attack had been brought to a standstill.

He wanted to disengage what was left of his three panzer divisions at Mortain and use them to blunt the Canadian drive at Falaise.[14]

Hitler was furious. He thought that Kluge had launched the attack prematurely, hastily, and carelessly. In Hitler's view, he should have waited for the arrival of three more armored divisions, on their way to Mortain, and then made a truly massive effort. From Hitler's point of view in East Prussia, that made sense; from Kluge's point of view in Normandy, to wait meant that the units already assembled would be destroyed in place by Allied artillery, air, and naval fire.

But Hitler was in charge, not Kluge, and Hitler gave the orders (they were read by Ike within an hour of Kluge's reading them). "I command the attack be prosecuted daringly and recklessly to the sea," Hitler began. "Regardless of risk," he wanted three panzer divisions withdrawn from the Fifth Army facing the Canadians and committed in the Avranches sector "to bring about the collapse of the Normandy front by a thrust into the deep flank and rear of the enemy facing Seventh Army." To consummate what to him had become the master stroke of the Western campaign, Hitler concluded, "Greatest daring, determination, imagination must give wings to all echelons of command. Each and every man must believe in victory."[15]

Kluge, despondent, told one of his subordinates, "I foresee that the failure of this continued attack can lead to collapse of the entire Normandy front, but the order is so unequivocal that it must be obeyed."[16]

The U. S. 30th Division could not by itself withstand an assault from six German armored divisions.* Bradley sent in the U. S. 2d and 3d Armored Divisions to meet the German spearheads, along with two infantry divisions to strengthen the flanks and provide additional artillery fire. Meanwhile other units continued to move through the gap between Avranches and the sea, then drive north toward the German rear or east toward Paris.

By nightfall of August 7, the battle that had begun at midnight was essentially over, despite Hitler's preemptory orders to Kluge.

---

* The 30th continued to fight magnificently, even though surrounded, in an action that ranks with that of the 101st Airborne at Bastogne in December; unfortunately the 30th Division has never received the credit it should have for this heroic stand.

American artillery batteries set new records for shells fired; they operated on the premise that it was better to waste shells than miss a possible target. The air forces had flown hundreds of sorties. As a result, of the two hundred or so German tanks involved in the initial assault, only twenty-five were left the next morning.[17]

Although Hitler continued to wallow in his fantasies and order attack after attack, the Battle of Mortain was over. Little remembered today, it was nevertheless a great Allied victory. The elements that made it possible included American mass-production techniques, which provided the fighting men with well-nigh unlimited artillery ammunition and virtually complete air cover, excellent tactical dispositions, the courage and skill of individual American soldiers (especially those in the 30th Division), and calm, cool, firm leadership at the top. But, clearly, the most important element in the victory was ULTRA.

Ironically, August 7 was the last day of the war that ULTRA would be decisive. The main reason for this development was that as Eisenhower went over to an all-out offensive, the Germans had to react to his moves, rather than the other way around, as had been the case during the battle of the buildup and at Mortain. Another reason was Monty's rather strange disregard of ULTRA information. Winterbotham complains throughout his book, *The Ultra Secret,* about Montgomery never acknowledging ULTRA, much less thanking all those involved in getting ULTRA's priceless information to him. That Monty hated to share the credit for a victory is clear enough, but why he frequently ignored ULTRA information (or other forms of intelligence, for that matter) remains mysterious. The best example of this phenomenon is Mortain.

By the morning of August 8, the Allied High Command knew that Hitler had ordered most of the armor in the Fifth Army to leave the Canadian front near Falaise and proceed to Mortain, there to participate in the attack. Although it was true that if this mighty force had managed to break through to the sea beyond Avranches it would have created serious problems for the Allies, especially Patton's Third Army, it was also true that Bradley had by then gathered together two armored and five infantry divisions to greet the German tanks. There was, in fact, almost no chance at all of a German breakthrough, as Kluge himself knew full well. Under these circumstances, Monty's most logical move would have been to hold back the Canadians until the panzers had departed from their front, wait for Kluge to commit his tanks at Mortain, and then unleash the Canadians for a drive to and through Falaise, which would completely sever the supply and communications lines of two entire German armies.

But Monty had been under extreme pressure from Ike for weeks to get going. He knew that Ike's impatience with his performance was shared by all the staff at SHAEF, British and American alike, and that even Churchill was beginning to growl. After all, Monty had promised to take Caen on D-Day, but he had not gotten it until nearly the end of July, and since then had hardly advanced beyond Caen. Tedder had urged Eisenhower to demand of Churchill that Monty be relieved of his command. He would not go that far, but as Butcher recorded, "Ike keeps continually after Montgomery to destroy the enemy now."[18]

So Montgomery, the general who usually waited until the last button on the last private was in place before attacking, attacked too soon. On the morning of August 8 he sent the Canadians forward again, toward Falaise. The attack came just after the 10th ss Panzer Division had started its move to Mortain, and just as the 9th and 12th ss Panzer Divisions were starting to follow along the same route. The Canadian attack gave Kluge the excuse he needed to cancel the whole movement; he kept the tanks in place to fight the Canadians. If Monty had only waited twenty-four hours, he could have had Falaise the next day. As it was, the Canadians ran into the massed fire of two German armored divisions and made little headway.[19]

Eisenhower and Bradley, meanwhile, were looking forward to the prospect of devouring two entire German armies whole. After hearing the latest intelligence reports on the morning of August 8, and after studying the map, Eisenhower decided that Patton ought to turn north in order to link up with the Canadians behind the German lines, thus encircling the enemy's Seventh Army and Fifth Army. He went to Bradley with the idea, only to find that "Brad had already acted on it," a typical example of the similarity of strategic thought between the two generals.

Bradley told Patton to drive on to Argentan, concentrate his forces there, and wait for the Canadians to come to him through Falaise. Eisenhower drove to Monty's headquarters "to make certain that Monty would continue to press on the British-Canadian front."[20]

Kluge, meanwhile, in accordance with his orders, continued to attack on the Mortain front. The men of the 30th Division who were encircled on Hill 317 continued to call in devastating artillery fire from the massed batteries of the division's artillery. By day's end there were one hundred wrecked tanks around the hill. The Germans had attacked again and again in an effort to take the high ground, and although they killed or wounded more than half the seven hundred men on Hill 317, the rest held out. The 30th Division as a whole lost almost two thousand men during the battle. German losses were much greater. As the closest student of the battle, Martin Blumenson, observes, "What the Mortain counterattack might have accomplished seemed in retrospect to have been its only merit."[21]

By continuing to attack, Kluge was doing exactly what Eisenhower and Bradley hoped that he would do—sticking his head farther into a noose that would be drawn tight when the Canadians and the U. S. Third Army linked up at Argentan. Patton was making spectacular progress toward that link-up; the Canadian offensive, however, was going slowly. By August 10, Kluge realized that his only hope for escape lay in an immediate withdrawal behind the Seine, but Hitler insisted that he continue the offensive at Mortain. Finally, after an exchange of messages and a telephone conversation, Hitler consented to allow Kluge to suspend the westward attack, shorten his lines, and then strike Patton's leading corps in order to keep the supply lines open. It seemed already to be too late. The German Seventh Army had lost its rear installations and was depending on the Fifth Army for supplies. The Germans were on the verge of an incredible debacle.

On August 12, Patton's Third Army spearhead, the XV Corps, reached Argentan. The Canadians were still eighteen miles to the north and making only slight progress. Patton, impatient, wanted to cross the boundary line Bradley had established in order to close the gap. He pleaded with Bradley on the telephone, "Let me go on to Falaise and we'll drive the British back into the sea for another Dunkirk."

Bradley refused to change the boundary, and Ike backed him up. Not until August 19 did the link-up occur, too late to do much good, according to Patton, who blamed Monty, and beyond him Ike. At times Patton could be almost idolatrous of Eisenhower; at other times he could be heard to complain, "Ike's the best damn general the British have got," meaning that Eisenhower was too much under Monty's and Churchill's influence.

Twenty-three years later, in 1967, when he was reviewing a summary of the criticisms of his generalship at Falaise, prepared as part of the annotation for his official papers, Ike wrote by hand, "Some of these writers forget that grand tactics and strategy must be decided upon by people who are in possession of the overall situation in such matters as relative strength, mobility and logistic possibilities. Patton was an *operational* officer—not an overall commander."[22]

What Eisenhower meant was that Patton seemed to think that all he had to do was send the XV Corps forward until it linked up with the Canadians, at which point the encirclement would be complete and the Germans would surrender. But as Eisenhower and Bradley knew, from all their intelligence sources, capped by ULTRA, there were two complete German armies inside the trap. Although they were short on supplies, they still could maintain a tremendous rate of fire, from heavy artillery through tank to small arms. To encircle is not to destroy. Already ULTRA indicated that the Germans would be fighting their way out. Hitler had relieved Kluge, but gave his successor, General Model, a free hand. Model started a full-scale retreat.

Beyond ULTRA revelations, Eisenhower was relying on intelligence estimates of the enemy's intentions that were, basically, his own. At its highest level, intelligence is more a hunch than a scientific matter. It has to be felt rather than studied, sensed rather than calculated. At this level, intelligence is an art form, a prediction about what the enemy will do before the enemy knows himself. Eisenhower was a master of it. One of his most notable traits as a human being was his sensitivity, his keen awareness of the other man's point of view. Those who worked with Ike have told of his concern for the well-being of his subordinates, of acts of kindness or awareness. One of the secrets of his success was his hardworking staff; his staff slaved for him precisely because he was concerned about them, as people. This tremendous concern gave him unmatched insights into other people's minds, and thus paid off with the most important kind of intelligence. From Hitler in 1945 to Khrushchev in 1959, Ike seldom misjudged his opponents.

As at Falaise, where Patton, and many others, assumed that the Germans in the West had had it, that their defeat was as obvious to them as to the Allies, and that surrender was imminent. Eisenhower held a press conference on August 15 and the reporters kept asking him how many weeks it would take to end the war. Furious, "Ike vehemently castigated those who think they can measure the end of the war 'in a matter of weeks.' He went on to say that 'such people are crazy.'" He reminded the press that Hitler could continue the war effort through the Gestapo and pointed out that the German leader knew he would hang when the war ended so he had nothing to lose in continuing it. Ike said that he expected Hitler would end up hanging himself, but before he did he would "fight to the bitter end" and most of his troops would fight with him.[23]

He was almost exactly right. All he missed was the method Hitler would use to kill himself.

Eisenhower was right in the short run, too, at Falaise. The Germans rejected the easy way out, surrender, and fought to hold open the jaws of the trap that were slowly closing on them. They, not Patton, made it a Dunkirk in reverse. Despite Eisenhower's plea, in an order of the day, for every man in his command "to make it his direct responsibility that the enemy is blasted unceasingly by day and by night, and is denied safety either in fight or flight," it was the Germans, not the Allies, who made the supreme effort at Falaise.[24]

Lewin puts the last phase of the battle that began at Mortain into its proper perspective. No one, he writes, "who has not faced a German panzer army fighting for its life has the right to criticize those who have done so and apparently failed." The Germans were "struggling for survival." The failure at Falaise, if it can be called a failure, "was due to . . . a simple inability, on the Allies' part, to destroy the German will to survive."[25]

The truth is that Mortain/Falaise was a great victory, thanks in largest part to the superb defense at Mortain, which was itself based in equal measures on the courage and fighting ability of the men of the 30th Division and on ULTRA. Together with the Allied air forces and the Canadians, they gave the Germans a hell of a licking. Some 50,000 German troops were captured, another 10,000 killed, while about 40,000 got away.

Those who escaped left their equipment behind. An officer who had observed the destruction of the World War I battlefields found that "none of these compared in the effect upon the imagination with what I saw near Falaise. As far as my eye could reach on every line of sight, there were vehicles, wagons, tanks, guns, prime movers, sedans, rolling kitchens, etc., in various stages of destruction. I stepped over hundreds of rifles in the mud and saw hundreds more stacked along sheds. I saw probably three hundred field pieces and tanks, mounting large-caliber guns, that were apparently undamaged."[26]

The full extent of the destruction is best measured in the August 28 strength report of the Fifth Army. It had only 1,300 men, twenty-four tanks, and sixty pieces of artillery.[27] The full magnitude of the victory is best seen in the events that followed, as described by Adolph Rosengarten, the SLU with the U. S. First Army: "Many German Seventh Army formations escaped from the pocket and fled, although not in good order, to the German frontier. As it was three hundred odd miles away, following them was fun. We drove through the lovely French countryside in the August sun and pitched our tents for stands of two or three nights in the kitchen gardens of some beautiful chateaux."[28]

IN THAT DASH THROUGH FRANCE, ULTRA played little role, mainly because the Germans were so disorganized it was almost a case of every man for himself, which in turn meant there was little in the way of direction or control being exercised by radio. When the Germans did not use the radio, ULTRA was useless. The French people, however, provided an alternative source of information that was as accurate and trustworthy as ULTRA. In every village between the Seine and the German border, GIs and Tommies could count on the local inhabitants telling them exactly when the last German formation went through the village square, in what direction, with what equipment, and in what numbers. This priceless information made the pursuit effective and continuous. The Germans never got a chance to catch their breath.

Until they reached the German border. Suddenly the Allies, who had seen all and known all, were blind. Local inhabitants were sullen and noncommunicative instead of friendly and informative. Inside their own country, the Germans had secure telephone lines, and ULTRA could consequently hear nothing. Eisenhower, who until now had been well informed about his enemies' strengths and dispositions, was suddenly shut off from such information as completely as he would have been had a steel wall descended between the contending sides. He needed to prove himself as a commander who did not need virtually a complete set of the enemy battle plans in order to win. But if he was now in the inferior position with regard to intelligence, he commanded the superior force, not only in air power, but in tanks, men, artillery, and fighting formations.

His biggest problem was overconfidence. After the dash through France, his officers and men felt that the Germans in the West were finished, done, kaput. All that was left was the formality of occupying Berlin. The heady success of the liberation of France had its effect everywhere, even in the mind of the supreme commander. He was quite confident he could wrap the whole thing up by Christmas. He even made a bet with Monty about it.

CHAPTER NINE

Ike, Strong, Monty, and the Bridge Too Far

SEPTEMBER 15, 1944. The 9th and 10th Panzer Divisions are missing from the SHAEF order of battle for the Wehrmacht. It is Ken Strong's job to find them.

IKE'S CHIEF SPY in World War II, and one of the best ever in the art of gathering intelligence, Major General Sir Kenneth Strong was a blunt, hardy Scot who got on famously with Eisenhower, Bradley, and Patton, not so well with Monty. Strong had an explosive laugh, an appreciation of the wisecrack, and an easy acceptance of the West Pointers' rough language and casual manner rare in British officers. In his memoirs, he endeared himself to all those from the New World side of the Atlantic Ocean who had been put off by British stuffiness and snobbery when he remarked, "The best time in a man's life is when he gets to like Americans."[1]

Strong had been Eisenhower's intelligence officer in North Africa. When Eisenhower moved to SHAEF in January of 1944, and asked Alan Brooke, Chief of the Imperial General Staff, to transfer Strong to London so that he could be G-2 at SHAEF, Brooke refused. He charged that Eisenhower and his chief of staff, Bedell "Beetle" Smith, had already robbed Allied headquarters in Algiers of its best officers and he insisted that Strong had to stay there to help fight the war in Italy.

Smith, who had come personally to make the request for Strong, let his always hot temper get away from him. He shouted at Brooke, demanding to know how in hell OVERLORD could be a success if the British refused to give Ike their best talent. Brooke, his voice icy cold, said the answer was still no. Smith started for the door, grumbling that Brooke was "not being helpful." Brooke called him back and "a bit of frank talk" ensued. That evening, Eisenhower apologized to Brooke for Smith and explained that Smith "fights for what he wants" but meant no disrespect.[2]

Whatever Brooke's feelings, Eisenhower still wanted Strong. He kept repeating the request, only to meet more rebuffs. Finally, in an unusual move that in itself was an indication of Ike's estimate of Strong's abilities, the supreme commander went over the head of the Chief of the Imperial General Staff to appeal directly to the Prime Minister. Churchill, who was anxious to give Eisenhower all the help he could for OVERLORD, got orders sent to Algiers directing Strong to come to London to take up his duties as SHAEF G-2.[3]

As Ike's chief intelligence officer, Strong was the man who briefed the supreme commander on the enemy order of battle, capability, and intentions. His sources were wide and varied. The information flowed backward from company to battalion to division to corps to army to army group and, finally, to Strong's staff at SHAEF. Strong integrated it, digested it, summarized it, and then presented it to Eisenhower at a daily briefing.

In his memoirs, Strong described his methods and the nature of his relationship with his boss. The memoirs are an excellent source not only for their main theme, *Intelligence at the Top,* but also as an insight into Eisenhower's leadership techniques.

Strong learned, first of all, that Ike did not want him to think of himself as chairman of a committee, which was the British practice, but rather to regard himself as the commanding officer at the head of the staff section dealing with intelligence. His judgments should obviously be based on information supplied to him by his subordinates, but they should be *his* judgments, not the consensus views of a committee. Strong records, "I remember on one occasion suggesting to Bedell Smith that I would like to obtain the committee's view on a certain problem. His reply was prompt and to the point: 'We've hired you for your knowledge and advice. If you are wrong too often we'll fire you and hire someone else in your place.'"[4]

Eisenhower had unshakable views on the subject of staff. He had written to Marshall, in February of 1943, "I am constantly on my guard to prevent any important military venture depending for its control and direction upon the 'committee' system of command. . . . I am sure my staff thinks I am getting tougher and more arbitrary day by day but, although I admit the impossibility of working without adequate staffs, they do seem to develop diseases that include obesity and elephantiasis. Apparently only a sharp knife, freely wielded, provides any cure." He was also adamant on the subject of decision-making, which he insisted belonged solely to the commander. He frequently told this writer that in all his career he never asked for a staff to vote on a decision (he insisted just as strongly that he always wanted every staff member's views, honestly expressed) and said that any leader who left his decisions up to a staff vote was not worthy of his job.[5]

Another difference between the American and British staff system was in access to the commanding officer. Monty was something of an extreme example, but his habits made a dramatic illustration of the point. Monty lived in splendid isolation. He rarely met with aides, leaving such mundane matters to his chief of staff, Freddie de Guingand, who would report to him the results of subordinates' labors. Monty would then study the reports alone, make his decision, and hand down the result. He considered himself superior to almost everyone, and let everyone know it; his curt manner, his pinched facial features, trim mustache, and everpresent beret all tended to put people off. Where Ike was warm and outgoing, Monty was cold and introverted.

Ike was in constant contact with the heads of his staff sections, meeting with them formally and informally, chatting, discussing, mulling over, considering this or that item. Although Strong was already a general officer and one of the top-ranking ones in the British Army at that, he was surprised to discover that "I had the right of direct access to Eisenhower and his Chief of Staff, and I could approach them whenever I wished." He was even more surprised—and pleased—to learn that "above all, under the American system I was a member of the 'inner circle,' where policy was decided and planning and other decisions taken. All my experience suggests that this status is vital to the efficient functioning of an Intelligence machine."[6]

Another difference between Ike and Monty was that Ike was a great believer in "the team." Back at West Point, before World War I, Eisenhower had been a potential All-American halfback, but a knee injury had cut his career short. In his first decade in the Army, however, he frequently coached the football team on the post. Partly as a consequence of these experiences, he was a self-described "fanatic" on the importance of teamwork. As supreme commander, he would not allow any of his American officers, not even Bradley or Patton, to get away with anti-British cracks. At SHAEF he insisted that his staff be not only a "team," but also a "family."

His principal method for welding the staff together, Strong wrote, was to intermingle British and American officers at all levels. If the head of a section was British, his deputy was always American, and vice versa down the line. Furthermore, Ike made them eat together and share living quarters. As a result, he hoped, national prejudices and approaches to problems would disappear, to be replaced by Allied attitudes.[7] In fact, for the most part, it did work out that way. For example, it was usually the British officers at SHAEF, led by the Deputy Supreme Commander himself, Air Marshal Arthur Tedder, who urged Ike to sack Monty.

Another feature of Eisenhower's leadership technique was to give authority to the man he was making responsible. In Strong's case, Ike told him that if anyone on the intelligence staff was not making the grade or was creating difficulties, Strong was "fully empowered to sack him on the spot whatever his nationality. 'Hire and fire' was the slogan." This stands in sharp contrast with Monty, who kept all the power in his own hands. Another of Ike's techniques was frequent visits to front-line units. "The first time I saw Eisenhower," Strong recalled, "he told me that it was my duty to get out of my office as much as possible in order to make contact with the commanders and their staffs in the field and gain their confidence."[8]

As everyone knows, Eisenhower could stand up to the British when he thought they were wrong. Throughout the war he had some real set-tos with Alan Brooke and Churchill. With regard to one of Churchill's proposals, Ike recalled after the war that "I said 'no' to him in one hundred different ways in ten different languages"[9]—without changing Churchill's mind, it should be added —and some of the most famous controversies of the war pitted Eisenhower against Churchill, Brooke, and Monty.

But Eisenhower was by no means too proud to learn from the British. Ike frequently complained to Strong about the poor quality of American intelligence officers. He explained that few officers had received any training in intelligence, that intelligence had ranked just about at the bottom of all military specialties in the prestige ranking of the U. S. Army, and that consequently no officer of ability had gone into intelligence work. The result was that "the United States Intelligence machine in Washington and in the field was ineffective." To remedy this shortcoming, Eisenhower had Strong create a training school for intelligence officers.

In the school Strong tried to get the Americans to dismiss from their minds the romantic, Hollywood approach to intelligence. His theme was, "Intelligence is now a scientific matter revolving around such things as air photography, interrogation, examination of documents and radio listening. We no longer depend on agents and such cloak-and-dagger sources for our information. These modern methods have completely transformed Intelligence."[10]

Eisenhower demanded much of his staff officers; he gave much in return. He was an absolute master at the handling of men, keenly sensitive to their needs and wants. Having been a staff officer for almost all the twenty-one years between the wars, Eisenhower had been there himself and knew how it felt. For example, when a rumor swept SHAEF that Tedder was going to be replaced as deputy, the staff assumed that the new deputy would insist on a new staff setup, both in personnel and organization. These speculations reached Eisenhower. He told Strong and the other heads of staff sections "that if Tedder were replaced it would make no difference to their positions." He assured them that they had his confidence "and that it would be his wish for us to carry on as hitherto."

To Strong personally, Eisenhower said "that I should remain in charge of Allied Intelligence at Supreme Headquarters, no matter what other changes might be made."[11] To have such complete backing from the boss does wonders for a man's morale and, as Eisenhower knew, makes a man work twice as hard as before.

STRONG'S INSISTENCE on a scientific, objective basis for intelligence was obviously wise, and obviously impossible. No matter how much data is collected, in the end intelligence requires a penetration of the enemy's mind and spirit. In the fall of 1944 that meant judging correctly the state of German defenses, not just in terms of numbers of tanks, artillery, aircraft, etc., but also— indeed, more important—judging the German will to resist. On this level everyone involved, from the supreme commander through his chief intelligence officer down to the lowest second lieutenant serving on a divisional G-2 staff in the field, was wrong.

They were wrong because they were too cocky, too over-confident, too likely to commit the oldest military sin—underestimating the enemy. The Japanese and Germans had done it at various times in the 1940–42 period. It had hit Montgomery hard, causing him to believe that he could break right through the German defenses and march on into Berlin in a single, narrow thrust across the north German plain. SHAEF planners, and Eisenhower, suffered too, although their hallucination was different—they thought that the Allied armies could advance abreast right up to and beyond the prepared defensive positions in the West Wall.

It was inevitable that Ike and his commanders should feel optimistic. The three weeks from August 15 to September 5 were among the most dramatic of the war, with great successes following one another in rapid succession, beginning with the destruction of the German armies in France and the liberation of that country. Rumania surrendered unconditionally to the Soviets, then declared war on Germany. Finland signed a truce with the Russians. Bulgaria tried to surrender. The Germans pulled out of Greece. The Allies landed in the South of France and drove to Lyons and beyond, while simultaneously attacking in Italy. The Russian offensive carried the Red Army to Yugoslavia, destroying twelve German divisions, inflicting 700,000 casualties. Both in the East and the West the Germans seemed to have crumbled. No wonder then that memories of November 1918 crowded in on everyone's mind.

IT WAS IN THESE CIRCUMSTANCES that Monty offered a bold plan to end the war. Code name MARKET-GARDEN, it involved three paratrooper divisions, the U. S. 82d and 101st and the British 1st, along with the British Second Army. It was designed to leap the Rhine River before the Germans could organize their defenses. The paratroopers would drop in a carpet out ahead of the Second Army, seize and hold bridges, and wait for the ground troops to come up to them. The British 1st Airborne would be farthest away, at Arnhem.

The plan involved a high degree of risk and only commanders who were convinced that the enemy was routed could have agreed to it. "Had the pious teetotaling Montgomery wobbled into SHAEF with a hangover," Bradley recalled after the war, "I could not have been more astonished than I was by the daring adventure he proposed. For in contrast to the conservative tactics Montgomery originally chose, the Arnhem attack was to be made over a 60-mile carpet of airborne troops. Monty's plan for Arnhem was one of the most imaginative of the war."[12]

At this moment, Eisenhower was bedridden, the result of twisting his knee during an emergency landing in a small plane on the beach after a reconnaissance mission. He was in Granville, where his second-story bedroom window held a magnificent view of Mont St. Michel. There, looking out at the supreme accomplishment of medieval architecture, Ike, Bradley, Smith, and Strong discussed Monty's proposal.

Bradley was opposed, in part because MARKET-GARDEN would cost him his First Army (lent to Monty to protect the Second Army's right flank), and partly because it would take supplies from Patton, whose Third Army was just starting across the Moselle River. But Smith said SHAEF could deliver a thousand additional tons of supply per day to MARKET-GARDEN, and Strong added that he believed the Germans had not yet recovered from their rout in France, so here was a chance to get across the Rhine at a relatively small cost. Eisenhower decided to approve Monty's plan.

Years later, in 1966, General Eisenhower read some annotation on MARKET-GARDEN in his official papers, then being prepared for publication. In a handwritten note, he commented, "I not only approved MARKET-GARDEN, I insisted upon it. What we needed was a *bridgehead* over the Rhine. If that could be accomplished I was quite willing to wait on all other operations. What this action proved was that the idea of 'one full-blooded thrust' to Berlin was silly."[13]

What Eisenhower, Bradley, Smith, Strong, and Monty did not realize was that Field Marshal Walter Model, Rommel's and Kluge's successor at the head of Army Group B and probably the best general in the Wehrmacht at this time, had established his headquarters in the Arnhem area. He had with him the 2d ss Panzer Corps, containing the 9th and 10th ss Panzer Divisions, veterans of both the Eastern and Western fronts. They had come to Holland from France to refit and regroup, not because they expected an attack there. Purely by chance, then, Monty's leading unit, the British 1st Airborne Division, would be dropping in the midst of two of the best divisions in the German army, commanded by a tough, experienced, and determined general.

The operation that ensued, after Ike insisted on MARKET-GAR-DEN, showed SHAEF intelligence operating efficiently, but it also showed the distinct limitations of the impact of the intelligence community on decision-making. Lewin's scathing judgment is that MARKET-GARDEN was "a failure of intelligence, whose roots are to be found in the prevailing attitude of complacency. Nobody wanted to know."[14] But that is far from the whole truth. Some intelligence officers, including Strong, did realize that there was a panzer corps in the Arnhem area and tried to warn the generals, but their warnings were ignored.

MARKET-GARDEN indicated that the Allies had come to rely too heavily on ULTRA, even though by September of 1944 ULTRA was producing little for the land forces. The one useful message ULTRA picked up showed that Model's Army Group B headquarters was four kilometers west of Arnhem, but when this information was sent out from Bletchley Park on the fifteenth, two days before the attack began, it was given a low priority rating, for the obvious reason that no one at BP realized a major operation was scheduled for the Arnhem area. The word did not arrive at higher headquarters until too late.[15]

But if Strong's sources at BP were letting him down, he had others in the field who were not. The Dutch Resistance was not as numerous, well-armed, or active as the French Resistance, but it could nevertheless provide valuable information. On September 11 elements of the Dutch Resistance got word to the intelligence officer at British Second Army headquarters about "battered panzer divisions believed to be in Holland to refit." This was an item too vague to be of any immediate or practical use. Strong did not include it in his daily briefing of Ike, nor did he put it into the weekly intelligence summary. But he did file it in the back of his mind.[16]

The information was also passed down the line, exactly as the SHAEF G-2 organization was supposed to operate, and it came to the desk of Major Brian Urquhart, the intelligence officer at 1st Airborne Corps (which consisted of the U. S. 82d and 101st Airborne and the British 1st Airborne). Urquhart was the officer most immediately concerned, for his job was to tell his superiors what they could expect to find in and around Arnhem. Although the reported German divisions were unidentified, their strength unknown, and although they might well be merely passing through Holland, the spot on earth that Urquhart was most concerned with might well have two enemy armored divisions on it. Urquhart, as he later recalled, "was really very shook up."[17]

Thus, unlike Strong (who had many more responsibilities than just MARKET-GARDEN), Urquhart did not file the report in his mind but rather followed it up. First Airborne Corps headquarters was in England, and Urquhart knew that there was a Spitfire fighter squadron equipped with special cameras for reconnaissance stationed nearby, in Oxfordshire. On the afternoon of September 12, he requested a sweep of the Arnhem area. The resulting photographs indicated the presence of tanks, although in what numbers (most were well camouflaged), and whether serviceable or not, could not be told.[18]

This information came to Strong, along with persistent reports from the Dutch Resistance. At SHAEF G-2, officers had been working for some time past in an attempt to locate the 9th and 10th SS Panzer Divisions. SHAEF G-2 kept track of all German units, and these particular divisions had been "lost" since the beginning of September. Putting all his information together, Strong came to the right conclusion—there was German armor in the MARKET-GARDEN area. Strong took his conclusion to Smith, saying that he did not know the fighting capability of either unit, but that he did not doubt the location of the 9th and 10th SS Panzer Divisions. He guessed that they were in Arnhem "to be refitted with tanks."

What happened next was told by Smith to the American military historian S. L. A. Marshall immediately after the war, who later retold it to Cornelius Ryan for use in his best-selling book, *A Bridge Too Far*. Strong also told the story in his memoirs.

Smith was deeply concerned, indeed "alarmed over the possibility of failure," in his own words. He took Strong with him to Ike's bedroom, where he told Ike that the British 1st Airborne Corps "could not hold out against two armored divisions." Smith told S. L. A. Marshall that "my feeling was that if we could not drop the equivalent of another division in the area, then we should shift one of the American airborne divisions, which were to form the 'carpet' further north, to reinforce the British."[19]

The suggestion, three days before the assault was scheduled to begin, seemed odd, especially coming from the man Eisenhower once described as "the perfect staff officer."[20] It would have been well-nigh impossible for the staff at 1st Airborne Corps to do all the necessary work in time, not to mention the problems of coordinating the new action with the Second Army. That Smith nevertheless recommended it to Eisenhower indicated how seriously he took Strong's information.

But Ike could hardly tell Monty how to use his divisions. American army practice was to give subordinates in the field a free hand. Monty was closer to the battle than Ike; Second Army commander and 1st Airborne Corps commander were closer than Monty; presumably they could best judge how to use their strength. As at OVERLORD, Eisenhower could have canceled the operation, but there were two good reasons not to do so. First, the Germans had not been able to stand and fight since the Falaise battle a month earlier. There was no overwhelming reason to believe that they could do so now, and the Allied troops and their commanders were all anxious to go.

Second, it would have exacerbated the bad feelings between SHAEF, Bradley, and Patton on the one hand, and Monty on the other. Tension was dangerously high already. "I cannot tell Monty how to dispose of his troops," Ike told Smith, nor could he "call off the operation, since I have already given Monty the green light." But he did want to make sure Monty had the benefit of Strong's information and Smith's recommendations. He told the two generals to "fly to 21st Army Group headquarters and argue it out with Montgomery."[21]

Strong and Smith flew to Brussels, where they met with Monty. Smith recommended that because of the unexpected presence of the 2d ss Panzer Corps in Arnhem, the landing zone of one of the American airborne divisions be switched there.

Montgomery, Smith later told S. L. A. Marshall, "ridiculed the idea. Monty felt the greatest opposition would come more from terrain difficulties than from the Germans. All would go well, he kept repeating, if we at SHAEF would help him surmount his logistical difficulties. He was not worried about the German armor. He thought MARKET-GARDEN would go all right as set." Smith added, "At least I tried to stop him, but I got nowhere. Montgomery simply waved my objections airily aside."[22]

The attack went as scheduled. It almost worked, but at a terrible price. Field Marshal Model and his panzers lived up to their reputation, counterattacking fiercely and skillfully, imposing on the British 1st Airborne Division the worst losses suffered by any Allied division in the war. Of the 10,005 men who dropped into Arnhem, casualties totaled 7,578. The division ceased to exist.[28]

Overall, the Allies took heavier casualties in MARKET-GARDEN than they did on D-Day. Their attempt to leap the Rhine had been thrown back. There would be no victory before Christmas. A long, tough winter campaign loomed ahead. Much had been lost, nothing gained by MARKET-GARDEN.

As Strong summed it up in 1979, "Our information was sufficient for me to utter a warning—Intelligence can seldom do much more than that—of potential danger from armoured troops. After that it is up to the decision makers and there is no guarantee that they will heed the Intelligence people."[24]

It is easy, today, to criticize Monty—and his boss, Eisenhower—for not heeding their intelligence people, but every attack carries with it the risk of heavy casualties and failure. Potential losses must be balanced against potential gains. As Strong himself put it in his memoirs, "The astonishing thing was that the great gallantry of those taking part brought the Arnhem operation so near to success. If it had not been for the quick and incisive reactions of the Germans, triggered off by the chance presence on the spot of that most energetic German commander, Field-Marshal Model, all our objectives might have been captured, in spite of the armoured divisions lurking in the background."[25]

Or, to put it into a cliché, with a little bit of luck it would have worked.

CHAPTER TEN

Ike's Intelligence Failure
at the Bulge

MIDNIGHT, DECEMBER 15–16, 1944, in the Eifel, the rough
mountainous country in western Germany, at the spot where
Belgium, Luxembourg, and Germany meet, directly opposite
the rugged forest area of the Ardennes. All through the Eifel
there is feverish activity. Squad leaders wake their men in
churches, town halls, cellars, and attics. They hustle the
sleepy-eyed soldiers off to their assembly points. Engines
roar, and out of haystacks come tanks, gigantic tanks with
long muzzles sniffing the air, looking in the mist like prehis-
toric monsters, to meet with other monsters emerging from
barns, from under trees, or camouflage netting. Elsewhere
soldiers throw back the tarps that cover their cannon, or
remove the brush they had piled up against the big guns, and
make ready for action.

For the first time since the spring of 1943, at Kursk in
faraway Russia, the German Army, the mighty Wehrmacht,
is about to take the offensive.

AS LONG AGO as the middle of September 1944, on the eve of
the Arnhem battle, Hitler had started planning his counterattack
against Eisenhower's armies. He had selected the Ardennes for
this, his masterstroke, for a number of good reasons. Eisenhower
was unlikely to station strong forces there, partly because the road
net was inadequate to supply many troops, more because of the nature of the terrain in the Eifel. The natural defensive strength of
the mountain country meant that Ike's armies would have to flow
to the north and south of the area. Further, the Allies would never

expect an attack through the Ardennes, even though that was where the German tanks broke through the French lines in 1940, because the Allies did not believe Hitler could collect sufficient fuel to sustain an attack through the Ardennes into the open country beyond the Meuse River.

Hitler's plan of attack was bold and daring, designed to win not just a local tactical victory but rather a strategic success that would reverse the fortunes of the war. The basic idea was for two panzer armies to break through the thinly held line of the U. S. First Army in the Ardennes, with two additional German armies providing flank protection and reinforcements. The panzers, once into the clear, would cross the Meuse River, then turn northwest, toward Antwerp, the largest port in Europe and Eisenhower's lifeline. The attack would split the British and American forces in Europe while cutting their supply lines. If Hitler's wildest fantasy then came true, the Western Allies would sue for peace, leaving Germany free to turn all of her forces against the Red Army, then pressing against Germany's eastern border. To succeed, Hitler needed to gather enough strength in the Eifel to strike with overwhelming force at the point of attack; he needed surprise; and he needed enough gasoline reserves to carry his tanks to Antwerp.

Security was a *sine qua non*, and security meant first of all keeping to an absolute minimum the number of those who knew of the offensive, those "in the know." This suited Hitler's inclination anyway, because after the July 20 attempt on his life, Hitler trusted almost none of his generals—with good reason.

One that he did trust was Rundstedt, whom he called out of retirement to serve as commander of the attack. In fact, however, Rundstedt's role in the Ardennes battle was similar to Patton's in the Normandy battle—he was a decoy. Hitler personally took charge of the tactical details; Rundstedt's presence was designed to make the Allies think that if a counterattack did come, it would be north of the Ardennes, because Rundstedt was too much the professional soldier to try anything so crazy as a tank attack through the Ardennes without sufficient gasoline.

Hitler oversaw everything, missing no detail. It was an impressive performance. Gathering two panzer armies in the Eifel was a gigantic logistical task. Men, tanks, cannon were brought in from all over Europe, from Norway to Austria. Other units were pulled away from the fighting in Holland, conveyed back over the Rhine, refitted and reinforced, and sent back again over the Rhine to the Eifel. Enormous quantities of fuel, ammunition, food, bridging equipment, camouflage netting, and other materials were moved into the assembly area, and all movement had to take place by night. Come dawn, everything was hidden from the Allied air forces.

The Germans took special precautions to prevent deserters from crossing the line with news of the activity in the Eifel. In the first two weeks of December, there were only five deserters on the whole Western front; usually there were ten or more per day. German officers with knowledge of the plan were not allowed to fly west of the Rhine for fear of capture in the event of an accident. Hitler counted on, and got, Europe's traditionally bad late-fall weather, which hindered Allied air reconnaissance.

Security covered everything. Along the Eifel front line, only units that had been in position for some weeks were allowed to fire, and even they at a reduced rate, to give the idea that they were low on ammunition. Radio communication was kept up at exactly the same rate, day after day for a month and more. Patrolling was kept down to a minimum.

Altogether, without the Allies ever suspecting a thing, Hitler gathered an impressive force in the Eifel, not so great as he had hoped, but much larger than his skeptical generals had thought possible when he first announced his plan. The total was nearly two hundred thousand combat troops with about five hundred tanks and nearly two thousand guns, organized into two panzer armies of twenty-four divisions.

Like Eisenhower, Hitler knew that to achieve surprise it is necessary not only to make sure the enemy does not know where you are attacking but to get him to look for an attack in another place. All the shifting of German troops, the movement of units across Europe, could not be totally hidden from Allied intelligence. Divisions do not disappear. It might be possible to make Strong and his subordinates think that two or three, or even five or six, divisions had been cannibalized—broken up and placed as reinforcements—but not ten or more. There had to be some believable explanation about what was happening to the divisions withdrawn from the front lines. Nor could the movement of all those guns, tanks, and trucks be kept a complete secret.

Hitler therefore tried to divert Allied attention to the north, in the Roer River area, where SHAEF G-2 already expected a counterattack. The Germans did what they could to encourage that idea. Troops' movements toward the Roer were not carefully concealed. As the Allies did in FORTITUDE, the Germans created a ghost army, the Twenty-fifth, with radio traffic, movement orders, and all the other activity associated with the organization of a new army. The existence of the Twenty-fifth helped in accounting for divisions actually attached to Sixth SS Panzer Army. Civilians were openly evacuated from the Roer area, and artillery fire was greatly increased.

From what the Germans could tell, the deception scheme had worked. The Americans in the Ardennes, only three divisions strong (VIII Corps, General Troy Middleton commanding), were cocky after the long string of successes they had won—overconfident and security-lax. VIII Corps radio chitter-chatter had told the Germans that nothing was suspected and that no reinforcements were on the way.

On December 15, Hitler got a prediction of bad weather for the next week, and gave the order to go. The final briefings came as a surprise to many of the officers and men, but their surprise soon gave way to elation. The Wehrmacht was on the move again! It would be just like the spring of 1940.[1]

MIDNIGHT, DECEMBER 15–16, 1944, at SHAEF headquarters, Trianon Palace Hotel, Versailles, outside Paris. General Eisenhower took one last sip of champagne, waved one last good-bye. He was in a fine mood. It had been a wonderful party, held at WAC quarters, to celebrate a marriage earlier that day between two enlisted personnel of the inner SHAEF staff.

Ike had something else to celebrate too—that day he learned that his nomination as General of the Army, with its five stars, had been sent by FDR to the Senate. In 1940 Ike had told his son John that he expected to retire within a year or so at the rank of lieutenant colonel, after having been a major for sixteen years. Since the war began, he had risen from light colonel to five-star general—six promotions in a little over three years.[2]

Christmas, promotions, weddings, parties—the mood was a gay one throughout the Allied Expeditionary Force. Monty had written Ike on December 15 to ask permission to "hop over to England" to spend the Christmas holidays with his son. Ike said he was delighted Monty had the chance and added a heartfelt, "I envy you."[3] In mid-November the U. S. First Army had moved its headquarters to Spa, just north of Malmedy on the edge of the Ardennes. An intelligence officer with the First Army later wrote, "Until then, we had been in the field in tents. I mention this because there is no doubt that once we moved into buildings we began to feel more civilized, and on the whole I don't think the headquarters was on its toes as well as it had been when the men were out in the swamps or fields. Spa, an almost untouched city, is one of the great European resorts, and the buildings into which we moved offered many luxuries."[4]

Buoyant, breezy, sure of itself, the AEF waited only for a break in the weather to finish the job against the Wehrmacht. When the First Army gathered into its POW cages the 250,000th German prisoner, a staff officer suggested that they hold a formal ceremony at which the lucky German would be given a War Bond.[5] In 1979, General Strong recalled "the general euphoria that existed among the top commanders. The German was already beaten and that was that!"[6]

It was difficult to think otherwise. On December 3, Eisenhower had written to the Combined Chiefs, "General Strong reports to me in his latest G-2 report that the attacks that began in November have eliminated at least 128,000 Germans. I know that there have been counted through the cages of the First, Ninth and Third Armies, more than 40,000 prisoners. Our losses have been nothing like the figures given above."[7]

Two days later, in a personal letter to Marshall, Ike said, "At present we have newly formed Divisions arriving on our front, and have attracted several Divisions directly from Hungary and East Prussia. In spite of all this, the enemy is badly stretched on this front and is constantly shifting units up and down the line to reinforce his most threatened points."

That was exactly what Hitler wanted Ike to believe. Indeed, if Hitler could have seen Eisenhower's letter to Marshall, he would have been delighted. From Hitler's point of view, there was even better to come. Eisenhower declared that G-2 studies "show that the German is more frightened of our operations" in the Roer and Saar—that is, north and south of the Eifel—"than anywhere else," and thus more likely to counterattack there.[8]

The SHAEF intelligence team, along with its subordinate units attached to the armies, corps, and divisions in the field, liked to think of itself as the best in the world. As Eisenhower's report to Marshall indicated, G-2 recognized that new divisions were coming into the line, that the Germans had been attempting to gather together an armored reserve, and that a counterattack was a distinct possibility. Indeed, First Army's G-2 Estimate No. 37 of December 10, 1944, declared that second among four possible German actions was "a concentrated counterattack with air, armor, infantry and secret weapons at a selected focal point at a time of his own choosing."[9]

Strong told Smith, early in December, that the German reserve might be transferred to the Eastern front, or that it might strike in the Ardennes or east of the Vosges, whenever the Germans had a prediction of six days of bad weather. Smith asked his G-2 head to go to Bradley to warn him of these possibilities. Strong did so, and Bradley said, "Let them come."

Bradley's G-2 at Twelfth Army Group concluded that the enemy was using the Eifel as a training ground, putting replacements into the line there in order to give them experience. First Army G-2 reported in early December, "During the past month there has been a definite pattern for the seasoning of newly-formed divisions in the comparatively quiet sector opposite VIII Corps prior to their dispatch to more active fronts." And VIII Corps' G-2 reported on December 9, "The enemy's present practice of bringing new divisions to this sector to receive front line experience and then relieving them out for commitment elsewhere indicates his desire to have this sector of the front remain quiet and inactive."[10]

In sum, at midnight on December 15–16, 1944, the Allies were as ignorant of German intentions and capabilities as the Germans had been of Allied plans at midnight on June 5–6, 1944. When, at dawn on December 16, the German artillery barrage began and the tanks started to grind their way westward through the mist and fog, the attack came as a complete surprise.

THE WORLD'S GREATEST intelligence establishment had been badly fooled. Attacking where they were not expected helped the Germans but it was the size, fury, and sustained power of the attack that came as the greatest surprise to SHAEF.

Forrest Pogue, SHAEF's official historian (and later General Marshall's biographer), has written a comprehensive analysis of the intelligence failure. His conclusion is that there were four major reasons for it. First, although Ike and Bradley realized the Germans were capable of some offensive action somewhere, they were reluctant to move their troops from point to point to meet every possible threat, not only because it was impractical but also because it would disrupt their own offensive plans. The second reason was SHAEF's emphasis on an offensive strategy. The third was the erroneous belief that Rundstedt, the cautious and traditional soldier, was controlling strategy and would not put his troops into the open where the Allied air force could destroy them. The fourth was the belief that the German fuel shortage would preclude any major counterattack.[11]

As noted earlier, ULTRA was of little help once the Germans stabilized the line and could use the telephone. What little ULTRA did reveal was, for purposes of predicting the Ardennes attack, misleading. Most ULTRA material came from the Luftwaffe, and most Luftwaffe traffic consisted of complaints about the fuel situation. The various Allied G-2s had come to rely excessively on ULTRA, rather like Mockler-Ferryman in the desert at Kasserine Pass. Because ULTRA did not reveal any preparations for an attack, while it did indicate a severe fuel shortage, the G-2s concluded that there was nothing to worry about.

Adolph Rosengarten, SLU with the U. S. First Army, in a 1978 article in the professional journal *Military Affairs* on his experiences with ULTRA, recalled one intercept that might have been decisive. "Dissected during a post-mortem of the Bulge with a reader from another headquarters, one signal in early December I remember from a Luftwaffe Liaison officer to his command had reported that he had reached his destination (if memory now serves, the headquarters of a named Panzer corps), where they were preparing for the forthcoming operations. Homer wrote that after the event even the fool is wise, and today one can infer from that signal that something on a large scale was planned. But, I submit, the American intelligence officer, who in early December 1944 used that isolated intercept to predict an offensive led by two Panzer armies with adequate flank support, would have been sent home."[12]

There was another hint that, properly interpreted, would have prepared the Allies for the assault. Operational Intelligence Centre at the British Admiralty detected, according to Patrick Beesly, "a very considerable southward movement of troops from Norway.

On October 30 it reported, 'the gross tonnage of shipping which has made the passage from Oslofjord to Denmark from the middle of October amounts to 95,000 GRT. It is estimated that this is sufficient to have lifted at least one division from Norway. Elements of the 269th Division previously stationed in the Bergen area have been identified on the Western Front during the last few days.' The movements continued throughout November and the first half of December." Beesly adds flatly, "Eisenhower's intelligence staff cannot have drawn the right conclusions from these reports."[13]

Overconfidence was one reason, looking in the opposite direction another. Ike was emphasizing the offensive. The Allied bombers were blasting German production facilities. The Red Army was pressing hard on the Eastern front. Rundstedt's only hope for holding the line once spring came was to husband his forces. To use them up in a German offensive that could achieve nothing more than a slight tactical success made no sense. What SHAEF, the army groups, and the armies were concerned with was not what the Germans might do to them but rather what they would do to the Germans.[14]

Only in the Eifel, in German territory, could the Wehrmacht assemble such a mighty force without SHAEF discovering its presence. Had the Germans tried to do it anywhere in France, Holland, or Belgium, local resistance groups would have gotten the word to SHAEF immediately. Indeed, the surprise the Germans achieved at the Bulge is one of the most telling comments on the value of the underground forces to Ike and his armies during the campaigns in France.

Spies inside Germany might have helped predict the attack, but both SOE and OSS had concentrated on cooperating with the French, and neither had an extensive spy network set up in enemy territory. OSS had only four men inside Germany and they had no communications with London and were producing no intelligence.[15]

Eisenhower personally insisted on accepting the blame for the surprise, and he was right to do so, for his failures were the crucial ones. He had failed to read correctly the mind of the enemy commander; he had failed to recognize that Hitler, not Rundstedt, was directing the strategy; he had failed to see that Hitler would try anything. He was the man responsible for the weakness of the line in the Ardennes, the one who had insisted on continuing the offensives north and south of that area. As a result of his policies there was no general SHAEF reserve available.

But despite his mistakes, Ike was the first Allied general to grasp the full import of the attack, the first to be able to readjust his thinking, the first to realize that although the surprise German offensive and the initial Allied losses were painful, in reality Hitler had given AEF a magnificent opportunity. On December 16, at Versailles, Bradley was inclined to think, on the basis of scattered reports, that the attack was a local one that could be stopped without difficulty. Ike insisted that he send armored divisions from the north and south toward the flanks of the attack. The next day Ike reported to Washington that the enemy had "launched a rather ambitious counterattack east of the Luxembourg area where we have been holding very thinly." He said he was bringing some armor in to hit the German flanks and concluded, "If things go well we should not only stop the thrust but should be able to profit from it."[16]

By December 19 the Germans were already dangerously behind schedule. Although they had crushed most of Middleton's VIII Corps, small units or groups of Americans continued to fight and hold up the advance. As expected, the poor road system was hurting the Germans, too, especially because Ike had rushed the 101st Airborne into the key road junction at Bastogne.

But in the Allied world, there was something close to panic. In Paris the French flags that in August had waved so proudly from nearly every window were now discreetly put back into storage. In Belgium people braced themselves for another German occupation nightmare. Jews who had survived the first occupation went back into hiding.

A special German detachment of English-speaking soldiers, dressed in American uniforms and infiltrated behind the lines, added to the panic. Some put on U. S. Military Police armbands and misdirected traffic, while others went on kidnaping and assassination missions, with Ike himself as the ultimate target. As one result, Harry Butcher recorded, "Ike is a prisoner of our security police and is thoroughly but helplessly irritated by the restrictions on his moves. There are all sorts of guards, some with machine guns, around him, and he has to travel to and from the office led and followed by an armed guard in a jeep."[17]

In spite of the disastrous beginning, it was at the Bulge that Eisenhower came into his own as a military commander. As General Strong has written, "The Ardennes shows Eisenhower at his very best—decisive, determined and in full control of the situation."[18] On December 19, when the threat appeared most alarming, he called a war council at Verdun, where the Allied High Command met in a cold, damp squad room in a French army barracks, with only a lone potbellied stove to ease the chill. Everyone looked glum and serious.

Ike opened the meeting by declaring, "The present situation is to be regarded as one of opportunity for us and not of disaster. There will be only cheerful faces at this conference table."

Patton picked up the theme. "Hell, let's have the guts to let the —— — ——— go all the way to Paris," he said, grinning. "Then we'll really cut 'em off and chew 'em up."[19]

Eisenhower next told his commanders what he had already said to Butcher: "It is easier and less costly to us to kill Germans when they are attacking than when they are holed up in concrete fortifications in the Siegfried Line, and the more we can kill in their present offensive, the fewer we will have to dig out pillbox by pillbox."[20]

Another mark of Eisenhower's self-confidence during this crisis was a conversation he had with Bradley, with only General Strong present to overhear it. Because the early German success had disrupted communications lines, Eisenhower had given command of the U. S. First Army to Monty, on a temporary basis only. Bradley was furious. He did not like Monty to begin with, and it was galling to have the First Army taken from him at the height of the battle.

"I cannot be responsible to the American people if you do this," Bradley told Ike—one of his oldest and best friends—and added for good measure that he wished to resign at once. Ike was shocked, according to Strong, but recovered quickly and declared flatly, "Brad, I, not you, am responsible to the American people. Your resignation therefore means absolutely nothing." Bradley hesitated a moment, then accepted the situation.[21]

THE BATTLE THAT FOLLOWED, the Battle of the Bulge, is the most written-about battle of World War II, and it need not be discussed any further here, except to point out that once the attack began, the Germans left behind them their telephone and tele-printer links, so they were forced to use the radio again. That brought ULTRA back into play. The SLUs could report to their com-mands the location of German units, the relief and replacement of top officers, the chain of command, division boundaries, the loca-tion of headquarters, and the movement of larger formations.

Hitler's bold bid failed, as Rundstedt knew it would. The Allies won a smashing victory in the Ardennes, and the chief result of the battle was that, when good weather came in the spring of 1945, Rundstedt had insufficient forces left to defend Germany. The Al-lies by then had such overwhelming strength that they no longer required exact, precise information about the enemy. They could simply overwhelm the Wehrmacht.

Strong's comment on the intelligence failure at the Bulge was that "the consequences were of course serious, but perhaps too much attention has been paid to this specific question." A major factor helping the Germans to achieve surprise was Strong's own estimate of German capabilities, not only in armored units but also in the fuel and the supply situation generally. Strong's information was such that he believed Rundstedt was incapable of sustaining a major offensive.

Strong was absolutely correct in this conclusion. As he writes, "It should not be forgotten that our estimate of German capabili-ties at this stage of the war was basically sounder than the estimate of those who launched the Ardennes offensive—the Germans themselves."[23]

AT THE END OF THE WAR, Colonel Telford Taylor, the man in command of the SLUs and the distribution of ULTRA material, asked all his SLUs to submit a full written report on their experi-ences. For a third of a century these reports were kept under lock and key at the National Archives, finally being declassified in Octo-ber of 1978. They provide a major source for the history of ULTRA, its uses, and effectiveness.

Lieutenant Colonel Adolph Rosengarten wrote the longest re-port, and the most self-critical. He stated bluntly "that the Ar-dennes Offensive, which was very costly, could have been fore-seen." He gave four basic reasons. First, "the enemy was defending on an artificial line with a major obstacle, the Rhine, astride his supply lines." Second, basic German army doctrine was an active defense. Third, "the German situation, in the big picture, was so desperate that he could afford to take the longest chances." Fourth, "the effect of our overwhelming air superiority was minimized by choosing a time when daylight was shortest, and the weather most likely to be bad." Rosengarten admitted that some clues came in from other sources, but were ignored because none came from ULTRA.

Once the Allies realized that they faced an all-out offensive with Antwerp as the strategic objective, Rosengarten wrote, "The tide swung precipitously from general optimism based on the long-term hopelessness of Germany's strategic position to calamity and woe, involving the imminent arrival of divisions believed to be in the East (as well as invented ones), and new secret weapons. The problem was to keep the record accurate and straight."[24]

THAT THE SLUS, and the G-2s and their commanders, took more care after the Bulge was clear on January 1, 1945, when the Germans launched another, secondary offensive. Major Donald Bussey, SLU to the U. S. Seventh Army, stated in his postwar report that shortly after the Ardennes offensive began, ULTRA started picking up GAF reconnaissance orders to cover the Saar-Palatinate area. It was clear that an attack was in the offing, and that its objective was to draw off Allied strength from the Bulge. But where would it come?

Bussey found that by putting together enemy order-of-battle information, along with the boundary lines between German units (information provided by ULTRA), he could "state with relative certainty that the main effort in the attack would be made west of the Hardt Mountains, with a secondary attack between the mountains and the Rhine." Bussey commented, "If there was ever an essential element of information this was it, for the passes through the Vosges Mountains were a serious obstacle to the rapid movement of Seventh Army reserves." Using the information Bussey had picked up from the GAF intercepts, Eisenhower reinforced the threatened sector with the 2d French Armored Division and the U. S. 36th Infantry Division (a veteran outfit and one of the best); these movements were not picked up by German intelligence.

Bussey described the result: "When the attack was launched on 1 January, the German main effort collapsed completely. Their only success was in the sector of the secondary effort, in and east of the Hardt Mountains. This German offensive was properly appreciated and preparations made to successfully meet the threat. Lacking ULTRA it seems very doubtful whether the attack would have been repulsed, or whether other sources of information would have given advance warning. Open sources provided only the most meager evidence of an attack, and there was much opposing evidence suggesting precisely the opposite—a thinning out in the sector and movement of units away from the Saar-Palatinate to reinforce the North."25

WHILE IKE'S ARMIES met and repulsed these last-gasp German attacks, his air forces were busy pounding Germany to bits. In the air war, ULTRA continued to be of great help because the Luftwaffe used the radio constantly and carelessly. There was so much ULTRA material that the Tactical Air Forces had not only a SLU attached to headquarters, but in addition a Special Adviser on ULTRA. Major Lucius Buck explained that "the necessity for the Special Adviser grew out of the failure . . . to recognize the capabilities and role of tactical air power, coupled with the unworkable and fallacious theory that it was the function of Armies and Army Groups to do target planning for the Tactical Air Forces and their Tactical Air Commands; and a 'Battle of Britain' emphasis on ULTRA at Air Ministry and War Station, that is, a stressing of Order of Battle aspects and a large discount of the target value. This was inconsistent with American concepts of offensive air power."26

Other Americans echoed Buck's complaint that the British concentrated too much on what the Germans might do to them, not enough on what air power might do to the Germans. Lieutenant Colonel Leslie Rood, SLU at the First Tactical Air Force, wrote in his report to Taylor, "If I have any criticism to make of Bletchley Park's amazing contribution to the War it is that it failed to recognize after D-Day that targets had replaced the German Air Force as the main interest of air intelligence. At BP I gained the impression that the GAF was a hot subject but at the commands the operations people were completely uninterested in its grandiose plans and ineffective operations. The Allied air superiority was too overwhelming to be affected by anything the GAF might do."

Nevertheless, Rood went on, "GAF news continued to come over the link in its carefully processed form while the target information arrived without the benefit of BP's usual dependable thought."

In his analysis of the situation, Rood pointed out that "target intelligence is naturally more controversial than order of battle because in it intelligence becomes operational. Perhaps I was seeking order where there could be no order. Yet I feel that had BP exercised the same careful and ubiquitous guidance in this field as it did in order of battle, some of the wasteful target arguments might have been eliminated and the bombers used more intelligently."[27]

Insofar as there was a GAF left after D-Day, ULTRA provided the clues that rendered it inoperative. Lieutenant Colonel James Fellers, SLU to the IX Tactical Air Command, noted that in attacking GAF facilities, "it was of key importance to produce bomb craters. Repair was no longer a simple process of bulldozer and roller. In the existing weather, the craters filled with water, drainage was poor, and considerable delay in restoring serviceability was affected. ULTRA revealed that the *real* way to render the GAF nonoperational was *not* in shooting up individual aircraft by strafing, but rather by destroying fuel stocks and supplies, rendering airfields unserviceable and delaying repairs. The significance of ULTRA in affecting such changes in Allied tactics is noteworthy."[28]

There was general agreement among the U. S. Army Air Force officers who served as SLUs that ULTRA was the best guide to target priorities. Within hours of a raid, BP would pick up the Germans' own damage report and assessment, thus telling the Allies whether they needed to hit that particular target again. And, as Major Ansel Talbert, SLU at U. S. Eighth Air Force, pointed out, ULTRA was "the agent which changed different viewpoints into a common policy." Throughout the war, both the British and American air forces complained that they had too many masters to serve—SHAEF, 21st Army Group, 12th Army Group, the various armies, and even corps headquarters. Each master had his own idea as to the proper use of Allied air power.

ULTRA served as the ultimate guide, rejecting this or that pet theory on the basis of the German reaction while embracing others. As Talbert noted, "The oil offensive was not undertaken until a few weeks before the invasion and there was considerable skepticism in many air force quarters whether it would pay off in time to affect German air and ground operations. By Fall 1944, ULTRA began to reveal shortages of fuel which grew in proportions rapidly and soon clearly were revealed by ULTRA as being general, NOT local. This convinced all concerned that the air offensive had uncovered a weak spot in the German economy and led to exploitation of this weakness to the fullest extent."[29]

BY THE SPRING OF 1945, Germany was finished. Ike's air forces dominated the sky overhead, his troops could go almost anywhere at will, the Russians were closing in on Berlin, and his need for information about the enemy's plans, intentions, and capabilities had all but disappeared. There was, however, to be one more minor flap over intelligence.

Allen Dulles, head of the OSS operation in Switzerland, and his agents became convinced that the Germans were building an Alpine redoubt, or fortress, in the Bavarian Alps, where Hitler intended to make a last-ditch, Wagnerian stand, a true *Götterdämmerung*. As early as September 1944, OSS reports had warned of the possibility that as the war neared its end the Nazis would probably evacuate key government departments to Bavaria.[30]

Then on February 16, 1945, Dulles' office sent to OSS headquarters in Washington a bizarre report obtained from agents in Berlin: "The Nazis are undoubtedly preparing for a bitter fight from the mountain redoubt. . . . Strongpoints are connected by underground railroads . . . several months' output of the best munitions have been reserved and almost all of Germany's poison gas supplies. Everybody who participated in the construction of the secret installations will be killed off—including the civilians who happen to remain behind when the real fighting starts."[31]

The various G-2s embellished on the supposed threat, possibly because they had little else to do by this stage of the war. Seventh Army G-2, for example, suspected the creation in the redoubt of "an elite force, predominately SS and mountain troops, of between 200,000 and 300,000 men." Already supplies were arriving in the area at the rate of "three to five very long trains each week. . . . A new type of gun has been reported observed on many of these trains. . . ." There were hints of an underground aircraft factory "capable of producing Messerschmitts."[32]

It all seemed to make sense, if only because the Bavarian Alps were the best natural defensive area the Germans could find, and there they could combine the fighting forces from Germany and Italy, perhaps even draw in some from the Eastern front. General

Strong ordered reconnaissance missions flown over the Alps, but the results were confusing. The Germans seemed to be installing extensive bunkers, and there was a definite increase in antiaircraft protection. It did seem likely that the fanatical Nazis would make a last-ditch stand somewhere, and there was no better place to make it.

As General Strong commented to Bedell Smith, "The redoubt may not be there, but we have to take steps to prevent it being there." Smith agreed. He said in his opinion there was "every reason to believe that the Nazis intend to make their last stand among the crags."[33]

All the rumors, the fragments of real evidence, and the genuine fears among the Allies that they would have to kill every last Nazi before the war would be over fed the March 11 SHAEF intelligence analysis: "Theoretically within this fortress, defended both by nature and the most efficient secret weapons yet invented, the powers that have hitherto guided Germany will survive to organize her resurrection. The area is, by the very nature of the terrain, practically impenetrable. The evidence indicates that considerable numbers of ss and specially chosen units are being systematically withdrawn to Austria . . . and that some of the most important ministries and personalities of the Nazi regime are already established in the Redoubt area."

At this point, Strong seems to have been carried away with his own verbiage. "Here armaments will be manufactured in bomb-proof factories, food and equipment will be stored in vast underground caverns and a specially selected corps of young men will be trained in guerrilla warfare, so that a whole underground army can be fitted and directed to liberate Germany from the occupying forces."[34]

Insofar as there never was a redoubt (although SHAEF G-2 did have a map pinpointing German defensive positions in the area, as reported by OSS), never any German plan to move troops into the region (although because of the pressure from their enemies they did tend to drift in that direction), Strong's report of March 11 must rank as one of the worst intelligence summaries of the war. He himself blamed Allen Dulles. In his memoirs, Strong wrote, "There was a period when Allen Dulles was responsible for passing a good deal of information directly to the Americans under Eisenhower—especially information concerned with the so-called 'National Redoubt' in Germany; if I had not taken steps to counter some of the less reliable information about this 'Redoubt' it could have had a considerable effect on Eisenhower's strategy."[35]

It has, however, often been charged that Dulles' flight of fancy about the redoubt did actually induce Eisenhower to change his strategy, specifically to leave Berlin to the Russians while he moved Patton's and Bradley's troops south toward the redoubt in the last weeks of the war. This charge immediately gets tied up in the broader issues of whether the Allies should have and could have taken Berlin before the Russians got there, controversies that will go on as long as people are interested in World War II. Suffice it to say here that whether Ike was right or wrong, his reasons for avoiding Berlin had little to do with imaginative intelligence rumors; he stayed away from the capital for what seemed to him—and to this writer—to have been solid military, diplomatic, and political reasons.

ON MAY 8, 1945, Germany surrendered unconditionally. The final intelligence report of the war, issued that day, read, "For the first time in eleven months there is no contact with the enemy. The victory which was won on Omaha and Utah Beaches reached its climax. Today belongs to the men of this Army who fought and conquered the enemy from Normandy to the Elbe. There is no enemy situation to report for there is no longer an enemy to defeat."[36]

INTERLUDE
1945-53

CHAPTER ELEVEN

Eisenhower Between SHAEF and the Presidency

EARLY SPRING, 1952. Ike has to decide whether or not to run for the presidency. He believes it is improper for a soldier to enter politics, but he does not want to shirk his duty, and he does believe his country faces grave threats.

FROM JANUARY OF 1942 UNTIL MAY OF 1945, Dwight Eisenhower was one of the dozen or so most powerful men in the world. From January of 1953 until January of 1961, he was the most powerful man in the world. In the interlude, from 1945 to 1953, Ike was not a decision-maker nor in a position to create policy. He was, however, near the center of power, first as Army Chief of Staff (November '45 to February '48), then as President of Columbia University ('48 to '51), where he added the New York financial and industrial elite to his list of friends, a list that already included many of the top government and military officials around the world, and finally as the first supreme commander of the NATO forces ('51 to '52). In retrospect, although not planned that way, the interlude was a perfect preparation for the presidency, a sort of finishing school at the highest level.

Although he frequently expressed a heartfelt desire for a quiet retirement, the truth was that Ike was much too vibrant, too passionate, too concerned to simply retire, even when in 1950 he reached sixty years of age.

He worked a brutal schedule. As Chief of Staff, he was constantly testifying before congressional committees, attending ceremonial functions, meeting with the Joint Chiefs, going on inspection tours, putting in long days in his office and putting off politicians who wanted him to run for the presidency. At Columbia, where he had hoped to get some rest in the supposedly calm atmosphere of ivy-covered walls, he found he was working almost as hard as he had in 1944.

Mentally, he was reaching toward a peak. He had a breadth of experience, with his knowledge of foreign leaders matched in America only by George C. Marshall, and in the world only by Churchill, de Gaulle, and Stalin. He had been to the Kremlin after the war, where he met with Stalin and all the top Russians. He had an intimate association with Churchill (who was voted out of power in 1945, but went back to Number 10 Downing Street in 1951). He had de Gaulle's respect, admiration, and—best of all—friendship. He knew the map of Western Europe as well as that of central Kansas; he had lived in the Philippines for four years before the war; he had journeyed through much of Asia. He was familiar with Central America, too, having served in Panama for three years in the 1920s.

He knew the United States Government, perhaps as well as any man living. First of all, he knew the White House and its operating procedures. Never personally close to either FDR or Harry Truman, Ike nevertheless spent more than enough time with each President to have a genuine insider's perspective and understanding of how the presidency worked. Second, he knew the armed forces and their ways of doing things, their capabilities and limitations, their personnel, their prejudices, and their traditions.

He also knew Congress and its peculiar ways of operating, so frustrating to outsiders. Ike knew about Congress as a result of having served MacArthur, in the thirties, as the Army's chief liaison officer with Congress. Further, his brother Milton was the number two man in the Department of Agriculture during the New Deal, and he shared his experiences with Ike four or five nights a week. Being at the center of one of the New Deal's most active agencies, and being a sharp observer of the congressional scene, Milton was able to give his brother a priceless education merely by recounting his day. Finally, as Army Chief of Staff after the war, Ike had his own experiences with the inner workings of Congress. For all these reasons he also knew the federal bureaucracy and its standard operating procedures.

Another asset was his firsthand knowledge of clandestine operations, of what they could and could not accomplish, how to set them up, how to control them, how to direct these covert actions so that they reinforced policy, how to tie them into a broader program of national action. He was up to date, too, on the state of the art in electronic intelligence gathering, air reconnaissance, cameras, and other devices used in scientific spying. He knew the British Secret Service's operation almost as well as Churchill or Menzies. He knew the right questions to ask of the spies, and how to ask them.

A further source of Eisenhower's strength was his tremendous popularity with the American people. His big grin, his open manner with reporters, his obvious sincerity, his speaking ability (he was a big hit with small groups of influential men, as well as with large audiences; many Britishers, including Churchill, rated Ike's 1945 Guildhall speech as one of the best they had ever heard), and his image as the leader of the crusade against Hitler all combined to make him trustworthy. Montgomery put it best: Ike, Monty said, "has but to smile at you, and you trust him at once."[1] Even those who never met or saw the man felt that way, believed that they could trust Ike.

Crusade in Europe, his war memoir published in 1948, added to his stature, prestige, and popularity. Often described as the second-best set of memoirs from an American professional soldier —pride of place goes to Ulysses Grant—Ike's book was an immediate best seller. It was Ike at his best—his common sense, his ability to communicate with different types at different levels, his decisiveness, his leadership capability, his outstanding generalship, his openness to new ideas, new techniques, new methods, all came through in nearly every chapter.

Small wonder, then, that both the Democrats and the Republicans were anxious to nominate him for the presidency in 1948. He turned them both down, partly because he thought he had done enough for his country, mainly because of Pershing's example after World War I. Pershing was one of Ike's few heroes, and he agreed with Pershing that soldiers ought not involve themselves in politics.

But, like most men, Ike was susceptible to flattery. Republicans began to tell him that if he did not run in 1952, as a Republican, it would be the end of the two-party system in America. It was, they said, his duty to his country to run.

The key word was "duty." The Republicans recognized, early on, that Ike, like George Marshall, could not resist that word (Truman had twice persuaded Marshall to give up his retirement by citing his "duty"). One of the Republicans to approach Eisenhower was the defeated 1948 candidate, Thomas Dewey. On July 7, 1949, Ike recorded in his diary, "Gov. Dewey visited me yesterday. He stayed at my house for 2 hours. He says he's worried about the country's future—and that *I* am the only one who can do anything about it.

"The Gov. says that I am a public possession—that such standing as I have in the affection or respect of our citizenry is likewise public property. All of this, therefore, must be carefully guarded to use in the service of all the people.

"(Although I'm merely repeating someone else's exposition, the mere writing of such things almost makes me dive under the table.)"[2]

On November 3, 1949, Ike again turned to his diary: "A message sent me by a very strong manufacturing association (not the N.A.M.) was to the effect that I had soon to let them know that, in the event of nomination, I'd be 'willing.' The argument was that this gang was ready to spend five million dollars—and they weren't going to do that if there was any later chance of my declining. So I told the man to say 'Nuts.' In fact the thing smacks of the same ineptitude that has characterized a lot of American business leadership over the past 40 years.

"I am not, now or in the future, going willingly into politics. If ever I do so it will be as the result of a series of circumstances that crush all my arguments—that there appears to me to be such compelling reasons to enter the political field that refusal to do so would always thereafter mean to me that I'd failed to do my duty."[3]

Like most great men, Ike was both self-assured and dynamic. He had no doubts of his ability to do the job and in fact to do it better than anyone he could think of as an alternative. His great energy required an outlet. Already a world figure, the truth was, whatever his protests, he needed a world stage to fully express himself, to exercise his abilities, to satisfy his intense and never-ending curiosity. He needed to lead his nation through perilous times. In 1952, he agreed to serve.

THAT THE TIMES WERE PERILOUS, that they demanded the best the nation could offer, he had no doubt. The menace of Stalin and the Communists was as grave to Ike as that of Hitler a decade earlier. In some ways it was greater. The Nazis had a limited ideological appeal outside Germany, while the Communists could and did appeal to entire classes of people in France, Italy, Germany, and throughout the world. The Nazis had been forced to buy their spies, and even then could not trust them, while the Communists could and did receive invaluable information—the best being how to set off an atomic bomb—from out of the blue, a gift from true believers who managed to convince themselves that giving Stalin military secrets would speed the coming of the inevitable socialist utopia.

In post-Vietnam America it became fashionable on some college campuses to sneer at Ike and his contemporaries for their seemingly excessive fear of Stalin and obsessive anti-communism. That generation of American leaders, however, felt—like Churchill in the thirties—that they were warning against dangers that were terribly clear to them but which their countrymen seemed determined to ignore. The evidence that Stalin did pose a threat to all the world, including the United States, seemed to them to be beyond dispute.

The facts spoke for themselves—Poland, East Germany, Rumania, Bulgaria, Estonia, Latvia, Albania, Yugoslavia, Czechoslovakia, North Korea, and China, all taken over by the Communists in the first half decade following Hitler's death. In every instance Communist dictatorships suppressed precisely those freedoms Ike and his comrades in arms had fought to defend—freedom of speech, of the press, of religion, of economic enterprise, and of personal movement. In the process, Stalin brought all these countries (except for China, Albania, and Yugoslavia) under his direct control, thereby adding enormously to the military potential of the Soviet Union. Thus by the early fifties, as Eisenhower and his friends saw it, Stalin had clearly demonstrated that he had the will to conquer, the ideology with which to do so, and the military strength to make world conquest conceivable.

With the single exception of World War II, the United States, after her wars, has indulged in splendid isolationism. The immediate postwar generation—in 1784, in 1816, in 1900, and in 1920—has turned away from active involvement in the world, relying on the oceans for the nation's defense. That did not happen after the Second World War. The isolationists were still there, to be sure, led by Senator Robert Taft. Ike's fear that Taft would be the Republican nominee if he himself did not run was the major factor in convincing him that his duty required him to enter politics. For the Americans to withdraw from Europe and Asia would have been to abandon those ancient civilizations to communism; Ike felt he had to do what he could to prevent such a catastrophe.

New weaponry magnified the Communist threat. World War II had brought great leaps forward in the arsenal of destruction and made America, for the first time, vulnerable to an attack launched from Europe. Most terrifying of all, of course, was the atomic bomb, which the Russians acquired in 1949. From that moment on, the Cold War was fought under the shadow of the mushroom-shaped cloud.

If the bomb highlighted the threat, so did the method by which the Soviets acquired it. The United States and Great Britain had made a stupendous effort to build the first atomic weapons, an effort that involved billions of dollars, hundreds of thousands of man-hours of their best scientists, and a huge industrial commitment. The Russians, thanks to their spies, who were for the most part motivated by ideology, were able to avoid much of that effort. If the Russians could so easily penetrate the top-secret Manhattan Project, it appeared that no scientific breakthrough would be safe for long.* The Russians had a worldwide network of spies, much the largest in history.

There were many obvious reasons to fear the Russians, not the least of which was the Red Army in Eastern Europe. Capable of mobilizing hundreds of divisions along the Elbe River, the dividing line in Germany between East and West, the Red Army could—according to estimates by the U. S. Army G-2—overrun all of Western Europe in two weeks. That was an exaggeration, Ike thought— he wrote on the margin of this 1948 estimate, "I don't believe it. My God, we needed two months just to overrun Sicily"[5]—but the general point was certainly valid.

Most frightening was what seemed most likely, a surprise attack. Pearl Harbor had burned itself into the minds of every American leader of the day. To a man they were determined that it would never happen again. A Russian-launched "Pearl Harbor" would involve a ground offensive by the Red Army in Europe

---

* U.S. scientists had estimated that it would take the Russians about four years to develop the bomb. Thus, as far as the scientists were concerned, espionage played a small role. To the politicians, however, the spies' role seemed crucial.[4]

and/or an atomic assault on the United States, and unlike the original Pearl Harbor, it would almost surely be decisive, at least in Europe. The Red Army, once entrenched in France, would be almost impossible to dislodge.

Ike's perception of these threats was keener than that of most leaders, partly because it was his business, mainly because he knew better than anyone else how close World War II had been.

The dangers America faced in the Cold War were even greater because Stalin and the Russians were better than Hitler and the Germans, better in the sense that they had more spies, more troops, and a similar lack of scruples. In short, as Ike saw it, the life and death struggle that began with Hitler's invasion of Poland in 1939 did not come to an end in 1945 with Hitler's death. Far from it— the struggle was now even more intense.

Eisenhower expressed his private thoughts on the subject from time to time in his diary. On January 27, 1949, he recorded, "Jim. F. [James Forrestal, Secretary of Defense] and I have agreed to try to keep the minds of all centered on the main facts of our present existence.

(a) The free world is under threat by the monolithic mass of Communistic Imperialism.

(b) The U.S. must wake up to prepare a position of strength from which it can speak serenely and confidently."[6]

And on June 11, 1949, shortly after Forrestal's tragic death, he wrote, "There is no use trying to decide exactly what I thought of Jim Forrestal. But one thing I shall always remember. He was the one man who, in the very midst of the war, always counselled caution and alertness in dealing with Soviets. He visited me in '44 and in '45 and I listened carefully to his thesis—I never had cause to doubt the accuracy of his judgments on this point. He said 'Be courteous and friendly in the effort to develop a satisfactory modus vivendi—but never believe we have changed their basic purpose, which is to destroy representative government.' "[7]

CHAPTER TWELVE

The Birth and Early Years
of the CIA, 1945–53

FALL, 1944. President Franklin Roosevelt asks General Donovan of the OSS to send him a secret memorandum on the subject of a postwar intelligence service. "When our enemies are defeated," Donovan writes in response, "the demand will be equally pressing for information that will aid us in solving the problems of peace." Accordingly, he proposes that FDR take immediate action to transform the OSS into a "central intelligence service" that will report directly to the President. The OSS, Donovan declares, has "the trained and specialized personnel needed for the task. This talent should not be dispersed."[1]

DONOVAN'S PROPOSAL WAS SIMPLE, straightforward, logical. He hoped it would be implemented directly upon the defeat of the Nazis, with Donovan in command. But the gestation period was years, not months, and by the time the CIA emerged, Donovan was long since gone.

He had been done in by America's most imposing bureaucrat, possibly the most feared man in Washington, the Director of the Federal Bureau of Investigation, J. Edgar Hoover. Hoover, ponderous, single-minded, and pugnacious, was a builder of empires. He wanted the FBI to be the most powerful agency in Washington, and he knew that the key to achieving his goal was by monopolizing intelligence. He who had the inside information had everything. At the beginning of the war, Hoover had tried to obtain for the FBI the exclusive right to collect and analyze intelligence on a worldwide basis. Donovan protested that domestic and foreign clandestine activities had to be handled by separate agencies. Roosevelt, in his usual fashion, decided to split the difference; he gave Donovan Europe and Asia while reserving South America for the FBI.

Donovan's partial victory strengthened Hoover's distrust of the OSS. Representatives of the British Secret Service in Washington were amazed to find that "Hoover keenly resented Donovan's organization from the moment it was established." The feud continued. Richard Harris Smith, author of an excellent history of the OSS, records that in 1942 Donovan's agents secretly broke into the Spanish Embassy in Washington and began photographing the code books. Hoover, furious at this invasion of his operational territory, waited until Donovan's men made another nocturnal entry into the embassy. While they were taking photographs, two FBI squad cars pulled up outside the embassy and turned on their sirens. Donovan's agents fled. Donovan protested to FDR, but rather than reprimand Hoover for his action, Roosevelt ordered the embassy infiltration project turned over to the FBI.[2]

Jabbing and sparring between the OSS and the FBI continued through the war. Late in 1944, Hoover saw a chance to rid himself of the OSS and Donovan for good. He seized the opportunity. He somehow acquired a copy of Donovan's recommendations for a postwar intelligence service and, in a flagrant breach of security, leaked the top-secret document to the bitterly anti-Roosevelt Chicago *Tribune*. The *Tribune*'s Walter Trohan then wrote a series of sensational articles, under even more sensational headlines, about Donovan's plans for a "super-spy system" in the "postwar New Deal." Trohan charged that Donovan wanted to create an "all-powerful intelligence service to spy on the postwar world and to pry into the lives of citizens at home. . . . The unit would operate under an independent budget and presumably have secret funds for spy work."[3]

A predictable congressional uproar resulted. One conservative congressman declared, "This is another indication that the New Deal will not halt in its quest for power. Like Simon Legree it wants to own us body and soul." Roosevelt decided it would be expedient to back off; the White House had Donovan's proposal put on the table. In April 1945, FDR decided to revive it, but a week later he was dead.

Roosevelt's successor, Harry Truman, was, unlike Roosevelt, no friend of Donovan's, and at the beginning of his administration

Truman was hardly strong enough to take on the redoubtable Hoover. In addition, Truman was determined to reduce the federal budget, which meant eliminating wartime agencies. When his venerable and conservative Director of the Budget, Harold Smith, indicated that a great deal of money could be saved by abolishing the OSS and putting its agents and activities into the hands of the older, established departments of the Navy, War, and State, Truman acted. Boldly declaring that America had no need for a peacetime "Gestapo," on September 20, 1945, Truman issued an executive order disbanding the Office of Strategic Services.[4]

The older departments were all delighted to have the OSS functions assigned to them, naturally enough, although they were resentful of the freewheeling Donovan agents who came along with the assignment. The covert and espionage side of OSS went to the War Department as a so-called Strategic Services Unit, but this was nothing more than a caretaker body to preside over the liquidation of the OSS espionage net. The Research and Analysis Branch of OSS went to State, where it was quickly decimated by congressional and presidential budget cutting, coupled with the hostility of older State Department hands. Assistant Secretary of State Spruille Braden told a congressional committee, "We resisted this invasion of all these swarms of people . . . mostly collectivists and 'do-gooders' and what-nots."[5]

The conservative reaction that dominates Washington after all of America's wars (best summed up by Warren Harding's classic call for a "return to normalcy") represented a hope for, rather than a realistic appreciation of, the future. Truman, like millions of his fellow citizens, yearned for "normalcy," which meant a return to isolationism. An isolationist America would not need huge military budgets or secret spy agencies.

Almost immediately, however, Truman realized that he was wrong. America could not escape the world, and to be effective in dealing with other countries, the United States had to have a centralized intelligence service, just as it had to have a more centralized military establishment, the Truman Doctrine, and the Marshall Plan. The attack at Pearl Harbor was a surprise because the Army and Navy frequently acted as if they were at war with each other, and because a fragmented intelligence apparatus, dominated by the military, had been unable to distinguish "signals" from "noise," let alone make its assessments available to senior officers in time for them to act.

In January 1946, therefore, Truman issued a presidential directive establishing the Central Intelligence Group. The CIG had a director of Central Intelligence, selected by the President, and was responsible for coordination, planning, evaluation, and dissemination of intelligence. It sounded impressive, but in fact the CIG's budget and personnel were drawn from War, Navy, and State, which meant that the old departments retained their autonomy over their own intelligence operations and thus had control over the CIG.[6]

This was an obviously unsatisfactory situation. The military intelligence services jealously guarded their sources while continuing to insist on their right to provide policy guidance to the President. In the words of a later Senate committee, the military thereby made the "CIG's primary mission an exercise in futility."[7] Not only would the armed services not provide information on overseas events, they would not even tell the CIG what American capabilities and intentions were. The State Department was equally unwilling to cooperate with the CIG. From the White House point of view, by 1947 America's intelligence organizations were no better coordinated, nor more professional, than they had been in 1941. It was as if there were no lessons to be learned from Pearl Harbor.

Change was clearly needed. It came in July 1947 with the passage of the National Security Act, a broadly based piece of legislation that established the basic defense organization for the United States for the Cold War. The act separated the Air Force from the Army, gave the Joint Chiefs of Staff a statutory basis, made an attempt to integrate the services by creating the office of Secretary of Defense, and provided the President with a committee responsible directly to him, the National Security Council (NSC).

One part of the act changed the name of CIG to Central Intelligence Agency (CIA) and, more important, made it an independent department, responsible to the NSC (and thus directly to the President), not to the Secretary of Defense. The act assigned five general tasks to the CIA: (1) to advise the NSC on matters related to national security; (2) to make recommendations to the NSC regarding the coordination of intelligence activities of the departments; (3) to correlate and evaluate intelligence and provide for its appropriate dissemination; (4) to carry out "service of common concern," and (5) "to perform such other functions and duties related to intelligence affecting the national security as the NSC will from time to time direct."[8]

The last function was decisive in giving the CIA a major and controversial role in the Cold War. It had been hotly debated and was deliberately worded vaguely because neither the Executive nor the Legislative branch of government could bring themselves to forthrightly advocate or authorize covert actions by the CIA. As George Kennan of the State Department later recalled, "We were alarmed at the inroads of the Russian influence in Western Europe beyond the point where the Russian troops had reached. And we were alarmed particularly over the situation in France and Italy. We felt that the Communists were using the very extensive funds that they then had in hand to gain control of key elements of life in France and Italy, particularly the publishing companies, the press, the labor unions, student organizations, women's organizations, and all sort of organizations of that sort, to gain control of them and use them as front organizations. . . .

"That was just one example that I recall of why we thought that we ought to have some facility for covert operations."[9]

Combining intelligence gathering and covert actions in one agency represented a victory for the Donovan heritage, as Edmond Taylor, an OSS veteran, pointed out in 1969. The OSS, Taylor wrote, established "a precedent, or a pattern, for United States intervention in the revolutionary struggles of the postwar age. The Donovan influence on U.S. foreign and military policy has continued to be felt ever since his death; for good or ill he left a lasting mark on the nation's power elite. However indirectly, many of our latter-day Cold War successes, disasters, and entrapments can ultimately be traced back to him."[10] Another OSS veteran, Francis Miller, agreed. "The CIA," he wrote in 1971, "inherited from Donovan his lopsided and mischievous preoccupation with action and the Bay of Pigs was one of the results of that legacy."[11]

According to critics, assigning the CIA a covert action responsibility was a twofold mistake. First, it gave license to an agency of the U. S. Government to carry out operations that were clearly illegal and, more often than not, counterproductive. Sabotage and subversion were one thing in wartime, another altogether during a period of general peace.

Truman himself spoke to this point in 1963, when he declared in a syndicated newspaper interview, "For some time I have been disturbed by the way CIA has been diverted from its original assignment. It has become an operational and at times a policy-making arm of the government. . . .

"I never had any thought that when I set up the CIA that it would be injected into peacetime cloak-and-dagger operations. Some of the complications and embarrassment that I think we have experienced are in part attributable to the fact that this quiet intelligence arm of the President has been removed from its intended role that it is being interpreted as a symbol of sinister and mysterious foreign intrigue—and a subject for cold war enemy propaganda."[12]

Kennan echoed Truman's complaint. "It ended up with the establishment within CIA of a branch, an office for activities of this nature, and one which employed a great many people," he declared in 1975. "It did not work out at all the way I had conceived it. . . ." Kennan said he had thought "that this would be a facility which could be used when and if an occasion arose when it might be needed. There might be years when we wouldn't have to do anything like this. But if the occasion arose we wanted somebody in the Government who would have the funds, the experience, the expertise to do these things and to do them in a proper way."[13]

The second error in combining intelligence gathering and covert operations was that, inevitably, covert ops (as they came to be known) took precedence over intelligence collection, especially in the mind of the director of the CIA. The one was dull, scholarly, painstaking work; the other was exciting and dramatic, providing immediate and tangible benefits and giving its practitioners prestige and glamour. Thus, critics charge, the irresistible tendency in the CIA has been to concentrate on the sensational covert action rather than the practical, but far more important, task of collecting and analyzing information.

In its first three years, under Admiral Roscoe Hillenkoetter as Director of Central Intelligence (DCI), the CIA engaged in a few selected covert activities. The first was an intervention into the Italian elections of April 1948. There was a great fear in Washington that Italy was on the verge of going Communist, by popular vote, which would have been an absolute disaster for American foreign policy, a policy based on Truman's containment doctrine (announced in 1947) and the Marshall Plan for European recovery. Dominoes were not yet being used as an analogy, but Assistant Secretary of State Dean Acheson did speak about rotten apples infecting the whole barrel. If Italy went Communist, Acheson argued, then France would go, and then West Germany, and then the Low Countries, and then Britain. America would stand alone, an island in a Communist world.

The Communist coup in Czechoslovakia in February 1948 was the event that shocked the free world into action. Nearly everyone remembered Hitler and Munich ten years earlier, and feared that the Red Army was about to march across Europe, as the Wehrmacht had done.

With the stakes so high, no wonder the Truman administration decided to act, especially since this first action was benign ("benign" in the sense that it was done not to overthrow an existing government but to support it). The Russians were known to be pouring money into the treasury of the Italian Communist Party; what could be more natural than an effort to counter that program? The NSC recommended to Truman that the United States provide campaign funds for the pro-Western Christian Democratic Party. Truman accepted the recommendation and authorized the CIA to contribute about one million dollars to the Christian Democrats. When they won the election, the CIA naturally took credit for the victory.[14]

What a bargain! For a paltry million dollars, Italy and Western Europe were saved. Or so at least the CIA could and did argue. It was a cautious, conservative venture into covert ops, but it was a start.

The next year, 1949, Congress passed the Central Intelligence Agency Act, which exempted the CIA from all federal laws requiring the disclosure or the "functions, names, official titles, salaries, or numbers of personnel employed by the Agency," and gave the DCI power to spend money "without regard to the provisions of law and regulations relating to the expenditure of government funds . . . such expenditures to be accounted for solely on the certificate of the director."[15]

With unlimited funds available, and no accounting required, the CIA began secretly to subsidize democratic organizations throughout Western Europe—labor unions, political parties, magazines, newspapers, professional associations, and so forth. Overall, the assistance program was a great success, enthusiastically supported by those few congressmen who knew about it and by every President from Truman to Nixon.

But the CIA's main reason for existence was not to provide a funnel for pouring money into the hands of America's European allies—it was, rather, to provide early warning of a Soviet attack. What came to seem absurd to later generations—that the Red Army would one day, without warning or provocation, cross the Elbe River and march into Western Europe—seemed in 1948 to be not only possible but even probable. That fateful year of 1948, the year of the Czech coup and the Italian elections and the Marshall Plan, also saw Stalin's attempt to drive the West out of Berlin by imposing a blockade on the German capital. In a now famous telegram, General Lucius Clay, Ike's successor as commander of American forces in Germany, declared, "Within the last few weeks, I have felt a subtle change in Soviet attitude which I cannot define but which now gives me a feeling that it [war] may come with dramatic suddenness."[16]

The 1948 war scare enhanced the CIA's growing reputation. U. S. Army intelligence flatly predicted an imminent Soviet invasion, "imminent" meaning within a matter of weeks, if not days. The CIA dissented. In the agency's view, based on its information, drawn mainly from agents behind the Iron Curtain, the Red Army was not ready to march. There was no need to panic. Time proved the CIA analysis correct.

To get advance information on Soviet intentions, the CIA began a program of overflights of Eastern Europe and the Soviet Union. Big, lumbering C-47s would parachute agents behind the enemy lines. The agents were political refugees from Hungary, Czechoslovakia, Poland, and elsewhere, men willing to risk their lives to fight communism. Their main function was to provide information on Soviet troop movements, mobilization activities, and other military intelligence. This program, according to the agent in charge, "was never cleared with the Department of State, though presumably it was with the President, and only in the early fifties was the Secretary of State informed."[17] Of course, the Russians knew about the illegal overflights, which were monitered by Soviet ground crews. Occasionally they shot at some, but the C-47s survived every flight.

To almost everyone's surprise, the Communist offensive, when it came in June 1950, was not in central Europe but in Asia, and was not mounted by the Russians but by the North Koreans. The CIA failed to predict the attack, but its excuse was unassailable— General Douglas MacArthur, commanding American forces in the Far East, refused to allow the CIA to operate in his theater, just as he had shut out the OSS during World War II. When the war started, MacArthur reluctantly gave the CIA permission to operate in Korea, and agents were air-dropped behind enemy lines, mainly Koreans but including some Americans. One such agent was a former high-ranking Chinese Nationalist officer who parachuted onto the mainland in the late summer of 1950. His detailed reports on the number and distribution of Chinese Communist troops along the Manchurian-North Korean border gave a fair warning of the imminent Communist crossing of the Yalu River in November 1950.

Nevertheless, MacArthur was caught by surprise again. His own overconfidence was the major reason, but he later denied having seen any CIA reports of a Chinese buildup along the Yalu. Truman contradicted the general. He stated publicly that he had seen and read CIA reports on Chinese troop concentrations along the Yalu.[18]

MacArthur was by no means the CIA's only foe within the American power structure. J. Edgar Hoover was predictably unhappy with the newly created agency. When the CIA exercised its rights and replaced the FBI network in Latin America, Hoover told his men there to destroy their intelligence files rather than bequeath them to the CIA. It was a real "scorched earth" policy, according to Howard Hunt, who had to pick up the pieces in Mexico City.[19] Hoover also promoted charges that the Communists had penetrated the CIA, with old do-gooders and one-worlders from the OSS leading the way.

Partly to counter such charges, in 1950 Truman appointed Walter Bedell Smith, Ike's wartime chief of staff, as DCI. Smith was about as right-wing as a professional army officer was ever likely to get. "I know you won't believe this," an ex-CIA agent later declared, "but Smith once warned Eisenhower that [Nelson] Rockefeller was a Communist."[20]

Precisely because he was so extreme on the Communist issue, Smith was a brilliant choice as DCI. Senator Joseph R. McCarthy had launched his anti-Communist crusade earlier in 1950, and had indicated in a number of ways that when he had finished with the State Department he intended to turn his attention to the CIA. Smith's appointment helped pacify McCarthy, as did the appointment of other right-wingers, such as Charles Black, husband of former child movie star Shirley Temple, and James Burnham, later an editor on William Buckley's *National Review*. Buckley himself was McCarthy's chief intellectual defender, co-author of *McCarthy and His Enemies*.[21]

Smith brought more to the job than an ability to appease McCarthy. Blunt, curt, outspoken, a strong and heavy user of curse words, Smith was a bureaucrat's bureaucrat. He knew precisely when to make a decision, when to say no, when to say maybe, when to buck the decision on up to his boss. Although he was almost unknown outside the top military and governmental circles, where it counted his reputation was almost as high as that of Eisenhower himself.

Smith did not suffer fools gladly, nor delays, nor excuses, nor shoddy performance. He did suffer from ulcers that produced almost continuous and nearly unbearable pain, which helped explain why his face seemed always to be pinched together in a crabby grimace. Physically small and too thin, he nevertheless terrified his subordinates and associates. The overall impression was of a very sour, very aggressive, very self-confident, very intelligent man. Summing up Smith's personality, Ike once told this writer, referring to Smith's ethnic stock, "You have to always keep in mind that Beetle is a Prussian."[22] As President, Ike took great delight in seeing Beetle go to Moscow as the American ambassador. "It served those bastards right," Ike commented, as he grinned at the idea of the Kremlin having to put up with Smith.[23]

The CIA, under Smith, became more aggressive in collecting information, in pressing its views on the President, and in conceiving and conducting covert operations. It was not, however, given over completely to the right-wing, or otherwise surrendered to McCarthy and his friends. This was primarily because of Allen Dulles, who Smith selected in 1951 as his deputy director.

Like Smith, Dulles had emerged from World War II with a reputation, among insiders, as one of the best men America produced in the struggle against the Nazis. Fifty-eight years old at the time of his selection, Dulles' background was well-nigh perfect for his new job. The son of a Presbyterian minister, he had studied at Auburn,

New York, Paris, and Princeton, where he graduated in 1914. After short stints teaching at missionary schools in India, China, and Japan, he joined the diplomatic service in 1916, serving in Vienna and Berne as an intelligence officer. He moved up rapidly, as did his older brother John Foster Dulles, in part no doubt because their grandfather had been Benjamin Harrison's Secretary of State, while an uncle had held the same post under Woodrow Wilson. The Dulles brothers were together in Paris in 1919 as members of the American delegation to the Versailles Peace Conference.

In 1920, Allen Dulles married Clover Todd, the daughter of a Columbia University professor. They had one son, who was wounded and permanently disabled in the Korean War. In 1926, after service in Berlin, Constantinople, and Washington, Dulles left the diplomatic service to join his brother in the famous Wall Street firm of Sullivan and Cromwell, specialists in international law corporate practice. With Sullivan and Cromwell, Dulles worked on a daily, intimate basis with the political and industrial elite of Europe and the United States.

In their work at Sullivan and Cromwell, the Dulles brothers came to know the world and its commerce as well as any men living. Although they shared a common workload, they were not much alike. William Macomber, who worked for both, said that "Allen from the beginning was less intellectual and more outgoing. He had a more developed personality, a warm personality." John Foster Dulles was more old-fashioned, a gentleman of the old school. "He always measured with a handkerchief on a globe, that's how he measured the distance. He always sharpened his own pencils. Incredible. He always finished the job with a pocket knife. When he was a little boy his father or his grandfather would ask if he were carrying his knife; and if he was carrying it he got a penny, if he weren't carrying it he owed a penny. He was brought up to think it important for a man to carry a pocket knife."

Both the Dulles brothers had gout, "terrible gout," but John Foster never failed to take his pills on schedule, while Allen "was always having trouble, because he would forget to take his pills. . . . Allen Dulles didn't have the brilliance of either his sister or his brother, but he had a perfectly good set of brains."

Both men were a little soft, dumpy, nonathletic. Huge, perfectly round eyeglasses gave them an owlish appearance. Allen had thinning hair, a large forehead, black bushy eyebrows, a prominent nose, and a strong, jutting chin. Allen's pipe, which he was constantly lighting, peering over, or waving around to make a point, gave him the appearance of a Princeton professor, perhaps of history or political science. He had a gray mustache, twinkling gray eyes, a booming laugh, and an advanced sense of irony that added to the impression of a detached intellectual. John Foster had more of a giggle than a laugh. Where Allen tended toward tweedy, Ivy League clothes, John Foster favored severe, double-breasted, conservative suits, giving the appearance of a successful banker.

Howard Hunt remembered Allen Dulles as "a man who was physically imposing. He had a very large head, almost white hair, a sort of a Teddy Roosevelt mustache." Dulles inspired great loyalty and affection among all those who worked for him. To a man, they praised him almost to excess, even twenty years after he left the CIA. Hunt said, "He was one of the most thoughtful, kindly men that I have ever known. In fact, I can't think, with the exception of my own father I can't think of anybody more deserving of such a description." Richard Bissell, who was in the CIA for over two decades, said, "I can't think of anybody in the agency who didn't like Allen. Everyone both liked and admired him. Which is quite a tribute over a period of years."

Macomber recalled that Allen was much more informal than John Foster. In 1951 he went to see Allen in his CIA office. "Allen Dulles in those days was number two, Beetle Smith was one, and Allen was deputy director. But he was eminent enough for me. I remember going in there, and my boss sat down, and the first thing I knew he put his feet up on Allen Dulles' desk. The only person who seemed to notice it was me."[24]

Because of his vast experience and innumerable contacts, Allen Dulles was a natural choice for the job assigned to him by Donovan when World War II began, chief of the OSS mission in Switzerland. His diplomatic cover was as an assistant to the minister in the American Legation, but in fact he operated his intelligence group from a fifteenth-century house in Berne overlooking the Aar River.

As a master spy, Dulles got more credit than he deserved. He was praised for two outstanding accomplishments—the penetration of the Abwehr, Hitler's intelligence service, and as the man responsible for the surrender of German troops in Italy. In fact, in both cases, Dulles was merely convenient. The Abwehr hardly needed penetrating, as its head, the bumbling Admiral Canaris, all but shoved top-secret material into Dulles' hands, and Field Marshal Kesselring turned to Dulles to arrange the surrender of his forces, not because Dulles was brilliant, but because he was there.

Everyone knew he was there, according to Kenneth Strong, which would normally be regarded as a disaster to a spy, but which in Dulles' case was a boon. The publicity he received helped him accomplish his task because, Strong points out, "often the difficulty with informants is that they have no idea where to take their information. What Switzerland needed during World War II was a well-known market for intelligence, and this is what Dulles provided." Indeed, he was "beseiged by a multitude of informants," which helped him add to his wide network of contacts and spies throughout Europe.

Unlike Smith, Dulles was soft-spoken, polite, easygoing. He had, Strong recalled, "an infectious, gusty laugh, which always seemed to enter a room with him." Where Smith was blunt and direct, Dulles seemed almost scatterbrained. "Even when I came to know him better in later years," Strong wrote, "I was seldom able to penetrate beyond his laugh, or to conduct any serious professional conversation with him for more than a few sentences."[25]

But there was, Strong also noted, "a certain hardness in his character." He was a great believer in the possibilities of covert operations. Robert Anderson, Eisenhower's Secretary of the Navy, regarded him as "one of the great intelligence figures in the century. And I think largely because he loved it so."[26] Strong said he was "the last of the great Intelligence officers whose stock-in-trade consisted of secrets and mysteries. He might without disrespect be described as the last great Romantic of Intelligence."[27]

Dulles was Smith's opposite in many ways, including politics. It usually comes as a surprise to Americans to learn that their most famous Director of Central Intelligence was a liberal—but he was. While Smith was bringing McCarthy's friends into the CIA, Dulles was just as busy bringing liberals on board. One CIA newcomer recruited by Dulles was William Sloane Coffin, later chaplain of Yale University and a leading dove during the Vietnam War. Another liberal was a Dartmouth College professor of English, art museum director, and OSS veteran, Thomas Braden. Lyman Kirkpatrick was a third. Tracey Barnes and Richard Bissell were others.

Under the influence of Dulles and his recruits, the CIA extended its financial support of foreign organizations to the non-Communist political left. Braden later recalled, "In the early 1950s, when the Cold War was really hot, the idea that Congress would have approved many of our projects was about as likely as the John Birch Society's approving Medicare. I remember, for example, the time I tried to bring my old friend Paul Henri-Spaak of Belgium to the U.S. to help out in one of the CIA operations." Allen Dulles mentioned Spaak's proposed journey to the Senate Majority Leader, William F. Knowland of California, one of McCarthy's chief supporters.

"Why," the senator said, "the man's a socialist."

"Yes," Dulles replied, "and the head of his party. But you don't know Europe the way I do, Bill. In many European countries, a socialist is roughly equivalent to a Republican."

"I don't care," Knowland growled. "We aren't going to bring any socialists over here."[28]

Richard Bissell, a Ford Foundation official who joined the CIA, where he had a spectacular career, and who characterized himself as an eastern liberal, later remembered the agency in the early fifties as "a place where there was still intellectual ferment and challenge and things going on." It was the one governmental agency that was not running scared from McCarthy, and as such it attracted some of America's best and brightest young men.[29] The CIA was the good way to fight communism. McCarthyism was the bad way.

Smith, the hard-boiled military man, was something of a McCarthyite, looking for Communists under his bed at night. At the height of the 1952 presidential election campaign, he told a congressional committee, "I believe there are Communists in my own organization. I do everything I can to detect them, but I am morally certain, since you are asking the question, that there are."[30]

Allen Dulles refused to join a witch hunt. John Foster Dulles was a great disappointment to many career Foreign Service officers because he failed to protect the State Department from McCarthy. Allen was a hero to CIA agents precisely because he did stand up to McCarthy. After Ike made him the DCI, Allen warned his employees that he would fire anyone who went to McCarthy with leaks or accusations against agency employees. He also persuaded Eisenhower to have Vice President Richard Nixon go to McCarthy to pressure the senator to drop his plan for a public investigation of

Communist infiltration into the CIA.* As one result, throughout Ike's term in office morale in the CIA was excellent, in sharp contrast to the State Department. The relaxed, freethinking atmosphere Dulles created was deeply appreciated.[31]

In summing up his impressions of the Dulles brothers, Bissell said, "They were quite different temperamentally. . . . Allen was a more open person. . . . He was a warmer, more outgoing individual, and I think he inspired much more loyalty. I admired certain aspects of Foster Dulles very much. He was a tough man, on occasion a very courageous person. He didn't choose to deploy his courage much against McCarthy, and I never liked that aspect."[32]

With Allen Dulles in place in the CIA, young idealists joined the "Company," underwent their training, and then sallied forth to save the world. It was all supersecret, superexciting, supernecessary. Professors at Yale, Harvard, and other prestigious institutions recommended their best students to the CIA, and the agency kept expanding.

UNDER THE SMITH-DULLES TEAM, the CIA covert action capability skyrocketed. The Office of Policy Coordination (OPC), the branch of the Agency in charge of such activities, leaped from a total personnel strength of 302 in 1949 to 2,812 in 1952, with an additional 3,142 overseas contract personnel. In 1949, OPC's budget was $4.7 million; by 1952 it was $82 million, a nearly twentyfold increase. In 1949, OPC had seven foreign stations; by 1952 it had forty-seven such stations.[33]

That was a lot of people turned loose with an awful lot of money. And the attitude in OPC was an early version of the infamous "body count" in Vietnam—agents were judged by the number of projects they initiated and managed. There was vicious internal competition between agents over who could start the most projects. By 1952 there were forty different covert-action projects under way in one central European country alone.[34]

Former agent Victor Marchetti points out that "one reason, perhaps the most important, that the agency tended to concentrate largely on covert-action operations was the fact that in the area of traditional espionage (the collection of intelligence through spies)

---

* McCarthy was after William Bundy, a member of the CIA's Board of National Estimates and Dean Acheson's son-in-law. Bundy, it seemed, had contributed $400 to the Alger Hiss Defense Fund.

the CIA was able to accomplish little against the principal enemy, the Soviet Union. With its closed society, the U.S.S.R. proved virtually impenetrable."[85]

The East European satellites were somewhat easier to penetrate, or so at least OPC liked to think. In the early Smith-Dulles years, the CIA set up a vast underground apparatus in Poland. Millions of dollars in gold were shipped there in installments. Agents inside Poland used radio, invisible ink, and other classic spy methods to get reports back to their controllers in West Berlin. These Polish operatives continually asked for additional agents and more gold; on occasion an agent would slip out to make a direct report on progress, and ask for even more agents and money.

It was a great achievement, or so the CIA thought, until late in 1952 when to its chagrin the agency discovered that it was all a hoax. The Polish secret service had almost from the beginning co-opted the entire network. There was no real CIA underground in Poland. The Poles kept the operation going in order to lure anti-Communist Polish exiles back into their homeland, where they were promptly thrown into prison or else run by controllers, just as the British had run German spies in the Double-Cross System. In the process, Marchetti writes, "the Poles were able to bilk the CIA of millions of dollars in gold."[86]

Such a contretemps would have been a major embarrassment, at best, for any other government agency, but the CIA could shrug it off because, in truth, almost no one in authority wanted to know the details of what the CIA was doing. On this occasion, Dulles called in the agents responsible, asked some somber questions, got the shocking answers, puffed on his pipe, and finally rose from his chair to go face an executive session of Senator Richard Russell's Armed Services Committee.

"Well"—Dulles shrugged—"I guess I'll have to fudge the truth a little." His eyes twinkled at the word "fudge," according to Tom Braden, who was there. Then he turned serious as he pulled his old tweed topcoat over his rounded shoulders. "I'll tell the truth to Dick [Russell]. I always do." Then the twinkle returned, and he added, with a chuckle, "That is, if Dick wants to know." But Dick did not want to know, either then or later, as he publicly stated on a number of occasions.[37]

It may be that Truman, too, did not want to know. That could be the explanation for his statement, "I never had any thought when I set up CIA that it would be injected into peacetime cloak and dagger operations." In April 1964, Allen Dulles challenged the former President on that remark, reminding Truman of various covert operations that the CIA carried out during his term. Another explanation is that Truman was misquoted, and a third has it that he was in his eighties by that time and may not have been responsible for what he was saying. In any event, much as he may have disliked dirty tricks and "Gestapo" tactics, it is abundantly clear that the CIA was fully involved in such activities during his presidency.[38]

Kennan, too, may have hoped that the CIA would merely be a funding agency for friendly overseas organizations, but eventually he almost certainly had to know better. That is, if he wanted to know.

The point is, as noted by the Church Committee, that "by 1953 the agency had achieved the basic structure and scale it retained for the next twenty years."[39] Created by Truman, shaped by Smith and Dulles, it was one of Eisenhower's chief assets when he became President—"the State Department for unfriendly countries," as Allen Dulles once described it. Like ULTRA or the Double-Cross System or the French Resistance, it was a weapon available to the Commander in Chief for the life or death struggle for freedom and democracy around the world.[40]

Part Two

THE PRESIDENCY

CHAPTER THIRTEEN

President Eisenhower and the Communist Menace

JUNE 19, 1953. Demonstrators march up and down in front of the White House, their signs pleading with the President to grant executive clemency to Julius and Ethel Rosenberg, who have been sentenced to death for giving atomic secrets to the Russians.

December 2, 1953. Secretary of Defense Charles Wilson calls the President on the telephone to inform him that J. Edgar Hoover has just sent him charges that it is "more likely than not that J. Robert Oppenheimer is a Communist spy."

January 15, 1954. Senator Mike Mansfield introduces a resolution to create a "Joint Congressional Oversight Committee for the American Clandestine Service."

THE MANNER in which Ike dealt with these three incidents is the measure of how gravely he regarded the Communist threat to the United States, and of the importance he attached to espionage and counterespionage activities. All involved hard decisions that had to be made on the basis of what the President thought was best for the country.

The Rosenberg case was on Eisenhower's desk when he took office.[1] Julius and Ethel Rosenberg were members of the Communist Party, U.S.A., and allegedly at the center of a Soviet spy ring. David Greenglass, Ethel's brother, had worked as a machinist on the Manhattan Project, and in January 1945 he supposedly gave the Rosenbergs rough drawings of the detonating device for the atomic bomb (how to set off an atomic bomb had been one of the most vexing problems of the Manhattan Project). Later in 1945, via a courier named Harry Gold, Greenglass gave the Rosenbergs drawings of the bomb itself, along with explanatory notes.

Four years later, the Russians exploded their first atomic device. Shortly thereafter, in England, Klaus Fuchs confessed to espionage for the Soviet Union. He put the finger on Gold, who in turn named Greenglass. In June 1950, Greenglass confessed. He named the Rosenbergs. Greenglass got a fifteen-year sentence, Gold got thirty years, while in England, Fuchs was sentenced to fourteen years.

But the Rosenbergs pleaded not guilty. They were tried, found guilty, and sentenced to death on the charge of espionage.* They appealed, unsuccessfully, to the Supreme Court. By January of 1953, when Ike took office, the Rosenbergs' only hope was executive clemency.

Communists and their fellow travelers, joined by innumerable liberals and such luminaries as Martin Buber, Pope Pius XII, Albert Einstein, and Bertrand Russell, launched a campaign to convince Ike to stay the execution. They charged that the Rosenbergs had been framed, that their death sentence was the result of anti-Semitism and runaway McCarthyism. They staged demonstrations in America and around the world. Humanitarians, meanwhile, objected to the severity of the sentence. Greenglass, Gold, and Fuchs had gotten off with their lives, and even without life imprisonment. In addition, the Rosenbergs had two small boys. Some of Ike's most trusted advisers told him he would have to grant a stay of execution because the nation simply could not put to death the mother of small children. Many in the Cabinet recommended clemency.[2]

Ike nevertheless decided to allow the executions to be carried out. He expressed his reasons in private letters to his son John and to a Columbia University friend, Clyde Miller. To John he wrote, "I must say that it goes against the grain to avoid interfering in the case where a woman is to receive capital punishment. Over against

* The Rosenberg case is almost the American Dreyfus affair. It has excited more controversy than the Hiss case, and continues to do so. In 1979 *The New Republic* (June 23) published an article that contended that Julius was involved in a Communist espionage ring, while Ethel—although certainly an active Communist—was innocent of any spying. The article brought forth a virtual avalanche of angry letters from both sides (see the August 4, 1979, issue of *The New Republic*). There is a very active National Committee to Reopen the Rosenberg Case.

this, however, must be placed one or two facts that have great significance. The first of these is that in this instance it is the woman who is the strong and recalcitrant character, the man is the weak one. She has obviously been the leader in everything they did in the spy ring. The second thing is that if there would be any commuting of the woman's sentence without the man's then from here on the Soviets would simply recruit their spies from among women."

To Miller: "As to any intervention based on consideration of America's reputation or standing in the world, you have given the case for one side. What you did not suggest was the need for considering this kind of argument over and against the known convictions of Communist leaders that free governments—and especially the American government—are notoriously weak and fearful and that consequently subversive and other kinds of activity can be conducted against them with no real fear of dire punishment on the part of the perpetrator. It is, of course, important to the Communists to have this contention sustained and justified. In the present case they have even stooped to dragging in young and innocent children in order to serve their own purpose.

"The action of these people has exposed to greater danger of death literally millions of our citizens. . . . That their crime is a very real one and that its potential results are as definite as I have just stated, are facts that seem to me to be above contention."[3]

THE CASE OF J. ROBERT OPPENHEIMER was nearly as difficult as the Rosenberg affair. Oppenheimer, the brilliant scientist who had been a central figure in the Manhattan Project, was chairman of the General Advisory Committee of the Atomic Energy Commission. In 1949 he had opposed the development of the hydrogen bomb on what were essentially political grounds—he thought it much too dangerous and a great mistake to create such a weapon—but had been overruled by President Truman. In 1953, Ike put him at the head of an advisory group to report to the President on what could be done about the arms race. Oppenheimer's attitude was that it would be madness to continue developing ever-bigger bombs and nuclear arsenals. In a memorable phrase, he compared the United States and the Soviet Union to "two scorpions in a bottle, each capable of killing the other, but only at the risk of his own life."[4]

Oppenheimer was tremendously popular with scientists and young intellectuals generally. On college campuses all across the country, students—especially those majoring in physics, in those years *the* hot subject—could be seen wearing the porkpie hats he favored, smoking pipes as he did. His stance on the hydrogen bomb elicited a strongly pro-Oppenheimer response.

Oppenheimer advised Ike that his first step in bringing the arms race under some kind of control should be candor about the horrors of nuclear war, starting with a report on the size of the American nuclear arsenal and a description of the amount of devastation it could cause. The recommendation set off an intense debate in Eisenhower's administration. Oppenheimer's leading opponent was Admiral Lewis Strauss, a Wall Street investment banker with close ties to the Republican right wing, and also the chairman of the Atomic Energy Commission. Despite their political differences, Strauss and Oppenheimer were old friends, frequently staying in each other's homes as houseguests. In 1946 it was Strauss who got Oppenheimer the post of Director of the Institute for Advanced Studies at Princeton.

But on the issue of Operation Candor, as it came to be called, Strauss was fiercely opposed to Oppenheimer. Strauss took the view that such candor "would not have advantaged the American public but certainly would have relieved the Soviets of trouble in their espionage activities."[5]

Ike was between Oppenheimer and Strauss in his thinking, "encouraging both without offending either." He viewed the so-called "Bang! Bang! papers," with their descriptions of atomic horrors leaving "everybody dead on both sides, with no hope anywhere," as too frightening to serve any useful purpose. "We don't want to scare the country to death," he said, fearing it would set off a congressional demand for outlandish and largely ineffective defense spending. Eventually, he tried—unsuccessfully—to find a way out of the arms race with his famous Atoms for Peace proposal to the UN.[6]

It was not Operation Candor that got Oppenheimer into trouble, however, although later it was charged that Oppenheimer's fight with Strauss, plus the general atmosphere of McCarthyism, was responsible for what happened.

The incident began on December 3, 1954, when Ike held a meeting in the Oval Office, with Strauss, the Attorney General, the Secretary of Defense, and a few other high-ranking officials in attendance. Allegations had been made against Oppenheimer's loyalty.

J. Edgar Hoover had a letter from the former director of the Joint Committee on Atomic Energy, William Borden, charging that it was "more likely than not that J. Robert Oppenheimer is a Communist spy." Senator McCarthy had become aware of the charges. It was thus potentially both a hot political issue and a dangerous security challenge, as Oppenheimer knew as much about atomic weapons as any man living, and McCarthy was locked in a struggle with the Administration (the Army-McCarthy Hearings were then going on).

Ike was furious. He first of all wanted to know how on earth Strauss could have cleared Oppenheimer for the AEC back in 1947, and why the man had been cleared for work on the Manhattan Project during the war, and why there had been no investigation of him since the Republicans took office. Strauss muttered some replies, the main point being that they could not have built the bomb without Oppenheimer. Ike then said that while he "wished to make it plain that he was not in any way prejudging the matter," he wanted a "blank wall" placed between Oppenheimer and any further access to top-secret information until such time as a hearing had been completed.[7]

The next morning, Ike wrote in his diary, "I directed a memorandum to the Attorney General instructing him to procure from the Director of the FBI an entire file in the case of Dr. Oppenheimer and to make of it a thorough study. . . . It is reported to me that this same information [the charges against Oppenheimer], or at least the vast bulk of it, has been constantly reviewed and re-examined over a number of years, and that the overall conclusion has always been that there is no evidence that implies disloyalty on the part of Dr. Oppenheimer. However, this does not mean that he might not be a security risk."[8]

Eisenhower set up a three-man committee to conduct the hearing. The committee discovered that Oppenheimer had a continuing friendship with a former French professor and Communist intellectual, Haakon Chevalier. In the 1930s Oppenheimer had been a frequent contributor to West Coast leftist organizations. He admitted that he had been a "fellow traveler" from 1937 to 1942. His fiancée, Dr. Jean Tatlock, was a member of the Communist Party in San Francisco. His former wife had been married to a Communist who was killed in 1937 fighting in the Spanish Civil War. His brother and sister-in-law had been Communists. Perhaps worst of all, Oppenheimer admitted that he had lied, under oath, about these associations.[9]

By a vote of two to one, the committee held that Oppenheimer, while not disloyal, had "fundamental defects of character" and therefore recommended that his security clearance be taken away. By a vote of five to one, with Strauss leading the way, the AEC then upheld that decision. Ike in turn concurred in the recommendation and refused to reinstate Oppenheimer's clearance.

The decision split the American scientific community into two bitter factions. Critics charged that refusing Oppenheimer access to top-secret material was like telling him he was not allowed to think. The ugly charge of anti-Semitism was hurled about. Many of Oppenheimer's supporters said Ike had done it only to appease McCarthy. Strauss came in for some particularly hostile remarks. The bitterness was such that some time later the Senate refused to confirm Strauss' nomination as Secretary of Commerce.

Ike's attitude, as always, was to try to find some compromise, some common ground on which all the contestants could stand, some way of leaving everyone happy and no one angry. At the height of the controversy, he sent a note to Strauss saying, "Why do we not get Dr. Oppenheimer interested in desalting sea water? I can think of no scientific success of all time that would equal this in its boon to mankind—provided the solution could do the job on a massive scale and cheaply."[10]

Oppenheimer, who had been publicly humiliated, never worked for the government again.

Whether or not a terrible mistake had been made and an injustice done cannot be settled here. In 1963, LBJ awarded Oppenheimer the AEC's highest honor, the Fermi Award—this act was generally taken to be a vindication. It should be noted that Oppenheimer was not "punished" in any direct way, merely denied the opportunity to continue working for the government on atomic matters on the grounds that such employment was not "clearly consistent with the interests of the national security." Strauss personally continued to support Oppenheimer; as a member of the board of directors, Strauss offered the motion to reelect Oppenheimer as Director of the Institute for Advanced Studies. And in his memoirs Ike insisted that the McCarthy aspect of the case had no bearing on his decision. It just seemed to him that a man who had such long and close association with Communists, and who had lied about it for years, had to be considered a security risk. As he put it in his first State of the Union address, "Only a combination of both loyalty and reliability promises genuine security."[11]

IF IKE'S DECISION in the Rosenberg and Oppenheimer cases demonstrated how seriously he regarded the threat to the United States posed by the Soviet espionage network, his acceptance of the Doolittle Report showed how far he was willing to go to counter that threat.

Early in Eisenhower's presidency, Senator Mike Mansfield introduced a resolution for a "Joint Congressional Oversight Committee for the American Clandestine Service." Eisenhower strongly opposed any such interference with executive control of the CIA. Stuyvesant Wainwright II, a freshman congressman from Long Island, and Peter Frelinghuysen, another Republican (from New Jersey), supported Mansfield in the House. Ike exploded. Wainwright later recalled that "he told both Peter and me that this kind of a bill would be passed over his dead body." One reason was "he felt that any Congressional Committee would end up being dominated by Senator McCarthy . . . and he was damned if he was going to let McCarthy have any other area wherein he might get a foothold."

Ike was also upset, Wainwright related, because he felt that Wainwright, as a former SLU and member of the SHAEF staff, should have known better. "I asked him one day," Wainwright recalled, "why the hell do you call me Wainwright and Peter, Peter? He said, 'Well, because you were on my staff and worked for me.'* Consequently he was really shocked and horrified that I would have chosen, in his view, to attack the intelligence services with this bill, or attack the CIA with a bill requiring a certain amount of disclosure to a select committee."[12]

Eisenhower tried to head off the Mansfield bill by appointing a committee to investigate the CIA and report to him personally. The

---

* Wainwright, in his early twenties during the war, was a very junior member of Ike's staff. He could recall seeing Eisenhower only four or five times in 1944 and 1945, and was much impressed that Ike remembered his name eight years later. "He had a politician's kind of memory," Wainwright said.

committee was headed by the famous World War II aviator General James Doolittle.

The prose of the Doolittle Report's conclusion was chilling: "It is now clear that we are facing an implacable enemy whose avowed objective is world domination by whatever means and at whatever cost. There are no rules in such a game. Hitherto acceptable norms of human conduct do not apply. If the United States is to survive, long-standing American concepts of 'fair play' must be reconsidered. We must develop effective espionage and counterespionage services and must learn to subvert, sabotage, and destroy our enemies by more clever, more sophisticated, and more effective methods than those used against us. It may become necessary that the American people be made acquainted with, understand, and support this fundamentally repugnant philosophy."[13]

The Doolittle Report was a concise summary of Ike's own views. As President, he intended to fight the Communists just as he had fought the Nazis, on every battlefront, with every available weapon. His arsenal was a mighty one, capped by the atomic bomb. One important element in it, the one the Doolittle Report had been designed to protect, was the newly born but rapidly growing Central Intelligence Agency.

CHAPTER FOURTEEN

Iran: The Preparation

MIDNIGHT, AUGUST 1–2, 1953. A large, ornate garden in Teheran, Iran. A medium-sized, medium-height, rather non-descript American, wearing a dark turtleneck shirt, Oxford-gray slacks, and Persian sandals, opens the gate to the garden, slips out, glances up and down the street, and silently climbs into the back seat of an ordinary-looking black sedan. Without a backward glance, the driver pulls away slowly, smoothly, and heads toward the royal palace. In the back seat, the American huddles down on the floor and pulls a blanket over him.

At the palace gate, the sentry flashes a light in the driver's face, grunts, and waves the car through. Halfway between the gate and the palace steps, the driver parks, gets out, and walks away. A slim, nervous man walks down the drive, glancing left and right as he approaches. The American pulls the blanket out of the way and sits up as the man enters the car and closes the door.

They look at each other. Then His Imperial Majesty, Mohammed Reza Shah Pahlavi, Shahanshah of Iran, Light of the Aryans, allows himself to relax, and even smile.

"Good evening, Mr. Roosevelt," he says. "I cannot say that I expected to see you, but this is a pleasure."

"Good evening, Your Majesty. It is a long time since we met each other, and I am glad you recognize me. It may make establishing my credentials a bit easier."

His Imperial Majesty laughs. "That will hardly be necessary. Your name and presence is all the guarantee I need."

Roosevelt—Kermit ("Kim") Roosevelt, Teddy Roosevelt's grandson and FDR's cousin—quickly explains that he has entered Iran illegally, that his cover name is James Lochridge, and that he is there as a personal representative of President Dwight Eisenhower and Prime Minister Winston Churchill. "President Eisenhower will confirm this himself," Roosevelt states, "by a phrase in a speech he is about to deliver in San Francisco—actually within the next twenty-four hours. Prime Minister Churchill has arranged to have a specific change made in the time announcement of the BBC broadcast tomorrow night. Instead of saying, 'It is now midnight,' the announcer will say, 'It is now'—pause—'*exactly* midnight.'"

Having established his bona fides, Roosevelt explains that his purpose in coming is to assure the Shah that he has the full backing of the American and British governments, that Washington and London are anxious to help him overthrow his prime minister and ensure that H.I.M. retains his throne.

The thirty-four-year-old Emperor smiles, as well he might. To have the complete, unquestioning support of a Roosevelt, Eisenhower, and Churchill is, after all, a reassuring feeling, especially to a shaky monarch surrounded by rumors of coups, countercoups, plots, and revolutions, with the additional problem of sharing a long, virtually undefended border with the Soviet Union. Even better than the general promise of support from Eisenhower and Churchill is Roosevelt's pledge that he would personally set in motion a series of events that would rid the Shah of his Iranian enemies.

After giving H.I.M. a brief outline of his proposed countercoup, Roosevelt indicates that they had best part before their meeting is discovered. They agree to meet again the following midnight under identical circumstances.

"Good night—or should I say good morning?—Mr. Roosevelt. I am glad to welcome you once again to my country."

"And I am very glad to be here, Your Majesty. I am full of confidence that our undertaking will succeed." The Shah leaves the car, the driver returns, Roosevelt pulls the blanket over his head again, and is returned to his garden. The CIA's first major covert action under Eisenhower's orders is launched.[1]

HOW HAD THINGS COME TO SUCH A PASS that a Roosevelt was sneaking around at midnight, hiding under blankets, while Eisenhower altered a speech and Churchill used the BBC for personal messages, all in support of a potential dictator whose sole political objective was to overthrow a highly popular prime minister in favor of a pro-Nazi general? A brief answer is that oil and communism make a volatile mixture. A fuller response takes into account the complexities of postwar international relations and the recent history of Iran.

There are only two facts about modern Persia—Iran—that truly matter to the rest of the world. It has oil, and it is Russia's southern neighbor. Because of the oil, the British had moved in on Iran in 1909, when the Anglo-Persian Oil Company (in which the British Government controlled 52 percent of the stock) obtained a sixty-year concession which gave it exclusive rights to explore and exploit the oil of Iran. Because of the border, Britain and Russia (with American support) had invaded Iran in 1941, where in a matter of hours they destroyed the Imperial Iranian Armed Forces. This was as much an act of great power highhandedness and brutality as Hitler's invasion of Denmark, although in this case the voices of outraged protest were exclusively Iranian. The purpose of the invasion was to provide a corridor for the shipment of American lend-lease goods into Russia.

The ruler of Iran in 1941 was Reza Khan, an illiterate officer in the Persian Cossack Brigade who had led a coup against the Qajar regime in the 1920s and established himself as Reza Shah, founder of the Pahlavi dynasty. Iran was a constitutional monarchy with a two-house Parliament.[2] The British and Russians believed that Reza Khan was potentially pro-Nazi, so they forced his abdication, sent him into exile, and put his twenty-three-year-old son on the throne. At the same time the British also kidnaped General Fazollah Zahedi, a dashing, handsome, six-foot-two ladies' man with a taste for silk underwear, expensive prostitutes, and opium. According to the British, Zahedi was also pro-Nazi, and they kept him in jail in Palestine for the duration.

The new, young Shah looked the part of a monarch. He carried himself stiffly and was strikingly handsome, despite—or perhaps because of—a highly prominent nose. But despite the impression of strength he gave, he had been a sickly boy, dominated by his stern and cruel father, and was filled with self-doubt and fears of his own weakness.[3] He was easily manipulated by the occupying powers (which after 1942 included the Americans).

The Allies gave the Shah a sense of importance. Churchill accepted an invitation to lunch at the palace, and the Big Three held one of their famous conferences in Teheran, where the young Shah met, briefly, both Stalin and Roosevelt. Stalin offered him arms (with Soviet advisers to go with them); Churchill pretended to discuss seriously military strategy; FDR displayed great interest in a reforestation program and offered to return to Iran after the war to advise the Shah on the subject.[4]

At the Teheran Conference, the occupying powers pledged themselves to withdraw their troops from Iran within six months of the end of hostilities. In late 1945, Britain and America kept their word, but the Russians stayed on in the northern Iranian province of Azerbaijan, where they attempted to inspire a revolt that would lead to a secession of the province and its incorporation as a "republic" into the Soviet Union. This was the first real crisis of the Cold War. President Truman sent America's newest aircraft carrier, the *Franklin D. Roosevelt,* to the eastern Mediterranean as a show of force to back his demand that the Russians get out of Iran. After negotiating a deal that gave the Russians access to Iranian oil, Stalin did pull his troops out. The Iranian Parliament then refused to ratify the deal, and Russia suffered a major diplomatic setback.[5]

The American attitude toward Iran in the immediate postwar years was set by Secretary of State Dean Acheson, who believed the United States should play a supporting role in Iran's resistance to the Soviet pressure. As a result, relations between America and Iran were excellent. The Shah visited the United States, where he had a successful audience with Truman and met Eisenhower, then president of Columbia University (Ike recorded in his memoirs, "At that time I developed—on short acquaintance—some confidence that he would prove an effective leader of his people").[6]

In 1947, Kim Roosevelt, Harvard graduate, historian, OSS Mideastern expert during the war, was writing a book called *Arabs, Oil and History,* and he had a long interview with the Shah in his palace. Roosevelt was then thirty-one, the Shah twenty-eight.

They impressed each other favorably, or so Roosevelt later claimed. The Shah, he wrote, was "an intense young man, with a wiry body and a wiry spirit also—dark, slim, with a deep store of barely hidden energy." Roosevelt did admit that "his [the Shah's] personality was subdued at that time."[7]

The most important American in the Shah's life in the mid-1940s was not Truman, nor Acheson, nor Kim Roosevelt, but rather a fabulous character named Schwarzkopf. Colonel H. Norman Schwarzkopf of the U. S. Army had been the chief of the New Jersey State Police and was internationally known for his success in handling the Lindbergh kidnaping case.

He was one of the first of those experts sent by the United States to underdeveloped countries to teach their governments how to maintain law and order and preserve themselves in power. The Iranians had asked for his help in reorganizing their police force. From 1942 to 1948 he commanded the Imperial Iranian Gendarmerie with firmness and determination, turning it into a modern, efficient force that was loyal to the Shah and extremely hostile to the Tudeh (Communist) Party. Schwarzkopf also helped organize the secret, or security, branch of the police, the notorious SAVAK. During the crisis in Azerbaijan the Gendarmerie helped ensure firm government control by arresting some three hundred Tudeh Party leaders. Schwarzkopf personally showed up wherever trouble was brewing and was thus singled out as a target for special attacks from the Soviet press, which accused him of being the front man for American imperialism.[8] In 1948, Schwarzkopf was promoted to brigadier general and left Iran for a new post in West Germany.

The United States, delighted at Iran's successful resistance to Soviet encroachment, rewarded the Shah's government with new programs of technical and financial aid, including a military mission of some eighteen officers who oversaw the distribution of weapons from American war surplus stocks worth some $60 million.[9] The badly burned Soviets, meanwhile, fearful of an increased American presence on their southern border (at this time the United States was replacing Britain as the chief supporter of the Greek monarchy, in accordance with the recently announced Truman Doctrine), adopted a cautious and rather conservative attitude toward Iran. The Russians preferred a weaker British presence in Iran to an aggressive American intrusion, but there was little they could do to stop the incoming Yanks.[10]

With the Russians checked and the Americans providing support, the Iranians were in a position to turn on their real enemies, the hated British. They had much to complain about. The Anglo-Persian Oil Company paid more in taxes to the British Government than it did in royalties to Iran. Equally galling, the company used the huge profits it earned in Iran to expand its oil output in other parts of the world. Further, to the British the Iranians were just another set of "wogs," to be treated with contempt and excluded from any but the most menial posts in the operation of the Abadan refinery.

The situation was intolerable. It presented a marvelous opportunity to any Iranian politician who had the courage to lead. The one who seized the chance was a remarkable old man, Dr. Mohammad Mossadegh, leader of the National Front. Seventy years old in 1951, he was a rich landowner, educated in France and Switzerland, worldly wise, a successful spellbinder of a speaker who had been elected to the Majlis (the second house of the Parliament) in 1915, and who was generally regarded by those Westerners who dealt with him as a completely unreasonable, demagogic, and xenophobic man.

Tall, thin, bent, a semi-invalid who often appeared in public clad only in pajamas, he would burst into tears at the most inappropriate moment, or faint dead away. He had a huge nose that was always dripping. (One State Department official said, "Mossadegh has a nose that makes Jimmy Durante look like an amputee!")[11] His favorite place for doing business was his bedroom, where he would recline, propped up by pillows, and alternatively cackle and cry.

Dean Acheson depicted Mossadegh as "small and frail, with not a shred of hair on his billiard-ball head; a thin face protruding into a long beak of a nose flanked by two bright shoe-button eyes. His whole manner and appearance was birdlike and he moved quickly and nervously as if he were hopping about on a perch. His pixie quality showed in instantaneous transformations."[12]

Mossadegh was the first Middle Eastern politician to demand the complete nationalization of his country's oil fields. The Shah's Prime Minister, General Razmara, opposed such drastic action. On March 7, 1951, a member of the Crusaders of Islam, one of the groups in Mossadegh's National Front, assassinated Razmara while he was attending a ceremony in a mosque. Mossadegh was the overwhelming popular choice to succeed Razmara. As the Shah later wrote, "How could anyone be against Mossadegh? He would enrich everybody, he would fight the foreigner, he would secure our rights. No wonder students, intellectuals, people from all walks of life, flocked to his banner."[13] Reluctantly, the Shah appointed him Prime Minister. The same day, May 2, 1951, the Parliament passed a bill nationalizing the oil industry. A week later the Majlis gave Mossadegh's government a vote of confidence by a majority of ninety-nine to three.

For the British, the wogs were on the rampage. For the Iranians, a war of liberation had begun against the colonialists.[14] For the Americans, here was an opportunity to get a foothold in the rich Iranian oil fields, and a window to Russia. The British refused to accept the compensation payment for the company offered by Mossadegh, shut down Abadan cold, refused to buy oil from Iran, and put various legal obstacles in the way of any country that was willing to purchase Iranian oil, arguing that such oil was in fact stolen goods and threatening to take any purchaser to court.

Truman and Acheson tried to serve as honest brokers, offering to mediate to bring about a compromise. Mossadegh came to Washington and was put up at the Blair House. Meeting with Truman, Mossadegh, looking old and pathetic, said in trembling tones, "I am speaking for a very poor country—a country all desert —just sand, a few camels, a few sheep . . ." Acheson, grinning, interrupted to say that with all its sand *and* oil, Iran reminded him of Texas. Mossadegh laughed delightedly. They talked of oil prices, with Mossadegh complaining about the vast gap between what the British paid Iran per barrel and what they charged for the product on the world market. Acheson "explained oil economics to him in terms of the wide spread between the price we got for beef cattle on the hoof on our farms and the price we paid for a prime roast of beef in the butcher's shop." Mossadegh responded that "peasants were always exploited."

Later, Acheson wrote that the United States was slow to realize that Mossadegh was "essentially a rich, reactionary, feudal-minded Persian inspired by a fanatical hatred of the British and a desire to expel them and all their works from the country regardless of cost."[15]

The shutdown at Abadan, meanwhile, forced a crisis in Iran. With no moneys coming in from oil royalties, the government was rapidly going bankrupt. In July 1952, Mossadegh demanded authority to govern for six months without recourse to Parliament, and that he be given the additional post of Minister of War. The Shah refused and instead demanded (and got) Mossadegh's resignation. Immediately the National Front, supported by the Tudeh Party, launched riots and demonstrations. Mossadegh's replacement inflamed the situation by indicating that he was going to give in to the British on the question of oil nationalization. The riots grew worse. Unable to control them, the new Prime Minister resigned. Five days after the Shah had fired Mossadegh, he had to reappoint him.[16]

In October 1952, Mossadegh broke off diplomatic relations with Britain. Meanwhile, Winston Churchill once again became Prime Minister of Great Britain, and, in November 1952, Eisenhower was elected President of the United States. The two comrades in arms from World War II now had their opportunity to solve the Iranian "problem."

IN JANUARY 1953, Mossadegh sent President-elect Eisenhower a three-page cable in which he congratulated Ike on his election victory, then plunged into an extended discussion of Iranian affairs. The theme was summed up in one sentence: "For almost two years," Mossadegh wrote, "the Iranian people have suffered acute distress and much misery merely because a company inspired by covetousness and a desire for profit supported by the British government has been endeavoring to prevent them from obtaining their natural and elementary rights." In a hand-drafted reply, Ike said his own position was impartial, that he had no prejudices in the case, and that he hoped future relations would be good.[17]

In fact, however, everything the President-elect was hearing was anti-Mossadegh. Churchill and the British seized on the Tudeh's support of the Prime Minister to make the point that the old man was either a Communist or a victim of Communist intrigue. The American ambassador to Iran, Loy Henderson, a career Foreign Service officer who had served in Moscow before the war, was bitterly anti-Communist. When asked to assess the extent of Mossadegh's support, Henderson told the incoming Eisenhower administration that "old Mossy" relied on "the street rabble, the extreme left . . . extreme Iranian nationalists, some, but not all, of the more fanatical religious leaders, intellectual leftists, including many who had been educated abroad and who did not realize that Iran was not ready for democracy."

Henderson also took a dim view of Mossadegh's action on the point at issue, the nationalization of the company. "We did not believe," he declared later in an interview, "that such an expropriation was in the basic interest of Iran, Great Britain, or the U.S. Acts of this kind tended to undermine the mutual trust that was necessary if international trade was to flourish."[18]

The British, meanwhile, had approached Kim Roosevelt, well known to them from OSS days and currently one of the top CIA agents. Sir John Cochran, acting as spokesman for the Churchill government, proposed that the British Secret Service and the CIA join forces to overthrow Mossadegh. "As I told my British colleagues," Roosevelt later wrote, "we had, I felt sure, no chance to win approval from the outgoing administration of Truman and Acheson. The new Republicans, however, might be quite different."[19]

Roosevelt expected a different approach because of the nature of Republican attacks on the Truman-Acheson foreign policy. Ike criticized the Democrats for spreading American resources too thin, accepting the status quo too willingly, and concentrating too heavily on Western Europe. Eisenhower contended that the United States must wrest the initiative from the Soviet Union, and if possible "liberate" areas from Communist control. Eisenhower seemed so much tougher than Truman that the New York *Times* wrote, "The day of sleep-walking is over. It passed with the exodus of Truman and Achesonism, and the policy of vigilance replacing Pollyanna diplomacy is evident."[20] Roosevelt also felt, based on his wartime experiences, that Eisenhower would be much more likely to use his covert-action capabilities than Truman had been.

The essence of the plan the British presented to Roosevelt was to keep the Shah while dumping his Prime Minister. Somehow Mossadegh learned of the plot. He then denounced the Shah for his intrigues with foreign interests and began to agitate for the Shah's abdication.

At this point the Shah lost his nerve. On February 28, 1953, he announced that he would leave the country, along with his queen and entourage. The announcement brought on riots in the streets of Teheran. The Tudeh Party, along with the United Front, marched in support of the Prime Minister; at the other end of town, as H.I.M. recorded in his memoirs, "the mass demonstrations of loyalty to the Shah were so convincing and affecting that I decided to remain for the time being." He canceled his agreement to abdicate.[21]

The active support of the Tudeh for Mossadegh fed the impression that the Prime Minister had gone over to the Communists, and for their own reasons the British—who had since the war lost colonies all around the world, a situation the new Churchill government was determined to reverse—clamored about the dangers of a Communist takeover in Iran. Strangely enough, no one seemed to notice that throughout this crisis, in which the stakes were nothing less than one of the world's greatest oil pools, the Russians were content to stand aside. Nor did anyone in the West ever point out that Mossadegh had not appealed to his northern neighbor for help.

The idea that this reactionary feudal landlord was a Communist was, in fact, quite ridiculous. The old man has his own explanation of what was going on. When Henderson complained to him about Communist mobs demonstrating against the West in the streets of Teheran, Mossadegh replied, "These are not real Communists, they are people paid by the British to pretend they are Communists in order to frighten the United States into believing that under my Premiership the country is going Communist." That may well have been true, but to Henderson it appeared that Mossadegh "had become a paranoiac so far as the British were concerned. He held them responsible for all of Iran's ills and gave them credit for almost superhuman machinations."[22]

Mossadegh's policy was to attempt to split the United States and Britain. To that end, in May 1953, he once again appealed to Ike. In a long personal message he begged the President to help remove the obstacles the British had placed on the sale of Iranian oil and to provide Iran with substantially increased American economic assistance. "I refused," Ike recorded bluntly, "to pour more American money into a country in turmoil in order to bail Mossadegh out of troubles rooted in his refusal to work out an agreement with the British."

To Mossadegh, Ike wrote directly. "I fully understand that the government of Iran must determine for itself which foreign and domestic policies are likely to be most advantageous to Iran. . . . I am not trying to advise the Iranian government on its best interests.

I am merely trying to explain why, in the circumstances, the government of the United States is not presently in a position to extend more aid to Iran or to purchase Iranian oil."[23] (It should be pointed out here that in those happy days, the United States was itself an exporter of oil, and in the world as a whole far more oil was being pumped out of the ground than was being consumed. Mossadegh's problem was that the world of the early 1950s could get along quite well without Iranian oil.

Iran was by now on the edge of financial and economic ruin. The Truman administration had increased American aid from $1.6 million before Mossadegh came to power to $23.4 million for the fiscal year 1953, but that was not even close to enough money to make up for the lost oil revenue. When Ike turned down his plea, Mossadegh was forced to draw money from the pension funds and the national insurance company.[24]

Moderates in Iran began to turn against the Prime Minister. In response, he suspended elections for the National Assembly and held a referendum to decide if the current National Assembly should be dissolved. He arranged the election so that those in favor of dissolution and those against it voted in separate, plainly marked booths, which were, of course, closely watched by his supporters. Under those circumstances, it was no surprise that Mossadegh won the referendum by 99 percent to 1 percent.

To Ike, the rigged election looked for sure like Communist tactics. He concluded that if old Mossy was not a Communist himself, then he was either a fool or a stooge for the Communists.[25] His ambassador (he had kept Henderson on the job) told him that if Mossadegh got rid of the Shah, "chaos would develop in Iran, a chaos that would be overcome only by a bloody dictatorship working under orders from Moscow."[26] This impression was very much strengthened when Mossadegh, having been spurned by Eisenhower, turned to the Soviets for help. On August 8 the Russians announced that they had initiated negotiations with Iran for financial aid and trade talks.

Mossadegh, Ike wrote in his memoirs, "believed that he could form an alliance with the Tudeh Party and then outwit it." To the President, this was improbable at best. He feared that "Mossadegh would become to Iran what the ill-fated Dr. Benes had been in Czechoslovakia—a leader whom the Communists, having gained power, would eventually destroy."[27] In addition to his determination to stop Communist expansion, the Republicans had just won an election, in part, by demanding to know "Who Lost China?" They were not going to expose themselves to the question "Who Lost Iran?"

Ike decided it was time to act. He ordered the CIA to go ahead with a plan that had been initiated by the British Secret Service, picked up by Kim Roosevelt, and approved five weeks earlier by his State Department in a high-level meeting in the Secretary of State's office.

That meeting inaugurated the CIA's covert-action program, going beyond simple financial support for America's overseas friends, to active intervention in the affairs of a foreign nation, to the point of overthrowing a government.

THE MEETING BEGAN when Kim Roosevelt laid before Secretary of State John Foster Dulles a thick paper outlining a plan of clandestine action, code name AJAX. Picking it up, the Secretary glanced around the room, smiled, and said, "So this is how we get rid of that madman Mossadegh!" No one laughed; indeed, some of those around the table flinched.[28]

Among those present were Bedell Smith, who Ike had moved from the CIA to the State Department, where he was now the Under Secretary of State. Bedell was a neighbor and old friend of Roosevelt's. He already knew of and had approved AJAX. Smith's replacement as director of the CIA, Allen Dulles, was also there. He, too, knew and approved of AJAX. A third insider was Loy Henderson, "a gentleman himself," Roosevelt recorded, "who preferred dealing with his foreign colleagues in a gentlemanly fashion. But Henderson was one of a small band of distinguished foreign-service officers of that era who understood the realities of life in this world we live in." In other words, Henderson too supported AJAX.[29]

There were a number of State Department officials present who were not in on the plot, including Robert Murphy, who had been Ike's first spy back in North Africa eleven years earlier. The new Secretary of Defense, Charles Wilson ("Engine Charlie," former head of General Motors) was there, ruddy-faced, white-haired, gruff, blunt to the point of embarrassment. Wilson had a habit of sitting through meetings with a cigarette in his mouth, letting it smolder right down until it started to burn his lips. He would toss it into the ashtray and light another and let it burn down. He had a way of getting to the heart of the matter. At one early Eisenhower cabinet meeting, there was a long discussion of America's military posture vis-à-vis Communist China. Finally Wilson stubbed out a cigarette butt, turned to Ike, and said, "Mr. President, I understand from what's been said that we could lick China. What I don't understand is what we would do with China after we got them licked."[30]

A group of hardheaded realists, in short, men of vast experience, able, cynical, accustomed to assessing evidence and making tough decisions, unafraid to take risks. Men Ike trusted to give him sound, practical advice. If Roosevelt could convince them that AJAX could work, they would convince Ike.

Roosevelt began by saying that, on Allen Dulles' instructions, he had made two trips to Iran since the election in order to make a judgment on two points. First, that "the Soviet threat is indeed genuine, dangerous, and imminent," and second, that in a showdown "the Iranian army and the Iranian people will back the Shah." Roosevelt said he was satisfied on both points. He reported further that the British had approved AJAX and agreed to provide whatever support they could, but given anti-British sentiment in Iran would stay as far in the background as possible.

The objective of AJAX was to remove Mossadegh from office. The Shah had indicated that he wanted to replace Mossadegh with General Zahedi. That was a bit much for the British to swallow, as they had kept Zahedi in prison throughout World War II and he was almost as anti-British as Mossadegh. But Churchill and his Foreign Secretary, Anthony Eden, realized that their choices were limited, and between Mossadegh and Zahedi they preferred Zahedi.

The first task, Roosevelt continued, was to organize military support for the Shah. The chief of staff, General Riahi, was a supporter of Mossadegh. He would have to be removed or circumvented. The key to AJAX was to be prepared to give the Shah prompt support, both military and public, when he announced the dismissal of Mossadegh and the appointment of Zahedi.

"We are quite satisfied, sir," Roosevelt concluded, turning to Secretary Dulles, "that this can be done successfully. All we wait upon is your decision."

Allen Dulles spoke first. "Kim, you had better cover two more points before the Secretary comments: first, on the estimated cost, and secondly, I think you should give your idea of the 'flap potential'—what could happen if things go wrong."

Roosevelt responded that the cost would be minimal, one or two hundred thousand dollars at the most. On the second point, he said again that he saw no danger of failure, but if he had totally misjudged the situation and things did go wrong, the consequences "would be very bad—perhaps terrifyingly so. Iran would fall to the Russians, and the effect on the rest of the Middle East could be disastrous. But I must add this: These are the same consequences we face if we do nothing."

Foster Dulles asked about General Guilanshah, the commander of the Iranian Air Force. Roosevelt said that although he was loyal to the Shah, he would not be a part of the plot because there was no role for the Air Force in AJAX and the conspirators wanted to keep the number of those in the know at the smallest possible figure.

The Secretary of State then polled the men around the table. Most signified consent with the least possible commitment. Roosevelt had no doubts about Bedell Smith—six months earlier, when Smith was still DCI, he had called Roosevelt into his office to demand, "When are those blanking British coming to talk to us? And when is our goddam operation going to get underway? Pull up your socks and get going, young man."[31] Now, when asked by Foster Dulles whether to go or not, Smith, surly as always, snarled that of course they should proceed.

Robert Murphy, the only man present with some experience in overthrowing governments, nodded his assent. Charles Wilson was enthusiastic. Loy Henderson spoke gravely: "Mr. Secretary, I don't like this kind of business at all. You know that. But we are confronted by a desperate, a dangerous situation and a madman who would ally himself with the Russians. We have no choice but to proceed with this undertaking. May God grant us success."

"That's that, then," the Secretary of State declared. "Let's get going!"

Later, Roosevelt recorded his conviction that "I was morally certain that almost half of those present, if they had felt free or had the courage to speak, would have opposed the undertaking."[32]

The next step was to get the approval of the heads of government. As noted, Ike gave his orders to go ahead after Mossadegh opened negotiations with the Soviets. On the British side, there was no problem—Churchill and Eden had been in on AJAX from the start; they had been the men who had initiated the operation.

HAVING CONVINCED HIS SUPERIORS that AJAX could work, and having obtained the President's go-ahead, Kim Roosevelt's next task was to persuade the Shah to act. This proved to be more difficult than convincing the Dulles brothers and Eisenhower. The Shah sensed that in trying to rid himself of Mossadegh, he could lose everything. In a showdown, the army and the people might very well support the Prime Minister rather than H.I.M.

When Roosevelt entered Iran in mid-July 1953 he knew that he had fudged a bit before the Dulles brothers in outlining AJAX when he guaranteed that the Shah was prepared for decisive action. In fact, the Shah was hesitant, confused, fearful. Two Iranian secret agents, who had once worked for the British, then joined with Roosevelt, had explained this quite carefully to him during one of his earlier visits.

H.I.M., the agents told Roosevelt, "is concerned over the apparent fact that he has no foreign support. Obviously the Russians . . . are his enemies. He knows they support Mossadegh. What about the West? As you know, as we know, they *are* with him. But how can he tell? Look at the terrific reception Mossadegh was given in Washington [by the Truman administration]. How can the Shah be sure, after that, that the U.S. will give him their backing? And the British, who are—whatever they may think—just about to be thrown out of Iran, why should he believe that they will come to his assistance? We hope you can find some way of convincing him, preferably not just of U.S. support but of British as well. We don't know just how we are going to arrange all this, but we tell you: It must be done!"[33]

Ambassador Henderson, at Roosevelt's urging, had tried to reassure the Shah of Western support. "I did have many frank private talks with the Shah during which I tried to encourage him," Henderson later recalled. "I can remember, for instance, that at one time, almost despairing at the position in which Mossadegh had pushed him, the Shah had decided to go abroad. I pled with him not to do so, pointing out that his departure might well lead to the loss of Iran's independence. I was greatly relieved when he decided that it was his duty to remain in the country regardless of the humiliations that Mossadegh was heaping on him."[34]

The simplest, most direct way to buck up the wavering Shah would have been for Roosevelt himself to go directly to the palace, but the Dulles brothers were determined to keep AJAX a clandestine operation. When they agreed to allow Roosevelt to serve as the agent in charge of AJAX, it was with the explicit understanding that he would remain completely out of sight. "He has a very prominent family name," Foster Dulles had declared, chuckling. "He will have to keep away from anyone who might know him." The Secretary did not want the American role revealed, under any circumstances.[85]

Roosevelt had therefore set up his command post in the basement of a "safe house" in Teheran, but there could be no coup if the Shah was afraid to act, and in early August the Shah was wavering more than ever. At this juncture, General Schwarzkopf appeared in Iran, "armed with a diplomatic passport and a couple of large bags" containing "millions of dollars."*

Schwarzkopf requested and was granted an audience with the Shah. But H.I.M., fearing spies in his own palace, was cautious, and Schwarzkopf's reassurances of Western support were not convincing. Meanwhile the Tudeh Party newspapers had learned of Schwarzkopf's presence. In special editions, they loudly denounced H.I.M. for his contacts with "brainless agents of international reaction." Mossadegh was furious. He threatened to hold another referendum, this time to depose the Shah. The crisis was at hand.

Obviously Schwarzkopf had to get out of the country, fast. Before leaving, he met with Roosevelt. "Kim," he said, "you simply are not going to be able to deal with the Shahanshah through *any* intermediary. I'm convinced that you will have to meet with H.I.M. personally." Nothing short of a direct meeting between the two men would convince the Shah to act.[87]

Roosevelt agreed emphatically. Using a communications network set up by the British on Cyprus, he got Ike to add a phrase to a speech he was making in San Francisco, and Churchill to alter

---

* Kim Roosevelt denies the figure; he claims there was only $1 million and only $100,000 actually spent. After his retirement in 1962, on a CBS television show, Allen Dulles was asked whether it was true that "the CIA people spent literally millions of dollars hiring people to riot in the streets and do other things, to get rid of Mossadegh. Is there anything you can say about that?" "Well," Dulles replied, "I can say that the statement that we spent many dollars doing that is utterly false."[86]

the BBC time announcement. That night he made the first in his series of clandestine visits to the palace, where he managed to convince the Shah that with Eisenhower, Churchill, and a Roosevelt standing behind him, H.I.M. could afford to act.

CHAPTER FIFTEEN

Iran: The Act

AUGUST 10, 1953. Prime Minister Mossadegh postpones prohibition for one year. Kennett Love of the New York *Times* reports that "wine jugs all over this land of Omar Khayyam [are] tilted today in celebration." Prohibition was voted in by the Majlis, under the leadership of Speaker Ayatollah Kashani, a few months earlier,* but Mossadegh has since then dissolved the Majlis and now, in a bid for popular support, Mossadegh—himself a teetotaler—overrides the law. Reporter Love guesses that his motive is to appease the Russians, who are continuing financial negotiations with Iran, a major export market for Russian vodka.

Obviously delighted himself, Love informs *Times* readers that "vodka is extremely important in Teheran life, being served in iced decanters with bowls of caviar beside splashing fountains under weeping willow trees in walled garden cafes. As the deadline for prohibition approached, thirsty patrons of Iranian taverns asked with the ancient tentmaker poet, 'I wonder often what the vintners buy one-half so precious as the stuff they sell.'"[1]

FOR KIM ROOSEVELT, hiding in his safe house, the big news was not the delay of prohibition, but rather the distressing word that the Shah had fled his capital. After agreeing to sign a royal decree dismissing Mossadegh and replacing him with General Zahedi, H.I.M. had lost his nerve. Together with his queen, he had

---

* Because the financial situation has been so bad, and because liquor taxes produced essential revenue, the implementation of prohibition had been set six months in the future.

flown off to his summer palace on the Caspian Sea—without signing the decree.

Roosevelt, double-crossed and furious, consulted with his two Iranian agents. He sent them to Colonel Nematollah Nassiry; they bullied Nassiry into flying to the Caspian with the royal decrees and instructions to make sure the Shah signed them. Nassiry got there safely and managed to convince the Shah to sign, but then the weather closed in and he was unable to fly back to Teheran.

So Roosevelt fumed. "We sat," he later wrote, "in the daytime around the pool, after dark in the living room, smoking, drinking mild vodkas with lime juice, playing hearts . . . or backgammon, and cursing heartfelt obscenities at unpredictable intervals."[2]

He also sent, via the British-controlled communications network on Cyprus, regular reports back to Washington. Ike recalled in his memoirs, "I conferred daily with officials of the State and Defense departments and the Central Intelligence Agency, and saw reports from our representatives on the spot who were working actively with the Shah's supporters." These reports, he added, "often sounded more like a dime novel than historical facts."[3]

At midnight, August 12, Colonel Nassiry returned with the signed documents. But to Roosevelt's dismay, they could not be delivered for two days because the Iranian weekend had begun. Thus he sat by the pool, smoking cigarettes, drinking vodka-limes, and playing a song from the current hit Broadway musical *Guys and Dolls*—"Luck Be a Lady Tonight."[4]

Mossadegh, meanwhile, had learned of the decrees dismissing him from office. So, when Colonel Nassiry appeared in the middle of the night of August 14–15 before the Prime Minister's home on Takht-i-Jamshid, a few blocks west of the American Embassy, he found it surrounded by American-made tanks, guarded by troops who were obeying orders from General Tazhi Riahi, the Iranian chief of staff and a Mossadegh loyalist. The troops had been instructed to keep Nassiry away, but he strode forward boldly, in full uniform, and announced that he had a royal decree to deliver. As the Shah later wrote, "The Colonel had judged correctly that the tank crews and other troops knew him so well, and were so accustomed to respecting his authority, that they could not bring themselves to shoot him down."[5]

Nassiry demanded access to Mossadegh. This was refused. He then demanded a receipt for the delivery of the royal decree. This was refused. Nassiry would not leave without a receipt. Finally, after an hour and a half wait, he got a receipt signed by a servant. The delay, however, was fatal—before Nassiry could withdraw, General Riahi had him arrested and brought to his office. Riahi stripped Nassiry of his uniform and put him behind bars.

The next morning at 7 A.M. Mossadegh made a radio broadcast. He announced that the Shah, encouraged by "foreign elements," had attempted a coup d'etat, and that he—Mossadegh—was therefore compelled to take all power unto himself. He sent out orders to arrest every known supporter of the Shah in Teheran. General Riahi's troops started turning the city upside down looking for General Zahedi, whom Mossadegh denounced as a traitor.

They could not find Zahedi because Kim Roosevelt had taken him to a safe house near the American Embassy, a place with a big basement and surrounded by a high wall. From that spot, Zahedi began making his own radio broadcasts, claiming that he was the rightful Prime Minister, by decree of the Shah, and that Mossadegh was the real traitor.[6]

At this juncture, the Shah fled Iran, with Queen Soraya, one aide, and the pilot of his Beechcraft. They had no luggage and no passports. They flew to Baghdad, where the Iraqi Government agreed to allow them to stay for a day.

In Teheran, meanwhile, the Tudeh hit the streets. Mobs swelled, chanted "Down with the Shah," "Death to the Americans," "Yankees, go home!" They surged up and down the streets, smashed statues of the Shah and his father, and joyfully looted everything they could grab.

"Frankly," Kim Roosevelt confessed, "it scared the hell out of me."[7]

The riots went on for two days. The Shah flew to Rome. Allen Dulles hopped a plane to Rome to confer with him. Foster Dulles, after consulting with Ike, told Loy Henderson (who had been on "vacation" as a part of the AJAX cover plan) to return to Teheran to see what he could do there.

Henderson's return proved to be the decisive stroke. He arrived on August 18. Kim Roosevelt, again huddled on a back seat under a blanket, made his way by car to the embassy to consult. "We've run into some small complications," Roosevelt ruefully confessed. He suggested that Henderson see Mossadegh, complain about harassment to Americans, and threaten to pull all American citizens out of the country if it did not stop.[8]

Henderson demanded and got an immediate audience with Mossadegh. The Prime Minister launched into a condemnation of the U. S. Government. He said that CIA agents had persuaded the Shah to issue the royal decrees, which he shouted were illegal, as only Parliament could remove him from office.

Henderson, brushing all the complaints aside, said he had come to talk about the presence of American citizens in Teheran. The Tudeh mobs were a threat to their lives and safety. In an interview years later, Henderson recalled, "I told the Prime Minister that unless the Iranian police were prepared to stop Communist pillaging and attacks, it would be my duty to order all Americans to leave the country at once."

Now it was old Mossy's turn to lose his nerve. He begged Henderson not to do it. An American evacuation would look just terrible, make it appear that his government was not able to govern. He asserted that he was perfectly capable of maintaining law and order. Henderson charged that he did not believe Mossadegh realized the extent to which the Tudeh had been given a free hand to ransack the city.

Mossadegh called in an aide and asked if it were true that the Tudeh people were roaming the streets in gangs, pillaging, destroying, and attacking foreigners. When the aide said it certainly was true, Henderson said, "In my presence Mossadegh picked up the telephone, called the Chief of Police, and gave orders that the police be instructed immediately to restore order to the streets, to break up the roving gangs who were engaging in violence."[9]

It was the old man's fatal mistake. The Schwarzkopf-trained police, previously under orders not to take steps that might offend the Tudeh, were delighted to be turned loose. Kennett Love reported to the New York Times, "Policemen and soldiers swung into action tonight against rioting Tudeh partisans and Nationalist extremists. The troops appeared to be in a frenzy as they smashed into the rioters with clubbed rifles and nightsticks, and hurled tear-gas bombs."[10]

The following morning, August 19, Kim Roosevelt sprang into action. The pro-Mossadegh forces were off the streets, the day was already hot, the atmosphere oppressive. Roosevelt gave his Iranian agents the order to strike. He had earlier described these agents to the Shah: "They are extremely competent, professional 'organizers' who have already demonstrated their competence. They have a strong team under them, they can distribute pamphlets, organize mobs, keep track of the opposition—you name it, they'll do it." Roosevelt also told the Shah, "We have a gigantic safe next to my principal assistant's office. It is in a big closet and occupies the whole space. This safe is jam-packed with rial notes. . . . We have the equivalent of about one million dollars in that safe."[11]

That was the money Schwarzkopf had brought in from the CIA. Roosevelt's Iranian agents now began to buy themselves a mob.

They started with the Zirkaneh giants, weight lifters who developed their physiques through an ancient Iranian set of exercises which included lifting progressively heavier weights. The Zirkanehs had built up tremendous shoulders and huge biceps. Shuffling down the street together, they were a frightening spectacle. Two hundred or so of these weight lifters began the day by marching through the bazaar, shouting "Long Live the Shah!" and dancing and twirling like dervishes. Along the edges of the crowd, men were passing out ten-rial notes, adorned with a handsome portrait of H.I.M. The mob swelled; the chant "Long Live the Shah!" was deafening. As the throng passed the offices of a pro-Mossadegh newspaper, men smashed the windows and sacked the place.[12]

"Do you think the time has come to turn General Zahedi loose to lead the crowd?" one of Roosevelt's assistants asked him.

Not yet, he replied. "There is nothing to be gained by rushing. Let's wait till the crowd gets to Mossadegh's house. That should be a good moment for our hero to make his appearance."[13]

Roosevelt's radio operator appeared, tears streaming down his face. He had a message from Bedell Smith, a message Smith had sent twenty-four hours earlier, but which the British on Cyprus had held up for a day. The message said, in effect, "Give up and get out."

With a hearty laugh and a broad grin, Roosevelt jotted down a reply for the radio operator to send back to Cyprus: "Yours of 18 August received. Happy to report Zahedi safely installed and Shah will be returning to Teheran in triumph shortly. Love and kisses from all the team."[14]

With that, Roosevelt left his basement hideout and went out into the streets. He was on his way to pick up Zahedi. He ran into General Guilanshah, chief of the Air Force, in full uniform. Guilan-shah recognized Roosevelt and eagerly offered to help. Roosevelt told him to pick up a tank. Guilanshah asked where Zahedi was, and Roosevelt gave him the address.

Arriving at Zahedi's hiding place, Roosevelt found the Prime Minister-designate in the cellar, wearing only his winter underwear. In broken German, Roosevelt told him to get dressed. The general put on his full-dress uniform. As he buttoned his tunic, Guilanshah burst into the room. He had a tank waiting outside.[15]

In telling the story years later, CIA agents embellished it until a myth developed that Kim Roosevelt, in the grand tradition of his Rough Rider grandfather, had mounted the lead tank and led the way to Mossadegh's home. In fact, he stayed out of sight. Zahedi led the mob, supported by tanks rounded up by Colonel Nassiry and General Guilanshah. According to the Shah (who of course was not there), an amazing cross section of the people of Iran led the assault on Mossadegh's forces—"students, artisans, manual labourers, professional men, policemen, members of the gendar-merie, and soldiers."[16] According to *Times* reporter Love (who was there), the two-hour battle that raged outside Mossadegh's home was fought between those soldiers loyal to Mossadegh, and acting under General Riahi's orders, and troops following Zahedi. One hundred were killed, three hundred injured. Zahedi's forces prevailed, as Riahi's men ran out of ammunition.[17]

At dusk, Royalist troops overwhelmed the remaining household guard and entered Mossadegh's home. The old man was gone—he had slipped out the back way.

Zahedi went to the officers' club, which was jam-packed and ri-otous, to celebrate. Kim Roosevelt went first to the American Em-bassy, where he and Loy Henderson opened champagne to toast "the Shah, Zahedi, Dwight Eisenhower, Winston Churchill, and one another." Then Roosevelt proceeded to the officers' club, where "everyone, total strangers as well as good friends, embraced me, kissed me on both cheeks."[18]

The Shah received the news the next day while he was lunching at his hotel in Rome. The *Times* reported that "he went pale and his hands shook so violently that he hardly was able to read when newspaper men showed him the first reports. 'Can it be true?' he asked. The Queen was far more calm. 'How exciting,' she ex-claimed, placing her hand on the Shah's arm to steady him."

A little later, in a press interview, the Shah declared, "It shows how the people stand. Ninety-nine per cent of the population is for me. I knew it all the time."[19]

That same day, August 20, Mossadegh, tears streaming down his face, his nose dripping, leaning heavily on his cane, and dressed only in his pink pajamas, accepted his fate and surrendered to Zahedi.[20]

With that, Zahedi sent a telegram to the Shah. "The Iranian people, and your devoted Army, are awaiting your return with the greatest impatience and are counting the minutes. I beg you to hasten your journey back in order that your people may show you their sentiments as they so ardently wish to do."[21]

H.I.M. decided to return. After such a touching display of affection and loyalty from his subjects, how could he do otherwise? On Saturday, August 22, His Imperial Majesty, the Shahanshah, Mohammed Reza Shah Pahlavi, Light of the Aryans, returned in triumph to his capital. Prime Minister Zahedi, all members of the new Cabinet, the entire diplomatic corps, "and mobs of deliriously happy citizens from all ranks of life" (at least according to Kim Roosevelt) were at the airport to greet him.

MIDNIGHT, AUGUST 23, 1953. Kim Roosevelt drove, one last time, to the palace. This time he sat up. His vehicle was plainly marked as belonging to the American Embassy. There was no blanket. Guards saluted with a flourish as he entered. Instead of sneaking into the car, the Shah received the American agent in his office. A frock-coated attendant appeared with vodka and caviar canapés. The Shah graciously motioned for Roosevelt to be seated.

His first words were, "I owe my throne to God, my people, my army—and to you!" He raised his glass in a toast.[22]

ON HIS WAY HOME TO THE STATES, Roosevelt stopped in London to brief Churchill. At Number 10 Downing Street, he found the Prime Minister propped up in bed—the seventy-nine-year-old Churchill had suffered a stroke. Roosevelt sat beside the bed.

"We met at your cousin Franklin's, did we not?" Churchill asked. Roosevelt nodded. "I thought so. Well, you have an exciting story to tell. I'm anxious to hear it."

When Roosevelt finished his tale, Churchill smiled. "Young

man," he said, "if I had been but a few years younger, I would have loved nothing better than to have served under your command in this great venture."

A few days later, Roosevelt reported in Washington to the Dulles brothers, Secretary of Defense Wilson, Admiral Arthur Radford, and General Andrew Goodpaster. In the best CIA fashion, he had an easel, maps, a chart, the works. He went into great detail. His audience, he later wrote, "seemed almost alarmingly enthusiastic. John Foster Dulles was leaning back in his chair. . . . His eyes were gleaming; he seemed to be purring like a giant cat."[23]

Then, and later, Eisenhower and his associates were extremely coy about Roosevelt's role in the coup. Ike did admit in his memoirs: "Throughout this crisis the United States government had done everything it possibly could to back up the Shah." Eisenhower was on vacation in Colorado when Kim Roosevelt returned. He was careful not to meet with Roosevelt or have any direct connection with AJAX. In his memoirs Ike did quote a portion of Roosevelt's report, but only that part that dealt with the aftermath ("The Shah is a new man. For the first time, he believes in himself . . ." etc.), and he stated flatly that the report was prepared by "an American in Iran, unidentified to me."[24]

In a private interview two decades later, when Loy Henderson was asked if he could identify this "unknown" American, he replied, "Yes, I think I know, but I'm not at liberty to tell you."[25] Over the following decades rumors flew, myths grew, until in 1979 Kim Roosevelt decided to set the record straight and wrote his own account of the coup.*

THE RECKONING IN IRAN went as follows: Mossadegh was tried, found guilty of treason, and sentenced to three years solitary confinement. Colonel Nassiry became Brigadier General Nassiry. Prime Minister Zahedi reestablished diplomatic relations with the British. An international consortium of Western oil companies signed a twenty-five-year pact with Iran for its oil. The old Anglo-Persian Oil Company got 40 percent, Royal Dutch Shell got 14 percent, the Compagnie Française des Petroles got 6 percent, and the Americans (Gulf, Standard of New Jersey, Texaco, and Socony-Mobil) got 40 percent. Under a special ruling by the Depart-

* See Note 1, p. 334.

ment of Justice, the American oil companies participated in the consortium without fear of prosecution under the antitrust laws.

So the British had failed to stop the inevitable—they lost their monopoly—while the Americans had managed to prevent the improbable, a Communist takeover in Iran.

In September 1953, President Eisenhower announced an immediate allocation of $45 million in emergency economic aid to Iran, with another $40 million to follow. On October 8, Ike wrote in his diary, "Now if the British will be conciliatory . . . if the Shah and his new premier, General Zahedi, will be only a little bit flexible, and the United States will stand by to help both financially and with wise counsel, we may really give a serious defeat to Russian intentions and plans in that area.

"Of course, it will not be so easy for the Iranian economy to be restored, even if her refineries again begin to operate. This is due to the fact that during the long period of shutdown of her oil fields, world buyers have gone to other sources of supply. . . . Iran really has no ready market for her vast oil production. However, this is a problem that we should be able to help solve."[26]

SIX YEARS AFTER THE COUP, President Eisenhower visited Iran. An American observer said that the drive from the airport to the Shah's palace was a tremendous triumph—the streets were packed with cheering throngs (the people were paid ten-rial notes to be there, or so the observer was given to understand). The entire distance, five or six miles, was covered with Persian rugs over which the limousine drove. Tens of thousands of Persian rugs. Whatever else might be said of the Shah, he was no cheapskate when it came to showing his gratitude.[27]

CHAPTER SIXTEEN

Guatemala

A BRIGHT, SUNNY DAY IN EARLY MAY, 1954. At the East German port of Stettin, longshoremen grunt as they work along the docks, moving heavy crates with Czechoslovakian markings onto a Swedish merchant vessel, the *Alfhem*. Sea gulls swirl overhead, their raucous cries blending in with the shouts of the longshoremen. From a nearby, unused dock, a bird watcher studies the gulls, scanning the scene with his binoculars, hoping to spot an exotic species.

The bird watcher blinks, lowers his glasses, rubs his eyes, raises and refocuses the binoculars. There is no mistake. The workers are using cranes to lift small artillery pieces into the hold of the *Alfhem*. The birder makes some notes on his species list, then slowly saunters off in the other direction, continuing to scan the sky for rare gulls.

RETURNING TO HIS APARTMENT, the bird watcher—who was in reality a CIA agent—wrote a seemingly innocuous letter to a French automobile parts concern in Paris. To it he attached a small microfilm dot. The agent in Paris translated the microfilm message into code—the message started with the twenty-second prayer of David in the Book of Psalms, which begins, "My God, my God, why has Thou forsaken me?" He sent it via radio to Washington. That evening in Washington another agent decoded the message, then reported to Allen Dulles. A shipment of Communist-block arms was on its way to Guatemala.

Dulles instructed still another agent to check out the report as the *Alfhem* passed through the Kiel Canal. He discovered that although the *Alfhem*'s manifest listed her cargo as optical glass and laboratory supplies, and her destination as Dakar, Africa, in fact the freighter was carrying two thousand tons of small arms, ammunition, and light artillery pieces from the famous Skoda arms factory in Czechoslovakia. Her real destination was Puerto Barrios, Guatemala.[1]

On May 15, 1954, the *Alfhem,* after changing course several times in an effort to confuse the CIA, tied up at Puerto Barrios. Two days later, as she was being unloaded, Secretary of State John Foster Dulles called a press conference, where he announced that a shipment of arms from behind the Iron Curtain had arrived in the western hemisphere, in defiance of the Monroe Doctrine. Immediately, Washington was in an uproar. Senator Alexander Wiley of the Foreign Relations Committee called the shipment "part of the master plan of world communism," and President Eisenhower asserted that this "quantity of arms far exceeded any legitimate, normal requirements for the Guatemalan armed forces."[2]

Ike was right, but the arms were not intended for the armed forces. Instead, the President of Guatemala, Jacobo Arbenz Guzmán, intended to distribute them to his supporters in order to create a people's militia, free of any control by the regular army officer corps. Arbenz no longer trusted the American-equipped and -trained Guatemalan armed forces.[3]

The American public response was swift. The Eisenhower administration announced that it was airlifting fifty tons of rifles, pistols, machine guns, and ammunition ("hardly enough to create apprehension" in Guatemala, Ike later wrote) to Guatemala's neighbors, Nicaragua and Honduras. In addition, Eisenhower declared a blockade of Guatemala, and called for a meeting of the Organization of American States to consider further steps.[4]

Those acts were backed up by a far more important decision, made at a secret, emergency session of the National Security Council, presided over by the President himself. Allen Dulles presented the CIA's assessment of the situation. It was, essentially, that the Communists were trying to establish a foothold in Central America as a base for operations throughout the New World, in blatant disregard of the Monroe Doctrine. He indicated that the CIA had not been caught unawares, that it was ready to move. Eisenhower approved the program Dulles outlined. The CIA-sponsored invasion of Guatemala was on.

LIKE VIRTUALLY EVERY ADMINISTRATION since Teddy Roosevelt's, Eisenhower's had come into power promising a new policy toward Latin America. No more gunboat diplomacy, no more big-bully tactics, no more Marines landing the moment a government to the south displeased Washington. In addition, Eisenhower's chief adviser on Latin America was his younger brother Milton, one of America's foremost experts on the area, a highly intelligent, keenly sensitive man who was well aware of Latin resentment of any American intervention for any reason into their internal affairs. How then could it be that Ike would approve—and enthusiastically at that—a clandestine operation designed to overthrow a democratically elected government in favor of a military regime?

To friendly observers, the answer was clear and straightforward. The threat of international communism overrode all other considerations. Ike was simply not going to allow the Communists to establish a base in Central America, a base from which they could subvert the governments of their neighbors.

To critics of the Eisenhower administration, the answer was also clear and straightforward. The Arbenz regime represented a threat to the financial interests of the United Fruit Company; the United Fruit Company had powerful friends in high places (including the Secretary of State and the director of the CIA); Eisenhower therefore acted to protect United Fruit.

The first view was stated in official form in October 1954 by the American ambassador to Guatemala, John E. Peurifoy, in testimony before the Subcommittee on Latin America of the House Select Committee on Communist Aggression: "The Arbenz government, beyond any question, was controlled and dominated by Communists. Those Communists were directed from Moscow. The Guatemalan government and the Communist leaders of that country did continuously and actively intervene in the internal affairs of neighboring countries in an effort to create disorder and overthrow established governments. And the Communist conspiracy in Guatemala did represent a very real and very serious menace to the security of the United States."[5]

The second view was expressed in an interview in December

1977 by the CIA's political director of the operation designed to overthrow Arbenz, E. Howard Hunt. Hunt declared, "I've often said of that project [Guatemala] that we did the right thing for the wrong reason. And I always felt a sense of distaste over that. I wasn't a mercenary worker for United Fruit. If we had a foreign policy objective which was to assure the observance of the Monroe Doctrine in the hemisphere then fine, that is one thing; but because United Fruit or some other American enterprise had its interests confiscated or threatened, that is to me no reason at all."[6]

UNITED FRUIT'S INVOLVEMENT in Guatemala began shortly after the turn of the century when, because the fertile country offered "an ideal investment climate," it became the site of the company's largest development activity. The quaint little banana republic, in which all but the few enjoyed what Mexicans used to call *la paz de la tumba* (the peace of the tomb), was safe for foreign companies, foreign merchants, wandering foreign students, scholars of Mayan antiquities, and missionaries. The company was the dominant economic institution in Guatemalan life.[7]

In 1931, as the Depression hit Guatemala, a new *caudillo* (dictator), Jorge Ubico, took power. Four years later the law firm that represented United Fruit, Sullivan and Cromwell, negotiated a ninety-nine-year contract with Ubico that improved the company's already favorable position. First, United Fruit got more land, bringing its total possession to more than the combined holdings of half of Guatemala's landowning population, including the Catholic Church. Second, the contract exempted United Fruit from virtually all taxes and duties; even the export tax on its major commodity, bananas, was insignificant. Additional concessions included unlimited profit remittances and a monopoly of the communication and transportation networks.

The Sullivan and Cromwell lawyer who negotiated the deal for United Fruit was John Foster Dulles.[8]

In 1944 a military junta overthrew the Ubico dictatorship. In October of that year, in Guatemala's first free election, Juan José Arévalo was elected President. Arévalo was an educator and an intellectual with leftist tendencies; he called his program "spiritual socialism," a concept which caused much derision. United Fruit agents made it synonymous with fuzzy political thinking and softness toward communism. His nickname was *"Sandia,"* or the watermelon, which everyone knows is green on the outside and red inside.[9]

Arévalo introduced reforms that were modeled, in part, on the New Deal, including health care, worker's compensation bills, and a social security system. He gave women the right to vote. He started a massive Indian literacy campaign. He allowed a completely free press and tolerated all political activity. The Catholic Church took advantage of this freedom to agitate against him, sending in anti-Communist priests from other Central American countries who adopted a bitterly anti-government line. Communists also flocked to the country, both previously exiled Guatemalans and foreign-born. The Communists had a flourishing newspaper, became increasingly active in the government, and began organizing labor unions.[10]

In 1947 the Arévalo government enacted a new Labor Code. The code called for compulsory labor-management contracts; it required collective bargaining in good faith; it expressly acknowledged the right of workers to organize; it established the principle of minimum salaries. At that time the FBI was still responsible for espionage in Latin America, and J. Edgar Hoover's men began compiling dossiers on Arévalo and other leading figures in the government. These documents, which have recently been declassified under the Freedom of Information Act, reveal that most of the FBI's informants were former Ubico supporters who naturally enough stressed the Communist influence in the new government. The main "proof" was Arévalo's encouragement of labor unions.[11]

Much of the FBI's evidence of Guatemala's penetration by international communism was equally silly. For example, in 1950, Tapley Bennett, the State Department's officer in charge of Central American Affairs, charged that Guatemala's failure to sign the 1947 Rio de Janeiro Treaty of Reciprocal Assistance (which called for American nations to come to each other's aid in the event of an armed attack) was "a pertinent example of the influence on Government thinking [in Guatemala] by Communist-minded individuals."[12] In fact, Guatemala's opposition stemmed from its historic controversy with Honduras over Belize. Even the military government that the United States set up in Guatemala in 1954, when it signed the Rio Treaty, added the reservation, "The present Treaty constitutes no impediment preventing Guatemala from asserting its right with respect to the Guatemalan territory of Belize by any means by which it may deem most advisable."[13]

There was, however, some real evidence of Communist infiltration. In the regularly scheduled elections of 1950, the campaign manager of winning candidate Jacobo Arbenz Guzmán was José Manuel Fortuny, founder of the Guatemalan Communist Party and editor of its newspaper. (But Arbenz vehemently denied that he himself was a Communist, and Fortuny lost his own bid for a seat in the National Assembly.) Arbenz was inaugurated on March 19, 1951; two weeks later Fortuny signed, for the first time, a public manifesto as the Secretary-General of the Communist Party of Guatemala. In October the Confederation General de Trabajadores de Guatemala became the single national labor federation, with a self-proclaimed Communist as Secretary-General. Two months later, the CGTG affiliated with the World Federation of Trade Unions, the Communist international labor front.[14]

One man who never questioned the Communist influence on Arbenz was the CIA's agent in Mexico City, E. Howard Hunt. Of medium height, Hunt was broad-shouldered, powerful, sure of himself. Casual of manner, soft of voice, he was nevertheless deliberate in his movements, straightforward in his actions. Articulate and intelligent, he had a flair for descriptive and imaginative writing and a penchant for action. He was quick to form judgments and brutal in expressing them.

In the early fifties, Hunt was sending in reports from Mexico stressing the dangers in Guatemala. Most of his information came from Mexican students who had conferees in Guatemala. Hunt was, in his own words, "subsidizing and directing a very powerful anti-Communist student organization in Mexico, and these young people, and it's not proper to call them agents because they didn't know who was behind them, were reporting student activities in Guatemala, and this was very alarming."

When asked about Arbenz himself, Hunt replied, "Well Fortuny was the principal Communist. He and Arbenz' wife, who came from a very good Salvadorean family (in fact they became neighbors of ours years later in Montevideo). Arbenz was a very weak individual. His two daughters were beautiful and nubile. . . . She [the wife] was really the agitator, and he was sort of one of those faceless persons. . . . She on the other hand represented the might of the Communist world. He was I would say their puppet.* Of course I had ample opportunity in later years to observe them in Montevideo. We even belonged to the same country club. He liked to live well."[15]

Whether or not Arbenz was the weakling Hunt thought he was—his portrait shows a man strikingly handsome, in a Spanish Don sort of way, with a high forehead and long, aristocratic nose, who looked like he might have been a bullfighter if he had not become a politician—the Guatemalan President did have enough courage to push through the Agrarian Reform Law of 1952. In the words of one careful historian of the Guatemalan revolution, "The law itself is widely accepted by critics writing in both Spanish and English as justified under Guatemalan conditions and as basically aimed at idle land."[16]

The bill redistributed all estates taken by the government from German owners during World War II. More important, it expropriated some 240,000 acres of United Fruit's Pacific coast holdings, all of it idle land, and (a year later) another 173,000 idle acres on the Atlantic coast. This left the company with 162,000 acres, of which only 50,000 were under cultivation. Arbenz offered to pay $600,000 for the land, but in long-term non-negotiable agrarian bonds.[17] Eisenhower, while admitting that "expropriation in itself does not, of course, prove Communism," nevertheless charged that the compensation offered was "woefully inadequate" for "this discriminatory and unfair seizure."[18] The figure $600,000, however, was not pulled out of thin air—it was United Fruit's own declared valuation for tax purposes.

The company, furious, struck back with all its considerable resources. Although it was not able to force the Truman administration to send in the Marines or otherwise actively intervene, it did use its contacts and influence to picture Arbenz as a Communist to be feared. These United Fruit contacts included Spruille Braden, Assistant Secretary of State for Latin American Affairs, later public relations director for the company, and Edward Miller, Jr., another assistant secretary who had been a member of Sullivan and Cromwell. They helped paint the picture of Arbenz that United Fruit wanted the American people to see. The company launched a sizable publicity campaign and sponsored junkets to Guatemala.

---

* Later in the same interview Hunt characterized Arbenz as "not a nervy guy, a weakling . . . [who drank too much] totally dominated by his actually very competent wife. . . ."

Truman's Guatemalan ambassador, Richard Patterson, Jr., said that he could tell a Communist by applying the "duck test." He explained, "Many times it is impossible to prove legally that a certain individual is a Communist; but for cases of this sort I recommend a practical method of detection—the 'duck test.' . . . Suppose you see a bird walking around in a farm yard. This bird wears no label that says 'duck.' But the bird certainly looks like a duck. Also, he goes to the pond and you notice that he swims like a duck. Then he opens his beak and quacks like a duck. Well, by this time you have probably reached the conclusion that the bird is a duck, whether he's wearing a label or not."[19]

Patterson's successor, appointed by Ike, was John Peurifoy. According to Howard Hunt, Peurifoy got the job for three reasons. First, the Republicans were stuck with him. "You know Peurifoy started out as an elevator operator," Hunt explained, "and with the oncoming Eisenhower administration he would have been cast out, but the Democrats did what they are so skillful at doing, they encapsulated their people, giving them civil service protection. . . . There was a hell of a stink at the time. In any event, Peurifoy was an unwanted man at the ambassadorial level." Second, he had been ambassador to Greece in the late forties, at the time of the Truman Doctrine, so he had experience fighting Communists. Third, "he was expendable. Nobody in the Eisenhower administration owed him a damn thing . . . and they needed a guy who could take the heat in case things went wrong."[20]

Peurifoy applied Patterson's duck test to Arbenz and it came out positive. "I spent six hours with him one evening," Peurifoy explained, "and he talked like a Communist, he thought like a Communist, and he acted like a Communist, and if he is not one, he will do until one comes along."[21]

Official Washington, in short, was convinced that with Arbenz the Communists had succeeded in establishing their first regime in the New World. Given what had recently transpired in China, Czechoslovakia, East Europe, and in Vietnam (the Geneva Conference on Vietnam was just then getting under way); given Ike's own views on Communist aggression, as well as the Dulles brothers' and that of nearly every senator and representative in Washington; given the CIA's recent success in Iran; given that the CIA had already set up an operation, code name PBSUCCESS, to overthrow Arbenz, it was probably inevitable that the United States would intervene in Guatemala, United Fruit or no United Fruit.

John Foster Dulles himself stated explicitly at the press conference called to announce the shipment of arms on the *Alfhem:* "If the United Fruit matter were settled, if they gave a gold piece for every banana, the problem would remain just as it is today as far as the presence of Communist infiltration in Guatemala is concerned. That is the problem, not United Fruit."[22]

Richard Bissell, Jr., who was intimately involved in PBSUCCESS, said in an interview in November 1977, "I have a strong conviction that United Fruit's interests would not have been particularly persuasive on Allen Dulles. I think by this time in his career my guess is that Foster Dulles was infinitely less interested in the United Fruit Company than he was with communism. . . . As for Mr. Eisenhower and Bedell Smith, two military men, I would bet very heavily that the issue was not United Fruit, but communism."[23]

All of which may very well be true, but what is also absolutely true is that United Fruit had some powerful supporters in the Eisenhower administration. Aside from the Dulles brothers, and their connection with Sullivan and Cromwell, there was John Moors Cabot, the Assistant Secretary of State for Inter-American Affairs. He was a major stockholder in United Fruit. His brother, Thomas Dudley Cabot, the State Department's Director of Security Affairs, had previously been a director of United Fruit and president of the First National Bank of Boston, the registrar bank for United Fruit. Eisenhower's Secretary of Commerce, Sinclair Weeks, had been another director of the First National Bank. Robert Cutler, Special Assistant to the President for National Security Affairs, had been board chairman of the Old Colony Trust Company, United Fruit's transfer agent. Others in the Eisenhower administration had direct financial interests in Guatemala, including Robert Hill, ambassador to Costa Rica, and Henry Cabot Lodge, Jr., U. S. Representative to the United Nations. Hill later became a director of United Fruit. So did Bedell Smith after he left the government.[24]

If one were to apply the duck test to this list of worthies, one might be forgiven for concluding that despite Dulles' disclaimers, despite Bissell's vehement denials, the United Fruit Company did play a significant role in convincing Ike that, whatever his scruples about not intervening in the internal affairs of a sister republic, the Arbenz regime had to be toppled.

But Eisenhower himself told one of his oldest friends, General Alfred Gruenther, that policies which defended individual companies without considering the adverse effects such policies had on nationalist movements were shortsighted and "Victorian." He believed that the Western powers should make gradual concessions to satisfy the spirit of nationalism in developing countries, thereby assuring their continued support. As he wrote his friend Bill Robinson of the New York *Herald Tribune,* if the United States followed policies inimical to the economies of the developing nations, "we will most certainly arouse more antagonism." Then the possibility of these countries "turning Communist would mount rapidly." But it was entirely another matter once a country had already turned Communist, as Ike thought had happened in Guatemala.[25]

Eisenhower made his decision and ordered the CIA to go ahead with PBSUCCESS. The CIA, flushed with its triumph in Iran, was about to overthrow another government.

PBSUCCESS ALMOST GOT STARTED in the Truman administration. In 1952, Anastasio Somoza, the Nicaraguan dictator, approached Bedell Smith, then director of the CIA, with a proposal. If the CIA would send him sufficient arms, he would take care of the Arbenz problem. Smith approved and got the shipment ready, but the State Department learned of the deal and vetoed it.

A year later, in August of 1953, Thomas Corcoran, former aide to FDR and then a lobbyist for United Fruit, approached the by-then Under Secretary of State Smith. "The intervention of Tommy the Cork with Bedell Smith was decisive," Howard Hunt said, "that is according to everything I've heard and I've never heard anything in contrast."[26]

Corcoran told Smith that both Nicaragua and Honduras were prepared to act against Arbenz, provided they were assured of American help. He also said that Colonel Carlos Castillo Armas and Miguel Ydígoras Fuentes (Arbenz's major opponent in the 1950 election) had met in Tegucigalpa, Honduras, to sign a "gentleman's pact" promising to cooperate to overthrow Arbenz. Castillo Armas told Ydígoras Fuentes that they could count on American support. In September, Castillo Armas wrote Somoza saying, "I have been informed by our friends here that the government of the North, recognizing the impossibility of finding another solution to the grave problem of my country, has taken the decision to permit us to develop our plans."[27]

Allen Dulles was the driving force behind PBSUCCESS in the United States. Richard Bissell stated in an interview that Dulles "was closer to the Guatemala operation than he was to the Bay of Pigs. . . . The Guatemalan operation was authorized at a higher level at the very beginning, like the Bay of Pigs operation, and was regarded as a very major operation, with potentially political overtones and the rest."[28]

When Ike approved PBSUCCESS in its original form, he did so strictly on the basis of making a plan and creating a force to carry it out, which he regarded as an asset that might or might not be used, depending on circumstances. He was accustomed to operating in that manner—his paratroopers, for example, had made literally dozens of plans in France and Germany in 1944–45, and more than half a dozen times had gotten to the point of actually loading up, but only one operation, MARKET-GARDEN, had gone forward to become reality. Ike vehemently and frequently insisted to his closest associates that approval of plans did not mean approval of actual operations. "He was very, very precise about that," General Andrew Goodpaster, Eisenhower's liaison officer between the CIA and the White House, stated in a 1979 interview.[29] Ike gave the order to go only after the arrival of the *Alfhem* in Guatemala.

The CIA had set up its headquarters for PBSUCCESS at Opa-Locka, Florida, outside Miami. There were about one hundred agents involved. The first head of the project was J. C. King, an FBI holdover, who, according to Bissell, "epitomized the old FBI approach, and that was an approach that concentrated almost exclusively on espionage." So King was replaced by Al Haney, who was not, according to Hunt, any improvement. "'Zaney' Haney . . . was a real nut. His Spanish was execrable, but that was the least of his deficiencies. . . ."[30]

At this point Dulles sent in four of his best men. Tracey Barnes, who had worked with Dulles in Switzerland during the war, became head of the operation, under the supervision of Frank Wisner, Deputy Director of Plans for the CIA, and Richard Bissell.

And Howard Hunt became Chief of Political Action for PBSUCCESS.*

Hunt's first and most important task was to select Arbenz' replacement. There was not much choice. "It's like talking about an opposition in the Soviet Union today," Hunt explained. "You can't really pick your people from the inside, where they are under harassment or possibly in prison. You had to deal with those who had managed to escape."

Ydígoras Fuentes, who had run against Arbenz in 1950, and who was in Honduras, was the obvious choice, but "the people in State said he was too reactionary. Anybody who doesn't like communism becomes an ultra-rightest in their vocabulary." But Hunt himself recognized that Ydígoras Fuentes would not do, because "he looked like a Spanish noble. And these were the little things we had to take into consideration. You don't rally a country made up of *mestizos* with a Spanish Don."[32]

Colonel Castillo Armas, by way of contrast, "had that good Indian look about him. He looked like an Indian, which was great for the people." Further, he had *machismo*. A professional soldier (and a graduate of the U. S. Army's Command and General Staff College at Fort Leavenworth, Kansas), Castillo Armas was something of a folk hero. Wounded in an abortive 1950 uprising against the Arévalo government, Castillo Armas was believed dead and was taken off to be buried. Only a fortuitous moan changed his destination to a hospital. After his release he was sentenced to prison, from which on June 11, 1951, he dramatically escaped by hand-digging a long tunnel. Subsequently he traveled throughout Central America contacting other counterrevolutionaries, including Ydígoras Fuentes. His military background, honest reputation, heroic image, and Mayan appearance made him a good choice to lead the invasion.[33]

The CIA created a base for Castillo Armas in Honduras. Via Opa-Locka, he received money and an "army," mercenaries recruited throughout Central America. At the training camp, an American reporter saw soldiers "receiving wads of dollar bills passed out by men who were unmistakably American." There was

---

* The program was separately administered—i.e., the regular CIA station chiefs were not involved. PBSUCCESS had its own budget and chain of command. According to Hunt and Bissell, the project cost between $5 and $7 million.[31]

another "rebel" center in Nicaragua, located on a personal estate of Somoza. Americans came in from Opa-Locka via an old-abandoned French airstrip in the Panama Canal Zone, then on to Nicaragua.

In May 1954 the United States signed military agreements with Nicaragua and Honduras, and the New York *Times* could report, "Militarily the United States is doing its utmost to draw a circle around this spot of Communist infection. . . . The charter aircraft business at Toncontin [Honduras] boomed so that it was virtually impossible to hire a private plane."[34]

Diplomatic support for PBSUCCESS was deep and far-reaching. Bedell Smith kept a close watch on the operation. Bissell said Smith "was the State Department official with whom we dealt almost hour by hour. . . . One of the occasions that I remember was a meeting in Smith's office, and several of us were there. We were trying to get permission to send four more of those little obsolescent aircraft, and Henry Holland, the Assistant Secretary responsible, was opposing and Bedell Smith overruled him."[35]

Smith had a team of diplomats in Central America under his direct orders. There was Peurifoy, of course, serving as "team leader" from his post as Ambassador to Guatemala. He communicated with the CIA via the agency's station there to Opa-Locka. Other members of the team included Whiting Willauer, the Ambassador to Honduras, who had been Claire Chennault's deputy in the Chinese Flying Tigers (the outfit that had fought so long against the Chinese Communists), along with Robert Hill, Ambassador to Costa Rica, and Thomas Whelan, Ambassador to Nicaragua.

The United States Information Agency (USIA) mobilized all its resources to support PBSUCCESS. Its main goal was to convince the Organization of American States that there was a genuine Communist threat in Guatemala, a difficult task since, as the USIA noted, most Latins "either regarded the Arbenz regime as a 'homegrown' revolutionary movement dedicated to improving the lot of the exploited Guatemalans, or preferred to dwell on the United Fruit issue and speculate as to United States motives of economic imperialism." The USIA flooded Central America with pamphlets, tape recordings, planted stories in newspapers and on radio programs, all designed to establish the point that Arbenz was indeed a Communist.[36]

The Secretary of State himself took the lead in providing legal justification for action. In March 1954 he flew to Caracas, Venezuela, to attend the Tenth Inter-American Conference. In his opening remarks, Dulles dealt at length with the threat of communism and Soviet aggression in the Americas. Then he introduced a draft proposal, "Declaration of Solidarity for the Preservation of the Political Integrity of the American States Against Communist Intervention," later known as the Declaration of Caracas. Denouncing communism as "alien intrigue and treachery," the declaration concluded by proposing that Communist domination or control of any country would justify "appropriate action."

That phrase, "appropriate action," aroused traditional Latin fears of Yankee intervention, and various amendments were added. During the debate the Guatemalan Foreign Minister denounced the resolution as "merely a pretext for America for intervening in our internal affairs," and he accused the United States of returning to Teddy Roosevelt diplomacy, internationalizing McCarthyism, and seeking to use the false issue of communism to suppress Latin American desires for economic independence. Nevertheless, the declaration passed by an overwhelming majority, although Uruguay's chief delegate seemed to speak for many when he told *Time* magazine, "We voted for the resolution but without enthusiasm, without optimism, without joy, and without the feeling that we are contributing to the adoption of a constructive measure."[37]

With the declaration safely adopted, Dulles flew off to Geneva for the conference on Indochina, where he continued to fight the never-ending battle against communism. Smith went with him. Arbenz, faced with invasion, rebuffed time after time in his attempt to buy arms from the United States, mistrustful of his own military, now turned to the Soviet Union for help. He intended to arm the peasants. The Russians, delighted at an opportunity to extend their influence to Central America, arranged for the shipment of arms from the Skoda factory to Puerto Barrios.

When Allen Dulles reported the shipment of arms to Ike, the President ordered the CIA to put PBSUCCESS into full operation.

THE MILITARY PREPARATIONS for the showdown, on both sides, were little more than a show. The Czechoslovakian arms were either worn out or ineffective for jungle warfare and completely inappropriate—because they were too complex or too cumbersome—for a militia force. Most of the arms were never used but stored in an arsenal, where they were eventually blown up.

On the American side, too, the Castillo Armas "army" was ridiculous, nothing more than a "rag-taggle" (Bissell's description), never intended for serious fighting. Instead the emphasis of PBSUCCESS was psychological warfare. The key project was to broadcast anti-Arbenz, pro-Armas radio pronouncements into Guatemala from the surrounding countries. It got started on May 1, 1954; the Labor Day holiday ensured a wide audience. Calling itself the Voice of Liberation, the station adopted the slogan *"Trabajo, Pan y Patria"*—Work, Bread and Country.

The broadcasters claimed that they were operating from within Guatemala itself, even though they never set foot on its soil. They would simulate a "raid" by government officials, only to broadcast again the next day, allegedly from a new location, thus providing "proof" of Arbenz' ineptness. The Voice of Liberation sounded so authentic that soon foreign correspondents, including those from the New York *Times* and *Life* magazine, accepted it as *the* source of information.

The CIA arranged for propaganda leaflets, criticizing the Arbenz government for selling the country out to the Communists, to be dropped on Guatemala. The agency also arranged for Cardinal Spellman of New York to have his associates hold clandestine meetings with Guatemalan priests, which led to a massive volume of anti-Arbenz pastoral messages each Sunday. Guatemalan Army officers who could not be convinced that Arbenz was a Communist were bought off by direct bribery.[38]

As the pressure mounted, Arbenz turned to the Soviets with a plea for more military aid. They responded by arranging to ship six tons of antiaircraft shells to Puerto Barrios. But Ike had already declared a blockade of Guatemala, and on June 14 the United States announced that German port policemen in Hamburg, acting under the direction of U. S. Army occupation officers, had prevented the loading of the shells aboard the Hamburg-American Line freighter *Coburg*. This action caused a tremendous uproar. The U. S. Army officer on the scene admitted that the documents accompanying the shipment were in perfect order and that the cargo was legitimate export; he said therefore that the *Coburg* had been "detained but not confiscated."[39]

The British were greatly alarmed. They rejected out of hand

John Foster Dulles' proposal that ships bound for Guatemala voluntarily submit to a search by U. S. Navy vessels. "There is no general power of search on the high seas in peacetime," Anthony Eden declared. Drew Middleton reported from London that the British wished to be polite to Mr. Dulles, but did want him to understand that they "cannot allow either the Atlantic or the Caribbean to become his private preserve."[40]

At this juncture Robert Murphy, Deputy Under Secretary of State (who had been kept ignorant of PBSUCCESS), upbraided Dulles for his "bankrupt" policy of blockade. "Instead of political action inside Guatemala we are obliged to resort to heavy-handed military action on the periphery of the cause of trouble," Murphy complained. "While I do not question the usefulness of a display of naval force in the Central American area under present circumstances, forcible detention of foreign flag shipping on the high seas is another matter. . . . In our past we asserted our right to deliver arms to belligerents." Murphy said that the American disregard for the high principle of freedom of the seas was a bad mistake, brought on by "inadequate staff action in the Department."[41] Henry Holland, Assistant Secretary of State for Inter-American Affairs, was also critical of the decision to impose a blockade.

All of which made Ike furious. He later told Goodpaster that "he and the National Security Council had gone quite deeply into the Guatemalan situation" and the decision to act had been made. At this "crucial period," Goodpaster recalled Ike saying, "some of those, of his principal associates . . . began to get nervous about it, after we had committed ourselves. And his answer to them, which stayed very clear in his mind, was that the time to have those thoughts was before we started down this course, that if you at any time take the route of violence or support of violence . . . then you commit yourself to carry it through, and it's too late to have second thoughts, not having faced up to the possible consequences, when you're midway in an operation."[42]

Ike told Dulles to push on. The following day, June 19, the New York *Times'* headline proclaimed, "REVOLT LAUNCHED IN GUATEMALA: LAND-AIR-SEA INVASION REPORTED: RISINGS UNDER WAY IN KEY CITIES."

That was putting it rather grandiloquently. In fact, Castillo Armas' "army" of 150 men had crossed the Honduran border, advanced six miles into Guatemala, settled down in the Church of the Black Christ—and waited for the Arbenz regime to collapse.

The CIA based its strategy on fear. Agents trained in Opa-Locka jammed Guatemalan radio communications so that the inhabitants of Guatemala City had little or no idea as to what was happening at the "front." Wild rumors circulated, reporting major defeats of government forces and the imminent arrival of well-equipped divisions of rebel troops. In fact, the Guatemalan Army remained safely in barracks throughout the rebellion.

Arbenz aggravated the situation when, in an effort to silence the Voice of Liberation, he ordered a total blackout of the capital and other large cities. This only increased the tension, making the threat seem more real. The incessant sound of police sirens and curfew bells frayed the people's nerves to the breaking point. The scene was one of mass confusion.

In this situation Castillo Armas' "air force," with pilots hired by the CIA, became the crucial factor. It consisted of a few small Cessnas along with some P-47 Thunderbolts. These planes buzzed Guatemala City, occasionally dropping a small bomb or two, or blocks of dynamite attached to hand grenades. They were called *sufatos,* the Guatemalan word for laxatives, due to the psychological effect they had on Arbenz and the residents of the city. One lucky hit on the citadel where the *Alfhem*'s cargo of munitions was stored made an impressive explosion.

The CIA used black propaganda effectively to ground Arbenz' air force, which was weak and unreliable to begin with. The Voice of Liberation broadcast accounts of Soviet aviators who had defected to the West with their planes. When a Guatemalan pilot did the same, CIA agents tried to persuade him to appeal publicly to others in the air force to follow his example. He refused, but the agents got him drunk, then persuaded him to make an "imaginary" appeal. This was secretly recorded, cut and spliced, and then broadcast triumphantly by the Voice of Liberation. From that moment, Arbenz grounded the remainder of his air force, fearful that other pilots would defect with their planes.[43]

Nevertheless, Arbenz' antiaircraft gunners were able to put up some resistance, and, on June 22, Allen Dulles reported to Ike that Castillo Armas had lost two of the three old bombers with which he was launching the "invasion." The *Times,* meanwhile, after keeping the Guatemalan revolt in the headlines for a week, was rapidly losing interest. No Guatemalan peasants were rallying to Castillo Armas' cause, the Guatemalan Army continued to sit in its barracks, the rebel "army" to sit in its church. Without some boost, the rebellion might soon die of boredom.

Late on the afternoon of June 22, Ike held a meeting in the Oval Office of the White House. Foster Dulles was there, and Allen, along with Henry Holland. Allen Dulles said that Somoza of Nicaragua had offered to supply Castillo Armas with two P-51 fighter-bombers if the United States would agree to replace them. Holland, perfectly innocent of any knowledge of PBSUCCESS, insisted that the United States should keep hands off because the Latin American republics would, "if our action became known, interpret our shipment of planes as intervention in Guatemala's internal affairs." The Dulles brothers argued that replacing the bombers "was the only hope for Castillo Armas, who was obviously the only hope of restoring freedom to Guatemala."

Ike turned to Allen Dulles. "What do you think Castillo's chances would be without the aircraft?"

"About zero."

"Suppose we supply the aircraft. What would the chances be then?"

Dulles did not hesitate. "About twenty percent."

Recalling the event years later, Ike said he thought of the "letter and spirit of the Caracas resolution." His duty was clear. He instructed Dulles to send the planes.

As Dulles began to walk out of the Oval Office, Ike went to the door with him. Smiling to break the tension, the President said, "Allen, that figure of twenty percent was persuasive. It showed me that you had thought this matter through realistically. If you had told me that the chances would be ninety percent, I would have had a much more difficult decision."

"Mr. President," Dulles replied with a grin of his own, "when I saw Henry walking into your office with three large lawbooks under his arm, I knew he had lost his case already."[44]

The planes were delivered, the rebels resumed their bombing, and five days later Arbenz resigned. He was replaced by a short-lived military junta that gave way to Castillo Armas a week later.

On June 30, Foster Dulles went on nationwide television and radio to report to the American people. In his conclusion he declared, "Now the future of Guatemala lies at the disposal of the Guatemalan people themselves."[45]

TO IKE'S CRITICS this was a sordid event, nothing more nor less than the overthrow of a democratically elected, popular government whose only interest was in improving the wretched lives of the Guatemalan people. To Ike's defenders this was a heroic event, nothing more nor less than the prevention of the rise of an early Castro in Central America. To United Fruit it was a godsend. The company got its land back, the labor reform laws were repealed, wages cut. To Castillo Armas it was only a temporary victory. He was assassinated three years later, to be replaced by Ydígoras Fuentes, whose cooperation with the CIA in permitting the agency to use Guatemala as a staging ground for the Bay of Pigs caused such widespread criticism that he was compelled to declare martial law.

For Peurifoy the result may well have been Castillo Armas' fate. Peurifoy went to Thailand as ambassador; a year later he died in an automobile accident. Hunt said that "a lot of people think that he was killed in Southeast Asia" because of his involvement in PBSUCCESS. "I have many friends who still think that."[46] For Hunt and Bissell, the result was greatly enhanced reputations and a big step forward in their CIA careers. For the CIA, the result was a huge success. At the cost of a few dozen lives and a few million dollars, it had overthrown another government.

In 1977, thinking over the event, Howard Hunt mused, "Of course I've often wondered in retrospect if we shouldn't have let the Guatemalans [i.e., Castillo Armas' Guatemalans] shoot that group we had out at the airport there, including Che Guevara. I'm glad they didn't have to shoot Arbenz though, I think that would have been bad. What happened was that there was an agent there and he said, 'Don't do it, we don't want a bloodbath.' "[47]

As a socially conscious, rebellious medical student in his early twenties, Guevara had entered Guatemala in February 1954. He was more a concerned observer than a dedicated revolutionary, at least at first, but then he became a supporter of Arbenz. When Arbenz fled, Che went with him, seeking asylum in Mexico. There he met Raúl Castro, who later introduced him to his brother Fidel.

The lesson Che learned in Guatemala was that no Latin American reform, no matter how justified, would be accepted by the

United States, not if it impinged on American economic interests. He was also convinced that Arbenz' failure to arm the peasants had caused his downfall. In his first political article, "I Saw the Fall of Jacobo Arbenz," Guevara outlined his tactics for revolutionary organization. Latin revolutionaries, he argued, must build an army whose loyalty is to the government, not independent of it, and they must spurn moderation, because moderation in the face of American hostility is futile.

"The struggle begins now," Che wrote in his concluding sentence. When, seven years later, the CIA went to Cuba to do to Castro what it had done to Arbenz, Guevara and the Castro brothers would be ready.[48]

CHAPTER SEVENTEEN

Hungary, Vietnam, and Indonesia

NOVEMBER 1, 1956. "Help! Help! Help!—SOS!—SOS!—SOS!" the radio from Budapest repeats over and over. "Any news about help? Quickly, quickly, quickly!" Explosions and gunshots can be heard in the background. "SOS! They just brought us a rumor that the American troops will be here within one or two hours." Another handmade Molotov cocktail goes off with a roar. "We are well and fighting. SOS! Where are the American troops?"[1]

THERE NEVER WOULD BE ANY AMERICAN TROOPS. The Hungarian Freedom Fighters of 1956 would have to fight it out on their own, with Molotov cocktails against tanks, slingshots and stones against machine guns and bullets. American promises to help liberate Hungary were hollow, meaningless, empty verbiage.

In a terrible blunder, the CIA had promised what it could not deliver, raised hopes that could not be realized, helped start a rebellion that could only be crushed. But it was by no means the exclusive fault of the CIA, which was merely repeating what the Secretary of State was saying and what the President had approved.

Republican promises to help free the Russian satellites induced thousands of Americans of East European parentage to vote for Eisenhower in 1952. The promises also raised unrealistic hopes among the peoples of Hungary, Poland, East Germany and elsewhere. These hopes were sustained and strengthened by broadcasts from Radio Free Europe, a CIA-controlled radio station in Munich that broadcast to all the East European countries. RFE encouragement to the captive peoples was backed up by the Eisenhower

White House, which sent out a stream of captive-nations resolutions. Each Christmas the White House radioed a Christmas greeting to the East Europeans to "recognize the trials under which you are suffering and to share your faith that right in the end will bring you again among the free nations of the world."[2]

Such statements made good campaign material, but unfortunately some of the captive people did not know how to distinguish between American campaign bombast and actual policy. The truth was that liberation talk was intended for the domestic political situation, not for the East Europeans themselves. There was precious little thought given to the RFE broadcasts or the White House pronouncements. The idea that the East Europeans could set themselves free by copying the example of the French Resistance was absurd. The French Resistance had been successful because, first, the SHAEF armies tied up nearly all German resources and, second, nearly every Frenchman and -woman supported the Resistance, and third, the French underground had a closely knit organization. None of these conditions were, or could be, present in East Europe in 1956. Under the circumstances, it was highly irresponsible for the Republicans to talk of liberation, but they could not resist the temptation.

The irony was that this awful failure in Hungary was a direct result of one of the CIA's great intelligence coups, the acquisition in 1956 of Premier Nikita Khrushchev's famous secret speech at the Twentieth Party Congress denouncing Stalin for his criminal cruelty and misgovernment. That speech dovetailed perfectly with the Republican Party platform pledges in the 1952 campaign to "liberate" the Communist satellites in East Europe. In one well-publicized incident during that campaign, John Foster Dulles had said the United States would "use every means" to achieve liberation. Ike had called him on the phone that evening and told him to be sure to insert the word "peaceful" between "every" and "means" from then on, but nevertheless the emphasis remained on liberation.[3]

According to Ray Cline (Harvard graduate, OSS officer, author of the CIA's National Intelligence Estimates, eventually Deputy Director of the CIA), Allen Dulles managed to get a copy of Khrushchev's secret speech by putting out the word that the CIA wanted it badly and that price was no object. It was finally acquired "at a very handsome price," according to one ex-CIA agent. But James Angleton, Jr., the former Chief of Counter Intelligence, declared in 1976 that "there was no payment." Angleton said the speech was acquired from an East European Communist whose motive was ideological. A third source, Howard Hunt, said that the speech was given to the CIA by Israeli intelligence.[4]

However acquired, the CIA had a copy of the speech. In it Khrushchev had been brutal in his denunciations of Stalin and seemed to promise that the future would be different, that a relaxation of Communist Party controls inside Russia would be matched by a moderation of policy toward the satellites. It even hinted that there might be a modicum of true independence for the satellites in the near future. It was, in short, an explosive document, and the Soviets had kept it a closely guarded secret. Only those who had heard Khrushchev deliver the speech at the Twentieth Party Congress knew of its existence.

The first question for the CIA was, is our copy authentic? Ray Cline, representing the intelligence-gathering and analysis side of the CIA, was able to provide Frank Wisner, Richard Helms, and Angleton, all from the operations side, with "convincing and most welcome internal evidence that the text we had was authentic. . . . This made everyone happy."[5]

The next question was, what to do with it? Cline wanted to release it at once, on the grounds that "it was a rare opportunity to have all the critical things we had said for years about the Soviet dictatorship confirmed by the principal leader of the Soviet Politburo. The world would be treated to the spectacle of a totalitarian nation indicted by its own leadership."

To Cline's amazement, Wisner and Angleton demurred. They were in charge of an operation, code name RED SOX/RED CAP, which involved training refugees from Hungary, Poland, Rumania, and Czechoslovakia for covert and paramilitary operations inside their homelands. Angleton and Wisner wanted to hold the secret speech until the RED SOX/RED CAP forces were "up to snuff," then release it to promote national uprisings.[6] But they could not convince Cline, and he could not convince them.

Shortly thereafter, on a Saturday, June 2, 1956, Cline was alone with Allen Dulles, working on a speech. Suddenly, Dulles swung his chair around, peered at Cline, and said, "Wisner says you think we ought to release the secret Khrushchev speech."

Cline said that he did and gave his reasons. As Cline later

recalled the scene, "The old man, with a twinkle in his eye, said, 'By golly, I am going to make a policy decision!' He buzzed Wisner on the intercom, told him he had given a lot of thought to the matter, and wanted to get the speech printed."[7]

Dulles then phoned his brother at the State Department. Foster Dulles concurred. Together, the Dulles brothers went to the Oval Office. Ike was enthusiastic and ordered it done. State sent a copy of the speech to the New York *Times,* which printed it on Monday, June 4, in its entirety.[8]

Publication of the speech caused tremendous excitement throughout East Europe. Riots in Poland led to the disbanding of the old Stalinist Politburo in Warsaw. Wladyslaw Gomulka, an independent Communist, took power. Poland remained Communist and a member of the Warsaw Pact, but it won substantial independence and set an example for the other satellites.

The excitement spread to Hungary. On October 23, 1956, Hungarian students took to the streets to demand that the Stalinist rulers be replaced with Imre Nagy, a Hungarian nationalist. The CIA sent RED SOX/RED CAP groups in Budapest into action to join the Freedom Fighters and to help organize them.

Hungarian workers joined with students to demonstrate against the Russian occupation forces. Khrushchev agreed to give power to Nagy, but that was no longer enough to satisfy the Hungarians, who now demanded the removal of the Russians and an end to communism. Radio Free Europe, and the RED SOX/RED CAP groups, encouraged the rebels. So did John Foster Dulles, who promised economic assistance to those countries that broke with the Kremlin.

On October 31, Nagy announced that Hungary was withdrawing from the Warsaw Pact. Khrushchev, furious, decided to invade. He sent 200,000 troops with 2,500 tanks and armored cars to crush the revolt. Bitter street fighting in Budapest left 7,000 Russians and 30,000 Hungarians dead.[9]

Those radio pleas for help from Budapest made the tragedy even more painful, but Ike did not even consider giving overt military support to the Hungarians. When Milton asked him about it, Ike merely pointed to a map and said, "Look for yourself. Hungary is landlocked. We can't possibly fight there."[10]

Liberation was a sham. It had always been a sham. All Hungary did was to expose it to the world, and to the CIA, which was furious at Ike for backing off. William Colby, at the time a junior CIA officer, later remarked that "there can be no doubt that Wisner and other top officials of his Directorate of Plans, especially those on the covert-action side, were fully prepared with arms, communications stocks and air resupply, to come to the aid of the freedom fighters. This was exactly the end for which the Agency's paramilitary capability was designed."

But Ike said no. "Whatever doubts may have existed in the Agency about Washington's policy in matters like this vanished," Colby wrote. "It was established, once and for all, that the U.S., while firmly committed to the containment of the Soviets . . . was not going to attempt to liberate any of the areas within their sphere."[11]

However deep Ike's hatred of communism, his fear of World War III was deeper. Even had this not been so, the armed forces of the United States were not capable of driving 200,000 Red Army combat soldiers out of Hungary, except through a nuclear offensive that would have left most of Hungary and Europe devastated. In the face of Russian tanks, the RED SOX/RED CAP groups were pitifully inadequate. The Hungarians, and the other East European peoples, learned that there would be no liberation, that they would have to make the best deal they could with the Russians. The Soviet capture and execution of Nagy made the point brutally clear.

Many ex-agents today believe that Frank Wisner's tragic mental breakdown and subsequent suicide date from the failure of the RED SOX/RED CAP program.[12]

After the event, President Eisenhower and General Lucian Truscott conducted a thorough review of the entire liberation policy. Truscott questioned the CIA's RED SOX/RED CAP operators to find out what they had told the freedom fighters about American intentions and promises of support. In Truscott's view the results of his investigation showed a basic failure on the part of the CIA to distinguish between insurrectional violence, mass uprisings, revolutionary action, and true guerrilla warfare in the twentieth century. To his horror, he discovered that the CIA was still pushing RED SOX/RED CAP. The agency wanted to try again, in Czechoslovakia. But as a result of his report to the President, Ike ordered RED SOX/RED CAP terminated.[13]

Eisenhower himself, however, was the man most responsible for the debacle. Not only had he given his approval to RED SOX/RED

CAP, it was his Administration, acting under his orders, that had made liberation "a major goal of American foreign policy." Liberation was good for domestic politics, but a disaster for the Hungarians. They ended up with 30,000 of their best and most courageous young people dead, and a tighter Soviet control than ever before.

SIMULTANEOUSLY WITH THE HUNGARIAN UPRISING came the Suez crisis. Britain and France, acting in conjunction with Israel, invaded Egypt in an attempt to recover control of the Suez Canal from Colonel Gamel Abdel Nasser. Ike was angry at the British and French for acting without consulting him, and furious at Allen Dulles for having failed to warn him in advance. He eventually forced the British and French to give the Canal back to Egypt.

Still, Ike was no friend of Nasser's. At one Oval Office conference, he listened to various suggestions on ways the CIA might "topple Nasser." Finally, according to the minutes of the meeting, "The President said that an action of this kind could not be taken when there is as much active hostility as at present. For a thing like this to be done without inflaming the Arab world, a time free from heated stress holding the world's attention as at present would have to be chosen."[14]

In that instance, the President himself said no to the CIA. In other cases, it was the 5412 Committee, chaired by Gordon Gray. Gray had been Truman's Secretary of the Army and then Eisenhower's Director of the Office of Defense Mobilization. In 1955 he became Ike's Special Assistant for National Security Affairs. He was the liaison between the White House and the State and Defense Departments, as well as Chairman of the 5412 Committee.

That committee (often referred to as the "Special Group") consisted of Gray, the Secretaries of Defense and of State, and the Director of Central Intelligence. Created in March of 1955 by the National Security Council, in Paper number 5412/1, it was the most secret committee of the U. S. Government. No covert action could be undertaken without the prior approval of the committee.[15]

The major function of the special group, according to Gray, was "to protect the President." It would scrutinize proposed CIA actions, policies, and programs to make certain they did not get the President or the country into trouble. The committee dealt with issues too sensitive to be discussed before the whole National Security Council, a large group that debated issues but never set policy.[16]

Richard Bissell explained how the committee worked. "When an operation was about to be undertaken, it would be written up within the clandestine service, and approved up the line, up to and including Allen, and then Allen himself almost always attended the 5412 and then he would present it." At that point the State Department, usually represented by Robert Murphy, Foster Dulles' deputy, would give its approval. When Bissell was asked if an operation, once approved by 5412, would go before the National Security Council, he replied, "No. These were much too sensitive. Remember that under Eisenhower the NSC was a whole big roomful of people."

Gordon Gray would bring the 5412 decision privately and informally to the President. Then, a day or two later, Gray would get back to Allen Dulles and say, "Look, my boss has this or that reaction to this operation." Only then would the CIA spring into action.[17]

During the early years of 5412, the CIA had tremendous confidence in itself, and Ike had tremendous confidence in it. It seemed that the agency could manipulate events anywhere in the world to suit the United States. Iran and Guatemala were the proof.

But Iran and Guatemala, if realistically assessed, would have indicated the unwelcome truth that there were limits on what the United States and the CIA could accomplish. Instead, as Ray Cline noted, "romantic gossip about the coup in Iran spread around Washington like wildfire. Allen Dulles basked in the glory of the exploit wtihout ever confirming or denying the extravagant impression of CIA's power that it created."

The trouble was, as Kim Roosevelt was the first to admit, "the CIA did not have to do very much to topple Mossadegh, who was an eccentric and weak political figure." Iran did not prove that the CIA could overthrow governments when and where it wished; rather "it was a unique case of supplying just the right bit of marginal assistance in the right way at the right time."[18]

In Guatemala "the legend of CIA's invincibility was confirmed in the minds of many by a covert action project that inched one step further toward paramilitary intervention." Again, however, as Cline insists, Guatemala was a unique situation. It required little use of actual force and succeeded mainly because of a shrewd exploitation of favorable local political circumstances. Nevertheless, the "mystique of CIA's secret power was well established by the tales from Teheran and Guatemala City," not least in the mind of Allen Dulles himself.[19]

The major result was that the CIA became even more of an action-oriented agency, which was certainly in accord with the Donovan-OSS legacy but which was, according to such well-informed critics as Cline and Morton Halperin, detrimental to the conduct of American foreign policy.[20] Detrimental because the covert operations backfired, as in Hungary in 1956 and later in Indonesia and Cuba, and because the emphasis on action meant that the CIA, under Dulles, failed to provide the President with the information he needed, when he needed it, as in the Suez crisis of 1956 or in Cuba in 1959.

Ike was painfully aware of these shortcomings. He wanted Dulles to serve him as General Strong had served him during the war, to be in fact as well as in name his chief intelligence officer, the man who would give him an overview, to be sure the President got the information he needed to act, while screening him from petty detail. He did not want Dulles wasting his time on minor clandestine operations. Ike had Gordon Gray talk to Dulles about these points, but it did little good.[21]

Dulles continued to spend most of his time on covert operations and remained hesitant to make intelligence summaries or judgments. Rather than come down on one side or the other on whether the French could hold out in Vietnam, for example, or whether Fidel Castro was a Communist, Dulles preferred to present vast amounts of raw intelligence material to the President and let him decide, while he directed his agents in their paramilitary activities. The trouble was twofold: the raw intelligence was usually contradictory, and always terribly bulky. The President simply did not have the time to read it and evaluate it.

In January 1956, Ike created the President's Board of Consultants on Foreign Intelligence Activities (PBCFIA), composed of retired senior government officials, to provide the President with advice on intelligence matters in general, and to recommend appropriate changes in the CIA. Omar Bradley, General Doolittle, and David Bruce were among the members. The PBCFIA recommended that Dulles separate himself from the CIA altogether and serve as the President's intelligence adviser by coordinating intelligence gathered from all sources, including the FBI, the military, and the State Department. In brief, Dulles would be to President Eisenhower what Strong had been to General Eisenhower.

But Dulles would not change. Despite the PBCFIA, and despite Ike's own pressure (the Church Committee found that "President Eisenhower himself repeatedly pressed Dulles to exert more initiative" in intelligence gathering and summary), Dulles held to his own concepts and methods. He could not or would not shake the Donovan legacy.[22]

A year later, in January of 1957, Ike held a review conference with the NSC. Always seeking new ways to balance the budget, he complained that intelligence was becoming a $1 billion-a-year operation. The minutes noted that "in discussion the President recalled that because of our having been caught by surprise in World War II, we are perhaps tending to go overboard in intelligence effort." Admiral Arthur Radford, Chairman of the Joint Chiefs, said that the various intelligence-gathering agencies, including the CIA, "are doing quite well in bringing in the material." But, he added, "we can do better as regards screening and pulling it together."

Ike said he agreed with the importance of screening material, but he did not want to go too far in that direction either. The DCI should not hold back important items, he declared, citing the example of Pearl Harbor, where the senior officers on the spot were not given information available in Washington.

The notes then record that Dulles gave his semiannual report on covert operations. As the meeting ended, the DCI told the President he wanted to get General Lucian Truscott to join the CIA "and take over the coordination duty." Ike replied that he wanted it the other way around—"that Mr. Dulles must perform the coordination, and that he should get a man who could manage the operations of the CIA."[23]

But when Truscott came to the CIA, he did so as Deputy Director for Community Affairs, with responsibility for coordinating intelligence gathered by the CIA, the military services, and the State Department. This did not work out, for, as the Church Committee noted, "the separate elements of the intelligence community continued to function under the impetus of their own internal drives and mission definitions."[24] As President, Ike never found the replacement for General Strong that he was looking for.

All of which raises the perplexing question, why didn't he fire Dulles? The man had violated his direct orders, in both letter and spirit, in the Truscott affair. Part of the answer is the nature of the beast. President Eisenhower could not impose his will on the federal bureaucracy to anything like the extent that General Eisenhower imposed his will on SHAEF. Another part of the answer lies in personality and influence. Ike's very high regard for John Foster Dulles undoubtedly played a major role in his retention of Allen Dulles.

Ike gave his own answer in this statement, quoted by the Church Committee: "I'm not going to be able to change Allen. I have two alternatives, either to get rid of him and appoint someone who will assert more authority or keep him [Allen] with his limitations. I'd rather have Allen as my chief intelligence officer with his limitations than anyone else I know."[25]

So Dulles stayed on, as Ike's chief spy, for the entire eight years of the Eisenhower administration. His reputation was consistently high. He was on the front lines in the Cold War, the man who could overturn governments with a snap of his fingers, foil the KGB with the back of his hand, uncover secrets no matter where or how deeply hidden. By pretending to avoid publicity, he attracted it. He was certainly the best-known spy in the world, the subject of feature articles in the *Saturday Evening Post* and *U.S. News & World Report*,[26] as well as a favorite guest of television interviewers. And throughout his tenure as DCI, he kept the emphasis of the CIA on covert operations.

AS IN VIETNAM. By the time Ike moved into the White House, in January 1953, the United States was already involved in Vietnam to the extent that it was paying for a considerable portion of the French war effort. One of the first foreign-policy decisions of the Eisenhower administration was to step up that support to include equipment as well as money.

In April 1953, Ike approved "the immediate loan of up to six 'Flying Boxcars' (C-119s) to the French for use in Indochina to be flown by civilian pilots." The President wanted the loan kept secret, so he had Allen Dulles and the CIA handle the arrangements. In May, Ike had Bedell Smith arrange to send a military mission to Vietnam "to explore ways and means through which American assistance can best be fitted into workable plans for aggressive pursuit of hostilities."[27]

The escalation was under way. By January 1954 the United States had sent in fifty heavy bombers (B-26s) to support the French at Dien Bien Phu. At a meeting of the "President's Special Committee on Indochina." Allen Dulles "wondered if our preoccupation with helping to win the battle at Dien Bien Phu was so great that we were not going to bargain with the French as we supplied their most urgent needs."[28]

He was expressing a widespread concern in Washington that if we are going to supply the equipment and pay the cost, we must control the strategy. Ike was impatient with the French, whose strategy was almost as badly executed as it was conceived. He once said, "Who could be so dumb as to put a garrison down in a valley and then challenge the other guy, who has artillery on the surrounding hills, to come out and fight?"[29]

To exert more American influence, the Pentagon had convinced the French commander, General Navarre, to accept a group of liaison officers. This was obviously a delicate matter—the French fiercely resented any hint that they needed military advice from the Americans, but they needed the American equipment so badly they could not say no.

Unknown to the French, Dulles had bigger plans. The committee notes state, "Mr. Allen Dulles inquired if an unconventional warfare officer, specifically Colonel Lansdale, could not be added to the group of five liaison officers. . . . Admiral Radford thought this might be done."[30]

Thus did the redoubtable Colonel Edward Lansdale make his entry into Vietnam, where he made a mark that was later enshrined in two semifictional works, *The Ugly American* and *The Quiet American*. Lansdale was a former San Francisco advertising man who believed in "selling" the American way of life when and where he could, and in covert actions when they were necessary. He was a veteran of guerrilla action against the Communist Hukbalahaps in the Philippines.

Dulles' instructions to Lansdale were to "enter into Vietnam quietly and assist the Vietnamese, rather than the French, in unconventional warfare." He was not to irritate the French, if possible, but he was to keep them at arm's length. In Vietnam, Lansdale was to set up the Saigon Military Mission (SMM) "to undertake paramilitary operations against the enemy and to wage political-psychological warfare."[31]

Lansdale entered Saigon on June 1, 1954. He had a small box of files, a duffle bag of clothes, and a borrowed typewriter. The prospects could not have been gloomier. Dien Bien Phu had just fallen to the Vietminh. At the Geneva Conference, the northern half of Vietnam had been given over to Ho Chi Minh and the Communists. Speaking for the United States, Under Secretary of State Bedell Smith promised that although his government had not signed the Geneva Accords, it would not use force to upset them. That put some limits on how much aid the Eisenhower administration could openly give to the South Vietnamese leader, Ngo Dinh Diem.

On Lansdale's first night in Saigon, Vietminh saboteurs blew up large ammunition dumps at the airport, rocking Saigon throughout the night. Lansdale had no desk space, no office, no vehicle, no safe for his files. He did have the use of the regular Saigon CIA station chief's communications system, but he had no assistants, no team. The SMM consisted of Lansdale alone.

But he made rapid progress. His reputation from the Philippines had preceded him, and high-ranking South Vietnamese officers made contact. Lansdale organized the Vietnamese Armed Psywar Company. This was in accord with his instructions "to develop homogeneous indigenous units with a native officer corps," for which purpose he had $124 million to spend.[32]

Lansdale trained his Psywar Company, then sent the soldiers, dressed in civilian clothes, to Hanoi. The city was in a state of near chaos as the French pulled out and the Vietminh took over. The Psywar Company's mission was to spread the story of a Chinese Communist regiment in Tonkin acting in a beastly fashion, emphasizing the supposed mass rapes of Vietnamese girls by Chinese troops. Since Chinese Nationalist troops had behaved in just such a fashion in 1945, and since the Vietnamese had hated and feared the Chinese for centuries, Lansdale was confident that the planted story would confirm Vietnamese fears of Chinese Communist occupation under Vietminh rule.

Alas, no member of Lansdale's Psywar Company ever returned from the mission. To a man, they deserted to the Vietminh.[33]

Lansdale, meanwhile, had jumped into the middle of the confused, nearly chaotic political situation in Saigon. In mid-1954, the French turned control of the government over to Emperor Bao Dai. His Prime Minister was Ngo Dinh Diem, a pudgy five-foot five-inch aristocrat, fifty-three years old, with a fierce ambition. The Army Chief of Staff was General Hinh, an impatient, disingenuous officer who wanted total control for himself. The struggle for power was between Diem and Hinh, as Bao Dai was enjoying himself in Paris and along the French Riviera.

Lansdale became involved because he was close to both Diem and Hinh. He had met them in the Philippines earlier, liked them both, and got on famously with their wives. He was also a friend of Hinh's mistress, who was a pupil in a small English-language class conducted by the CIA mission for the mistresses of various VIPs in Saigon.

Because of his connections, Lansdale learned of a plot by Hinh and other high-ranking officers to overthrow Diem. He informed Ambassador Donald Heath, who asked him to see what he could do to prevent an armed attack on the Presidential Palace, where Diem had his office. Lansdale went to Hinh and bluntly told him that United States support for South Vietnam would end if the attack took place. Then he went to the Palace to give the presidential guards tactical advice on how to stop a tank attack. The SMM official history records, "The advice, on tank traps and destruction with improvised weapons, must have sounded grim. The following morning, when the attack was to take place, we visited the Palace: not a guard was left on the grounds; Diem was alone upstairs, calmly getting his work done."[34]

The SMM, by mid-August 1954, had ten agents. Eight had been rushed in at the last minute, just before the cease-fire went into effect. The newcomers, rounded up in Korea, Japan, and Okinawa, were old OSS hands, with some experience in paramilitary operations but none at all in psywar. Their zeal made up for their inexperience. They formed clandestine units of anti-Communist Vietnamese, then went north to disrupt the Communist takeover in Hanoi. One team tried to destroy the largest printing plant there, but Vietminh guards frustrated the attempt. They then tried a so-called black psywar strike, printing leaflets, attributed to the Vietminh, that instructed residents on how to behave for the immediate future. They proclaimed a three-day holiday, outlined a phony monetary reform, and so on. Vietminh currency the next day fell 50 percent in value, and most of Hanoi was on the streets celebrating the "holiday."[35]

Another team spent the night before the Vietminh takeover at the city bus depot contaminating the oil supply so that the bus engines would gradually be wrecked. The team had to work quickly in an enclosed storage room. Fumes from the contaminant came close to knocking them out. "Dizzy and weak-kneed," the SMM history records, "they masked their faces with handkerchiefs and completed the job."[36]

Back in Saigon, Lansdale's efforts were somewhat more positive. He served as an adviser to Diem, supporting the Prime Minister in his decision to crush the Binh Zuyen, a quasi-criminal sect which controlled gambling, the opium trade, and prostitution in Saigon. Lansdale also persuaded Diem to hold a referendum designed to give his regime a popular legitimacy. The ballot allowed the South Vietnamese to choose between Diem and Emperor Bao Dai, who had thoroughly discredited himself as a playboy tool of the French. Diem got 98 percent of the vote on October 23, 1955, and became President of South Vietnam, which became a republic.[37]

Lansdale had ambitious plans for the new republic. He proposed to Allen Dulles that the CIA provide the money to support a program he called "Militant Liberty." He described it as a concept he had used successfully in the Philippines. As Lansdale explained it to Dulles, it sounded like a high school civics exercise: "The heart of any plan to implement 'Militant Liberty' is the progressive training of groups of indigenous personnel in an understanding of the meaning of a free society to the individual and the individual's responsibilities in creating and maintaining such a society." He wanted to concentrate the program in the South Vietnamese Army because "the induction-training-discharge cycle provides ready access to indigenous personnel who can play an important role in a revitalization of Vietnam both during their period of military service and subsequently after they have returned to civilian life."[38]

Through the second half of the fifties, Lansdale continued to involve himself in the Byzantine politics of Saigon, a city full of plots, filled with intrigue, and jammed with spies. All his activity could not hide the fact that the United States had been unable to prevent the Communist takeover in North Vietnam and that the CIA was incapable of toppling Ho Chi Minh's government in

Hanoi. In the Far East there were to be no cheap victories, as there had been in Iran and Guatemala.

THE CIA'S FAILURE IN VIETNAM did not deter the agency from trying again to topple an Asian government, this time in 1958 in Indonesia. President Sukarno, a fifty-six-year-old ladies' man who had had four wives and who was linked by gossip to such movie stars as Gina Lollobrigida and Joan Crawford, was somewhat like Mossadegh, a spellbinder of a speaker but erratic and mercurial as a leader. Like many Third World presidents, Sukarno had drifted toward the left. He had expropriated most of the private holdings of the Dutch (who had held Indonesia as a colony for 350 years), he had turned to the Russians for help in obtaining weapons for his armed forces, and he had brought the Communist Party of Indonesia into his coalition government.

Since winning its independence in 1949, Indonesia had been a parliamentary democracy. But in February 1957, following a tour of Russia and its satellites, Sukarno declared that democracy did not suit his diverse nation. Indonesia was indeed diverse—its nearly 100 million people lived on 3,000 islands. Sukarno dissolved Parliament and took semidictatorial powers for himself under the euphemism "Guided Democracy." His chief support came from the one-million-member Communist Party and the Indonesian Army.

Moderates in Indonesia, headed by political leaders outside of Java, wanted to overthrow Sukarno. The CIA encouraged them to act. On February 15, 1958, the Revolutionary Council in Sumatra proclaimed a new government with a multiparty, coalition cabinet. The rebels had hoped the armed forces would join them, but instead the head of the army, General Abdul Haris Nasution, dishonorably discharged six generals who had sided with them while the air force bombed, strafed, and destroyed two radio stations that had joined the rebels.

Civil war began. The United States took the high road. "We are pursuing what I trust is a correct course from the point of international law," John Foster Dulles told Congress in early March. "We are not intervening in the internal affairs of this country."[39]

The next week the rebels asked the United States for arms, and appealed to the Southeast Asia Treaty Organization for recognition. Again, Dulles declared American neutrality: "The U.S. views this trouble in Sumatra as an internal matter. We try to be absolutely correct in our international proceedings and attitude toward it."

The rebels' best weapon was their air force, which carried out a series of raids against the government. On April 30, Sukarno accused the United States of supplying the bombers and the pilots. He warned Washington "not to play with fire in Indonesia. . . . Let not a lack of understanding by America lead to a third war."

"We could easily have asked for volunteers from outside," Sukarno continued. "We could wink and they would come. We could have thousands of volunteers, but we will meet the rebels with our own strength."[40]

That same day, Ike held a press conference. He was asked about Sukarno's charges. "Our policy," the President replied, "is one of careful neutrality and proper deportment all the way through so as not to be taking sides where it is none of our business.

"Now on the other hand," Ike continued, "every rebellion that I have ever heard of has its soldiers of fortune. You can start even back to reading your Richard Harding Davis. People were going out looking for a good fight and getting into it, sometimes in the hope of pay, and sometimes just for the heck of the thing. That is probably going to happen every time you have a rebellion."

Boys will be boys, in short, and no one could expect the President to change human nature. The trouble with Ike's offhanded explanation was that it was a lie. The Americans flying bombing missions for the rebels were not soldiers of fortune acting on their own, but CIA agents acting at the direction of the Eisenhower administration.[41]

When Sukarno made his deal with the Indonesian Communist Party and began receiving arms from the Soviet Union, the CIA decided to do to him what it had done to Mossadegh and Arbenz. Ike checked over the plan, which was almost identical with PBSUCCESS, and approved the operation.

The pilots and planes came from the Civil Air Transport (CAT), originally formed in China by the CIA to support Chiang Kai-shek, later used by Lansdale in the Philippines and Indochina. Most of the CAT equipment and manpower came out of Claire Chennault's Flying Tigers. Lansdale described CAT in a top-secret memorandum on "unconventional-warfare resources in Southeast Asia," which he gave to General Maxwell Taylor in 1961 (and which was later published in the Pentagon Papers): "CAT, a CIA proprietary, provides air logistical support under commercial cover to most CIA and other U. S. Government agencies' requirements. . . . CAT has demonstrated its capabilities on numerous occasions to meet all types of contingency or long-term covert air requirements. . . . During the past ten years, it has had some notable achievements, including support of the Chinese Nationalist withdrawal from the mainland, air drop support for the Indonesian operation, air lifts of refugees from North Vietnam, more than 200 overflights of Mainland China and Tibet, and extensive air support in Laos during the current crisis."[42]

CAT supplied the Indonesian rebels with a half dozen or so B-26 two-engine bombers. They flew harassing raids intended to frighten Sukarno's military supporters into deserting him. All was going well until May 18, 1958, when a pilot named Allen Lawrence Pope was shot down during a bombing and strafing run on the Ambon Island airstrip in the Moluccas. The American ambassador to Indonesia, Howard P. Jones, followed Ike's lead and dismissed Pope as "a private American citizen involved as a paid soldier of fortune," but that fiction could not survive long. Allen Dulles lost his enthusiasm for the venture; Ike no longer wanted any part of it. The CIA withdrew CAT and the Indonesian rebellion collapsed.

It was an ignominious failure. As Ray Cline has noted, it made Sukarno increasingly dictatorial and led to much misery for Indonesia. Sukarno's atrocious political and economic mismanagement led to a crisis in the mid-1960s that saw the Communists murder many of the politically conservative leaders in an attempt to seize total control. That attempt resulted in the widespread massacre of thousands of Communists themselves. The University of Indonesia, after an investigation, placed the number killed at 800,000, making this one of the worst bloodbaths of all time.[43]

Cline has an excellent summary of the debacle in Indonesia: "The weak point in covert paramilitary action is that a single misfortune that reveals CIA's connection makes it necessary for the United States either to abandon the cause completely or convert to a policy of overt military intervention. Because such paramilitary operations are generally kept secret for political reasons, when CIA's cover is blown the usual U.S. response is to withdraw, leaving behind the friendly elements who had entrusted their lives to the U.S. enterprise."[44]

CHAPTER EIGHTEEN

The National
Intelligence Estimates

THE MOST IMPORTANT WORK THE CIA DOES takes place in the Washington office of the Deputy Director for Intelligence (DDI). There the CIA carries on the old research and analysis functions of the OSS, tapping America's prestigious universities for specialized personnel with intimate acquaintance with the languages, history, economics, and social conditions of foreign countries. R & A has none of the glamour of an Operation PBSUCCESS, none of the excitement of an Operation RED SOX/RED CAP, none of the rewards of an Operation AJAX, but it is the heart of the matter, what the CIA is all about. For it is the DDI who provides the information that the President relies upon when he makes a policy judgment.

Allen Dulles, as noted, was relatively uninterested in acquiring and analyzing intelligence—he left it up to the DDI.

One of the best men ever to work on the intelligence side of the CIA was Ray S. Cline, an OSS veteran of the R & A branch and ultimately the Deputy Director of the CIA. Cline is a scholar's scholar. After the war he wrote *Washington Command Post: The Operations Division,* one of the most widely praised volumes in the highly regarded series *The U. S. Army in World War II,* and after his retirement he wrote *Secrets, Spies and Scholars: Blueprint of the Essential CIA,* which was praised in the professional journals as the best book yet on the CIA.

In the 1950s, Cline worked deep in the labyrinth of the CIA's intelligence branch. There he had the greatest, and rarest, satisfaction that can come to a bureaucrat—his work actually had an impact on policy. It did so because Cline's ultimate boss, President Eisenhower, was able to force the bureaucracy to serve him as he wanted it to, rather than as it wanted to do.

In an NSC meeting early in 1954, Ike complained that there were two things wrong with the intelligence he was getting. First, it failed to make a clear distinction between Russian capability and actual intentions. This is a classic problem because the professional military, who are charged with the defense of the nation, always exaggerate the extent of the threat the nation faces. The military cites the enemy's capabilities—what the Russians might do in arms production—while ignoring the enemy's intentions—what the Russians are in fact doing.

The second complaint Ike had was that not enough was being done to put the Russian threat into a proper perspective. He was bombarded with news that the Russians were building up here, there, everywhere, without weighing the Russian capabilities and intentions against an estimate of America's capabilities. An overall view was absent because the CIA was responsible for gauging the Russian threat, while the Joint Chiefs of Staff (JCS) were responsible for estimates of the American ability to respond. The two had to be brought together.

What Ike wanted was a "net" evaluation, or what the military called a "commander's estimate," the kind of effort General Kenneth Strong produced throughout World War II. In 1954 the President asked Allen Dulles and Admiral Arthur Radford, Chairman of the JCS, to prepare such a commander's estimate on the probable outcome of a war between the U.S.S.R. and the United States.[1]

Dulles delegated Cline to do the CIA side of the study, while Radford chose Rear Admiral Thomas Robbins, whom Cline characterized as "a brilliant but somewhat lackadaisical" officer. Robbins, in the best military tradition, delegated two staff assistants to represent him. These young officers, Cline wrote, "had not a clue as to what we were supposed to do," so Cline took over.

He immediately discovered the tremendous power of the

military in the Washington bureaucracy. Cline could invoke Admiral Radford's name "and have things happen instantaneously." There was a vast vacuum-tube first-generation computer filling the basement of the Pentagon. He also learned that the only experienced war-gaming staff the services had was outside Washington. Cline mentioned this to Radford on Friday; on Monday, he had full-time use of the computer, and the war-gaming staff was on station in the Pentagon. Cline then prepared to play a computerized war game and, for the first time, make it part of a net estimate.[2]

In that second year of the Eisenhower administration, at the height of the Cold War, the Pentagon was full of tension and fear. It was commonly said that communism was bent on "world domination" and that the "time of greatest danger" of attack was two years hence. The Russians would march across the Elbe River into West Germany and on to France, while the Chinese would march across the Yalu River into Korea and launch an amphibious assault against Formosa. The unexamined assumption was that the Communists had both the capability and intention of carrying out such ambitious offensives.

But when Cline played his war games on that giant computer, he made some fascinating discoveries, the chief being that "it was a pretty desperate move for the U.S.S.R. to attack us with their substantially inferior long-range air force." U.S. radar tactical warning systems in Europe and Asia were good enough to preclude the possibility of the Communists achieving surprise. An incidental discovery was that the characteristics of defense radar made it more profitable to attack at low levels, where "ground clutter" confused the radar, than at the high altitudes for which American bombers were designed. This discovery led to a revision of U. S. Air Force bombing tactics, a fortuitous revision as the development over the next few years of Soviet ground-to-air missiles made it imperative for the United States to go to low-level attack.[3]

With the results of the war game before him, Cline then wrote the commander's estimate for 1954. He prepared a briefing on the subject, complete with the usual visual aids and charts. The military insisted on pride of place and Admiral Robbins, not Cline, made the oral presentation at the White House. Ike insisted that all the top officials in the Defense Department attend this special briefing.

"The encomiums were great," Cline wrote with justifiable pride. What Ike had suspected all along was confirmed—using such terms as the "ultimate" intention of "world domination" was a poor indicator of specific near-term military action.* The Communists were neither ready nor able to resort to direct military action. The figure of speech that "the time of greatest danger of attack is two years hence" disappeared from JCS papers. Military intelligence officers and civilian analysts became more sophisticated, their language more moderate, their descriptions of the Communist threat more accurate and less scary.

The commander's estimate, Cline summarized, along with others in the following years, "succeeded in reducing the Soviet military threat to the United States to reasonable proportions in the minds of war-planning staffs." This in turn allowed Ike to hold steady to his "New Look" in defense policy, at an immense financial savings to the nation while simultaneously reducing fears and slowing the arms race. The CIA, Cline boasts, "probably never accomplished more of value to the nation than this quiet, little-remarked analytical feat."[4]

Cline's accomplishment was a victory for analysis. It was matched by the CIA's greatest triumph of intelligence gathering, the U-2 program, discussed in the following chapter. A third function of the DDI's side of the CIA was prediction, to anticipate events around the world and report them to the President before they happened. Even when the President could not do anything one way or another about the event, which was usually the case, he always wanted to know in advance. American Presidents hate to be caught by

---

* Eisenhower's defense policy, which he called the "New Look," cut back drastically on Truman's expenditures for defense, primarily because Ike refused to be bamboozled into seeing the Russians as some sort of supermen. Ike thought the greatest threat was an uncontrolled arms race that would lead to uncontrollable inflation and ultimate bankruptcy.

surprise. It is the CIA's job to tell the President what is going to happen, and it is an almost impossible assignment.

IN 1956, ON THE EVE of the Eisenhower vs. Stevenson presidential election, France and Britain joined with Israel to attack Egypt. White House Press Secretary James Hagerty told reporters that the President got his first information on the invasion "through press reports." The attack "came as a complete surprise to us." Simultaneously, the Russians sent their tanks into the streets of Budapest; Administration spokesmen told the press that the Russian attack on Hungary was also a complete surprise.

Such reports made Allen Dulles furious. A month later he leaked stories to the Washington press corps that the CIA had predicted Hungary in detail. He also complained to reporter Andrew Tully, "My brother said the State Department was taken by surprise. That was only technically correct. What he meant was that the British, French and Israeli governments had not informed our ambassadors. But we had the Suez operation perfectly taped. We reported that there would be a three-nation attack on Suez. And on the day before the invasion CIA reported it was *imminent*."[5]

Dulles' leaks made Ike, in his turn, furious. The President had a legendary temper, which he struggled—usually successfully—all his life to control. When angry, he could not keep the bright red color out of his face, and the back of his neck would become red as a beet, but he did manage to sit perfectly still. Under his desk, however, he would tear his handkerchief into tiny bits, down to the individual strands of cotton. When he finished, there would be a loose ball of cotton strands at his feet, and no handkerchief.

What upset Ike was, first, the fact of the leak itself—all Presidents dislike leaks. Second, Dulles' claims to have predicted Suez and Hungary simply were not true. But the ultimate insult to Ike was Dulles' hint that the President was too lazy to do his homework. Throughout his presidency, Ike smarted under the criticism that he took too many vacations, that he did not work hard enough, that he neglected his duties for a golf game or a fishing expedition, and most of all that he refused to read any report that was more than one page long.

In an April 1958 article on Hungary, *Harper's Magazine* repeated Dulles' charges that Ike would have known what was going to happen if he had only read the CIA reports. Eisenhower, according to *Harper's*, "showed great annoyance at this, announcing that the reports were too ponderous to read and asking that henceforth the CIA append maps, with red arrows pointing to strategic points, and headline summaries to its daily intelligence digest."[6]

Nightclub comedians, late-night TV comics, and the Democratic Party all had great fun with Ike's red arrows and headline summaries. The truth was, however, that the CIA reports *were* too ponderous for anyone to read. It can be argued that the President is the busiest man in the world, operating on the tightest schedule, carrying the most responsibilities, and having the least amount of time for serious reading, or indeed reading of any kind. He wants his intelligence summaries to be brief, straightforward, accurate.

But the world is much too complex and the CIA's task much too difficult to meet those requirements. The honest intelligence officer knows that he can never be completely sure. He is trying to predict the actions of men and organizations that are resourceful, have every reason to hide their intentions, and have vast experience in doing so. And, obviously, many of the world's great events are unpredictable, taking everyone by surprise. Inevitably, the CIA wants to cover itself, to qualify its predictions, to introduce nuances into its reports, to say that "such and so might happen if this takes place, but then on the other hand . . ." etc.

A long, ponderous report, filled with qualifications, is an honest report. It is also of little use to the President. In predicting Communist reactions to possible American initiatives, however, the CIA was often quite exact, and most helpful, especially in giving Ike a reason not to do something he did not want to do anyway.

Vietnam makes a good case study of this development. From 1953 to 1961 the CIA filed voluminous reports on the prospects in Vietnam. Called "National Intelligence Estimates," they were issued at regular intervals. The estimates were submitted to the President and the NSC by Allen Dulles, who was careful to note on the cover page that "the following intelligence organizations participated in the preparation of this estimate: The CIA and the intelligence organizations of the Departments of State, the Army, the Navy, the Air Force, and the Joint Staff." Some of the estimates were over thirty pages long, none less than ten.

The first estimate Ike saw on Vietnam was published on June 4,

1953. It was interesting but, for the President, of little use. The report said that the military situation might or might not get better. Who could tell if new French generals would help or not? The Chinese might or might not invade. There was one good, solid, straightforward prediction: "If present trends in the Indochinese situation continue through mid-1954, the French political and military position may subsequently deteriorate very rapidly."[7] But then, that was hardly a secret.

On June 15, 1954, the agency dealt with one of the most explosive problems the NSC ever handed it—to estimate Communist reactions to the use of nuclear weapons by the United States in Vietnam. The request came about because various members of the Eisenhower administration, led by Chief of Staff of the Air Force General Nathan Twining, and including all the JCS (except for Army Chief of Staff Matthew Ridgway), as well as the Secretary of Defense, and the Vice President, had urged the President to use atomic bombs. Twining said that the use of two or three "nukes" on the Vietminh around Dien Bien Phu would "clean those Commies out of there and the band could play the Marseillaise and the French would come marching out in fine shape."[8]

Ike said that he would not use atomic weapons for the second time in less than a decade against Asians, partly because it would put the United States in the worst possible light in Asia and throughout the Third World, mainly because he hated what he called "those terrible things."[9]

Nothing could have budged Ike from that position, but he was thankful for CIA support. The CIA warned flatly that "the Chinese would take whatever military action they thought required to prevent destruction of the Viet Minh, including when and if necessary open use of Chinese Communist forces in Indochina." The agency pointed out that "U.S. use of nuclear weapons in Indochina would hasten the ultimate Chinese decision whether or not to intervene."[10]

Dien Bien Phu fell to the Vietminh. In Geneva, in July of 1954, France, Ho Chi Minh, and the great powers (except for the United States) signed the Geneva Accords. The parties agreed to a truce and to a temporary partition of Vietnam at the 17th parallel. Neither the French in the south (who soon handed over the government to Diem) nor Ho Chi Minh's Communists in the north could join a military alliance or allow foreign military forces or equipment onto their territory. There would be elections within two years to unify the country.

The United States did not sign the accords, nor did any representative of a South Vietnamese government. Bedell Smith was in Geneva as an observer, not a participant in the conference. He issued a letter stating that his government "took note of" the accords and promising that the United States would support free elections and would not use force to upset the agreements.

This was a major embarrassment to the Republicans, who had come to power pledged to a policy of "liberation," and who now had to watch as yet another Asian country, North Vietnam, fell to the Communists. Desperate to save something from the debacle, in late July, General Twining, Admiral Radford, Secretary Dulles, and others worked out an invasion scheme that would have landed American troops at Haiphong, followed by a march to Hanoi.

Again General Ridgway opposed. On the basis of Army intelligence estimates, he argued that the adventure would require at least six divisions, even if the Chinese did not intervene. Eisenhower's defense policy was to reduce the Army, not expand it. The President refused to act.[11]

Secretary Dulles then moved on the diplomatic front. Ike was a great believer in alliances, and in September of 1954 he encouraged Dulles to sign up allies in Asia. Dulles persuaded Britain, Australia, New Zealand, France, Thailand, Pakistan, and the Philippines to join the Southeast Asia Treaty Organization (SEATO). It was a defensive alliance in which the parties agreed to act together to meet an aggressor. Protection for Cambodia, Laos, and South Vietnam, the independent nations that had come into being when the French withdrew from Indochina, was covered in a separate protocol.

Bringing South Vietnam into SEATO was a *de facto* violation of the Geneva Accords. The United States had already decided, in any event, that those accords would have to be ignored, especially the section that called for free nationwide elections. The CIA had reported in August that "if the scheduled national elections are held in July, 1956, and if the Viet Minh does not prejudice its political prospects, the Viet Minh will almost certainly win."[12]

Ike was more precise in his memoirs. He stated, "I have never talked or corresponded with a person knowledgeable in Indochinese affairs who did not agree that had elections been held

. . . possibly 80 per cent of the population would have voted for the Communist Ho Chi Minh as their leader rather than Chief of State Bao Dai."[13]

Ike's statement, so frequently quoted by doves in the second half of the 1960s, had a major qualifier to it. Bao Dai was then living in France. He had no interest in his native land, and all the CIA reports indicated that his popularity was nonexistent among his subjects. In addition, Ike often pointed out, when confronted with this statement, that North Vietnam had nearly twice the population of South Vietnam, and he assumed that Ho Chi Minh would get 100 percent of the vote in his half of the country.[14]

Nevertheless, the stark fact remained that Ho Chi Minh had more popularity than any non-Communist leader. Under the circumstances, no one in the U. S. Government could have been expected to support free elections. So the decision was made to find an alternative to Ho, meanwhile avoiding elections. Ngo Dinh Diem became the favored alternative, and with the help of Colonel Lansdale and the CIA, he managed to win the power struggle, eliminating his opponents in the Vietnamese military and Bao Dai.

The CIA, on September 15, 1954, judged Diem a good prospect for American support, indeed "the only figure on the political scene behind whom genuine nationalist support can be mobilized." Although he was "confronted with the usual problems of inefficiency, disunity, and corruption in Vietnamese politics," he was honest and energetic. Diem, the CIA felt, had "considerable unorganized popular support, particularly among Catholic elements of South Vietnam." It predicted he would survive the present crisis but said that his ability to create a government that could last depended on "early and convincing" outside support.[15]

Eisenhower then made his decision to back Diem. On October 1, 1954, he wrote a letter of support to him, a letter often cited later by Presidents Kennedy, Johnson, and Nixon as proof that it was Ike who got us into Vietnam.

"We have been exploring ways and means . . . to make a greater contribution to the welfare and stability of the Government of Viet-Nam," Ike began. He was therefore instructing the American ambassador in Saigon to confer with Diem to see "how an intelligent program of American aid given directly to your Government can serve to assist Viet-Nam in its present hour of trial, provided that your Government is prepared to give assurances as to the standards of performance it would be able to maintain in the event such aid were supplied."

The purpose of the offer, the President said, was to assist Diem "in developing and maintaining a strong, viable state, capable of resisting attempted subversion or aggression through military means." There was a condition to the aid. "The Government of the United States expects that this aid will be met by performance on the part of the Government of Viet-Nam in undertaking needed reforms." Such a government would be, the President hoped, "so responsive to the nationalist aspirations of its people, so enlightened in purpose and effective in performance, that it will be respected both at home and abroad and discourage any who might wish to impose a foreign ideology on your free people."[16]

The reforms never took place. The CIA reported that Diem's regime was increasingly repressive. American aid nevertheless continued to support Diem's government. One of the reasons was the lack of an alternative; another was the optimistic picture the CIA painted of South Vietnam. In Saigon, there was a high standard of living, political stability, economic progress—according to the CIA.

In May 1957, Diem came to the United States for a triumphant welcome. He spent three days in Washington, where he conferred with Ike, Dulles, and other high officials. He addressed a joint session of Congress and met with such supporters as Cardinal Spellman, Senator John Kennedy, Justice William O. Douglas, and Mayor Robert Wagner of New York. Wagner hailed Diem as a man "to whom freedom is the very breath of life itself." Ike loaned Diem his personal plane to fly to the West Coast. In the press, on television, at banquets, everywhere Diem was hailed as the miracle worker who provided living proof of what could be accomplished in the Third World without Communist regimentation.[17]

CIA reports continued to echo that view. In its 1959 National Intelligence Estimate, the agency contrasted the two Vietnams. The north was "organized along strict Communist lines. The standard of living is low; life is grim and regimented; and the national effort is concentrated on building for the future." In the south, meanwhile, "the standard of living is much higher and there is far more freedom and gaiety." Security in the south was much improved; the number of Communist guerrillas was down from

10,000 to 2,000, "scattered along the Cambodian border and in the remote plateau region of the north."

The agency did admit that there were problems, although one had to go to the fine print of the bulky document to find them. One was that Diem concentrated on building his armed forces, not long-term economic development. Consequently, American aid dollars were used to buy consumer goods from Japan or the United States, which inhibited the development of local industry.

Another problem was that "a façade of representative government is maintained, but the government is in fact essentially authoritarian. . . . No organized opposition, loyal or otherwise, is tolerated, and critics of the regime are often repressed." The strongly centralized one-man rule provided stability at the expense of alienating the nation's educated elite and inhibiting the growth of political institutions that had popular support.

Overall, however, the CIA's conclusion was that "Diem will almost certainly be President for many years," and that with Diem there would be stability and continued prosperity in South Vietnam.[18]

In briefing President-elect Kennedy on January 19, 1961, on Southeast Asia, Ike did not even mention Vietnam. It was not a "problem area."

Nearly two decades later, by which time the United States had sent 4.25 million of her young men to Vietnam, and then brought them home, and lost the war, General Goodpaster placed part of the blame for Ike's shortsightedness on Vietnam at the feet of the intelligence agencies. Goodpaster characterized our information on Vietnam as "inadequate, poor, terrible."[19]

That judgment seems unfair if it is directed solely toward the CIA. America's policy toward Vietnam was made in the White House and the State Department, not in CIA headquarters. The chief feature of the CIA reporting was that it could usually be read either way. Ike could have supported Diem on the basis of the intelligence he received, or he could have adopted an anti-Diem policy on the basis of those same reports. The choice was his. All the CIA did was to supply him with information. That was all it was supposed to do.

On the question, who got us into Vietnam? the Eisenhowers could be as quick to point the finger of blame as Ike's successors. In an interview in 1979, Milton Eisenhower said, "One of the hardest things I had to do with Lyndon Johnson was that he kept saying, as the criticism of the Vietnam war mounted, 'I'm only carrying out the policy of Truman, Eisenhower and Kennedy.'

"And on one occasion I said, 'President Johnson, you're making a terrible mistake. President Eisenhower was bitterly opposed to any participation in the Vietnam war. He was importuned by the Air Force and everybody else, and he declined time and again.'

"And Johnson looked at me, and took me by surprise. He said, 'Well, then why is it that now that we're in there he's never spoken a word of opposition?'

"I said, 'Well, there are two things to be said about that. Before we get into a fight it's quite a different matter. And furthermore, now that we're in it and you are making all the statements that you are, if President Eisenhower differed with you, it would be the greatest comfort to the enemy that you can imagine, and it would prolong the war.'

"He said, 'My God, I never thought of such a thing. I'll never say that again.'

"I said, 'You just remember that Truman gave monetary help, Eisenhower put in a few men as advisers, but Kennedy put the first men in to start shooting, and you're the one that expanded the war. So don't blame it on anybody else.' He took it like a man."[20]

Ike, too, could be critical of his successors, although as Milton pointed out he never uttered a word against the President in public on the subject of the war. But in 1968, immediately after LBJ made his startling announcement that he was not going to run for reelection and simultaneously announced that he was stopping the bombing north of the DMZ, Ike wrote in the privacy of his diary:

"April 1, 1968. Last evening President Johnson went on the television on a national hookup. He talked a great deal about the war and made these points: 1. He defended earnestly the reasons for America being in the war. 2. He said America would persevere until the limited objectives he outlined should be realized and that those objectives did not include conquering North Viet Nam, using such methods that would convince Hanoi that we would not be defeated and therefore to induce them, sooner or later, to come to the bargaining table. He reiterated the Administration's determination to achieve these limited objectives and thereafter to assist that corner of Asia.

"Next he said that he had ordered a cessation of bombing of North Viet Nam in the hope that this would lead to satisfactory peace. This abrupt change in policy, without any quid pro quo from Hanoi, will, of course, further bewilder the United States. It appears to be not only contrary to the President's announced determination in the matter, but a partial capitulation, at least, to the 'peace at any price' people in our own country.

"The final and most puzzling feature of his talk was his declaration that he would not seek and would not accept the nomination of his Party for the Presidency of the United States. The inclusion of this statement seems to be almost a contradiction to his plea for a more unified America in attaining our limited objectives in Viet Nam. His speech is virtually an effort to surrender to another the Presidential responsibilities in the conflict. The conclusion seems inescapable that though he is convinced of the worthiness of our purposes in Southeast Asia, he, himself, is unwilling to remain, personally, in the fight.

"To me it seems obvious that the President is at war with himself and while trying vigorously to defend the actions and decisions he has made in the past, and urging the nation to pursue these purposes regardless of cost, he wants to be excused from the burden of the office to which he was elected."[21]

CHAPTER NINETEEN

The U-2 and Ike's
Defense Policy

NEARLY MIDNIGHT, a balmy June evening, Washington, 1956. An almost full moon shines on the Lincoln Memorial and down the length of the reflecting pool. A tall, stoop-shouldered, long-faced, long-legged man, very deliberate in his movements, strides along the shadows beside the pool. He has an air of self-confidence that shows in every step. He stops when he reaches Building K, one of those dismal, ugly World War II "temporary" buildings. Buildings J, K, and L stretch the entire length of the reflecting pool, from Seventeenth to Twenty-third streets. They serve as the headquarters for the Deputy Director of Plans of the CIA and his staff.

The man, Richard Bissell, draws himself up to his full six-feet-four-inch height, glances up and down the pool, then hurriedly moves inside K. He walks quickly down the corridor to his office. Six hours earlier he had approved mission plans for a spy flight over the Soviet Union. Now he has returned for the "go-no-go" briefing.

In his office, Bissell's project team has been waiting for him. He sits behind his desk, picks up a paper clip, and leans back in his chair, swinging his long legs and big feet up onto his desk. As is his habit, he twiddles the paper clip, bending it into fantastic shapes. Tossing it aside, he fidgets with a pencil, polishes his glasses, looks up at the ceiling, all the while listening to reports, occasionally interjecting an "O.K." or a "Right, right!" and less frequently shaking his head and mumbling "No, no."

He's like an atomic bomb, a tremendous bundle of energy bound up in one small space, always on the verge of bursting.

His weatherman reports that conditions over Russia have not changed since the previous briefing—the weather remains favorable. That is the key. The President authorized the flight four days earlier, for a ten-day period. If Bissell cannot get it off the ground in those ten days, he will have to scrub the mission and return to the White House to start all over again. He has already postponed the flight three times because of cloud cover over Russia.

The liaison man with the airbase in Wiesbaden, West Germany, reports that the plane and pilot are ready. The technical man says that the camera and film are properly set up for the operation. Other experts confirm that they are ready to bring the film from Germany to the labs in Washington for immediate processing.

Nodding vigorously, Bissell lets a little of his tremendous energy burst forth. "All right," he announces. "Let's go."

AND WITH THAT the most elaborate, technologically advanced, and spectacularly successful spy mission in the history of espionage to that date was launched. The word was flashed to Wiesbaden, and within minutes the first U-2 was airborne on its initial flight over Soviet territory.[1]

Bissell was accustomed to high-risk situations. He had been in the middle of the PBSUCCESS operation in Guatemala and involved in other CIA activities. He went home after making his decision and enjoyed a good night's sleep. The following morning, at a quarter to nine, he walked into Allen Dulles' office.

Dulles eagerly asked if Bissell had gotten the U-2 mission off the ground.

"Yes," Bissell replied. "It's in the air now."

"Where is it going?" Dulles asked.

"Going first over Moscow," Bissell replied, "and then over Leningrad."

"My God!" Dulles exclaimed. "Do you think that was wise, for the first time?"

"It'll be easier the first time than any later time," Bissell assured his boss.

The remainder of the morning, Bissell and his project people sat around, rather like Walter Cronkite and the men at Mission Control in Houston during a rocket launching, waiting for a report. Toward noon, a cable from Wiesbaden came in. The U-2 was back. The weather had been perfect, the pilot had used all his film, the film was on its way to Washington. A cheer went up. Bissell, all smiles, hurried down the hall to tell Dulles.

The director of the CIA went to the White House, where he had the great pleasure of reporting the successful flight to the President and seeing one of Ike's famous grins spread across his face.

THE U-2 PROGRAM was the CIA's greatest coup. It got its start because Ike insisted that the U. S. Government keep itself at the cutting edge of technology and saw to it that his nation's best scientists were working for the government on matters of national security. On the basis of his own World War II experience, Eisenhower had great faith in aerial reconnaissance, and had been deeply impressed by the miracles that could be performed by photographic interpretation. As President, one of his great fears was that the United States might again be caught by another surprise attack, as at Pearl Harbor, but this time on the mainland and far more devastating, as it would be carried out with nuclear bombs.

In early 1954, about a year after he took office, Ike appointed a Surprise Attack Panel, under the chairmanship of James R. Killian, president of MIT from 1948 to 1959 and Eisenhower's Special Assistant for Science and Technology from 1957 to 1959. The Surprise Attack Panel had three subcommittees, one of which was concerned with intelligence. Its leading members were Edwin H. Land and Edward Purcell.

Land was the inventor of the Polaroid camera, and president, chairman of the board, and director of research for the Polaroid Corporation. During World War II he had worked for the Navy on plastic lenses. Purcell was a Harvard professor of physics, winner of the Nobel Prize (1952), and an expert in such areas as microwave phenomena, nuclear magnetism, and radio-frequency spectroscopy.

The subcommittee met regularly. It was greatly impressed by the work of Arthur Lundahl, a PI (photo interpreter) of World War II who had joined the CIA and ran the small photo interpretation office of the DDI. Lundahl was a farsighted visionary who constantly touted the potential of the picture that told more than 10,000 words, or than 1,000 spies. Ray Cline called Lundahl "the supersalesman of photo interpretation." At the start, he had only twenty men under him; by the end of the 1950s, there were 1,200 PIS in the CIA.[2]

Lundahl showed Killian, Land, and Purcell some astonishing developments in photography. Land was much impressed by the new cameras, lenses, and special films that made high-level photography practical. Seeing what Lundahl could accomplish, the subcommittee of the Surprise Attack Panel began casting about for a way to fly over Russia to take pictures.

Land learned that six months earlier Clarence "Kelly" Johnson, a designer at Lockheed, had proposed to the Air Force a high-altitude single-engine reconnaissance aircraft. Johnson had even submitted a design concept and a few drawings. The Air Force, unimpressed, contracted instead for a new version of the Candara bomber, with new wings and redesigned for weight reduction. Four of these lightweight Candaras were built and flown, but they proved to be unsatisfactory.

Discouraged, the Air Force had turned to a balloon project. Unmanned balloons, equipped with the latest cameras, were to float across the U.S.S.R., to be recovered in the Pacific. Two or three balloons were actually built, and the attempt was made, but those flights, like the Candaras, were unsuccessful.

Land, meanwhile, had decided that the Air Force made a mistake when it turned down Kelly Johnson and Lockheed. He and Purcell went to Allen Dulles for a private meeting. They convinced Dulles. The day before Thanksgiving, 1954, Land, Purcell, Dulles, and Killian went to the Oval Office to meet with the President. They took no papers with them, and no minutes were kept.

Ike listened, considered, and approved immediately. This was unusual for him, as he ordinarily liked to sleep on a decision. He told Allen Dulles to get on it. Dulles called Richard Bissell on the phone and told him to get over to the White House.

Bissell was there in half an hour. "Because all the discussion had been conducted at such a high level in the executive branch," he later explained, "nobody had really worked out how anything was to be done. Nobody knew where the money was coming from. Nobody knew how much it would cost. Nobody knew who would procure the aircraft. Nobody had even given any thought to where it could develop, where flight testing could be done, where people could be trained or by whom, who would fly it or anything."

Washington has a reputation as a town in which it is difficult to get anything done, and nothing gets done quickly, but with a presidential mandate to act, the pieces tend to fall into place. That afternoon—still the day before Thanksgiving, 1954—Bissell went to the Pentagon to meet with the Air Force people who had been working on the Candara, balloon, and other high-altitude projects. As Bissell succinctly put it in an interview in 1979, "the program was kicked off then and there." Trevor Gardiner of the Air Force called Kelly Johnson long-distance and gave Lockheed the go-ahead to build a U-2.

Immediately the question of funding arose. Bissell said he would recommend to Dulles that the cia fund the procurement of the airplane out of the Reserve Fund, which money could be released on presidential authority or by the Director of the Budget. He went back to see Dulles. Dulles approved. Then over to the Director of the Budget, and he also approved. So the money was found to make covert procurement possible.

Bissell had a genius for administration. He set up his project office in a downtown Washington office building. He started off with four men—a finance officer, a contracting officer, an operations officer, and an administrative officer. Two or three others were later added, but the project office staff never went above eight men.

Lockheed called the plane the U-2. It was built in a separate little hangar in California called the "skunk works," because no one not working on the craft was allowed near the hangar. Pratt-Whitney built the engine, a modified J-57, and Hycon built the cameras.[3]

The speed with which the plane and cameras were made ready for operations was simply incredible. By early 1955, only a few months after Ike said to build it, the first U-2 was ready—and Bissell had brought it in at a cost $3 million below the original cost estimate.[4]

The plane itself, as Ray Cline described it, "looked more like a kite built around a camera than an airplane; it was nearly all wing and its single jet engine made it shoot into the air like an arrow and soar higher than any other aircraft of its day." To hold down the weight, it landed on one set of tandem wheels rather than the nor-

mal pair. As a result, when forward momentum was lost on landing, the U-2 simply fell over on one of its long wing tips. Taking
off, the wings had to be held up by little pogo sticks on wheels that
dropped off when the plane was airborne.[5]

The plane could fly miles high in the sky, attaining altitudes of
better than 70,000 feet for cruising. From that immense distance,
the cameras were so good they could take a picture of a parking lot
and the PI could actually count the lines for the stalls or the number of cars parked in the lot.

Bissell went to the White House, along with Dulles and two Air
Force generals, to report that the U-2 was ready for test flights. He
asked Ike to extend the boundaries of an atomic-energy test site in
the southwestern United States, which the President immediately
did. Then Bissell had a small airbase built on the edge of a salt-lake
bed, and he was ready to start test flights.

At this point an inevitable jurisdictional dispute began. The Air
Force, by now well aware of Ike's wholehearted support for the
project, tried to take it over. General Curtis LeMay of the Strategic
Air Command argued that SAC ought to take charge of the operational phase of the project. Dulles and Bissell refused and Ike
backed them up. The most the President would give SAC was a
deputy's post under Bissell.

The President also insisted that although the pilots would be
recruited from SAC, they would have to acquire civilian status and
fly under contract with the CIA. Ike wanted the entire project conducted as a civilian intelligence-collecting operation rather than as
a military operation.

Eisenhower, meanwhile, used his foreknowledge of the U-2 to
make the boldest proposal for peace in the history of the Cold War.
At the Geneva Summit Conference in July 1955, a week or so after
the first U-2 test flight, Ike described the new program to British
Prime Minister Anthony Eden, "who was most enthusiastic." The
next day, July 21, 1955, Eisenhower spoke to the full conference.
He made an offer, which came to be called "Open Skies," that was
an extraordinary, farsighted proposal. Had the Russians been
equally farsighted, Open Skies might well have put a lid on the
arms race. It certainly would have lowered tension.

Ike told the conference, to the astonishment of everyone present except for Eden and a half-dozen top advisers, that the United
States was prepared to exchange military blueprints and charts

with the Soviets. He was making the offer, he said, to show American sincerity in approaching the problem of disarmament. The world's great fear was a surprise nuclear attack. An exchange of all military information would ease that fear.

The President said he was willing to go further. He invited the Russians to build airfields in the States, from which their people could freely fly over American military installations to reassure themselves that no surprise first strikes were in the offing. Each plane would carry an American representative along on the reconnaissance flights. The United States would want the same privileges in Russia.

Of course, as soon as the U-2 was operational, the United States would be able to spy unilaterally over the U.S.S.R. Ike's offer of a reciprocal agreement was quite remarkable, the clearest proof of what chances and risks he was willing to take for peace.

The immediate reception was remarkable, too. As Ike recorded in his memoirs, "As I finished, a most extraordinary natural phenomenon took place. Without warning, and simultaneous with my closing words, the loudest clap of thunder I have ever heard roared into the room, and the conference was plunged into Stygian darkness. . . . For a moment there was stunned silence. Then I remarked that I had not dreamed I was so eloquent as to put the lights out."

Despite the thunder, Premier Nikita Khrushchev turned him down. He said the idea of Open Skies was nothing more than a bald espionage plot against Mother Russia. Ike argued, to no avail.[6]

The U-2 tests, meanwhile, went well, with a minimum of hitches. By early 1956 Bissell was satisfied. He ordered twenty-two U-2s from Lockheed. The pilots were ready, too, having flown missions which Bissell directed from Washington that simulated overseas conditions. As the Church Committee noted, quite correctly, getting the plane, the pilots, the cameras, and the film prepared for actual missions so quickly "was a technical achievement nothing short of spectacular."[7]

Bissell flew to London, where he conferred with Eden, who agreed to allow the CIA to fly U-2 missions from the SAC base at Lakenhurst in the United Kingdom. Bissell sent over a few U-2s, which flew some practice missions over East Europe, but then the British grew skittish.

An incident in Portsmouth Harbor involved a Russian cruiser that was paying a courtesy call. The British Secret Service sent a frogman under the ship to get a look at its signaling gear and underwater apparatus. His body was found, three days later, floating in the harbor. Whether the Russians killed him or not no one knew. In any event, Eden indicated to Ike that he did not want Lakenhurst-based U-2s flying over Russia.

So Eisenhower sent Bissell to West Germany, where he met with Konrad Adenauer. The German Chancellor gave him permission to base the U-2 in Wiesbaden. Later the base moved to a small World War II Luftwaffe airfield that had been deactivated, close to the East German border but far from any city or town.

In early June 1956, Bissell and the Dulles brothers went to the Oval Office to request permission to overfly the Soviet Union itself. Ike listened, asked some questions, and said he would give Bissell his decision. A day later, General Goodpaster called Bissell on the phone and said that the President had authorized the flight for a period of ten days. Bissell said he assumed that meant ten days of good weather, not just ten calendar days. Goodpaster said, "No, you have just ten calendar days and you will have to take your chances with the weather." The flight went, successfully, five days later.

In the next five days, Bissell ran six additional missions. Then came a great shock—the Russians sent in a private but firm diplomatic protest. Much to the CIA's disappointment, it turned out that Russian radar was tracking the U-2 flights. The agency had assumed the spy planes flew too high to be spotted—American radar could not follow them, but the Russians, the CIA discovered, had better radar than the United States. Ike told Bissell to slow down, "and it was quite a few months before he was ready to authorize another flight." From then on, the President authorized flights one by one.

As Bissell explained in 1979, the entire program "was controlled very tightly by the President personally." Before each flight, Bissell would draw up on a map the proposed flight plan. They would spread the map on the President's desk in the Oval Office. With John Eisenhower standing behind one shoulder, Andy Goodpaster behind the other, Ike would study the route. Bissell, the Dulles brothers, Secretary Wilson, and the chairman of the JCS would all be present.

When Bissell's presentation was over, after he had explained why the CIA wanted pictures of specific spots, "the President would ask a lot of questions. He would ask me to come around and explain this or that feature of the flight, and there were occasions, more than once, when he would say, 'Well, you can go there, but I want you to leave out that leg and go straight that way. I want you to go from B to D because it looks to me like you might be getting a little exposed over here,' or something of that kind."

"So we had very, very tight ground rules," Bissell continued, "very tight control by the President. Then, once the mission was approved, it was my responsibility to watch the weather forecasts three times a day, and select the actual time, and then notify all concerned that the mission was about to take off."[8]

When the President felt it was necessary, he would initiate the flights himself, rather than waiting for Bissell to come to him with a proposal. On November 6, 1956, for example, at 8:37 A.M., he met with Allen Dulles and Goodpaster. The Suez crisis was at its height. It was also Election Day, Eisenhower vs. Stevenson. The President ordered Dulles to conduct U-2 flights over Syria, Egypt, and Israel to make certain that the Russians were not moving airplanes into Egypt. Goodpaster's minutes record, "The President said that if reconnaissance discloses Soviet Air Forces on Syrian bases he would think that there would be reason for the British and French to destroy them. The President asked if our forces in the Mediterranean are equipped with atomic anti-submarine weapons."

To Dulles, Ike said, "If the Soviets should attack Britain and France directly, we would of course be in a major war."[9]

With that, Ike and Mamie drove up to Gettysburg to vote. At noon they returned to Washington by helicopter. On the way into the White House from the airport, Goodpaster reported that the U-2 flights revealed no Soviet aircraft were moving into Syria, or from Syria to Egypt. World War III was not about to begin.[10]

Simultaneously, U-2s were flying over East Europe to monitor Red Army activity during the Hungarian crisis. Khrushchev protested, privately but firmly. Secretary of State Dulles called the President on the telephone to say "we are in trouble about these overflights." Ike said he was considering a "complete stoppage of the entire business."

Dulles said, "I think we will have to admit this was done and say we are sorry. We cannot deny it. Relations with Russia are getting pretty tense at the moment." All this was taken down verbatim by the tape recorder Ike had installed in his office.

Dulles said he had "always been afraid that as their [the Russians'] problems at home increased, they might get reckless abroad." Ike said he would call Charles Wilson and "have him stop it" until the crisis receded.[11]

By the beginning of 1957, the U-2 program was securely in place, including flights over the Soviet Union when the President authorized them. Bissell had about five hundred people in his organization. There were one hundred in Washington, another one hundred at the western testing facilities (Bissell was already looking ahead to the next generation of spy in the sky planes, and to the development of even better cameras).[12] Overseas, there were 150 men each at the two active airbases, which had been moved to Turkey and Japan. "We quite literally had the ability to cover almost any part of the surface of the earth for photograph reconnaissance, within twenty-four hours of notice . . ." Bissell declared.

Francis Gary Powers was in the first group recruited from SAC by Bissell. Powers began flying regularly in September 1956. His initial assignment was to fly over the Mediterranean, where he was to "watch for and photograph any concentration of two or more ships." The ships he was looking for were British and French; what the CIA, and Ike, wanted to know was how quickly and in what strength London and Paris were preparing for an attack on Egypt. Powers flew a number of such missions, taking off from the U-2 base at Adana, Turkey, flying over Cyprus, on to Malta, and back to base, or to Cyprus, then over to Egypt, across the Sinai, then north to Israel, and back to Turkey. On a flight on October 30, 1956, Powers saw and photographed black puffs of smoke in the Sinai—the first shots in the Israeli invasion of Egypt.[13]

Another U-2 pilot, making a pass over Egyptian airfields, saw Egyptian planes lined up wing tip to wing tip. He made a loop to get on the correct course for the next leg of his flight plan and passed over the airfield again. This time—five minutes had elapsed —he saw the Egyptian Air Force in flames. The Israelis had struck while he was making his turn.[14] All this information gave the President an accurate picture of what was going on and thus allowed him to make his policy decisions on the basis of facts, not guesses.

Ike made immediate practical use of the results of other U-2 flights. As one example, in September 1958 the Chinese were making the most dreadful threats against Formosa. The immediate issue was the tiny offshore pair of islands, Quemoy and Matsu. Chou En-lai warned that if Chiang Kai-shek did not abandon them, the Communists would invade Formosa. America would then be drawn into the conflict, and World War III might be under way. The China lobby warned that there had better not be any appeasement; the British and other NATO allies warned that they were not ready to go to war to defend a couple of tiny Nationalist Chinese islands.

U-2 flights revealed that there was no Chinese buildup for an invasion. Armed with that intelligence, Ike went on national television to report, "There is not going to be any appeasement, and . . . there is not going to be any war." The "crisis" disappeared.[15]

The U-2s paid off in the long-range strategic sense, as well as for short-term tactical decisions. In fact, the U-2 photographs undoubtedly saved the American taxpayer more money than any other government initiative of the 1950s, because those photographs gave Ike the essential information he had to have to hold to his New Look in defense policy.

As President, Eisenhower was responsible first and foremost for the defense of his country. As a professional soldier, he was keenly aware of the military threat the Soviets presented. As a statesman, however, he had long ago concluded that the greatest threat was that the Russians would frighten the United States into an arms race that would lead to unmanageable inflation and ultimate bankruptcy. He believed that America's greatest strength lay in her economic productivity, not in bombs and missiles. He believed further that a sound economy depended on a balanced federal budget, which he thought was the key to stopping inflation. To balance the budget, he had to cut back on defense spending.

To do that, he cut back on conventional arms, reducing the Army and the Navy, while relying increasingly on nuclear weapons for massive retaliation. As a result, Ike was able to hold Defense spending to an annual expenditure of around $40 billion throughout his eight years in office. This figure was some $10 billion under what Truman had proposed, and what the Democrats were advocating be spent. By holding down the defense costs, Ike was able to balance his budget more often than not, with one result being an annual inflation rate of 1.25 percent, or a total of 10 percent for his whole eight years in office.

This accomplishment was based on Ike's understanding of how massive retaliation worked. He argued that to deter the Russians what one had to do was be in a position to drop one or two bombs on Moscow. No Russian gain anywhere would be worth the loss of Moscow. The United States did not need thousands of bombers and missiles to make the threat believable. It was by no means necessary to be able to destroy the Soviet Union to deter the Kremlin.

Ike's fundamental insight, in short, was that in the nuclear age, Clausewitzian strategy, with its emphasis on the destruction of the enemy's fighting forces, no longer applied. The United States and the Soviet Union were in exactly the position Oppenheimer had said they were, two scorpions in a bottle.

Under those circumstances, the United States did not have to go into an all-out, fabulously expensive program of producing atomic bombs and ICBMs to deliver them. Indeed, Ike believed that the more the nation spent on defense, at least after a certain point, the less secure the nation became. That flew in the face of common sense, but was of course exactly true, for the obvious reason that the more the Americans built, the more the Russians would build, and there was no defense against ICBMs tipped with nuclear warheads. No arms race ever made much sense, Ike often said, but an arms race in the nuclear age was absolute madness.[16]

Eisenhower's Democratic critics, led by three Senate hawks, John F. Kennedy, Lyndon B. Johnson, and Hubert H. Humphrey, assailed him. They charged that he was allowing his Neanderthal fiscal views to endanger the national security. By 1958 they were claiming that a "bomber gap" existed; in 1959 it became a "missile gap." The Russians had gotten ahead of the United States in strategic weapons. America was suddenly vulnerable to a Soviet first strike.

Ike knew that the "gaps" were all nonsense. He knew because of the U-2 flights. They revealed, in 1957 and 1958 and 1959, that the Russians had by no means gone into a crash program of building either missiles or bombers. They proved that the United States, even with its modest bomber fleet and relatively small ICBM fleet (around two hundred by 1961), had a clear lead over the Soviets, a lead of about two to one.

As Bissell pointed out, the U-2 flights were the heart of a "very elaborate program of identifying Russian nuclear facilities." The photographs showed where the sites were located, their physical size and shape, the number of missile launchers, and so on. One or two firing ranges that had not been suspected were uncovered; in addition, the U-2 photos revealed the location of Russian radar installations. All this was basic, priceless knowledge.

In addition, as Andrew Goodpaster said in a 1979 interview, the flights showed what the Russians were *not* doing. If Khrushchev had been building bombers and rockets at maximum capacity, the "bomber gap" and the "missile gap" might have become reality. But photographic intelligence showed conclusively that the Soviets were building at a rate considerably short of capacity, and there was nothing in the pipeline, such as movement of basic supplies to construction sites, to indicate that they intended to speed up. There was no need to panic.[17]

The President would not be forced into spending money for weapons that were not needed. Of course, it was easier for Eisenhower to say no on such matters than any President before or since because—as one Senate hawk put it—"How the hell can I argue with Ike Eisenhower on military matters?"

The JCS could, and did, argue with the President. They could not win the argument, and two Army chiefs of staff—Matthew Ridgway and Maxwell Taylor—resigned in protest over Ike's reduction of the Army. Ike had been there himself, and he knew perfectly well that the Pentagon had to argue that not enough was being done for the nation's defenses. In August of 1956 he wrote his oldest friend, Swede Hazlett, an advocate of more defense spending, "Let us not forget that the Armed Services are to defend a 'way of life,' not merely land, property or lives." The President said he wanted to make the JCS accept the need for a "balance between minimum requirements in the costly implements of war and the health of our economy."[18]

Or, as he told the American Society of Newspaper Editors, "Every gun that is made, every warship launched, every rocket fired signifies, in the final sense, a theft from those who hunger and are not fed, those who are cold and are not clothed."[19]

Persuading the JCS to accept that position was one of the most difficult and frustrating tasks Eisenhower undertook as President. In a typical telephone comment to Foster Dulles, a month after the Hungary/Suez crisis, Ike said that "he was going to crack down on Defense people tomorrow, that he is getting desperate with the inability of the men there to understand what can be spent on military weapons and what must be spent to wage the peace."[20]

One remarkable aspect of Eisenhower's involvement with the U-2 was that he never revealed his sources, even after Powers was shot down, when it would have been greatly to his personal advantage to do so. Throughout 1960, Kennedy and the Democrats cried "missile gap" again and again, until it became almost the central theme of JFK's presidential campaign. Ike contented himself with responding that it simply was not true, without indicating how he knew.

He was badly disappointed, even hurt, when two of his own men, Nelson Rockefeller and Richard Nixon, turned against him on this issue. Rockefeller issued a "report" that repeated most of the charges the Democrats had made with regard to Defense spending. Nixon, at the height of the presidential campaign of 1960, went to New York, conferred with Rockefeller, and emerged to tell reporters that he, too, believed not enough was being done for America's defense. Their joint statement declared that "the U.S. can afford and must provide the increased expenditures to implement fully this necessary program for strengthening our defense posture. There must be no price ceiling on America's security."

In his memoirs, Ike put it politely when he commented, "That statement seemed somewhat astonishing, coming as it did from two people who had long been in administration councils."[21]

During the campaign, Eisenhower did nevertheless speak for Nixon. His one major address took up the question of increased Defense spending, and might have been pointed at both candidates, although he referred only to the Democrats: "If they would pay for these programs by deficit spending, raising the debt of our children and grandchildren, and thereby debase our currency, let them so confess."[22]

Kennedy won the election. As President, he began a crash program to build ICBMs. When Ike left office, the United States had about two hundred ICBMs. When Kennedy was assassinated, the number was one thousand and growing daily. Four years later Kennedy's Secretary of Defense, Robert S. McNamara, confessed that there never had been a "missile gap," or if there had, it was in America's favor. By then it was too late; the modern arms race was under way.

CHAPTER TWENTY

Francis Gary Powers and the Summit That Never Was

MAY 1, 1960. A beautiful day in Russia. At Adana, Turkey, Francis Gary Powers dresses in his pressurized flying suit, climbs into the cockpit of his plane, and takes off for Bodo, Norway. Midway through an uneventful flight there is a flash, followed by a boom and an explosion. The U-2 rocks, starts to crash. Powers ejects. His parachute opens and he floats to earth near Sverdlovsk. He is immediately captured and taken away for questioning.

"THE CIA PROMISED US that the Russians would never get a U-2 pilot alive," John Eisenhower declared, his eyes flashing. "And then they gave the S.O.B. a parachute!"[1]

His father put it less vehemently, but was equally firm. The U-2 program, Ike declared in his memoirs, operated under "the assumption that in the event of a mishap the plane would virtually disintegrate. It would be *impossible*, if things should go wrong, for the Soviets to come in possession of the equipment intact—or, unfortunately, of a live pilot. This was a cruel assumption, but I was assured that the young pilots undertaking these missions were doing so with their eyes wide open and motivated by a high degree of patriotism, a swashbuckling bravado, and certain material inducements."[2]

Richard Bissell, too, thought no pilot would ever emerge alive from a crash, whether brought about by a malfunction of the U-2 or as a result of a Russian attack. The CIA did provide the pilots with cyanide, but told them that whether to take it or not was their decision. The idea was to boost pilot morale by letting them think they had a chance to survive; the truth was that the CIA did not believe they had one chance in a million.[3]

So, the cover story in the event a U-2 went down, worked out years in advance, was based on the assumption that the pilot would be dead. "We were quite prepared to say, if the Russians showed photographs of it, either that it wasn't the U-2 or that they had taken the plane and moved it. We believed that we would make a pretty plausible case for the cover story. And we felt that it would be very difficult for them to disprove that," Bissell declared. "So the whole point of the story was to explain what had happened— that a pilot had inadvertently crossed the border and had been shot down and landed inside, and that they had moved the wreckage."[4]

But the CIA gave Francis Gary Powers a parachute, never expecting that he would be able to use it, and as a result the Paris Summit Conference of May 1960, which had once seemed so full of promise, was wrecked, and the United States suffered one of its most embarrassing moments in the entire history of the Cold War.

The event made Ike look indecisive, foolish, and not in control of his own government. It also led to the charge, widely believed, that the CIA had engaged in a conspiracy to sabotage Ike's search for peace by arranging for Powers' crash.

IN THE SPRING OF 1960, hope had bloomed around the world. It seemed that the Cold War might be ending, to be replaced by a period of growing cooperation and trust between the Super Powers. Mr. Khrushchev had made a trip to the United States in September 1959 that was a huge success, a media event of the first magnitude. He almost seemed to be an American politician out for votes. A jolly fat man, he roared with laughter at jokes and was duly impressed by American productivity. To the delight of photographers, he matched his girth against that of a portly Iowa farmer. He spoke constantly of the need for peace. Nearly as old as Ike and fully as bald, Khrushchev—again like Ike—had a grandfather image. He seemed, somehow, comforting.

At Camp David, the serene presidential retreat in the Maryland mountains that Ike had named after his grandson, Khrushchev added to the impression that he was a reasonable man whose sole interest was movement toward genuine peace. He had previously issued an ultimatum on West Berlin—if the United States, Britain, and France did not withdraw their occupation troops from that city, he threatened, he would turn over the access routes to the East Germans and then the Allies would have to fight their way through to Berlin. Now, at Camp David, Khrushchev said that he had not meant it to be a threat. The ultimatum was not an ultimatum. There could be negotiations.

The two leaders then agreed to meet in mid-May 1960 at a summit conference in Paris, where—it was hoped—"the Spirit of Camp David" could engulf the world. Afterward, Ike would repay Khrushchev's visit, taking along his family for a tour of the Soviet Union. Small wonder hopes were high for an end to the Cold War, for the beginning of peace.

IKE DID NOT SHARE THOSE HOPES. He was always suspicious of media events. He had told Khrushchev that political summits tended to be like real mountain summits—barren.[5] He had always expected Khrushchev to back down on his Berlin ultimatum, as long as the President of the United States stood firm, as he had during the Camp David talks. Ike was unimpressed by Khrushchev's public calls for peace. He would be convinced that Khrushchev was serious only when he saw some real indication that the Soviets were ready for peace. But the Soviets operated a closed system—Westerners could not even get a road map of the Soviet Union, much less an indication of their military dispositions—so the only way to see what they were up to was to spy on them. Therefore, as the date for the summit approached, Eisenhower ordered increased U-2 reconnaissance over Russia.

He did so with some reluctance. A series of recent National Intelligence Estimates from the CIA had indicated that the Soviets were developing, or had developed, surface-to-air missiles (SAMs) capable of intercepting the U-2. The SAMs, according to the CIA's information, could get up as high as the U-2, although they were optimized for use against manned bombers flying below 60,000 feet. The SAMs did not have much maneuverability above 60,000 feet, while the U-2 flew at 68,000 feet and higher. "There was therefore the thought," Bissell recalled in 1979, "that if the missile were fired it would be a near-miss, rather than a hit." But Gordon Gray personally told Ike that sooner or later "a U-2 would surely be shot down."[6]

However, the President's other advisers, from the CIA, the Department of Defense, and the State Department, downgraded the danger. Foster Dulles, for example, once told Ike, laughing, "If the Soviets ever capture one of these planes, I'm sure they will never admit it. To do so would make it necessary for them to admit also that for years we had been carrying on flights over their territory while they had been helpless to do anything about the matter."[7]

Of all those concerned, Ike later wrote, only John Eisenhower, Richard Bissell, and Andrew Goodpaster agreed with him that "if ever one of the planes fell in Soviet territory a wave of excitement mounting almost to panic would sweep the world, inspired by the standard Soviet claim of injustice, unfairness, aggression, and ruthlessness."[8]

After the event, in a July 1960 postmortem, Ike said that "all his advisers, including Foster Dulles, had missed badly in their estimate regarding the U-2. . . . He did not wish to say 'I told you so' but recalled that he was the one and only one who had put much weight on this factor, and that he had given it great emphasis. Being only one person, he had not felt he could oppose the combined opinion of all his associates. He added that the action that was taken was probably the right action, and what he would have done anyhow even if his advisers had correctly assessed the potential reaction."[9]

In other words, the President, like his advisers, was extremely anxious to make more flights, whatever the risk. The purpose, in the spring of 1960, was to fly over territory that had not been covered previously, territory that the CIA believed might be being used by the Soviets to build new ICBM sites. Ike wanted to know, before the summit, what the facts were.[10]

There was also a feeling that the United States had best fly as many missions as it could before the SAMs got any better. Francis Gary Powers thought that was the major reason for his May 1, 1960, flight. There had been two flights in close succession in April, Powers later wrote, and "the pilots believed the resumption of the flights was due at least in part to the agency's fear that Russia was now close to solving her missile-guidance problem."[11]

Powers also believed that the CIA had not informed Ike "of the many dangers involved, lest he consider the advisability of discontinuing the overflight program entirely." Powers further had the impression that "Eisenhower believed the pilots had been ordered to kill themselves rather than submit to capture."[12]

On this last point, Powers was certainly wrong. Eisenhower had no such impression. What he did believe was that no pilot could escape alive from a SAM hit.

MID-APRIL 1960, THE WHITE HOUSE. In the world's most famous office, John Eisenhower and Andrew Goodpaster leaned over the President's shoulders, tracing out for him on a huge map of Russia the proposed flight pattern for a U-2 mission. Ike asked a few questions. Bissell, across the President's desk, explained why the CIA thought there might be new missile sites along the route. Eisenhower grunted, then turned to the Secretary of State, Christian Herter (Dulles had died of cancer the previous year).

Herter was worried about the timing, with the Summit meeting only a month away. Ike's attitude was that "there would never be a good time for a failure." Still, he too was worried. The President told Bissell he had an authorization to fly for the following two weeks.[13]

Every day for the next fourteen days, Russia was covered by clouds. The U-2 needed near-perfect weather to fly. The weather never improved. Bissell applied for an extension. Ike had Goodpaster call Bissell and tell him the flight was authorized for one more week, that is, up to May 2. If he could not get it off the ground by then, it was scratched for good, because it would be too close to the Paris meeting to risk it.

"And that means," as Bissell summed it up in 1979, "that all of those stories implying that nobody gave any thought to the timing or that the White House forgot that the summit was going on are a bunch of nonsense."[14]

The afternoon of May 1, 1960, Goodpaster called Eisenhower on the telephone to report that a U-2 flying a mission over Russia was "overdue and possibly lost."[15] Whether it had malfunctioned, run out of fuel, or been shot down was unknown and unknowable.

There was no reason to panic. First, everyone assumed that Powers was dead. Second, the CIA had assured the President "that if a plane were to go down it would be destroyed either in the air or on impact, so that proof of espionage would be lacking. Self-destroying mechanisms were built in."[16] Third, Khrushchev would probably say nothing about it anyway, just as he had not mentioned the many previous flights, including the two in April.

On the first and second points, the CIA had given Ike bad information. Powers had survived and in any case it would have been impossible to destroy the conclusive evidence that he was engaged in spying on the Soviet Union. That evidence was the film itself. As Lyman Kirkpatrick, a CIA career man who became executive director of the agency, wrote in 1968, "Nobody has ever yet devised a method for quickly destroying a tightly rolled package of hundreds of feet of film. Even if Francis Powers had succeeded in pressing the 'destruction button' which would have blown the plane and the camera apart, the odds would still have been quite good that careful Soviet search would have found the rolls of film."[17]

The CIA had fudged when it told the President that the plane had a "self-destruct mechanism." The device had to be activated by the pilot. Further, it was only a two-and-one-half-pound charge, hardly sufficient to "destroy" a craft as big as the U-2.[18]

But the biggest mistake of all turned out to be the assumption behind point three, that Khrushchev would keep quiet. For a while, he did. Then, on May 5, four days after the SAM knocked Powers out of the sky, Khrushchev broke the news, and in such a manner as to ensure the wrecking of the Paris Summit, thereby destroying the bright hopes for an end to the Cold War. Whether that was his intention or not, no one in the West knows or can know, but it *was* the result.

Speaking before the Supreme Soviet, in a blistering speech, Khrushchev said that the Russians had shot down an American plane that had intruded Soviet airspace. He angrily denounced the United States for its "aggressive provocation" in sending a "bandit flight" over the Soviet Union. In the course of a long harangue, Khrushchev said the Americans had picked May Day, "the most festive day for our people and the workers of the world," hoping to catch the Soviets with their guard down, but to no avail.

In analyzing the event, Khrushchev suggested interpretations that were later picked up in the United States and remain very much alive in the 1980s as conspiracy theories. The Russian Premier charged that militarists in the United States, in the CIA and in the Pentagon, fearful of an outbreak of peace at Paris, had sent Powers over Russia precisely to wreck the conference. "Aggressive imperialist forces in the United States in recent times have been taking the most active measures to undermine the summit or at least to hinder any agreement that might be reached."

Then Khrushchev offered an explanation that still finds wide support among American intellectuals and liberals—that Ike did not know what the militarists were doing behind his back. "Was this aggressive act carried out by Pentagon militarists?" he asked. "If such actions are taken by American military men on their own account, it must be of special concern to world opinion."[19]

Ike did not deny the charges or reply to the innuendos. Meanwhile, the National Aeronautics and Space Administration went ahead with the long-established cover story. It issued a statement on May 5 that began, "One of N.A.S.A.'s U-2 research airplanes, in use since 1956 in a continuing program to study meteorological conditions found at high altitude, has been missing since May 1, when its pilot reported he was having oxygen difficulties over the Lake Van, Turkey, area." The pilot was identified as thirty-year-old Francis Gary Powers, a civilian flying under contract to Lockheed Aircraft Corporation. Presumably, the U-2 had strayed off course, perhaps crossing the border into Russia. The unstated assumption was that Powers' weather plane was the one the Russians had shot down.[20]

The following day, Khrushchev released a photograph of a wrecked airplane, describing it as the U-2 Powers had flown. It was not, however, a U-2, but another airplane. The Premier was setting a trap. He wanted Eisenhower to continue to believe that Powers was dead, the U-2 destroyed, so that the United States would stick to its "weather research" story, as it did. On May 7, Khrushchev sprang his great surprise. He jubilantly reported to a "wildly cheering" Supreme Soviet that "we have parts of the plane and we also have the pilot, who is quite alive and kicking. The pilot is in Moscow and so are the parts of the plane."

Khrushchev made his account a story of high drama and low skullduggery interspersed with bitingly sarcastic remarks about the American cover story. Cries of "Shame, Shame!" rose from the deputies as Khrushchev heaped scorn on the CIA, mixed with cries of "Bandits, Bandits!"[21]

Upon receiving this news, which he found "unbelievable,"[22] Eisenhower made a serious mistake. At Secretary Herter's urging, he authorized the State Department to issue a statement denying that Powers had any authorization to fly over the Soviet Union.

As James Reston reported in the New York *Times*, "The United States admitted tonight that one of this country's planes equipped for intelligence purposes had 'probably' flown over Soviet territory.

"An official statement stressed, however, that 'there was no authorization for any such flight' from authorities in Washington.

"As to who might have authorized the flight, officials refused to comment. If this particular flight of the U-2 was not authorized here, it could only be assumed that someone in the chain of command in the Middle East or Europe had given the order."[23]

Critics on one side blamed the President for admitting that the United States had spy planes. Critics on the other side blasted him for not being in command of his own military. Whichever way one examined it, the President looked terrible. The statement only made a bad situation worse.

In his memoirs, Eisenhower passed over that part of the statement that denied any authorization from Washington. He simply did not mention it. He did explain the "unprecedented" acknowledgment of espionage activities by pointing out that since the Russians had the plane in hand, he could hardly deny its existence.

Eisenhower also pointed out that the Soviets were notorious for spying on the United States, that their activities in espionage "dwarfed" those of the Americans, and that to charge that flying over a nation in an airplane carrying only a camera was "warmongering" was "just plain silly."[24]

Nevertheless, as Reston reported from Washington in the *Times* of May 9, "This was a sad and perplexed capital tonight, caught in a swirl of charges of clumsy administration, bad judgment and bad faith.

"It was depressed and humiliated by the United States having been caught spying over the Soviet Union and trying to cover up its activities in a series of misleading official announcements."[25]

Over the next few days, humiliation gave way to fright, as the headlines became more and more alarmist. "KHRUSHCHEV WARNS OF ROCKET ATTACK ON BASES USED BY U.S. SPYING PLANES," the *Times* announced on May 10. The following morning, the headline read, "U.S. VOWS TO DEFEND ALLIES IF RUSSIANS ATTACK BASES."

Ike, meanwhile, indicated that he would not make a trip to Russia after the Paris Summit Conference. Khrushchev replied that he would not be welcome anyway. The fate of the conference itself was in doubt. Khrushchev told an impromptu news conference in Moscow that he was putting Powers on trial and added, "You understand that if such aggressive actions continue this might lead to war."[26]

Eisenhower held his own news conference. He read a carefully worded statement, saying that the Soviet "fetish of secrecy and concealment was a major cause of international tension and uneasiness." In firm, measured tones, without a hint of regret or apology, Ike said Khrushchev's antics over the "flight of an unarmed non-military plane can only reflect a fetish of secrecy." The President then declared that he was assuming personal responsibility for the flights. He said they were necessary to protect the United States from surprise attacks.[27]

Although Ike defended America's right to find out all that it could about Russian military dispositions, and cited the need for the U-2 program, he also indicated that no more flights would go forth in the immediate future. There were two good reasons for this suspension. First, the obvious one—the Soviets had demonstrated a capacity to shoot down the aircraft. Second, the United States was making progress in photography of the earth from satellites, so the U-2s were not as crucial as they had been.[28]

That fact deepens the mystery as to what Khrushchev was up to, with his histrionics, wild charges, and pretended outrage. Soviet satellites were flying over America daily by 1960, and Russian newspapers had even published photographs of the United States taken by cameras aboard such satellites.[29]

Reston guessed in the *Times* that Khrushchev was pretending to be shocked and outraged because he realized that Eisenhower was not going to pull out of Berlin, so he was using the U-2 "to blame the United States for the breakdown of the Paris meeting."[30]

Charles de Gaulle later told Ike he thought the reason Khrushchev made such a fuss about the U-2 was that he feared a presidential visit to Russia, and used the U-2 incident as a way of preventing it. In de Gaulle's interpretation, Khrushchev did not want to give Ike the opportunity—as Ike had given to Khrushchev when he visited the United States—to speak directly to the Russian people over Soviet television.[31]

Whatever his motives, in the week before the Paris meeting Khrushchev kept saying that he doubted that Eisenhower personally knew about the flights. At one point, he even said that the KGB often carried on activities that he did not know about. Several of

Ike's associates, and some members of Congress, urged him to take advantage of this interpretation by dismissing Bissell and/or Allen Dulles, with the thought that this would show that the President had been a "victim of overzealous subordinates."

Ike refused, first because it was untrue, second because it would indicate that the CIA was operating irresponsibly, was even out of control, and third because it would allow Khrushchev to say that Eisenhower could not speak for his country since he could not control his own government. Thus, Ike recorded, "I rejected the whole notion out of hand."[32]

On May 14, 1960, Ike flew to Paris. De Gaulle, as host, had already checked with Khrushchev to make certain the Russian leader wanted to go ahead with the meeting. Khrushchev had said that he was ready. When Ike called on de Gaulle on May 15, however, de Gaulle reported that Khrushchev was now making trouble. He had been to see de Gaulle and indicated that he was highly agitated about the U-2 flights. He could not understand why Eisenhower had admitted publicly that he knew about the missions. By Khrushchev's standards this indicated not American truthfulness, but rather contempt for the Soviets. De Gaulle told Khrushchev that he could not seriously expect Ike to apologize.

De Gaulle discussed these matters, according to Ike's interpreter, General Vernon Walters, "with a sort of Olympian detachment. . . . He did not think that the peccadilloes of intelligence services were appropriate matters to be discussed at meetings of chiefs of government."[33]

The following morning, de Gaulle, presiding, had not even finished calling the initial meeting to order when Khrushchev was on his feet, red-faced, loudly demanding the right to speak. De Gaulle nodded, and Khrushchev launched into a tirade against the United States. Soon he was shouting.

De Gaulle interrupted, turned to the Soviet interpreter, and said, "The acoustics in this room are excellent. We can all hear the chairman. There is no need for him to raise his voice." The interpreter blanched, turned to Khrushchev, and began to translate. De Gaulle cut him off and motioned to his own interpreter, who unfalteringly translated into Russian. Khrushchev cast a furious glance at de Gaulle, then continued to read in a lower voice.

He soon lashed himself into an even greater frenzy. He pointed overhead and shouted, "I have been overflown."

De Gaulle interrupted again. He said that he, too, had been overflown.

"By your American allies?" asked Khrushchev, incredulous.

"No," replied General de Gaulle, "by you. Yesterday that satellite you launched just before you left Moscow to impress us overflew the sky of France eighteen times without my permission. How do I know you do not have cameras aboard which are taking pictures of my country?"

Khrushchev's jaw dropped. Then he smiled. He raised both hands above his head and said, "God sees me. My hands are clean. You don't think I would do a thing like that?"

De Gaulle grunted.

Khrushchev returned to reading his speech. Soon he exclaimed, "What devil made the Americans do this?" De Gaulle observed that there were devils on both sides and that this matter was not worthy of the consideration of chiefs of government to whom the world was looking for signs of peace.

Khrushchev then announced that unless Eisenhower would apologize he would walk out of the conference. Ike refused to apologize. Khrushchev repeated his threat to walk out.

De Gaulle looked at Khrushchev, according to translator Walters, "as one would look at a naughty child." He adjourned the meeting. As Eisenhower started to leave the room, de Gaulle caught him by the elbow and drew him aside, with Walters to interpret. He then said to the President, "I do not know what Khrushchev is going to do nor what is going to happen, but whatever he does, or whatever happens, I want you to know that I am with you to the end."[34]

The next day Khrushchev returned to Moscow. The Paris Summit Conference was over.

In summing up the event in his memoirs, Eisenhower admitted that "the big error we made was, of course, in the issuance of a premature and erroneous cover story. Allowing myself to be persuaded on this score is my principal personal regret."[35]

THERE HAVE BEEN many interpretations of the Powers incident and the failure of the summit conference. A prominent one is that the CIA deliberately sabotaged Powers' plane in order to prevent an outbreak of peace. This conspiracy theory reached such respectability that in October 1975 the professional quarterly journal

Military Affairs published an article on the subject that concluded, "The anomalies in the Powers case suggest that the U-2 'incident' may have been staged. Moreover, the management of the crisis gives further warrant to the hypothesis that the U-2 was a device deliberately chosen to destroy an emerging détente."[36]

Powers was eventually exchanged for Colonel Rudolf Abel, a master Soviet spy caught in Brooklyn. Powers worked for Lockheed as a test pilot for a few years, then became a pilot of a helicopter that watched rush-hour traffic for a television station in Los Angeles. In August 1977 he crashed and died in an accident. Inevitably, it was suggested that his crash was no accident—that the CIA had done him in, presumably because he was about to "talk."[37]

Powers in fact had already "talked," in his memoirs, entitled *Operation Overflight,* which he published in 1970. He had his own conspiracy thesis. It was based on the following facts: In 1957 the U-2s were based in a new location, Atsugi, Japan. In September 1957 a seventeen-year-old Marine private was assigned to a radar unit at Atsugi. After two years of extensive radar work for the Marines, he was discharged from the Corps. In October 1959 he defected to the Soviet Union, where he presumably told the Soviets everything he knew about American radar operations, and what he had learned, including—perhaps—the supposedly crucial information about the flying altitude of the U-2s.

The name of that Marine was Lee Harvey Oswald.[38]

One of Powers' "proofs" of Oswald's involvement was the fact that the Warren Commission had refused to release a top-secret CIA memorandum of May 13, 1964 (prepared by Richard Helms) to J. Edgar Hoover on the subject of "Lee Harvey Oswald's Access to Classified Information About the U-2." Powers complained that the document was still classified and he had been refused access to it.

In 1979, in response to a Freedom of Information Act request, this writer obtained the document. It recorded that the U-2 station at Atsugi was a "closed" base, with restricted flight lines and hangar areas. Oswald *"did not have access* to this area." Helms's conclusion was that "there is no evidence or indication that Oswald had any association with, or access to, the U-2 operation or its program in Japan." He may have seen the airplane but if he did "it is most unlikely that Oswald had the necessary prerequisites to differentiate between the U-2 and other aircraft engaged in classified missions which were similarly visible at Atsugi at the same time."[39]

When Richard Immerman asked Bissell about the possible Oswald connection, Bissell scoffed at it. There was no way that Oswald could have known the date of the flight, obviously, and Soviet radar had long since been tracking U-2 flights, so the Russians already knew how high the planes were flying. Bissell agreed with Goodpaster, John Eisenhower, and Kelly Johnson (the man who designed the U-2) that Powers was downed by a near-miss explosion from a SAM.[40]

The *Military Affairs* article made the point that because satellites were in operation by May 1960 further U-2 flights were unnecessary. Therefore, Powers must have been sent out by the CIA in order to be shot down.

Bissell's response to this charge is that "the first U.S. reconnaissance satellite did not occur until late August of 1960. Prior to that flight there had been some thirteen unsuccessful launches of the reconnaissance satellite, no one of which yielded usable photography, by reason either of vehicle or camera malfunction."

A second reason for using the U-2 was that "an aircraft mission can be programmed, as to choice of targets and timing over targets, so a mission could be laid out and timed in such a way as to achieve coverage of selected targets at specified times when it was expected that they would be visible." By contrast, satellite missions "had to be planned and prepared days in advance before reliable weather predictions were available. They could of course be aborted up to the last minute but they could not be greatly modified."

Finally, "the resolution of U-2 photographs was considerably higher than that of satellite photography. (That situation has changed in the intervening years.) Since the purpose of Powers' flight was to verify or disprove the existence of a number of ICBM sites in East Central Russia, and to obtain high resolution photography of them if discovered, a case could have been made for the use of the U-2 even if a satellite capability had been in existence."[41]

THE CHARGE THAT BISSELL, Allen Dulles, and others in the CIA deliberately sabotaged the Powers flight in order to wreck the summit conference and thus prevent détente is absurd. It ignores the obvious fact that it was Khrushchev who took the initiative. He was the one who made the Powers incident public, not Ike or Dulles or Bissell. He was the one who made a fuss, not the Americans. He was the one who wanted to wreck the summit, for whatever reason, and he succeeded.

CHAPTER TWENTY-ONE

Ike and the CIA's Assassination Plots

AUGUST 18, 1960, Léopoldville, the Congo. Prime Minister Patrice Lumumba has just made a deal with Khrushchev that will give the Congo forces Soviet military planes, which Lumumba says he needs to bring rebellious Katanga Province back under the control of the central government. Victor Hedgman, CIA station chief in Léopoldville, sends a telegram to Allen Dulles: "BELIEVE CONGO EXPERIENCING COMMUNIST EFFORT TAKEOVER GOVERNMENT. MANY FORCES AT WORK HERE: SOVIETS, COMMUNIST PARTY, ETC. ALTHOUGH DIFFICULT DETERMINE MAJOR INFLUENCING FACTORS TO PREDICT OUTCOME STRUGGLE FOR POWER, DECISIVE PERIOD NOT FAR OFF. WHETHER OR NOT LUMUMBA ACTUALLY COMMIE OR JUST PLAYING COMMIE GAME TO ASSIST HIS SOLIDIFYING POWER, ANTI-WEST FORCES RAPIDLY INCREASING POWER CONGO AND THERE MAY BE LITTLE TIME LEFT IN WHICH TAKE ACTION."

August 26, 1960. Allen Dulles sends a cable over his own signature (a highly unusual action) to Hedgman in Léopoldville: "IN HIGH QUARTERS HERE IT IS THE CLEAR-CUT CONCLUSION THAT IF LUMUMBA CONTINUES TO HOLD HIGH OFFICE, THE INEVITABLE RESULT WILL AT BEST BE CHAOS AND AT WORST PAVE THE WAY TO COMMUNIST TAKEOVER. . . . CONSEQUENTLY WE CONCLUDE THAT HIS REMOVAL MUST BE AN URGENT AND PRIME OBJECTIVE AND THAT UNDER EXISTING CONDITIONS THIS SHOULD BE A HIGH PRIORITY OF OUR COVERT ACTION."[1]

LUMUMBA WAS NOT THE ONLY TARGET. One of the CIA's plots was to poison Fidel Castro's cigars. Another was to drop a poison pill in his coffee. A third bright idea was to rig an exotic seashell with an explosive device to be placed in Castro's favorite skin-diving area; a fourth was to dust his diving suit with a skin contaminant.

Bissell brought the Mafia in on the plot. He thought the gangsters would be efficient and would keep their mouths shut. It turned out that they blundered every attempt to kill Castro and then sang like canaries, to everyone's embarrassment, especially after it was said that one of the Mafia leaders and John F. Kennedy shared a girl friend.[2]

There is no doubt, in either of these cases, that CIA Director Allen Dulles ordered Castro and Lumumba murdered. Whether he did so with Ike's knowledge, or not, is hotly debated. Whether he did so under Ike's orders, or not, is even more hotly debated. Eisenhower loyalists, and there are many, swear that Ike did not and could not have known about these assassination plots. In their opinion, it is inconceivable that he could have ordered the murders. Yet these same loyalists insist just as firmly, with regard to the U-2 and other CIA programs, that Ike was absolutely in charge, the man in command, and that Allen Dulles would never have dared move without the President's orders.

IN NOVEMBER 1975, the U. S. Senate's Select Committee to Study Governmental Operations With Respect to Intelligence Activities, popularly known as the Church Committee, conducted widely publicized and highly controversial hearings into CIA activities, including the assassination plots against foreign leaders. One of the committee's conclusions was, "The chain of events revealed by the documents and testimony is strong enough to permit a reasonable inference that the plot to assassinate Lumumba was authorized by President Eisenhower."[3]

Two months later, in January 1976, a number of Eisenhower administration insiders, including Gordon Gray, Douglas Dillon, Andrew Goodpaster, and John Eisenhower, challenged this finding. In a statement to the Senate, they requested that the committee "disavow" the finding that President Eisenhower had authorized an assassination. In a reply of February 2, 1976, the committee chairman, Frank Church, and the vice chairman, John

Tower, responded, "After reviewing the evidence in the Lumumba case once again, we remain convinced that the language used in the Committee's findings was warranted."[4]

The committee itself had noted in its original report, however, that "there is enough countervailing testimony . . . and enough ambiguity and lack of clarity in the records of high-level policy meetings to preclude the Committee from making a finding that the President intended an assassination effort against Lumumba." The committee did state directly and clearly that "Allen Dulles authorized an assassination plot." In explanation, it wrote, "Strong expressions of hostility toward Lumumba from the President and his national security assistant, followed immediately by CIA steps in furtherance of an assassination operation against Lumumba, are part of a sequence of events that, at the least, make it appear that Dulles believed assassination was a permissible means of complying with pressure from the President to remove Lumumba from the political scene."[5]

Those close to Ike deny directly and vehemently that the President ever authorized a murder. John Eisenhower, who attended NSC meetings as Assistant White House Staff Secretary, said he had no memory of his father ever ordering an assassination at one of them, as was alleged, and pointed out that "if Ike had something as nasty as this to plot, he wouldn't do it in front of twenty-one people," the number present at NSC meetings.

Goodpaster testified unequivocally to the Church Committee, "At no time and in no way did I ever know of or hear about any proposal, any mention of such an activity. It is my belief that had such a thing been raised with the President other than in my presence, I would have known about it."[6]

In an interview in the Superintendent's office at West Point in 1979, Goodpaster said he recalled some assistant once making a joking reference to bumping off Lumumba. Ike reddened, the sure sign of anger in the man, and said sternly, "That is beyond the pale. We will not discuss such things. Once you start that kind of business, there is no telling where it will end."[7]

Yet Robert H. Johnson, a member of the NSC staff from 1951 to 1962, told the Church Committee, "At some time during that discussion in the NSC, President Eisenhower said something—I can no longer remember his words—that came across to me as an order for the assassination of Lumumba. There was no discussion;

the meeting simply moved on. I remember my sense of that moment quite clearly because the President's statement came as a great shock to me."[8]

At an August 25, 1960, meeting of the 5412 Committee, covert operations against Lumumba were discussed. Gordon Gray, after hearing about attempts to arrange a vote of no confidence against Lumumba in the Congolese Senate, commented that "his associates had expressed extremely strong feelings on the necessity for very straightforward action in this situation."

Gray later admitted that his reference to his "associates" was a euphemism for Ike, employed to preserve "plausible deniability" by the President.

Dulles replied to Gray's comment by saying "he had every intention of proceeding as vigorously as the situation permits or requires but added that he must necessarily put himself in a position of interpreting instructions of this kind within the bounds of necessity and capability."

The minutes of the 5412 meeting concluded, "It was finally agreed that planning for the Congo would not necessarily rule out 'consideration' of any particular kind of activity which might contribute to getting rid of Lumumba."[9]

One of the major functions of 5412, Gordon Gray declared in a 1979 interview, was to "protect the President." In one sense, this meant its task was to carefully scrutinize policies and programs to make sure they did not get the President into trouble. The 5412 Committee also provided a forum for the discussion of operations too sensitive to be discussed before the whole NSC.[10] The committee also provided a perfect device for obscuring the record, making it impossible for the historian to say that this man ordered that action, or otherwise fix responsibility.

The CIA's record, and Ike's, with regard to assassination, is therefore purposely ambiguous. This is true not only with regard to Lumumba but also in the cases of Chou En-lai and Fidel Castro. A review of the whole delicate subject of assassinations and the CIA is thus in order before any conclusions can be attempted.

HOWARD HUNT IS THE SOURCE for the charge that the CIA, in the mid-fifties, had an assassination unit. Hunt said that the unit, which "was set up to arrange for the assassination of suspected double agents and similar low-ranking officials," was under the command of Colonel Boris T. Pash, a U. S. Army officer assigned to the CIA.[11] Pash's title was Chief of Program Branch 7 (PB/7), a "special operations" unit within the Office of Policy Coordination (OPC), the original clandestine services organization that eventually became the Directorate of Plans.

Frank Wisner, director of OPC and thus supervisor of Program Branch 7, said that Pash's PB/7 functions included assassinations and "kidnapping of personages behind the Iron Curtain . . . if they were not in sympathy with the regime, and could be spirited out of the country by our people for their own safety; or kidnapping of people whose interests were inimical to ours." This was, Wisner explained in a memorandum, "a matter of keeping up with the Joneses. Every other power practiced assassination if need be." The written charter of the unit read, "PB/7 will be responsible for assassinations, kidnapping, and such other functions as from time to time may be given it by higher authority."

Hunt told the Church Committee that at one point in 1953 he had a meeting with Pash and his deputy to discuss "wet affairs," i.e., liquidations, with regard to a double-agent who had penetrated the CIA's operation in West Berlin. Hunt said that Pash "seemed a little startled at the subject. He indicated that it was something that would have to be approved by higher authority and I withdrew and never approached Colonel Pash again."[12]

One attempt was almost made, in 1955, but PB/7 was not involved, the target was not a low-ranking double-agent, and Ike knew nothing about it. A station chief in East Asia sent a cable to CIA headquarters outlining a proposed media propaganda campaign. To it he added a plan to assassinate Communist China's number two man, Chou En-lai. Chou was attending a conference of Third World countries at Bandung. The plan was to have an indigenous agent place an undetectable poison in Chou's rice bowl at the Bandung Conference's final banquet. Chou would die two days later, after his return to Peking.[13]

Allen Dulles vetoed the plan. He had CIA headquarters send out a cable that "strongly censured" the station chief for even suggesting assassination and indicating "in the strongest possible language this Agency has never and never will engage in such activities."

The cable added orders to "immediately proceed to burn all copies" of any documents relating to the plan.[14]

FOR THE NEXT FIVE YEARS, the CIA stayed away from any discussion of political assassination. The subject came up again in 1960. Patrice Lumumba was the target. A brief history of developments in the Congo during the fifties is necessary to an understanding of the Lumumba assassination attempts.

The Belgian Congo, a European colony located in central Africa, was governed by the Belgians as if it were the eighteenth century. There was no local government of any kind; not even the 100,000 Belgians employed in the Congo had any political rights. All power resided with the Governor General, who was appointed by the Belgian Government and derived his powers from it. The Belgians made no attempt to prepare the Congo for independence until 1956, when at the urging of the United Nations some local elections were held to choose African advisers to the municipal governments. These elections led to the formation of political parties in the Congo. Joseph Kasavubu, leader of the Bakongo tribe in Léopoldville, formed one party drawn mostly from his tribe. Patrice Lumumba, a post-office clerk, founded another, which, unlike Kasavubu's, tried to attract supporters on a nationwide basis. Moise Tshombe formed a third party in the mineral-rich province of Katanga.

The coming of political parties naturally increased the pressure for independence, as no politician could hope to win votes unless he attacked the Belgians and demanded immediate independence. By the beginning of 1960 the Belgians had come to the conclusion that there was only one way they could keep the goodwill of the Congolese after independence, and thus keep possession of the mines, and that was to grant independence as early as possible and trust that the Congolese would recognize that their total inexperience made it necessary for them to rely on Belgian advisers and managers. Elections were quickly arranged, with independence promised for June 30, 1960. The elections would choose a National Assembly, which would then select a head of state and a prime minister.

Kasavubu and Tshombe urged the Belgians to create a federal state, which was natural as they had mainly local support. Lumumba demanded that the existing unitary state, with a strong central government, be continued. He argued that it was the only way to keep such a huge and disparate country together. The Belgians supported Lumumba, whose party won the most seats in the National Assembly in the ensuing election, although not enough to enable him to form a government. The Belgian Governor General gave both Lumumba and Kasavubu an opportunity to form a government. When both failed, a deal was made whereby Kasavubu became President, while Lumumba became Prime Minister.[15]

In early July, the army—called the Force Publique—mutinied against its Belgian officers. Kasavubu and Lumumba attempted to reason with the soldiers, but abandoned the effort when Belgian paratroopers entered the country for the purpose of protecting Belgian nationals. Lumumba charged that Belgium was preparing to restore colonial rule. On July 11 he appealed to the United Nations for help. That same day Tshombe, premier of Katanga Province, declared the independence of that province from the Congo, with himself as President. Meanwhile the Force Publique, under the nominal command of its sergeants, had been rapidly disintegrating, committing numerous atrocities against both black and white.

Katanga, the richest part of the Congo and thus the area of most concern to the Belgians, settled down under Tshombe's rule. He was discreetly backed by the Belgian mining companies, who paid their taxes to him and not to the central government. The United Nations, meanwhile, responding to Lumumba's plea for help, sent a peace-keeping force to the Congo.

In late July, Lumumba flew to the United States to consult with UN and State Department officials. He made a very bad impression on Under Secretary of State C. Douglas Dillon. "He would never look you in the eye," Dillon reported. "He looked up at the sky. And a tremendous flow of words came out. He spoke in French, and he spoke it very fluently. And his words didn't have any relation to the particular things that we wanted to discuss. You had a feeling that he was a person that was gripped by this fervor that I can only characterize as messianic. . . . He was just not a rational being."

The State Department had hoped that it would be able to work with Lumumba, but those hopes vanished after his meeting with Dillon, who concluded that "this was an individual whom it was impossible to deal with."[16]

Rebuffed, Lumumba returned to the Congo. Unable to obtain

arms and support in the United States, he turned to the Soviet Union. Khrushchev had already been shaking his fist at the West in general and the Belgians in particular, warning them not to attempt to reassert colonial control in the Congo. The Russian leader responded positively to Lumumba's request for military planes.

On August 18, 1960, Dillon reported on developments in the Congo to a meeting of the NSC, at which Ike was present. Both Lumumba and Khrushchev were demanding that the UN peace-keeping force get out of the Congo. Dillon, according to the minutes, said that "the elimination of the U.N. would be a disaster which . . . we should do everything we could to prevent." If the UN were forced out, he warned, the Soviets would come in. The minutes went on, "Secretary Dillon said that Lumumba was working to serve the purposes of the Soviets and Mr. Dulles pointed out that Lumumba was in Soviet pay."[17]

Ike then said it was "simply inconceivable" that the United States could allow the UN to be forced out of the Congo. "We should keep the U.N. in the Congo," the President said, "even if such action was used by the Soviets as the basis for starting a fight." Henry Cabot Lodge, Jr., Ambassador to the UN, said he doubted that the UN force could stay in the Congo if the government of the Congo was determined to kick it out. The President responded, the minutes record, by stating "that Mr. Lodge was wrong to this extent—we were talking of one man forcing us out of the Congo; of Lumumba supported by the Soviets." The Congolese people wanted the UN force there, Ike declared.[18]

THE FIRST DIRECT REFERENCE to assassination as a solution came from Hedgman, the station chief in Léopoldville who had sent the alarmist telegram of August 18. On August 24 he reported that anti-Lumumba leaders in the Congo had approached Kasavubu with a plan to assassinate Lumumba, but Kasavubu had refused to endorse it because he was reluctant to resort to violence and in any case there was no other leader of sufficient stature to replace Lumumba.[19]

The next day, August 25, the 5412 Committee met to discuss CIA plans for political actions against Lumumba. It was at this meeting that Gordon Gray, Ike's personal representative on 5412, reported that the President "had expressed extremely strong feelings on the necessity for very straightforward action in this situation, and he wondered whether the plans as outlined were sufficient to accomplish this." The minutes state that the committee "finally agreed that planning for the Congo would not necessarily rule out 'consideration' of any particular kind of activity which might contribute to getting rid of Lumumba."[20]

The following morning, Allen Dulles sent his own cable to Hedgman in Léopoldville telling him that the "removal" of Lumumba was an "urgent" objective.

Before Hedgman could act, the swirling events inside the Congo intervened. On September 5, President Kasavubu dismissed Lumumba from the government. He evidently was afraid that Lumumba would make the Congo into a Cold War battleground. Lumumba's dismissal should have solved the problem, but Hedgman wired Dulles, "LUMUMBA IN OPPOSITION IS ALMOST AS DANGEROUS AS IN OFFICE."

In response, Dulles told Hedgman that the United States was apprehensive about Lumumba's ability to influence events in the Congo by virtue of his personality, irrespective of his official position. A week later, on September 14, General Joseph Mobutu seized power via a military coup. Lumumba then placed himself in UN custody.

Hedgman thought that by turning to the UN peace-keeping force for protection, Lumumba had strengthened his position (at least he was temporarily safe from Hedgman and the CIA). Hedgman wired Dulles, "ONLY SOLUTION IS REMOVE HIM [Lumumba] FROM SCENE SOONEST."[21]

At this stage Richard Bissell asked a CIA scientist, Joseph Scheider, to make preparations to assassinate or incapacitate an unspecified "African leader." Bissell told Scheider that the assignment had the "highest authority" behind it. Scheider procured toxic biological materials and reported that he was ready.[22]

On September 19, 1960, Bissell cabled Hedgman, telling him to expect a messenger from Washington in the near future. Two days later, at an NSC meeting, Allen Dulles stated that Lumumba "would remain a grave danger as long as he was not yet disposed of." On September 26, Scheider flew to Léopoldville with the lethal substances, which he gave to Hedgman. Scheider told Hedgman that President Eisenhower personally had ordered the assassination of Lumumba.[23]

The substance was never used. Lumumba remained under UN protection until November 27, when he decided to go to Stanleyville to engage in political activity. Hedgman found out about Lumumba's plans and reported them to Mobutu. In addition, he cooperated with Mobutu in setting up roadblocks to help capture Lumumba.

A few days later, Lumumba was captured. Mobutu held him in prison until January 17, 1961, just three days before Ike left office, when he put Lumumba aboard an airplane that took him to Elisabethville in Katanga Province. So many of Lumumba's followers had been butchered at the Elisabethville airport that the place was known as the "slaughterhouse."

At the slaughterhouse, Lumumba was murdered. Eyewitnesses to his appearance as he was dragged off the plane testified later that he might well not have survived the beatings to which he had already been subjected anyway.[24]

So, in the end, the CIA was not directly involved in Lumumba's murder, although it had been in on his capture. That begs the question as to whether Ike ordered the man killed, however, or if Allen Dulles took it upon himself to put out the contract. It is simply one man's word against another's. John Eisenhower pointed out to the Church Committee that assassination was contrary to his father's philosophy that "no man is indispensable," and as noted Andrew Goodpaster was unequivocal in denying that Ike ever gave any order to assassinate anyone, and positive in his belief that he would have known about it had such orders been given.

Gordon Gray, who was present at all the crucial meetings, testified that "I agree that assassination could have been on the minds of some people when they used these words 'eliminate' or 'get rid of.' I am just trying to say it was not seriously considered as a program of action by the President or even the 5412 Committee." Gray also said that "there may well have been in the CIA plans and/or discussions of assassinations, but at the level of 5412 or a higher level than that, the NSC, there was no active discussion in any way planning assassinations."[25]

But to Richard Bissell, who was after all the number two man in the CIA, Dulles' cable to Léopoldville was a clear signal that the President had authorized the CIA to kill Lumumba. At the Church Committee, this exchange occurred:

"Q: Did Mr. Dulles tell you that President Eisenhower wanted Lumumba killed?

Mr. Bissell: I am sure he didn't.

Q: Did he ever tell you even circumlocutiously through this kind of cable?

Mr. Bissell: Yes, I think his cable says it in effect."

Bissell went on to say, "I think it is probably unlikely that Allen Dulles would have said either the President or President Eisenhower even to me. I think he would have said, this is authorized in the highest quarters, and I would have known what he meant."[26]

FIDEL CASTRO WAS THE NEXT CIA TARGET and the object of numerous assassination attempts. Some of the operations against Fidel crossed the border into pure lunacy. A part of the explanation as to how things got so completely out of hand is that the CIA was, by the end of the Eisenhower administration, at the peak of its power, prestige, influence, and cockiness. Another part is that having a Communist regime so close to the States, literally thumbing its nose at Uncle Sam, and this on an island that owed its independence to the United States and that had always had a special relationship with Washington, infuriated American policy-makers. Quite simply, it drove them mad. The result was lunatic actions.

Item: The CIA's Office of Medical Services treated a box of Fidel's favorite cigars with a botulinus toxin so potent that Castro would die the instant he put one in his mouth. The cigars were given to an agent who claimed he could get them into Cuba and into Fidel's hands.[27]

Item: Richard Bissell enlisted the Mafia in a plot to kill Castro. Bissell liked the idea of bringing the Mafia in on it because the gangsters would be highly motivated, having been cut out of their very lucrative gambling operation in Havana. Thus they had "their own reasons for hostility." Further, the Mafia provided "the ultimate cover" because "there was very little chance that anything the syndicate would try to do would be traced back to the CIA." Bissell thought the Mafia was extremely efficient and it had an unquestioned record of successful "hits."

Contacts were made with Johnny Rosselli, who had learned his trade under Al Capone, and Salvatore Giancana (also known as "Sam Gold"), who was on the FBI's list of ten-most-wanted criminals. The CIA wanted a "gangland-style killing" in which Castro would be gunned down. Giancana opposed the idea because it would be difficult to recruit a hit man for such a dangerous operation, and Rosselli said he wanted something "nice and clean, without getting into any kind of out-and-out ambushing." Giancana suggested a poison that would disappear without a trace. The CIA then prepared a botulinus toxin pill that "did the job expected of it" when tested on monkeys. Pills were given to a Cuban for delivery to the island. Obviously, none were ever dropped into Fidel's coffee.[28]

The various CIA plots to destroy Castro's public image were even more ridiculous. One scheme was to spray Castro's broadcasting studio with a chemical similar to LSD, thus undermining his charismatic appeal by sabotaging his speeches. That idea was discarded because the chemical was unreliable. Next the Technical Services Division of the CIA impregnated a box of cigars with a chemical that produced temporary disorientation, hoping to induce Fidel to smoke one of the cigars before delivering a major speech.

Another plan involved a trip out of Cuba that Castro was scheduled to take. The Technical Services Division prepared some thallium salts that could be dusted onto Castro's shoes when he left them outside his hotel room to be shined. The salts were a strong depilatant that would cause Fidel's beard to fall out, thus destroying his *machismo* image.[29]

HOW MUCH IKE KNEW about this nonsense is unclear. Dulles was certainly informed. In December 1959, J. C. King, the former FBI agent who was head of the CIA's Western Hemisphere Division, sent a memorandum to Dulles recommending that "thorough consideration be given to the elimination of Fidel Castro." King said that neither Raúl Castro nor Che Guevara had "the same mesmeric appeal to the masses" and that Fidel's elimination "would greatly accelerate the fall of the present Government." Dulles gave the recommendation his approval.[30]

Whether Dulles told Ike or not is the point at issue. Richard Bissell testified before the Church Committee that he did not inform either the 5412 Committee or President Eisenhower of the Castro assassination operation. Bissell added that to his knowledge, neither did Dulles tell Ike. However, Bissell said he believed that Dulles would have advised the President (but not the 5412 people or the NSC) in a "circumlocutious" or "oblique" way. Bissell admitted that his observation was "pure personal opinion" based on his understanding of Dulles' standard operation procedure in sensitive covert operations. But Bissell also said that Dulles never told him that he had so advised Eisenhower, although he ordinarily did let Bissell know when he had used the "circumlocutious" approach with the President.[31]

Other testimony before the Church Committee strongly denied that the President had any knowledge of a CIA connection with the Mafia or any assassination plots against Castro. Gordon Gray said that he had direct orders from the President to the effect that "all covert actions impinging on the sovereignty of other countries must be deliberated by the Special Group (the 5412 Committee)." Like Bissell, Gray said that the 5412 people never discussed any assassination plans for Castro. "I find it very difficult to believe," Gray testified, "and I do not believe, that Mr. Dulles would have gone independently to President Eisenhower with such a proposition without my knowing about it from Mr. Dulles."[32]

As to the possibility that Ike and Dulles conferred privately about the plot, General Goodpaster—who ordinarily was the first person to see the President in the morning—testified, "That was simply not the President's way of doing business. He had made it very clear to us how he wanted to handle matters of this kind, and we had set up procedures to see that they were then handled that way." SOP was to clear everything with 5412, then get the President's direct approval, as in the U-2 program. Bissell's assumption of a "circumlocutious" personal conversation between Ike and Dulles was to Goodpaster "completely unlikely."[33]

Thomas Parrott, Secretary for the 5412 Committee, said, "I just cannot conceive that President Eisenhower would have gone off and mounted some kind of covert operation on his own. This certainly would not have been consistent with President Eisenhower's staff method of doing business."[34]

John Eisenhower, who was Goodpaster's assistant, testified that his father had confided secret matters to him "to a very large extent." As examples, John said Ike had told him about the atomic bomb a month before Hiroshima. He then said that his father "never told him of any CIA activity involving an assassination plan or attempt concerning Castro and it was his opinion that President Eisenhower would have told him if the President had known about such activity." John also said that his father "did not discuss important subjects circumlocutiously." He added that his father believed "that no leader was indispensable, and thus assassination was not an alternative in the conduct of foreign policy."[35]

Finally, Admiral Arleigh Burke, Chief of Naval Operations, told the Church Committee, "It is my firm conviction, based on five years of close association with President Eisenhower . . . that he would never have tolerated such a discussion, or have permitted anyone to propose assassination, nor would he have ever authorized, condoned, or permitted an assassination attempt."[36]

All of which is strong testimony to Ike's innocence. The fact remains, however, that Dulles did approve at least two assassination plots, and the CIA did do its best to carry them out. It is highly unlikely, almost unbelievable, that Dulles would have done so unless he was certain he was acting in accord with the President's wishes. It may be that Dulles was too zealous or liberal in his interpretation of what the President wanted done. With both Eisenhower and Dulles dead, we will never know.

CHAPTER TWENTY-TWO

Ike and the Bay of Pigs

APRIL 17, 1961. Some two thousand Cuban rebels land at the Bay of Pigs. They are hit immediately by Castro's armed forces. A debacle is in the making. Around the world people want to know who is responsible for this terrible plan.

GENERAL ANDREW GOODPASTER, in Ike's opinion, was not only the best officer in the U. S. Army, but also one of the two or three smartest men in the country.[1] Well over six feet tall, ramrod straight, impeccable in his perfectly pressed uniform, with rugged features, broad shoulders, and a powerful chest, he was graceful in his movements, polite yet firm in his attitude. He was second in the West Point class of 1939 and earned a series of combat medals plus two Purple Hearts in Italy during the war.

Goodpaster's bearing, manner, shock of hair, and good looks reminded some observers of his namesake, another general, Andrew Jackson. When he emerged from retirement in 1977 to take up the duties of Superintendent of the Military Academy, to restore West Point to its full integrity, he reminded other observers of Sylvanus Thayer, the legendary founder of the academy.

Goodpaster was a man who spoke carefully, meaning exactly what he said, saying exactly what was on his mind. Late in 1960, in the Oval Office, Goodpaster expressed concern that the assembling and training of an organization of Cuban refugees, authorized by Eisenhower months earlier, might well be building up a problem with difficult consequences.

Eisenhower had given authority only to form and train the force, reserving any decision whether actually to use it and, if so, how. In his view, it was only a small training base, really not much more than a place to keep an eye on some of the hotheaded Cubans who were so anxious to return to their homeland and overthrow Castro. Goodpaster's fear, however, was that the operation would build up a momentum of its own, which would be hard to stop.

Ike refused to see any danger. He said he was only creating an asset, not committing the United States to an invasion of Cuba or anything like that. Whether this paramilitary force of Cuban exiles, trained by the CIA, would be used or not would depend entirely on circumstances, specifically on political developments. In any event, the decision would be made in the White House, not by the CIA or the Cubans themselves.

THE CUBAN TRAINING PROGRAM had its beginning in December 1959 at the same time that the CIA began its assassination plotting against Fidel. J. C. King wrote a memorandum to Allen Dulles observing that the Castro dictatorship in Cuba was expropriating American property at an alarming rate, and warning that if it were permitted to stay in power, the Castro regime would encourage similar actions against other U.S. holdings in other Latin American countries. He recommended a broad-based program to eliminate Fidel, including assassination and paramilitary activities.[3]

On January 13, 1960, Dulles took King's recommendations to the 5412 Committee. Dulles told the committee that "a quick elimination of Castro" was not contemplated by the CIA, but he also "noted that over the long run the U.S. will not be able to tolerate the Castro regime in Cuba, and suggested that covert contingency planning to accomplish the fall of the Castro government might be in order."

The State Department representative on 5412 commented that "timing was very important." The CIA should not move against Castro until a "solidly based Cuban opposition" was prepared to take over. Dulles then "emphasized that we do not have in mind a quick elimination of Castro, but rather actions designed to enable responsible opposition leaders to get a foothold."[4]

In February, Dulles came to the Oval Office to discuss with Ike possible moves against Castro. The President was sympathetic but hardly enthusiastic. Dulles had brought some U-2 photos of a Cuban sugar refinery, along with plans to put it out of action by using guerrilla saboteurs. Ike scoffed at this, pointing out that such damage could be easily repaired. The CIA had to come up with something better than this. Ike said that Dulles should go back to his people and return when they had a "program" worked out.[5]

The CIA then created a task force, under the direction of Richard Bissell, to take charge of Cuban operations. That group was tempted to try for a quick fix—Castro's assassination—as a solution. J. C. King's attitude, as recorded in a memorandum of a meeting on March 9 with the task force, was "that unless Fidel and Raúl Castro and Che Guevara could be eliminated in one package —which is highly unlikely—this operation can be a long, drawn-out affair and the present government will only be overthrown by the use of force."[6]

The following day, March 10, 1960, the NSC discussed American policy to "bring another government to power in Cuba." The minutes of that meeting record that "the President said we might have another Black Hole of Calcutta in Cuba, and he wondered what we could do about such a situation." Admiral Arleigh Burke, Chief of Naval Operations, said the chief immediate requirement was to find a Cuban leader around whom anti-Castro elements could rally. Dulles reported that the CIA was working on a plan to rid the island of Fidel. Burke suggested that any plan for his removal should be "a package deal, since many of the leaders around Castro were even worse than Castro."[7]

Bissell, meanwhile, had drafted a policy paper, "A Program of Covert Action Against the Castro Regime," and on March 14 brought it to the 5412 Committee. It called for four steps: (1) creation of a "responsible and unified" Cuban government in exile; (2) "a powerful propaganda offensive"; (3) "a covert intelligence and action organization in Cuba" that would be "responsive" to the government in exile, and (4) "a paramilitary force outside of Cuba for future guerrilla action."[8]

The 5412 people were impressed. Although Bissell warned that it would take six to eight months to put his program into action, what he proposed was more solid and helpful than the earlier talk about assassination. The committee did have "a general discussion as to what would be the effect on the Cuban scene if Fidel and Raúl Castro and Che Guevara should disappear simultaneously." Admiral Burke observed that the only organized group in Cuba was the Communist Party, and that if the Castros were eliminated the Communists would move into the vacuum. Dulles thought "this might not be disadvantageous" because it would give the United States and the Organization of American States an opportunity to move in on Cuba in force. J. C. King suggested that nothing be done hastily, as so far no anti-Castro Cuban leader had appeared who was capable of winning popular support.[9]

Three days later, on March 17, Ike approved Bissell's four-point program. The President put his emphasis on Bissell's first step, finding a Cuban leader living in exile (probably in Miami) who would form a government in exile that the United States could recognize.[10]

Through the spring and summer of 1960, Bissell worked on several fronts. As noted in Chapter Twenty-one, various attempts to assassinate Castro were made, possibly without Ike's knowledge, certainly without success. Meanwhile, the flow of anti-Castro Cuban refugees into Miami was becoming a flood. Many of these refugees were eager to return to their homeland and, with American military help, overthrow Fidel. Unfortunately, they bickered among themselves. Some were pro-Batista, most were anti-Batista, all were hot-tempered and hardheaded, few were willing to cooperate or take second place in a government in exile. No genuine leader emerged.

Bissell, meanwhile, began to put step four, the creation of a paramilitary force, into action. If nothing else, it was a way to give the most active refugees a sense of movement, a feeling that something was being done. The original training camp was outside Miami, but it was too public, so Bissell sent the group down to the Panama Canal Zone.

There the CIA trained an initial cadre of thirty Cuban leaders for guerrilla warfare inside Cuba. As Bissell explained in an interview, "The notion was that when a larger group was assembled subsequently for training, that larger group would be trained by Cubans, thus insulating the U.S. from any direct involvement."[11]

By July, it was obvious that the plan was no good. It was based on the concept of a strong guerrilla movement inside Cuba, which "began to appear less and less possible." One reason was that the anti-Castro Cubans never developed a command and control net, a true organized underground. There were virtually no communications between Miami and Cuba. There were resistance groups on the island but, as Bissell explained, "they were so poorly organized and their security practices were so poor that . . . they were rounded up quickly," except in the Escambrey Mountains.

And in the mountains, Bissell said, "what Castro did was to put a cordon of militia around the whole area, using enormous numbers, and in effect he starved these people out. They had to come out to forage, and they were picked up at that time."

The CIA did infiltrate a few small groups of guerrillas onto the north coast of Cuba during the summer, but because there was "no command and control net, no underground, no organization, no way they could be sheltered from informers, it was simply impossible to build up the basis of a resistance movement in the island."[12]

Assassination had failed. Infiltration had failed. Something bigger, something better planned and executed, was clearly necessary. On August 18, 1960, Ike approved an expanded program, with a $13 million budget. He was willing to take more active steps because the CIA had obtained photographs of Czech arms in Cuba.[13]

The same day, Ike approved the use of Department of Defense personnel and equipment in the Cuban operation, although he insisted that "no United States military personnel were to be used in a combat status."[14]

After giving his approval to Bissell's expanded plans, Ike asked again, "Where's our government in exile?" Bissell and Allen Dulles explained that it was difficult to get the Cubans to work together. Ike, impatient, replied, "Boys, if you don't intend to go through with this, let's stop talking about it." Nothing could happen, he insisted, without a popular, genuine government in exile.[15]

As Bissell's operation grew, it had to move to larger quarters. None were available in the Canal Zone, so he made contact with his friends in the Guatemalan Government, whose President, Miguel Ydígoras Fuentes, had helped to overthrow Arbenz seven years earlier. Ydígoras agreed to allow the CIA to establish its training base on Guatemala's Caribbean coast. By October the agency had four hundred guerrillas-in-training at the base.

The whole concept of the operation, meanwhile, had undergone a radical transformation, although neither Ike nor the 5412 people were informed of the change until months later.[16] The original idea had been to rely primarily on the anti-Castro resistance forces already on the island, but by the fall of 1960, Bissell had reluctantly accepted the fact that such a plan was impossible, because there was no resistance force that could be counted on. Bissell's new plan was to land a fairly large, well-equipped, heavily armed force that would secure a beachhead and be able to hold it against Castro's counterattack.[17]

The next stage would be a repeat of the CIA's performance in Guatemala in 1954. That is, the invasion force would hold its position, as Castillo Armas' "army" had sat in the Church of the Black Christ, while CIA airplanes carried out raids on Havana and CIA radio stations bombarded Cuba with propaganda and rumors. Then, as in Guatemala, it was hoped there would be defections by Castro's army and air force, Castro would lose his nerve and flee the island, and the CIA would have another triumph.[18]

As the training went forward, Bissell built his radio station on Swan Island, 110 miles off the coast of Honduras and 400 miles southwest of Cuba. Swan Island, a mile and a half long and half a mile wide, with a population of twenty-eight humans and thousands of lizards and gulls, was claimed by both Honduras and the United States. Bissell put up a fifty-kilowatt radio station which was powerful enough to cover the whole Caribbean area at night. It could also be heard in Miami. To give the appearance of even-handedness, it attacked both Trujillo of the Dominican Republic and Castro.[19]

In the United States, meanwhile, the Cuban operation became an issue in the Kennedy-Nixon presidential contest. Nixon was urging Ike to act: He felt that the overthrow of Castro before Election Day would be "a major plus, a real trump card." But Ike was unwilling to order action before the Cubans had agreed among themselves as to the government that would replace Fidel. The President continued to press Bissell and Dulles about the government in exile; they assured him that progress was being made. Ike was skeptical. "I'm going along with you boys," he said, "but I want to be sure the damned thing works."[20]

Bissell later confessed in an interview that no real progress had been made. "We had to virtually force a kind of alliance among the Cubans," he said. "They never achieved sufficient unity at the political level to make possible the formation of a cohesive, effective

Cuban-manned organization, that could direct the training, much less conduct it, that could plan for operations, that could do any of the logistic planning or support, or that could be entrusted with sensitive Intelligence or anything of this kind. So the impossibility of constructing such a Cuban organization left no alternative, if the operation was to be continued, but to have a U.S. organization [the CIA] that in effect made all the decisions."[21]

Democratic nominee Kennedy, meanwhile, thrust Cuba to the front of the campaign. On October 20 the New York *Times* headline ran, "KENNEDY ASKS AID FOR CUBAN REBELS TO DEFEAT CASTRO. URGES SUPPORT OF EXILES AND 'FIGHTERS FOR FREEDOM.' "[22]

Nixon later wrote that, when he saw the headline, "I could hardly believe my eyes." He checked with Dulles, who said he had informed Kennedy about the training operation in Guatemala and Bissell's plans. Nixon, furious, felt that Kennedy had jeopardized the operation while winning votes from the millions of Americans who wanted Castro toppled and who thought the Republicans too weak to do it. But despite his anger, Nixon believed that "the covert operation had to be protected at all costs." He therefore went to the other extreme, attacking Kennedy's proposal "as wrong and irresponsible because it would violate our treaty commitments."

In his campaign debate with Kennedy the following night, Nixon predicted that if the United States supported the Cuban exiles in a military adventure, it would be "condemned in the United Nations" while failing to "accomplish our objective." It would be "an open invitation for Mr. Khrushchev . . . to come into Latin America."[23] The irony, of course, was that precisely what Nixon predicted would happen—although he never really believed it himself—did happen. The United States did fail, it was condemned, and the Bay of Pigs operation was an invitation for the Russians to move military forces into Cuba, an invitation Khrushchev quickly accepted.

Kennedy, meanwhile, won the closest election in decades. The week after the election was a tense one in Central America. Riots in Guatemala, brought on by the government's decision to allow the CIA to use that country as a base of operations, raised fears in Washington that the Communists might take over there. Ike told

Secretary of State Herter that "if we received a request from Guatemala for assistance, we would move in without delay."[24]

The State Department, meanwhile, always more sensitive to Latin American feelings than the CIA or the White House, was urging the President to order the whole Cuban brigade out of Guatemala. Ike asked Bissell about it. "We thought of moving them by airlift out to one of the islands in the Pacific," Bissell later recalled, "we were so desperate to find a more secure base for them." One solution would have been to bring the Cubans back to southern Florida, but as Bissell said, "There was a reluctance to move them back and to face the fact that since the U.S. was doing the training, it might as well be done in the U.S." It seemed to Bissell that it was important to maintain the fiction that the United States was not involved. He convinced Ike. The brigade stayed in Guatemala.[25]

Its presence there practically invited Castro to send his own paramilitary forces, led by Che, into Guatemala. To guard against that possibility, Ike sent U. S. Navy vessels to the Caribbean to patrol the Guatemalan coast. Anastasio Somoza in Nicaragua was also worried about Che and other Cuban guerrillas invading his country, so Ike extended the patrols to include Nicaragua and added air cover to the sea patrols. The American servicemen were ordered to "refrain from combat unless specifically authorized or unless necessary to bar a direct Communist invasion attempt."[26]

In December, Dulles finally briefed Ike on Bissell's evolving concept of the operation. The new idea called for landing a relatively strong, self-contained force that could seize and hold a beachhead. Ike listened, then asked once again about political progress. Did the Cubans have a recognized leader yet? The President wanted a government in exile formed that would have enough popular support among Cuban exiles to allow him to recognize it as the new government.[27]

The following day, December 8, Dulles told the 5412 Committee of the new concept. By then the brigade was up to seven hundred men and still growing. The committee "encouraged" Dulles to continue "development" of the force. Someone warned that it was becoming common knowledge throughout Latin America that a United States-backed force was being trained in Guatemala.[28]

It was such common knowledge, in fact, that on January 10, 1961, the New York *Times* carried an article, with a map, describing the force, its location, and its purpose. The Eisenhower administration ignored the article.[29]

Ike's attitude toward the brigade remained one of wait and see. Douglas Dillon, Under Secretary of State, who discussed the brigade with the President on a number of occasions, reported that Eisenhower maintained "a certain skepticism until such time as the Cubans' training was completed, and then a willingness to look at it."[30] As always, he insisted on political unity before attempting paramilitary operations. In his memoirs, Ike declared, "Because they had as yet been unable to find the leader they wanted—a national leader known to be both anti-Castro and anti-Batista—it was impossible to make specific plans for a military invasion."[31]

Bissell later reported that "it wasn't until about January 1961 that the force in training reached as many as eight or nine hundred in strength, and of course at that time there had been *no firm decision* that they would be employed."[32]

But, as Goodpaster had suggested to Eisenhower, the momentum was there—and it was unstoppable. As Bissell put it, "It's only fair to say that the Kennedy administration did inherit a military organization here that would have been difficult to dispose of and embarrassing to dispose of in any way other than by allowing it to go into action."[33]

In his retirement, Eisenhower insisted that the distinction between creating an asset and approving a plan remained sharp and clear. He said he never discussed a tactical or operational plan with Bissell, Dulles, or anyone else, because the program had never gotten that far along.[34] And various members of Ike's administration insist to this day that had Eisenhower been in the White House, the Bay of Pigs operation either never would have gone forward or, if it did, there would have been massive American military backup support.

Perhaps so. But there was that momentum, a big part of which was the CIA's intense desire to help the refugees while simultaneously pretending that the United States was not involved. Ike was technically correct in saying he had not given his approval to any specific plan, but only technically. Bissell, Dulles, the State Department, and the incoming Kennedy administration all felt that the plan had General Eisenhower's professional backing.

The Kennedy people felt so because they had it from the best possible source, Ike himself. On January 19, the day before Eisenhower left office, he had an all-morning transition meeting in the Cabinet Room of the White House with the top echelon of the incoming administration. Clark Clifford, Harry Truman's special counsel and later Lyndon Johnson's Secretary of Defense, took notes.

According to Clifford's notes, Eisenhower, with JFK sitting on his left, made it clear that the project was going very well and that it was Kennedy's "responsibility" to do "whatever is necessary" to make it work. Clifford saw no "reluctance or hesitation" on Ike's part. Indeed, five days later Clifford sent a memorandum to President Kennedy reminding him that Ike had said "it was the policy of this government" to help the Cubans "to the utmost" and that this effort should be "continued and accelerated."[35]

The result, as everyone knows, was the disaster of the Bay of Pigs. The momentum Ike had allowed the CIA to build proved irresistible.

CHAPTER TWENTY-THREE

Ike and His Spies

THE LONG BLACK LIMOUSINE pulls up outside the CIA's headquarters building. Sitting in the back seat are the Attorney General of the United States, Robert F. Kennedy, and the Director of Central Intelligence, Allen Dulles. The door opens. Slowly, painfully, Dulles gets out. The limousine drives off.

Dulles' shoulders are slumped. He is very dejècted, deeply depressed. He has just finished another in a series of morning meetings with the committee that is investigating the Bay of Pigs disaster. Created by John Kennedy and chaired by Maxwell Taylor, the committee's real purpose, according to Howard Hunt, is "simply to whitewash the New Frontier and to lay the blame on the CIA." In Hunt's view, Dulles is "being harassed by Bobby Kennedy, harassed by the President, by Dean Rusk, and Bob McNamara."

Back with his own people at CIA headquarters, free for the remainder of the day from the hostility of the New Frontiersmen, Dulles' spirits revive. Turning away from Kennedy's departing limousine, his pace quickens, his step becomes a little lighter.

HUNT RECALLED, "By the time he emerged on the third floor from his private elevator and walked into the office, he would have a cheery grin on his face. He'd be rubbing his arthritic hands together, and would be cheerful and outgoing, giving none of us any reason to believe that he was under strain, that he was depressed about the fate that awaited him, and the very harsh and unwarranted criticism that the agency was being subjected to.

"And he would come into the mess for lunch (we would be already inside and seated) and give a shoulder-pounding to somebody, and shake hands here and there, and take his place at the head of the table and begin commenting on the World Series game the day before, ask for news of one thing or another. Very little business—mostly on events in the outside world. He was a pretty avid sports fan, so that is what he chatted about."[1]

ALLEN DULLES became the scapegoat for the Bay of Pigs. President Kennedy accepted his resignation. After that, his health failed rapidly. Within a few months he had a stroke.

More bad news followed. Dulles' son had been living with him in Washington. The boy had been a brilliant student at Princeton but had suffered a grievous wound in the Korean War, where he served in the Marine Corps. A Chinese bullet had blown away a good portion of his head. Dulles' son's condition naturally preyed on his mind. The burden became intolerable when the boy became extremely violent. Dulles had to have him taken off to a sanitarium in Switzerland.

As Hunt summed up, "The last years of Allen Dulles' life were very sad and unrewarding ones, although he and his wife maintained their beautiful Georgetown home in their customary style, with gracious hospitality. But he was at the end, a very tragic, sad, and unfulfilled figure of a man."[2]

HE HAD BEEN IKE'S CHIEF SPY FOR EIGHT YEARS. More than any other individual, he had shaped and molded the CIA. For better or for worse, it was his agency. He gave it a sense of importance and a sense of mission. The CIA under Allen Dulles fought on the front lines of the Cold War, its purpose nothing less than to save the world from the Communists. Morale was consistently high inside the agency, as was its reputation on the outside.

Two decades later, former agents looked back on the fifties with strong feelings of nostalgia. Gone were the greats—Frank Wisner, Richard Bissell, Tracey Barnes—and Allen Dulles. Nearly to a man, veterans felt that never again did the CIA have a leader to match Dulles. His motives were pure, his loyalty to his subordinates complete, his cause inspiring, his methods brilliant—or so at least it seemed to the ex-agents, in retrospect.

To the outside world, he seemed more difficult to assess. To some commentators, he appeared to be a rather bumbling imitation of the British master spy, a man who used the twist of a knife here, or a well-staged riot there, to gain and hold an empire. A somewhat contrary view regarded Allen Dulles as the evil genius who was at the center of the capitalist conspiracy to rule the world for the benefit of American corporations, the epitome of the immoral imperialist. Others saw him as a man who could be relied upon to protect American interests around the world, by whatever means were necessary.

Dulles was a leader who made some mistakes, enjoyed many triumphs. Nothing says more about Ike's view of Dulles than the fact that the President kept him on the job for eight years, a job that was crucial to the success of the Eisenhower administration, and a job that was clearly the most sensitive in the government. Ike decided he would rather have Allen Dulles as his chief spy, even with his limitations, than anyone else he knew. By itself, that was a powerful endorsement and recommendation.

INTERVIEWING IKE ABOUT HIS SPIES in his Gettysburg office, when he was in his mid-seventies, it was obvious that he enjoyed dwelling on the war years more than on the years with the CIA. Like many old men, he could remember events of thirty years past more vivdly than those of ten years past. When thinking about the war, he would grin and laugh as he recalled how the Allies won a victory, grimace and redden as he remembered something that had gone wrong.

Talking about Operation FORTITUDE, he would point out where Patton had created a dummy tank corps, or how the strategic bombing pattern convinced the Germans that the Allies would land at the Pas de Calais rather than Normandy. In the middle of discussing one or another of the myriad of elements that went into FORTITUDE, he would look skyward, frown, then smile, turn toward me with that wonderful grin, slap his hand down on his thigh, and exclaim, "By God, we really fooled them, didn't we!"

And he would laugh that big gusty Eisenhower laugh, and still get a kick out of remembering it, after all those years and all those rememberings. "By God, we really fooled them, didn't we!" You would have thought he was Tom Sawyer, pulling off a fast one on Aunt Polly.

And indeed Ike's spies did fool the Germans, generally throughout the war but especially so in the crucial OVERLORD battle. Make no mistake about it. OVERLORD was no sure thing. It was about as even a battle, taking all things into consideration, as ever happens. Either side could have won, without the victory being a fluke or the result of some piece of sheer luck. If intelligence and subterfuge did not win the war for the Allies, as might be argued, it is clear that without the edge in intelligence and subterfuge that they achieved and maintained, the Allies might not have won the war.

"WE REALLY FOOLED THEM." With Ike, the emphasis was always on the "we," even though he of all men in the Allied world had the right to claim, "I really fooled them." Partly that "we" was due to native modesty, but mainly it was a recognition of fact. Ike headed a team. He was not a professional intelligence officer, never had been. But through the war he learned how to command an intelligence effort, as he progressed from Robert Murphy and Mark Clark to Mockler-Ferryman and finally to Kenneth Strong.

Strong and his people let their boss down only once, at the Bulge. Otherwise, SHAEF G-2 compiled an enviable record. Strong could brag, with justice, that he knew the German order of battle better than the German High Command did from mid-August to the end of the war (even in December 1944), which was a feat unmatched by any other intelligence operation in this or any other war.

The "we" who helped fool them included all those nameless people associated with Bletchley Park and ULTRA. Churchill said of the RAF pilots in the Battle of Britain that never had so many owed so much to so few. It could be said with equal or more truth of the men and women of BP. Without them, the war could not have been won, or at least as quickly as it was.

Another part of the "we" was the French Resistance, which Ike guided and steered primarily through his adroit handling of General de Gaulle, partly through his judicious distribution of arms and supplies to the Maquis. The Resistance not only helped fool the Germans, it also delayed by force of arms the passage of major

German divisions to the Normandy battlefield, which was always the aim of FORTITUDE—delay the German reinforcements.

Success in FORTITUDE owed much to General Patton and his acting abilities. He made the wholly fictional FUSAG seem real. was helped by stagehands who could create, out of nothing but cardboard and plywood and some glue and nails, oil depots and tank divisions and barracks and whatever else one might want. He was also aided by those overage British and American officers, spread about Scotland and the east coast, constantly signaling to each other on the radio to hurry up with the ski bindings or get ready for General Patton's inspection or send more maps of the Pas de Calais coastline. A boring task, but one of those dull jobs that, had there been one slipup over the radio, could have led to disaster.

There could have been no FORTITUDE without the British Secret Service and the Double-Cross System. Garbo's message of June 5, warning his German controller that OVERLORD was coming, and his message of June 9, in which he argued that the real invasion would come later at the Pas de Calais, may have been the two most important messages of the war.

Obviously, Ike had no personal contact with Garbo or Brutus or any of the other turned spies, or with the radio officers in Scotland, or with the people of BP, although he commended them all.

But he was grateful to them all, just as he was to those who were intimately involved with SHAEF, or those he saw on a daily or weekly basis—such men as Bedell Smith and Kenneth Strong and Omar Bradley, and of course Monty.

Of all those who were part of the "we," Winston Churchill surely stood tall. He had cooperated handsomely on the Diplomatic Ban, with such distasteful tasks as moving British citizens out of their homes, and in countless other ways, but his real contribution was the unfailing support he gave to BP, to the Double-Cross System, and to all the other ranks in the Battle of Wits.

OVERLORD pitted the best Germany had to offer against the best the United States and the United Kingdom had to offer. It was Churchill and Roosevelt vs. Hitler, Eisenhower vs. Rundstedt, Bradley vs. Rommel, American sergeants and British privates vs. their German counterparts. In a sense, OVERLORD pitted the German educational system against the democratic educational system.

The Allies won. They won most of all because of the success of FORTITUDE and OVERLORD, which in turn depended on a culture, a political system, a tradition, a belief, an understanding of what democracy is and what it means. That kind of understanding and commitment come only when the threat to democracy is real and perceived, but when it does come, it is an awesome thing.

FORTITUDE required trust among the participants, up and down the line, a kind of trust that simply did not exist in Nazi Germany. Nearly every general in the Wehrmacht knew of the various plots to kill Hitler, while dozens of the generals were actively involved. Not a single one of them went to Hitler with the information. Such a situation in the Allied world is unimaginable.

People who do not trust each other, or believe in the cause they are fighting for, cannot equal the effort made by the people in Bletchley Park, at Strong's G-2, among the French Resistance and the British Secret Service, and throughout Ike's command.

FORTITUDE and OVERLORD were triumphs for Western democracy. I think that is what Ike had in his mind when he would grin that wonderful grin and slap his thigh and exclaim, "By God, we really fooled them, didn't we!"

If such a test of Western democracy ever comes again, it is that spirit that we can and will draw upon to defend ourselves.

NOTES

CHAPTER ONE

1. The whole secret war is magnificently described in R. V. Jones, *The Wizard War*.
2. Ibid., p. 215.
3. Anthony Cave Brown, *Bodyguard of Lies*, and Ronald Lewin, *Ultra Goes to War: The Secret Story*, are basic sources on ULTRA.
4. Brown, *Bodyguard*, p. 22.
5. Lewin, *Ultra*, p. 248.
6. Interview with Filby.
7. Jones, *Wizard War*, pp. 139, 204.
8. Lewin, *Ultra*, p. 281.
9. Adolph G. Rosengarten, Jr., "With Ultra from Omaha Beach to Weimar, Germany—a Personal View," *Military Affairs*, vol. XLII (October 1978), p. 129.
10. Patrick Beesly, *Very Special Intelligence: The Story of the Admiralty's Intelligence Centre, 1939–1945*, p. 69.
11. F. W. Winterbotham, *The Ultra Secret*, p. 135.
12. Lewin, *Ultra*, p. 19.

CHAPTER TWO

1. Alfred D. Chandler, ed., *The Papers of Dwight D. Eisenhower: The War Years*, p. 545. Hereinafter cited as Eisenhower Papers.
2. Robert Murphy, *Diplomat Among Warriors*, pp. 102–3; Harry Butcher, *My Three Years with Eisenhower*, pp. 105–10; Stephen E. Ambrose, *The Supreme Commander: The War Years of Dwight D. Eisenhower*, pp. 98–99; Dwight D. Eisenhower, *Crusade in Europe*, pp. 86–87; Arthur Funk, *The Politics of Torch*, pp. 106–9.
3. Eisenhower Papers, pp. 253–54.
4. Anthony Cave Brown, ed., *The Secret War Report of the OSS*, pp. 42–62.
5. Butcher, *My Three Years*, pp. 98–99.
6. Eisenhower Papers, p. 448.
7. Eisenhower Papers, pp. 562–63; Funk, *Politics of Torch*, p. 107; Murphy, *Diplomat Among Warriors*, p. 106.

8. Eisenhower Papers, p. 699.
9. Butcher, *My Three Years*, p. 106.
10. Ray Cline, *Secrets, Spies and Soldiers*, pp. 44–45.
11. Funk, *Politics of Torch*, p. 18.
12. Brown, *Secret War Report of the OSS*, p. 135.
13. Murphy, *Diplomat Among Warriors*, p. 117.
14. The oss reports on Dubreuil are in a Military Attaché Report of July 13, 1944, from Madrid, Record Group No. 3020, in Modern Military Records, National Archives; and in report No. MFT 3.3., June 19, 1944, Record Group No. 3700, in ibid., and in Richard Harris Smith, *OSS: The Secret History of America's First Central Intelligence Agency*, p. 40; see also Murphy, *Diplomat Among Warriors*, p. 116.
15. Funk, *Politics of Torch*, p. 89; Smith, *OSS*, p. 51.
16. Smith, *OSS*, pp. 42–43; Murphy, *Diplomat Among Warriors*, p. 92.
17. Smith, *OSS*, pp. 43–44.
18. Eisenhower Papers, pp. 469–71.
19. Brown, *Secret War Report of the OSS*, p. 134.
20. Ibid., pp. 140–42.
21. Smith, *OSS*, p. 57.
22. Eisenhower Papers, p. 590.
23. Butcher, *My Three Years*, pp. 106–7.
24. Funk, *Politics of Torch*, pp. 106–7; Murphy, *Diplomat Among Warriors*, p. 104; Butcher, *My Three Years*, pp. 108–9.
25. The document is in Record Group No. 226, OSS, Entry 5, cables, Modern Military Records, National Archives.
26. Winston Churchill, *The Hinge of Fate*, p. 630.
27. Funk, *Politics of Torch*, p. 21.
28. Butcher, *My Three Years*, p. 110; Murphy, *Diplomat Among Warriors*, p. 105; Ambrose, *The Supreme Commander*, pp. 100–1.
29. Eisenhower Papers, p. 567.

CHAPTER THREE

1. Mark Clark, *Calculated Risk*, p. 66.
2. Arthur Funk, *The Politics of Torch*, pp. 133–34; Robert Murphy, *Diplomat Among Warriors*, p. 118; Harry Butcher, *My Three Years with Eisenhower*, pp. 144–47; Clark, *Calculated Risk*, p. 67; Stephen E. Ambrose, *The Supreme Commander: The War Years of Dwight D. Eisenhower*, pp. 105–6; Smith, *OSS: The Secret History of America's First Central Intelligence Agency*, p. 58.
3. Interview with Eisenhower, October 7, 1965; Clark, *Calculated Risk*, pp. 67–68.
4. Clark, *Calculated Risk*, pp. 71–72.
5. Ambrose, *Supreme Commander*, p. 106.
6. Butcher, *My Three Years*, pp. 147–54.
7. Ibid., pp. 152–57; Clark, *Calculated Risk*, pp. 73–89.
8. Clark, *Calculated Risk*, p. 90.
9. Dwight D. Eisenhower, *Crusade in Europe*, p. 88.
10. The best discussion is in Funk, *Politics of Torch*, pp. 149–59.
11. Murphy, *Diplomat Among Warriors*, p. 120.
12. Ibid., pp. 120–21.

13. Eisenhower Papers, p. 666.
14. Eisenhower Papers, pp. 668–69; Ambrose, *Supreme Commander*, pp. 113–15.
15. Brown, *Secret History of the OSS*, pp. 143–45.
16. Ronald Lewin, *Ultra Goes to War: The Secret Story*, p. 244.
17. Eisenhower Papers, p. 606.
18. Ambrose, *Supreme Commander*, p. 117.

CHAPTER FOUR

1. Eisenhower Papers, p. 677.
2. Eisenhower Papers, p. 680.
3. Eisenhower Papers, p. 693.
4. Stephen E. Ambrose, *The Supreme Commander: The War Years of Dwight D. Eisenhower*, pp. 116–17.
5. Details are available in a secret OSS Report, M.I.9 (R.P.S.), 1218, January 20, 1943, in Modern Military Branch, National Archives.
6. Harry Butcher's diary, November 8, 1942, in Eisenhower Manuscripts, Abilene, Kansas.
7. Eisenhower Papers, pp. 686–88.
8. Eisenhower Papers, p. 699.
9. Butcher's diary, November 13, 1942.
10. Ambrose, *Supreme Commander*, p. 123.
11. Arthur Funk, *The Politics of Torch*, p. 255.
12. Eisenhower Papers, p. 711.
13. Funk, *Politics of Torch*, p. 252.
14. Eisenhower Papers, p. 707.
15. For a typical text, see RG 226, Records of the OSS, ⚡28564, November 11, 1942, Modern Military Records, National Archives.
16. Ambrose, *Supreme Commander*, pp. 130–32.
17. Interview with Milton Stover Eisenhower.
18. Ibid.
19. Ibid.
20. Robert Murphy, *Diplomat Among Warriors*, pp. 150–51.
21. Ambrose, *Supreme Commander*, p. 134.
22. Eisenhower Papers, p. 1,048.
23. Harold Macmillan, *The Blast of War*, p. 174.
24. Murphy, *Diplomat Among Warriors*, p. 143.
25. Richard Harris Smith, *OSS: The Secret History of America's First Central Intelligence Agency*, p. 64.
26. Ibid., pp. 62–65.
27. Rosfelder's remarkable story is in an obscure memo publication called *Today in France* (No. 99, January 1972), the newsletter of the Society of French-American Affairs in New York City. I want to thank Dr. Arthur Funk for bringing this document to my attention.
28. New York *Times*, December 26, 27, and 28, 1942.
29. Butcher's diary, December 26, 1942.
30. Ibid.
31. M. R. D. Foot to author, February 26, 1979; author's possession.
32. Ambrose, *Supreme Commander*, p. 148; *Newsweek*, January 4, 1943.
33. *Today in France*, No. 99, January–February 1972.

34. *Newsweek,* January 4, 1943.
35. New York *Times,* December 26, 1942.
36. Smith, *OSS,* p. 64.
37. Eisenhower Papers, p. 869; Arthur Funk, *Charles de Gaulle—The Crucial Years,* pp. 61–62.
38. Eisenhower Papers, p. 870.
39. Smith, *OSS,* p. 65.
40. London *Times,* December 30 and 31, 1942, and January 1, 1943; evidently the *Times* did not have a man in Algiers, for it took its stories from Charles Collingwood's radio broadcasts.
41. See document XL 6203, Record Group 226, Records of the OSS, Modern Military Branch, National Archives.
42. Smith, *OSS,* pp. 65–66.
43. Letter, Collingwood to author, September 13, 1978, author's possession.
44. Peter Tompkins, *The Murder of Admiral Darlan: A Study in Conspiracy,* pp. 270–71.
45. Ibid.
46. The full message is in U. S. Dept. of State, *Foreign Relations of the U.S., Diplomatic Papers,* 1943, 6 vols., Washington, 1963–65, vol. II, *Europe,* pp. 23–24.
47. XL 923, Record Group 226, Records of the OSS, June 19, 1944, in Modern Military Branch, National Archives.
48. Ibid.
49. Tompkins, *Murder of Darlan,* pp. 270–71.
50. Murphy, *Diplomat Among Warriors,* p. 143.
51. Tompkins, *Murder of Darlan,* p. 272.
52. Clark, *Calculated Risk,* p. 130.
53. Butcher's diary, January 4, 1943.

CHAPTER FIVE

1. Martin Blumenson, *Kasserine Pass,* pp. 1–71; Stephen E. Ambrose, *The Supreme Commander: The War Years of Dwight D. Eisenhower,* pp. 167–69.
2. Dwight D. Eisenhower, *Crusade in Europe,* pp. 141–47.
3. Blumenson, *Kasserine,* pp. 94–95; Eisenhower, *Crusade,* p. 142.
4. Ambrose, *Supreme Commander,* p. 170.
5. Blumenson, *Kasserine,* p. 163.
6. Ambrose, *Supreme Commander,* p. 171.
7. Eisenhower Papers, p. 969. After this book had gone to the galley proof stage, Michael Foot informed me that it was all a cover. Mockler-Ferryman had correctly picked up from Ultra the impending attack, but the American corps commander would not listen. Ike fired the American general. To give balance for the sake of Anglo-American relations, he also "fired" the Mock, sending the message to Marshall, quoted above in a low-level cipher in the hope the Germans would pick it up. According to the cover story, the Mock returned to London in disgrace, where he took up work with the Boy Scouts. In fact, he became head of the Special Operations Executive (SOE) that ran the French Resistance.
8. Eisenhower Papers, p. 971.

9. Harry Butcher's diary, February 20, 1943; see also Ronald Lewin, *Ultra Goes to War: The Secret Story*, pp. 273–74.
10. Harold Deutsch, "The Influence of Ultra on World War II," in *Parameters: Journal of the U. S. Army War College*, Vol. VIII (December 1978), p. 6.
11. Eisenhower Papers, p. 1,034.
12. Butcher's diary, February 20, 1943.
13. Eisenhower Papers, p. 1,014.
14. Ronald Lewin, *Ultra Goes to War*, pp. 311, 370.
15. Ibid., p. 280.
16. F. W. Winterbotham, *The Ultra Secret*, p. 158.
17. Eisenhower Papers, p. 1,249.
18. Eisenhower Papers, pp. 1,253–54.
19. Lewin, *Ultra Goes to War*, p. 281; letter, Gavin to author, March 26, 1979. Gavin admitted that only British six-pounders would have done the job, and they were not readily available.
20. Lewin, *Ultra Goes to War*, pp. 248–49.
21. Marshall's letter to Eisenhower of March 15, 1944, is in Modern Military Records, National Archives.
22. Lewin, *Ultra Goes to War*, p. 250.
23. Adolph G. Rosengarten, Jr., "With Ultra from Omaha Beach to Weimar, Germany—A Personal View," in *Military Affairs*, vol. XLII (October 1978), p. 131.
24. "Synthesis of Experiences in the Use of Ultra Intelligence by U. S. Army Field Commands in the European Theater of Operations," Record Group 457, Modern Military Records, National Archives.
25. Ibid.
26. Lewin, *Ultra Goes to War*, p. 262.
27. Anthony Cave Brown, ed., *The Secret War Report of the OSS*, pp. 189–90.
28. Ibid., pp. 190–91; Richard Harris Smith, *OSS: The Secret History of America's First Central Intelligence Agency*, p. 86.
29. Smith, *OSS*, p. 105.
30. Ibid., p. 86; Brown, ed., *Secret War Report of OSS*, p. 191.
31. Brown, ed., *Secret War Report of OSS*, pp. 192–93.
32. Smith, *OSS*, pp. 88–89.
33. Winterbotham, *The Ultra Secret*, pp. 164–65; Lewin, *Ultra Goes to War*, p. 281.
34. Ambrose, *Supreme Commander*, pp. 270–71.
35. Lewin, *Ultra Goes to War*, p. 283.
36. Ibid., pp. 285–86; Deutsch, "The Influence of Ultra . . . ," p. 9.

CHAPTER SIX

1. Eisenhower Papers, p. 1,673.
2. Anthony Cave Brown, *Bodyguard of Lies*, p. 426.
3. Eisenhower Papers, p. 1,656; Dwight D. Eisenhower, *At Ease: Stories I Tell to Friends*, p. 269.
4. Brown, *Bodyguard of Lies*, p. 409.
5. J. C. Masterman, *The Double-Cross System in the War of 1939–1945*, p. xiv.

6. Ibid., p. 145.
7. Earl Ziemke, "Operation Kreml: Deception, Strategy, and the Fortunes of War," *Parameters; Journal of the U. S. Army War College,* Vol. IX (March 1979), pp. 72–81.
8. Harry Butcher's diary, May 12, 1944; Eisenhower to Swede Hazlett, January 23, 1956, Dwight D. Eisenhower, Papers as President, 1953–1961 (Whitman File), Diary Series, "1956, Misc. (2)," Eisenhower Library, Abilene, Kansas. (Hereafter cited as Dwight D. Eisenhower Library).
9. Brown, *Bodyguard of Lies,* p. 436.
10. David Kahn, *Hitler's Spies: German Military Intelligence in World War II,* pp. 488–89.
11. Brown, *Bodyguard of Lies,* p. 464.
12. Ibid., p. 465.
13. Ibid., pp. 466–67; Masterman, *Double-Cross,* pp. 150–56.
14. Brown, *Bodyguard of Lies,* p. 472; Ronald Lewin, *Ultra Goes to War,* p. 333.
15. Masterman, *Double-Cross,* p. 146.
16. Eisenhower to Marshall, September 20, 1943, Eisenhower Papers, p. 1,439.
17. Eisenhower Papers, p. 1,840; Stephen E. Ambrose, *The Supreme Commander: The War Years of Dwight D. Eisenhower,* pp. 343–45.
18. Butcher's diary, June 12, 1943.
19. Eisenhower Papers, p. 1,853; Forrest C. Pogue, *The Supreme Command,* Appendix A, "SHAEF and the Press."
20. Sir Kenneth Strong, *Intelligence at the Top: The Recollections of an Intelligence Officer,* p. 118.
21. Ibid., p. 182.
22. Masterman, *Double-Cross,* p. 156.
23. Kahn, *Hitler's Spies,* p. 496.
24. G-2 Estimate of the Enemy Build Up Against OVERLORD, May 5, 1944, SHAEF SGS 350.09/3, Record Group 331, Modern Military Records, National Archives.
25. Ibid. See also German Appreciation of Allied Intentions Regarding OVERLORD, May 29, 1944, SHAEF SGS 350.09/2, Record Group 331, Modern Military Records, National Archives.
26. Ibid.
27. Eisenhower Papers, p. 1,746.
28. Eisenhower Papers, p. 1,761–62; Ambrose, *Supreme Commander,* p. 402.
29. Eisenhower Papers, p. 1,814; Ambrose, *Supreme Commander,* pp. 401–2; Kahn, *Hitler's Spies,* p. 507.
30. Ambrose, *Supreme Commander,* p. 403.
31. Ibid., p. 404; Brown, *Bodyguard of Lies,* pp. 532–33.
32. Ambrose, *Supreme Commander,* p. 403.
33. Brown, *Bodyguard of Lies,* pp. 540–41.
34. Leslie Groves, *Now It Can Be Told—The Story of the Manhattan Project,* pp. 199–206; Eisenhower Papers, pp. 1,859–60.
35. Dwight D. Eisenhower, *Crusade in Europe,* p. 249.
36. Kahn, *Hitler's Spies,* p. 615.
37. Eisenhower Papers, pp. 1,894–95.

CHAPTER SEVEN

1. J. M. Stagg, *Forecast for Overlord*, p. 67.
2. David Kahn, *Hitler's Spies: German Military Intelligence in World War II*, p. 514; J. C. Masterman, *The Double-Cross System in the War of 1939–1945*, pp. 156–57.
3. Walter Warlimont, *Inside Hitler's Headquarters*, p. 422; Anthony Cave Brown, *Bodyguard of Lies*, p. 639.
4. Masterman, *Double-Cross*, pp. 156–57; Kahn, *Hitler's Spies*, pp. 515–16.
5. Ronald Lewin, *Ultra Goes to War*, p. 317; Masterman, *Double-Cross*, p. 157; Kahn, *Hitler's Spies*, p. 515.
6. Masterman, *Double-Cross*, pp. 160–61.
7. These summaries are all in SHAEF SGS 350.09/2, Record Group 331, Modern Military Records, National Archives.
8. Masterman, *Double-Cross*, pp. 158–59.
9. Ibid., p. 163.
10. Richard Harris Smith, *OSS: The Secret History of America's First Central Intelligence Agency*, p. 163.
11. Anthony Cave Brown, ed., *The Secret War Report of the OSS*, p. 399.
12. Eisenhower Papers, pp. 1,927, 1,932.
13. Brown, ed., *Secret War Report of OSS*, p. 403; Smith, *OSS*, p. 175.
14. Smith, *OSS*, p. 179.
15. Eisenhower Papers, pp. 1,771, 1,852, 1,857.
16. M. R. D. Foot, *SOE in France: An Account of the Work of the British Special Operations in France*, p. 350.
17. Brown, *Bodyguard*, p. 567; Brown, ed., *Secret War Report of OSS*, p. 391.
18. "AFHQ History of Special Operations," MTO 1942–45, in Modern Military Records, National Archives.
19. Foot, *SOE*, p. 389.
20. Ibid., p. 398.
21. Brown, ed., *Secret War Report of OSS*, p. 459.
22. Foot, *SOE*, p. 399.
23. Brown, ed., *Secret War Report of OSS*, p. 453.
24. *Report by the Supreme Commander to the CCS on Operations in Europe of the Allied Expeditionary Force* (London, 1946), pp. 52–53.
25. Eisenhower Papers, pp. 1,926, 1,932.
26. Forrest C. Pogue, *The Supreme Command*, pp. 236–37.
27. Quoted in Foot, *SOE*, pp. 441–42. Foot adds, "It is impossible to overlook the contrast [with Montgomery]. Resistance is barely mentioned in either of the volumes in which Montgomery recounts the triumphs that, but for resistance, would not have been so easily won."
28. Wainwright interview.
29. Ibid.

CHAPTER EIGHT

1. Stephen E. Ambrose, *The Supreme Commander: The War Years of Dwight D. Eisenhower*, pp. 459–60.
2. F. W. Winterbotham, *The Ultra Secret*, p. 200.

3. Ibid., p. 199.
4. Ambrose, *Supreme Commander,* p. 466.
5. Interview with Eisenhower.
6. Martin Blumenson, *Breakout and Pursuit,* p. 460.
7. Ronald Lewin, *Ultra Goes to War,* p. 337.
8. Winterbotham, *The Ultra Secret,* p. 215.
9. Arthur W. Tedder, *With Prejudice: The War Memoirs of Marshall of the Air Force, Lord Tedder,* p. 575; Omar N. Bradley, *A Soldier's Story,* pp. 369–72; Eisenhower Papers, pp. 2,059–60.
10. Blumenson, *Breakout and Pursuit,* p. 461.
11. Ibid., pp. 462–63.
12. Lewin, *Ultra Goes to War,* p. 339.
13. Blumenson, *Breakout and Pursuit,* p. 464.
14. Winterbotham, *The Ultra Secret,* p. 220.
15. Blumenson, *Breakout and Pursuit,* p. 464.
16. Ibid., p. 465.
17. Ibid., p. 474; Winterbotham, *The Ultra Secret,* p. 227, writes, "It had been an epic story. The ULTRA signals between Hitler and von Kluge which led up to the Battle of Falaise and the destruction of a large part of the German Army in the West were probably ULTRA's greatest triumph."
18. Harry Butcher's diary, August 5, 1944.
19. Winterbotham, *The Ultra Secret,* p. 221; Blumenson, *Breakout and Pursuit,* p. 481. In Montgomery's defense, it should be noted that a heavy air bombardment preceded the Canadian attack and it would have been difficult to reschedule the participation of the bombers. Difficult, but not impossible.
20. Ambrose, *Supreme Commander,* pp. 473–75.
21. Blumenson, *Breakout and Pursuit,* p. 491.
22. Eisenhower Papers, p. 2,060.
23. Butcher's diary, August 16, 1944; Ambrose, *Supreme Commander,* p. 477.
24. Ambrose, *Supreme Commander,* pp. 476–77.
25. Lewin, *Ultra Goes to War,* p. 345.
26. Blumenson, *Breakout and Pursuit,* p. 558.
27. U. S. Military Academy, Department of Military Art and Engineering, *West Point Atlas of American Wars,* vol. II, map 55.
28. Adolph G. Rosengarten, Jr., "With Ultra from Omaha Beach to Weimar, Germany—A Personal View," in *Military Affairs,* vol. XLII (October 1978), p. 129.

CHAPTER NINE

1. Sir Kenneth Strong, *Intelligence at the Top: The Recollections of an Intelligence Officer,* p. 112.
2. Stephen E. Ambrose, *The Supreme Commander: The War Years of Dwight D. Eisenhower,* p. 339.
3. Strong, *Intelligence,* p. 176.
4. Ibid., p. 116.
5. Eisenhower Papers, p. 944; interview with Eisenhower.
6. Strong, *Intelligence,* p. 117.

7. Strong, *Intelligence*, p. 176.
8. Ibid., p. 114.
9. Interview with Eisenhower.
10. Strong, *Intelligence*, p. 135.
11. Ibid., p. 230.
12. Omar N. Bradley, *A Soldier's Story*, p. 416.
13. Ambrose, *Supreme Commander*, p. 518.
14. Ronald Lewin, *Ultra Goes to War*, p. 347.
15. Ibid., p. 348.
16. Interview with Strong; Cornelius Ryan, *A Bridge Too Far*, p. 104.
17. Ryan, *Bridge Too Far*, p. 105.
18. Ibid., p. 131.
19. Ibid., p. 130; Strong, *Intelligence*, p. 202.
20. Interview with Eisenhower.
21. Ryan, *Bridge Too Far*, p. 130.
22. Ibid., pp. 130–31.
23. Ibid., p. 517.
24. Strong to author, March 19, 1979.
25. Strong, *Intelligence*, p. 202.

CHAPTER TEN

1. This account of German preparations for the Bulge is based on Peter Elstob, *Hitler's Last Offensive*, pp. 46–50, and John S. D. Eisenhower, *The Bitter Woods*, and Ronald Lewin, *Ultra Goes to War*, pp. 355–57.
2. Harry Butcher's diary, December 16, 1944.
3. Eisenhower Papers, p. 2,350.
4. Adolph G. Rosengarten, Jr., "With Ultra . . . ," *Military Affairs* vol. XLII (October 1978), p. 130.
5. Ibid., p. 129.
6. Strong to author, March 19, 1979.
7. Eisenhower Papers, p. 2,329.
8. Eisenhower Papers, p. 2,335.
9. Rosengarten, "With Ultra," p. 132.
10. Stephen E. Ambrose, *The Supreme Commander: The War Years of Dwight D. Eisenhower*, p. 554; Forrest C. Pogue, *The Supreme Command*, pp. 361–65.
11. Pogue, *Supreme Command*, pp. 361–65.
12. Rosengarten, "With Ultra," p. 130.
13. Patrick Beesly, *Very Special Intelligence: The Story of the Admiralty's Intelligence Centre, 1939–1945*, pp. 242–43.
14. Rosengarten, "With Ultra," p. 130.
15. Richard Harris Smith, *OSS: The Secret History of America's First Central Intelligence Agency*, p. 225.
16. Eisenhower Papers, p. 2,117.
17. Butcher's diary, December 23, 1944.
18. Strong to author, March 19, 1979.
19. Ambrose, *Supreme Commander*, p. 558.
20. Butcher's diary, December 23, 1944.
21. Sir Kenneth Strong, *Intelligence at the Top: The Recollections of an Intelligence Officer*, p. 233.

22. Rosengarten, "With Ultra," p. 131.
23. Strong, *Intelligence,* p. 245.
24. Rosengarten's report is part of a series, "Reports by U. S. Army ULTRA Representatives with Army Field Commands in the European Theater of Operations," Record Group 457, N.S.A., SH H-023 Part 1, Modern Military Records, National Archives.
25. Ibid.
26. Buck's report is in ibid.
27. Rood's report is in ibid.
28. Fellers' report is in ibid.
29. Talbert's report is in ibid.
30. Cornelius Ryan, *The Last Battle,* p. 210.
31. Ibid., p. 212.
32. Quoted in ibid., p. 213.
33. Stephen E. Ambrose, *Eisenhower and Berlin: The Decision to Halt at the Elbe,* pp. 75–76.
34. Quoted in ibid., p. 75; see also, Rodney G. Minott, *The Fortress That Never Was.*
35. Sir Kenneth Strong, *Men of Intelligence,* p. 124.
36. Quoted by Rosengarten in his report to Taylor.

CHAPTER ELEVEN

1. Stephen E. Ambrose, *The Supreme Commander: The War Years of Dwight D. Eisenhower,* p. 325.
2. Eisenhower diary, Eisenhower Library, Abilene, Kansas.
3. Ibid.
4. Herbert F. York, *The Advisers: Oppenheimer, Teller, and The Superbomb,* pp. 31–37.
5. Policy Planning Staff Paper No. 32, January 10, 1948, Modern Military Records, National Archives.
6. Eisenhower diary.
7. Ibid.

CHAPTER TWELVE

1. Richard Harris Smith, *OSS: The Secret History of America's First Intelligence Agency,* p. 363.
2. Ibid., p. 20.
3. Ibid., p. 363.
4. Ibid., p. 364.
5. Ibid., p. 364.
6. *Final Report of the Select Committee to Study Governmental Operations With Respect to Intelligence Activities,* U. S. Senate, book IV, Senate Report No. 94-755, 94th Congress, 2d session, pp. 6–9. Hereinafter cited as Church Committee.
7. Ibid., p. 12.
8. Ibid., p. 13.
9. Ibid., p. 31.
10. Edmond Taylor, *Awakening From History,* p. 350, as quoted in Smith, *OSS,* p. 361.

11. Francis P. Miller, *Men From the Valley*, as quoted in Smith, *OSS*, p. 362.
12. Washington *Post*, December 22, 1963; there is a good discussion in David Wise and Thomas Ross, *The Invisible Government*, pp. 95–98.
13. Church Committee, book IV, p. 31.
14. Harry Rositzke, *The CIA's Secret Operations: Espionage, Counterespionage, and Covert Action*, pp. 186–87.
15. Wise and Ross, *Invisible Government*, pp. 96–97.
16. Quoted in Herbert Feis, *From Trust to Terror: The Onset of the Cold War*, p. 296.
17. Rositzke, *CIA's Secret Operations*, p. 23.
18. Ibid., p. 53.
19. Hunt interview.
20. Smith, *OSS*, p. 367.
21. Ibid., p. 367; William Buckley and L. Brant Bozell, *McCarthy and His Enemies*.
22. Eisenhower interview.
23. Ibid.
24. Macomber interview; Hunt interview; Bissell interview.
25. Sir Kenneth Strong, *Men of Intelligence*, pp. 124–25.
26. Anderson interview.
27. Strong, *Men of Intelligence*, p. 135.
28. Thomas Braden, "I'm Glad the CIA is 'Immoral,'" *Saturday Evening Post*, May 20, 1967, as quoted in Smith, *OSS*, pp. 368–69.
29. According to the Church Committee, which investigated the CIA in the mid-seventies, "during the early 1950's the CIA attracted some of the most able lawyers, academicians, and young, committed activists in the country." Church Committee, book IV, p. 43.
30. Smith, *OSS*, p. 369.
31. Ibid., pp. 370–71.
32. Bissell interview.
33. Church Committee, book IV, pp. 31–32.
34. Ibid., pp. 33–36.
35. Victor Marchetti and John Marks, *The CIA and the Cult of Intelligence*, pp. 46–47.
36. Ibid., p. 47.
37. Tom Braden, "What's Wrong with the CIA?" *Saturday Review*, April 5, 1975, as quoted in Church Committee, book I, p. 547.
38. Rositzke, *CIA's Secret Operations*, p. 151.
39. Church Committee, book IV, p. 40.
40. For a balanced and insightful essay on the role of intelligence in the modern world, the best this author has read, see M. R. D. Foot, "Intelligence Services," *The Economist* (London), March 15, 1980.

CHAPTER THIRTEEN

1. This section is based on interviews with Eisenhower and on Dwight D. Eisenhower, *Mandate for Change*, pp. 223–25.
2. Brownell interview.
3. Eisenhower, *Mandate*, p. 225, reprints these letters; the originals, to John Eisenhower, June 16, 1953, and to Miller, June 10, 1953, are in the Eisenhower Library in Abilene.

4. Quoted in Herbert Parmet, *Eisenhower and the American Crusades,* p. 386.

5. Lewis Strauss, *Men and Decisions,* p. 356.

6. Parmet, *Eisenhower,* p. 387.

7. Strauss, *Men and Decisions,* p. 268; Eisenhower, *Mandate,* p. 311.

8. Eisenhower, *Mandate,* p. 311, reprints this diary entry.

9. Parmet, *Eisenhower,* p. 344; Strauss, *Men and Decisions,* pp. 281–91.

10. Eisenhower to Strauss, June 16, 1954, Eisenhower Library, Abilene; Eisenhower, *Mandate,* p. 313.

11. Eisenhower, *Mandate,* p. 312.

12. Wainwright interview.

13. Quoted in Book IV, *Final Report of the Select Committee to Study Governmental Operations with Respect to Intelligence Activities,* U. S. Senate, Senate Report No. 94-755, 94th Congress, 2d Session, pages 52–53.

CHAPTER FOURTEEN

1. Kermit Roosevelt, *Countercoup: The Struggle for the Control of Iran,* pp. 155–57. Shortly after its publication, McGraw-Hill withdrew from circulation, until a later unspecified date, this memoir of the CIA's project to overthrow Mossadegh. Accounts of the withdrawal in *The Wall Street Journal* (November 6, 1979) and the New York *Times* (November 10, 1979) quote McGraw-Hill's publicity director, Donald Rubin, as explaining that the recall was due to "defective production and errata" and ". . . problems of accuracy at the time of shipping." Both articles emphasized that Roosevelt's volume had cleared the mandatory CIA review, and, although there is no direct evidence that the British Petroleum Company influenced McGraw-Hill's decision, these news reports assumed that BP had objected strongly to the former CIA operative's allegation that the Anglo-Iranian Oil Company—BP's predecessor company—had initially proposed the coup. Since this chapter in the CIA's history cannot be related accurately without Roosevelt's information, his work *Countercoup* is being cited here.

2. The most articulate critic of Reza Khan's decision to assume the throne was Mohammed Mossadegh, then a member of the Iranian Parliament. Marvin Zonis, *The Political Elite of Iran,* p. 19.

3. See ibid., p. 21, and Mohammed Reza Shah Pahlavi, *Mission For My Country.* pp. 49–65.

4. Pahlavi, *Mission For My Country,* p. 80.

5. Stephen E. Ambrose, *Rise to Globalism: American Foreign Policy Since 1938,* p. 131.

6. Dwight D. Eisenhower, *Mandate for Change,* p. 160.

7. Roosevelt, *Countercoup,* p. 59.

8. George Lenczowski, *Russia and the West in Iran, 1918–1948,* pp. 272, 313–14.

9. Ibid., p. 312.

10. Sharam Chubin and Sepehr Zabih, *The Foreign Relations of Iran,* p. 42.

11. Roosevelt, *Countercoup,* p. 87.

12. Dean Acheson, *Present at the Creation,* p. 503.

13. Pahlavi, *Mission For My Country*, pp. 90–91.
14. Leonard Mosley, *Power Play*, p. 204, as quoted in Roosevelt, *Countercoup*, p. 87. See also, Richard Cottam, *Nationalism in Iran*.
15. Acheson, *Present at the Creation*, pp. 504, 510.
16. Pahlavi, *Mission For My Country*, pp. 94–95.
17. Eisenhower, *Mandate*, pp. 160–61.
18. Henderson interview.
19. Roosevelt, *Countercoup*, p. 107.
20. New York *Times*, February 25, 1953; Nashville *Banner*, May 21, 1954.
21. Pahlavi, *Mission For My Country*, p. 97; Eisenhower, *Mandate*, p. 161.
22. Henderson interview.
23. Eisenhower, *Mandate*, p. 162.
24. Pahlavi, *Mission For My Country*, p. 98; Henderson interview.
25. Eisenhower interview.
26. Henderson interview.
27. Eisenhower, *Mandate*, p. 163.
28. Roosevelt, *Countercoup*, p. 8.
29. Ibid., p. 8.
30. Robert Anderson interview.
31. Roosevelt, *Countercoup*, p. 116.
32. Ibid., pp. 11–19.
33. Ibid., p. 94.
34. Henderson interview.
35. Roosevelt, *Countercoup*, p. 122.
36. Eric Sevareid, "CBS Reports: The Hot and Cold Wars of Allen Dulles," CBS-TV, April 26, 1962.
37. Roosevelt, *Countercoup*, pp. 148–49.

CHAPTER FIFTEEN

1. New York *Times*, August 11, 1953.
2. Kermit Roosevelt, *Countercoup: The Struggle for the Control of Iran*, p. 170.
3. Dwight D. Eisenhower, *Mandate for Change*, p. 164.
4. Roosevelt, *Countercoup*, pp. 171–72.
5. Mohammed Reza Shah Pahlavi, *Mission For My Country*, p. 100.
6. This reconstruction is based on the New York *Times* reports and Pahlavi, *Mission For My Country*, p. 101, and Roosevelt, *Countercoup*, pp. 175–79.
7. Roosevelt, *Countercoup*, p. 179.
8. Ibid., pp. 182–85.
9. Henderson interview.
10. New York *Times*, August 19, 1953.
11. Roosevelt, *Countercoup*, p. 166.
12. Ibid., pp. 186–87; Henderson interview.
13. Roosevelt, *Countercoup*, p. 188.
14. Ibid., pp. 190–91.
15. Ibid., pp. 192–93.
16. Pahlavi, *Mission For My Country*, p. 103.
17. New York *Times*, August 20, 1953.
18. Roosevelt, *Countercoup*, p. 18.

19. New York *Times*, August 21, 1953.
20. Ibid.
21. Ibid.
22. Roosevelt, *Countercoup*, p. 199.
23. Ibid., p. 209.
24. Eisenhower, *Mandate*, p. 164.
25. Henderson interview.
26. Eisenhower, *Mandate*, p. 166.
27. Harwood interview.

CHAPTER SIXTEEN

1. Andrew Tully, *The CIA: The Inside Story*, pp. 62–64; Hunt interview; James Hagerty diary, May 20, 1954, Eisenhower Library, Abilene, Kansas; Richard and Gladys Harkness, "The Mysterious Doings of the CIA," *Saturday Evening Post*, October 30, 1954.
2. New York *Times*, May 19, 1954; Dwight D. Eisenhower, *Mandate for Change*, p. 424.
3. Keith Monroe, "Guatemala, What the Reds Left Behind," *Harper's Magazine*, vol. 211 (July 1955), pp. 60–65.
4. Dwight D. Eisenhower, *Mandate for Change*, p. 424.
5. Quoted in ibid., pp. 422–23.
6. Hunt interview.
7. Walter Payne, "The Guatemalan Revolution, 1944–1954," *Pacific Historian*, vol. 17, no. 1 (1973), p. 3.
8. Thomas P. McCann, *An American Company: The Tragedy of United Fruit*, p. 45; Thomas and Marjorie Melville, *Guatemala; The Politics of Land Ownership;* Stacy May and G. Plaza, *The United Fruit Company in Latin America.*
9. Payne, "Guatemalan Revolution," p. 11.
10. Ibid., pp. 14–15; Louis McDermott, "Guatemala, 1954: Intervention or Aggression?" *Rocky Mountain Social Science Journal*, vol. 9, no. 1 (1972), p. 79.
11. FBI reports to the State Department are quite extensive and had remained closed to the public until we requested they be declassified under the Freedom of Information Act. The documents can be found in the correspondence between Hoover and Frederick B. Lyons in the NA814.00B file.
12. Tapley Bennett, State Department memorandum, "Some Aspects of Communist Penetration in Guatemala," March 23, 1950, in Carrollton Press, Inc., *The Declassified Documents Quarterly*, vol. I, no. 3 (January 1975), p. 179B.
13. U. S. House of Representatives, Committee on Foreign Affairs, 92d Congress, 2d Session (October 10, 1972), *Inter-American Affairs*, p. 131.
14. McDermott, "Guatemala," p. 14.
15. Hunt interview.
16. Payne, "Guatemalan Revolution," p. 18.
17. Max Gordon, "History of U. S. Subversion: Guatemala, 1954," *Science and Society*, vol. XXXV, no. 2 (1971), p. 142.

18. Eisenhower, *Mandate*, p. 421.
19. Richard Patterson, draft of speech to Rotary Club, March 24, 1950, Patterson Papers, box five, Truman Library, Independence, Missouri.
20. Hunt interview.
21. U. S. House of Representatives, Subcommittee on Latin America of the Select Committee on Communist Aggression, Ninth Interim Report, *Communist Aggression in Latin America*, p. 124.
22. U. S. Department of State, *American Foreign Policy, 1950–1955, Basic Documents*, vol. I, p. 1,310.
23. Bissell interview.
24. Much of this information is from the appropriate volumes of *Who's Who in America*. See also, Frederick J. Cook, "The CIA," *The Nation*, vol. 192 (June 24, 1961), pp. 537–41.
25. Eisenhower to Alfred Gruenther, November 30, 1954, Dwight D. Eisenhower, "November, 1954"; Eisenhower to William Robinson, August 4, 1954, Dwight D. Eisenhower, "August, 1954."
26. Bissell interview; Hunt interview.
27. Hunt interview; Spruille Braden interview; Miguel Ydígoras Fuentes, *My War With Communism*, p. 50.
28. Bissell interview.
29. Goodpaster interview.
30. Hunt and Bissell interviews.
31. Hunt interview.
32. Hunt interview.
33. *Hispanic American Report*, vol. VII (July 1954), pp. 11–12; New York *Times*, June 16, 1954.
34. New York *Times*, May 23, June 19, 1954; Bissell interview.
35. Bissell interview.
36. USIA, "Report on Actions Taken by the U. S. Information Agency in the Guatemalan Situation," Secret, August 2, 1954, NA714.00/8-254.
37. U. S. Department of State, *Tenth Inter-American Conference*, pp. 8–9; "After the Vote," *Time*, vol. 68 (March 29, 1954), p. 32.
38. David A. Phillips, *Night Watch: Twenty Years of Peculiar Service*, pp. 40–46; Hunt interview.
39. New York *Times*, June 15, 1954.
40. Ibid., June 19, 1954.
41. Quoted in Stephen Schlesinger, "How Dulles Worked the Coup d'Etat," *The Nation*, vol. 227, no. 14 (October 28, 1978), p. 441.
42. Goodpaster interview.
43. Fedro Guillen, *Guatemala, Prologo y Epilogo de una Revolución*, pp. 62–64; Phillips, *Night Watch*, pp. 43–44.
44. Eisenhower, *Mandate*, pp. 425–26.
45. Quoted in ibid., p. 427.
46. Hunt interview.
47. Hunt interview.
48. John Gerassi, "Introduction," *Venceremos: The Speeches and Writings of Che Guevara*, pp. 45–47.

CHAPTER SEVENTEEN

1. Stephen E. Ambrose, *Rise to Globalism: American Foreign Policy Since 1938*, p. 252.

2. Ibid., p. 253.
3. Ibid., pp. 244–45.
4. Ray Cline, *Secrets, Spies, and Scholars,* pp. 162–63; New York *Times,* November 30, 1976; William Corson, *The Armies of Ignorance,* p. 367; Hunt interview.
5. Cline, *Secrets, Spies, and Scholars,* p. 163.
6. New York *Times,* November 30, 1976; Corson, *Armies of Ignorance,* pp. 367–68.
7. Cline, *Secrets, Spies, and Scholars,* p. 164.
8. Corson, *Armies of Ignorance,* p. 368; New York *Times,* June 4, 1956.
9. Ibid., pp. 369–70.
10. Interview with Milton Eisenhower.
11. William Colby, *Honorable Men: My Life in the CIA,* pp. 134–35.
12. Hunt interview.
13. Corson, *Armies of Ignorance,* p. 371.
14. Memorandum of conference, October 6, 1956, Dwight D. Eisenhower, Staff Notes, "October, 1956."
15. Corson, *Armies of Ignorance,* p. 382.
16. Gray interview.
17. Bissell interview.
18. Cline, *Secrets, Spies, and Scholars,* p. 132.
19. Ibid., p. 133.
20. Halperin told the Church Committee, "I believe that the U.S. should no longer maintain a career service for the purpose of conducting covert operations." Church Committee, vol. 7, p. 58.
21. Gray interview.
22. Church Committee, book IV, p. 62.
23. Memorandum of a conference with the President, January 19, 1957, Dwight D. Eisenhower Notes, "January, 1957."
24. Church Committee, book IV, p. 63.
25. Ibid., p. 62.
26. Washington *Post* of November 13, 1954, and *U. S. News* of March 19, 1954.
27. *Pentagon Papers,* book 9, pp. 38–41.
28. Ibid., p. 241.
29. Eisenhower interview.
30. *Pentagon Papers,* book 9, p. 244.
31. *Pentagon Papers,* as published by the New York *Times,* July 5, 1971.
32. *Pentagon Papers,* book 9, pp. 334–36.
33. *Pentagon Papers,* New York *Times,* July 5, 1971.
34. Ibid.; *Pentagon Papers,* book 10, pp. 753–55.
35. *Pentagon Papers,* New York *Times,* July 5, 1971.
36. Ibid.
37. David Wise and Thomas Ross, *Invisible Government,* pp. 157–58.
38. *Pentagon Papers,* book 10, pp. 776–79.
39. Wise and Ross, *Invisible Government,* p. 140.
40. Ibid., p. 141.
41. Victor Marchetti and John Marks, *The CIA and the Cult of Intelligence,* p. 128; Wise and Ross, *Invisible Government,* p. 137.
42. *Pentagon Papers,* New York *Times,* July 5, 1971.
43. Wise and Ross, *Invisible Government,* p. 136.

44. Cline, *Secrets, Spies, and Scholars*, p. 182.

CHAPTER EIGHTEEN

1. Ray Cline, *Secrets, Spies, and Scholars*, p. 141.
2. Ibid., p. 142.
3. Ibid., pp. 142–43.
4. Ibid.
5. Andrew Tully, *CIA: The Inside Story*, p. 110.
6, Warren Unna, "CIA: Who Watches the Watchman?" *Harper's Magazine*, April, 1958.
7. *Pentagon Papers*, book 9, p. 47.
8. Stephen E. Ambrose, *Rise to Globalism: American Foreign Policy Since 1938*, p. 232.
9. Interview with Eisenhower.
10. *Pentagon Papers*, book 9, pp. 564–65.
11. Interview with Matthew Ridgway; Ambrose, *Rise to Globalism*, p. 233.
12. Pentagon Papers, book 10, p. 692.
13. Dwight D. Eisenhower, *Mandate for Change*, p. 372.
14. Interview with Eisenhower.
15. *Pentagon Papers*, book 10, p. 752.
16. *Public Papers of the Presidents: DDE, 1954* (Washington, 1960), pp. 948–49.
17. Marvin Kalb and Elie Abel, *Roots of Involvement: The U. S. in Asia*, p. 102.
18. *Pentagon Papers*, book 10, pp. 1,190–98.
19. Goodpaster interview.
20. Interview with Milton Eisenhower, Baltimore *Sun*, September 9, 1979.
21. Eisenhower diary.

CHAPTER NINETEEN

1. This chapter is heavily based on two long interviews with Richard Bissell, one by the Columbia University Oral History Project, the other by Richard Immerman. All statements of fact and quotations not otherwise footnoted come from one or the other of the Bissell interviews.
2. Ray Cline, *Secrets, Spies, and Scholars*, p. 156.
3. Ibid., p. 157.
4. Church Committee, book IV, p. 59.
5. Cline, *Secrets, Spies, and Scholars*, p. 157.
6. Dwight D. Eisenhower, *Mandate for Change*, pp. 520–21.
7. Church Committee, book IV, p. 59.
8. Bissell's testimony on these matters is fully corroborated, in detail, in separate interviews with John Eisenhower and Andrew Goodpaster.
9. Memo of conference, November 6, 1956, Whitman File, Eisenhower Library, Abilene, Kansas.
10. Dwight D. Eisenhower, *Waging Peace*, p. 91.
11. Dwight D. Eisenhower, "Phone calls, 12/56." Ike recorded, or had Ms. Whiteman take shorthand notes of, almost all his phone conversations.
12. Cline, *Secrets, Spies, and Scholars*, p. 158.
13. Francis Gary Powers, *Operation Overflight*, pp. 308–9.
14. Bissell interview.

15. Eisenhower, *Waging Peace*, p. 301; Goodpaster interview.
16. Based on many discussions with Eisenhower during interviews.
17. Goodpaster interview.
18. Quoted in Stephen E. Ambrose, *Rise to Globalism: American Foreign Policy Since 1938*, p. 223.
19. Ibid.
20. Dwight D. Eisenhower, "Phone calls, 12/56."
21. Eisenhower, *Waging Peace*, p. 595.
22. Ibid., p. 601.

CHAPTER TWENTY

1. Interview with John Eisenhower.
2. Dwight D. Eisenhower, *Waging Peace*, p. 546; italics mine.
3. Bissell interview.
4. Ibid.
5. Eisenhower, *Waging Peace*, p. 446.
6. Bissell interview; Gray interview.
7. Eisenhower, *Waging Peace*, p. 546.
8. Ibid.
9. Memorandum of a conference with the President, July 11, 1960, Whitman file, Eisenhower Library, Abilene, Kansas.
10. Bissell interview.
11. Francis Gary Powers, *Operation Overflight*, p. 229.
12. Ibid., p. 353.
13. Bissell interview; Eisenhower, *Waging Peace*, p. 547.
14. Bissell interview.
15. Eisenhower, *Waging Peace*, p. 543.
16. Ibid., p. 547.
17. Lyman Kirkpatrick, *The Real CIA*, p. 97.
18. Powers, *Operation Overflight*, p. 353.
19. The text of Khrushchev's speech is in the New York *Times*, May 6, 1960.
20. Ibid.
21. Ibid., May 8, 1960.
22. Eisenhower, *Waging Peace*, p. 549.
23. New York *Times*, May 8, 1960.
24. Eisenhower, *Waging Peace*, p. 551.
25. New York *Times*, May 9, 1960.
26. Ibid., May 13, 1960.
27. Ibid., May 12, 1960.
28. Eisenhower, *Waging Peace*, p. 552.
29. Vernon Walters, *Silent Missions*, p. 342.
30. New York *Times*, May 8, 1960.
31. Eisenhower, *Waging Peace*, pp. 558–59.
32. Ibid., p. 553.
33. Walters, *Silent Missions*, p. 341.
34. Ibid., pp. 344–47.
35. Eisenhower, *Waging Peace*, p. 558.

36. James A. Nathan, "A Fragile Détente: The U-2 Incident Re-examined," *Military Affairs*, vol. XXXIX (October 1975), pp. 97–103.
37. Los Angeles *Times*, August 28, 1977.
38. Powers, *Operation Overflight*, p. 357.
39. Helms to J. Edgar Hoover, May 13, 1964, Warren Commission Document 931, National Archives, Washington.
40. *Hearing Before the Committee on Armed Services, on Francis Gary Powers*, U. S. Senate, 87th Congress, 2d session, March 6, 1962.
41. Bissell to Immerman, October 29, 1979, Immerman's possession.

CHAPTER TWENTY-ONE

1. Church Committee, "Alleged Assassination Plots," pp. 14, 15.
2. Harry Rositzke, *The CIA's Secret Operations: Espionage, Counterespionage, and Covert Action*, p. 197; Thomas Powers, *The Man Who Kept the Secrets: Richard Helms and the CIA*, pp. 145–49.
3. Church Committee, "Alleged Assassination Plots," p. 51.
4. Church Committee, book IV, p. 138.
5. Church Committee, "Alleged Assassination Plots," p. 52.
6. Ibid., p. 64.
7. Goodpaster interview.
8. Church Committee, "Alleged Assassination Plots," p. 55.
9. Ibid., p. 60.
10. Gray interview.
11. New York *Times*, December 26, 1975.
12. Church Committee, book IV, p. 131. Both Wisner and Hunt testified to the Church Committee that they knew of no assassination missions or planning by PB/7, beyond the general discussion among Pash and others in the process of establishing OPC. The capability was there, but it was never used. Pash testified that "I was never asked to undertake such planning."
13. Church Committee, book IV, p. 133.
14. Ibid.
15. This discussion relies heavily on Stewart C. Easton, *World History Since 1945*, pp. 685–91.
16. Church Committee, "Alleged Assassination Plots," p. 53.
17. Ibid., p. 58.
18. Ibid.
19. Ibid., p. 15.
20. Ibid.
21. Ibid., pp. 16–17.
22. Ibid., p. 19.
23. Ibid., p. 48.
24. Ibid., pp. 64–65.
25. Ibid., p. 66.
26. Ibid., p. 73.
27. Ibid., pp. 73–81; Peter Wyden, *Bay of Pigs: The Untold Story*, pp. 40–43.
28. Church Committee, "Alleged Assassination Plots," p. 72.

29. Ibid., p. 92.
30. Ibid., pp. 109–11.
31. Ibid., p. 112.
32. Ibid., pp. 112–13.
33. Ibid., p. 113.
34. Ibid.
35. Ibid., p. 115.
36. Ibid.

CHAPTER TWENTY-TWO

1. Interview with Eisenhower. Ike put Goodpaster in a category with Robert Anderson and his brother Milton.
2. Goodpaster interview.
3. Church Committee, "Alleged Assassination Plots," p. 92.
4. Ibid., p. 93.
5. Peter Wyden, *Bay of Pigs: The Untold Story*, p. 24.
6. Church Committee, "Alleged Assassination Plots," p. 93.
7. Ibid.
8. Wyden, *Bay of Pigs*, p. 25.
9. Church Committee, "Alleged Assassination Plots," p. 93; Wyden, *Bay of Pigs*, p. 25.
10. Dwight D. Eisenhower, *Waging Peace*, p. 533.
11. Bissell interview.
12. Ibid.
13. Eisenhower, *Waging Peace*, p. 537.
14. Taylor Report. Immediately after the Bay of Pigs, President Kennedy had General Maxwell Taylor make a full investigation and report to him. In 1977 a part of this report, in an expurgated form, was made available to scholars through the John F. Kennedy Library, Boston, Massachusetts.
15. Wyden, *Bay of Pigs*, p. 31.
16. Ibid., p. 69.
17. Bissell interview.
18. Ibid.
19. Eisenhower, *Waging Peace*, p. 534; Wyden, *Bay of Pigs*, pp. 22–23.
20. Wyden, *Bay of Pigs*, p. 68; Gray interview.
21. Bissell interview.
22. New York *Times*, October 20, 1960.
23. Wyden, *Bay of Pigs*, pp. 67–68.
24. Eisenhower, *Waging Peace*, p. 613.
25. Bissell interview.
26. Eisenhower, *Waging Peace*, p. 613.
27. Ibid., p. 614.
28. Wyden, *Bay of Pigs*, p. 69.
29. New York *Times*, January 10, 1961.
30. Wyden, *Bay of Pigs*, p. 73.
31. Eisenhower, *Waging Peace*, p. 614.
32. Bissell interview. Italics mine.
33. Ibid.

34. Eisenhower interview. See also Earl Mazo, "Ike Speaks Out: Bay of Pigs was all JFK's," *Newsday*, September 10, 1965; Gray interview.
35. Wyden, *Bay of Pigs,* p. 88.

CHAPTER TWENTY-THREE

1. Howard Hunt interview.
2. Ibid.

GLOSSARY

Abwher: The military intelligence division of the German General Staff.

AJAX: Code name for the CIA covert operation to oust Iran's Premier Mohammed Mossadegh and reinstate the Shah.

ANVIL: The Allied landing at Marseilles, 1944.

BI-A: Counterespionage arm of MI-5, responsible for handling double-agents.

"Bomb": The device used at BP to break Enigma's code.

BP: Bletchley Park. The British estate where Enigma's code was broken and deciphered.

COBRA: U.S. General Omar Bradley's plan that led to the successful breakthrough of the German lines at St. Lô in late July 1944.

Church Committee: Headed by Frank Church, the 1975 Senate Committee which investigated CIA clandestine operations.

CIA: Central Intelligence Agency. The modern United States intelligence agency, created in 1947.

CIG: Central Intelligence Group. Created by President Truman in 1946, the largely ineffectual precursor to the CIA.

COI: Coordinator of Information. The first United States intelligence agency, established in 1941 under William Donovan.

Corps Franc d'Afrique: A commando group of young French patriots organized in part by OSS officer Major Carleton Coon.

DCI: Director of the Central Intelligence Agency.

Double-Cross System: The BI-A operation of turning captured German spies into double-agents.

Enigma: The German encoding machine, thought by them to be undecipherable.

ETO: European Theater of Operations.

FORTITUDE: Code name for OVERLORD deception plan.

FUSAG: The First United States Army Group. The imaginary force purportedly preparing for the Allied invasion at Pas de Calais.

G-2: SHAEF intelligence division.

G-3: SHAEF operations division.

GAF: German Air Force, or Luftwaffe.

H.I.M.: His Imperial Majesty. Common reference for the Shah of Iran.

HUSKY: Allied invasion of Sicily, July 1943.

JCS: Joint Chiefs of Staff. Combined heads of the United States Army, Navy, and Air Force.

JED: Short for JEDBURGH, the code name for the three-man Allied teams that armed and trained the French guerrilla underground and coordinated activities with SHAEF.

JSC: Joint Security Control. U.S. counterpart of LCS. Responsible for devising and coordinating strategic cover and deception schemes.

LCS: London Controlling Section. British organization responsible for devising and coordinating strategic cover and deception schemes.

MacGregor Unit: OSS code name for a sabotage team.

Maquis: The French guerrilla underground, or Resistance.

Manhattan Project: United States effort to build the atomic bomb.

MARKET-GARDEN: Field Marshal Bernard Law Montgomery's plan to cross the Rhine, September 1944.

MI-5: British Secret Service section responsible for security within Great Britain.

MI-6: British Secret Service section responsible for security outside Great Britain.

MULBERRY: Code name for concrete platforms that created an artificial port for OVERLORD.

NSC: National Security Council. Organized in 1947 along with the CIA, the White House agency integrating those departments responsible for advising the President on national security affairs.

ONI: Office of Naval Intelligence.

OPC: Office of Policy Coordination. The branch of the CIA initially in charge of covert operations.

OSS: Office of Strategic Services. The successor to the COI, the U.S. intelligence and covert action agency during World War II.

OVERLORD: Allied invasion of France, June 1944.

PBSUCCESS: Code name for CIA operation in Guatemala.

PWB: Psychological Warfare Branch, SHAEF.

RAF: British Royal Air Force.

SAVAK: The security branch of the Iranian police force.

SHAEF: Supreme Headquarters, Allied Expeditionary Force.

SLU: Special Liaison Unit. British and U.S. officers charged with relaying and interpreting ULTRA information to the field commanders.

soe: Special Operations Executive. The branch of mi-6 responsible for liaison with the French underground Resistance.

torch: Allied invasion of North Africa, November 1942.

U-2: Plane used to overfly the Soviet Union for intelligence gathering.

ultra: British code name for the systematic breaking of the German code.

AN ESSAY ON THE SOURCES
by Richard H. Immerman

THE BIBLIOGRAPHY lists the works cited in this book, but a study of covert intelligence operations is incomplete without some additional explanation of sources used. This is particularly true if the book deals with Dwight D. Eisenhower. Ike was so circumspect when it came to discussing—or writing about—his involvement in deception and clandestine activities that the author must be both researcher and sleuth. To uncover a secret operation is one thing; to reveal Ike's knowledge and participation is another.

Our investigation of Ike's conduct as Supreme Commander during World War II was made much easier by the excellent work of others, particularly the British historians, who are justifiably proud of their intelligence services and have written extensively about the subject. The British Government commissioned scholars like Michael Foot to make public previously unknown but critically important facets of the war effort, and recently the first volume of F. W. Hinsley's official history of British intelligence activities appeared. After F. W. Winterbotham broke the silence about ULTRA in 1974, R. V. Jones and Ronald Lewin brought to light a side of the war more intriguing than the most exciting and imaginative novel. These studies, along with the others included in the Bibliography, proved invaluable to our own work.

But learning of the United States' involvement, and especially Ike's still presented problems. There is no American official history, and almost all United States accounts of World War II intelligence are confined to the Office of Strategic Services. As explained in our book, the OSS was just one of several intelligence networks. Memoirs by Ike's subordinates, including his G-2, General Kenneth Strong, filled in much of the story, and Sir Kenneth kindly consented to answer our questions by letter. We found out about the role of the SLUs through the Telford Taylor reports, deposited in the Modern Military Records branch of the

National Archives, and helpful interviews with the participants listed in the Bibliography. Ike's role emerged. The final ingredient was the Johns Hopkins University edition of Eisenhower's papers, an exhaustive collection of Ike's personal correspondence and memoranda, without which our task would have been virtually impossible.

Our task became more difficult when we began the presidential years. Fortunately our timing was opportune. After the Watergate break-in and the disclosure of CIA "dirty works," there appeared a plethora of memoirs and scholarly investigations describing over two decades of intelligence operations. Interviews added to our knowledge, for an increasing number of former government officials welcomed an opportunity to set the record straight.

I want to express our thanks to all those who did cooperate so extensively, especially Richard M. Bissell, Jr., Howard Hunt, General Andrew Goodpaster, Milton Eisenhower, John Eisenhower, and Stuyvesant Wainwright III. These are all exceedingly busy men who took time out to spend hours discussing a myriad of subjects and often suggested additional avenues for us to pursue. Their collective memories comprise a great deal of our history, for they both described and explained what really went on.

We used our personal interviews in conjunction with the Columbia Oral History Collection and Princeton's Dulles Oral History Project, essential source material for any scholar of the Eisenhower presidency. The post-Watergate period produced two other essential sources: the *Pentagon Papers* and the transcript of the Church Committee's study of government operations. The value of these two publications to the student of the spies cannot be overemphasized.

The Johns Hopkins compilation of Eisenhower's papers has not yet gone beyond the chief-of-staff period, and we still await the publication of the *Foreign Relations* volumes for Ike's administration. To make matters worse from our standpoint, many of the documents relating to CIA activities were either never published or, as was more commonly the case, remained security-classified. Again we were helped by post-Watergate sentiment. By going through Record Group 59 of the National Archives Diplomatic Branch, we discovered numerous previously unused memoranda and dispatches and identified those still not released to the public. We obtained hundreds of these through the Freedom of Information Act.

For Ike himself, however, the main source was the Eisenhower Library in Abilene, Kansas. Director John Wickman, Dr. James Lyerzapf, and the rest of the library staff have expertly catalogued the thousands upon thousands of papers resulting from the Eisenhower White

House, and assembled detailed finding guides as to their contents. The bulk of this collection—known as the Whitman File—provides insights into Ike's administration and personality never before thought possible. Special mention should be made of Ike's personal diary. Although obviously too busy to record a day-by-day account of his activities, Ike kept the diary periodically from the 1930s up until his death. Perhaps no other document reveals with such clarity the mind of this man who for so many years supervised our complex intelligence community.

One final note on the sources. We have attempted to obtain as much of the information as possible, but we will not pretend that the story is complete. The files from the White House Special Assistant for National Security Affairs and the National Security Council series are still primarily closed, as are many other documents in the Eisenhower Library's holdings. It is unlikely, even with the newly instituted Executive Order 12065, that these documents will be declassified in the near future. Ike took many of his secrets with him to his grave. But he left enough for us to know that he believed in the intelligence community, that he used it to its fullest potential, and that it was never the same again after he retired.

BIBLIOGRAPHY

UNPUBLISHED SOURCES

Dwight D. Eisenhower, Papers as President of the United States, 1953–1961 (Whitman File), Dwight D. Eisenhower Library, Abilene, Kans.
James C. Hagerty Papers, Dwight D. Eisenhower Library, Abilene, Kans.
National Archives, Diplomatic Branch, Washington, D.C.
————. Judicial and Fiscal Branch, Washington.
————. Modern Military Records, Washington.
Richard G. Patterson, Jr., Papers, Harry S. Truman Library, Independence, Mo.
Taylor Report (Paramilitary Study Group), National Security Files, John F. Kennedy Library, Boston.

INTERVIEWS AND CORRESPONDENCE

Anderson, Robert (Columbia University Oral History Project).
Bissell, Richard M., Jr. (Columbia University Oral History Project).
————. (Richard H. Immerman).
————. (Princeton University).
————. Letter to Immerman, October 29, 1979.
Braden, Spruille (Richard H. Immerman).
Bradley, General Omar (Stephen E. Ambrose).
Collingwood, Charles, letter to Ambrose, September 13, 1978.
Coon, Carleton, letter to Ambrose, November 20, 1978.
Eisenhower, Dwight D. (Stephen E. Ambrose).
Eisenhower, John S. D. (Stephen E. Ambrose).
Eisenhower, Milton S. (Stephen E. Ambrose).
Filby, William (Stephen E. Ambrose).
Gavin, General James, letter to Ambrose, March 26, 1979.
Goodpaster, General Andrew (Stephen E. Ambrose).
————. (Columbia University Oral History Project).
Gray, Gordon (Richard H. Immerman).
Henderson, Loy (Columbia University Oral History Project).
Hunt, E. Howard (Richard H. Immerman).
Macomber, William B., Jr. (Richard H. Immerman).
Ridgway, General Matthew (Stephen E. Ambrose).

Strong, Sir Kenneth (Stephen E. Ambrose).
————. Letter to Ambrose, March 19, 1979.
Wainwright, Stuyvesant, III (Richard H. Immerman).

PUBLISHED SOURCES

Acheson, Dean. *Present at the Creation.* New York: Norton, 1971.
"After the Vote." *Time,* Vol. 68 (March 29, 1954).
Ambrose, Stephen E. *Eisenhower and Berlin: The Decision to Halt at the Elbe.* New York: Norton, 1967.
————. *Rise to Globalism: American Foreign Policy Since 1938.* London: Penguin Books, 1971.
————. *The Supreme Commander: The War Years of Dwight D. Eisenhower.* Garden City, N.Y.: Doubleday, 1970.
Beesly, Patrick. *Very Special Intelligence: The Story of the Admiralty's Intelligence Centre, 1939–1945.* Garden City, N.Y.: Doubleday, 1978.
Blumenson, Martin. *Breakout and Pursuit.* Washington: Department of the Army, 1961.
————. *Kasserine Pass.* Boston: Houghton Mifflin, 1967.
Braden, Thomas. "I'm Glad the CIA is 'Immoral.' " *Saturday Evening Post,* Vol. 240 (May 20, 1967).
————. "What's Wrong with the CIA?" *Saturday Review,* Vol. 2 (April 5, 1975).
Bradley, Omar N. *A Soldier's Story.* New York: Holt, 1951.
Brown, Anthony Cave. *Bodyguard of Lies.* New York: Harper & Row, 1975.
————, ed. *The Secret War Report of the OSS.* New York: Berkeley Publishing, 1976.
Buckley, William, and Brant, Bozell L. *McCarthy and His Enemies.* Chicago: Regnery, 1954.
Butcher, Harry. *My Three Years with Eisenhower.* New York: Simon & Schuster, 1946.
Carrollton Press, Inc. *The Declassified Documents Quarterly,* Vol. I (January 1975).
Chandler, Alfred D., ed. *The Papers of Dwight D. Eisenhower.* Baltimore: Johns Hopkins Press, 1970, 1978.
Chubin, Sharam, and Sepehr, Zabih. *The Foreign Relations of Iran.* Berkeley: University of California Press, 1972.
Churchill, Winston. *The Hinge of Fate.* Boston: Houghton Mifflin, 1950.
Clark, Mark. *Calculated Risk.* New York: Harper, 1950.
Cline, Ray. *Secrets, Spies, and Soldiers.* New York: Acropolis Books, 1976.
Colby, William. *Honorable Men: My Life in the CIA.* New York: Simon & Schuster, 1978.
Corson, William R. *Armies of Ignorance.* New York: Dial Press, 1977.
Cottam, Richard. *Nationalism in Iran.* Pittsburgh: University of Pittsburgh Press, 1964.
Deutsch, Harold. "The Influence of Ultra on World War II." *Parameters: Journal of the U. S. Army War College,* Vol. VIII (December 1978).
Easton, Stewart C. *World History Since 1945.* San Francisco: Chandler Publishing, 1968.

Eisenhower, Dwight D. *At Ease: Stories I Tell to Friends.* Garden City, N.Y.: Doubleday, 1967.

——. *Crusade in Europe.* Garden City, N.Y.: Doubleday, 1948.

——. *Mandate for Change.* Garden City, N.Y.: Doubleday, 1963.

——. *Waging Peace.* Garden City, N.Y.: Doubleday, 1965.

Eisenhower, John S. D. *The Bitter Woods.* New York: Putnam, 1969.

Eisenhower, Milton S. *The President Is Calling.* Garden City, N.Y.: Doubleday, 1975.

Estob, Peter. *Hitler's Last Offensive.* London: Macmillan, 1971.

Feis, Herbert. *From Trust to Terror: The Onset of the Cold War.* New York: Norton, 1970.

Foot, M.R.D. *SOE in France: An Account of the Work of the British Special Operation in France.* London: Her Majesty's Stationery Office, 1966.

Funk, Arthur. *Charles de Gaulle—The Crucial Years.* Norman: University of Oklahoma Press, 1960.

——. *The Politics of Torch.* Lawrence: University of Kansas Press, 1976.

Gerassi, John, ed. *Venceremos! The Speeches and Writings of Che Guevara.* New York: Macmillan, 1968.

Gordon, Max. "History of U. S. Subversion: Guatemala, 1954." *Science and Society,* Vol. XXXV (Summer 1971).

Groves, Leslie. *Now It Can Be Told: The Story of the Manhattan Project.* New York: Harper & Row, 1962.

Guillen, Fedro. *Guatemala, Prologo y Epilogo de una Revolución.* Mexico: Cuadernos Americanos, 1964.

Harkness, Richard and Gladys. "The Mysterious Doings of the CIA." *Saturday Evening Post,* Vol. 227 (October 30, 1954).

Hinsley, F. W. *British Intelligence in the Second World War.* Cambridge, England: Cambridge University Press, 1979.

Jones, R. V. *The Wizard War.* London: Coward, McCann & Geoghegan, 1978.

Kahn, David. *Hitler's Spies: German Military Intelligence in World War II.* New York: Macmillan, 1978.

Kalb, Marvin, and Abel, Elie. *Roots of Involvement: The U.S. in Asia.* New York: Norton, 1971.

Kirkpatrick, Lyman. *The Real CIA.* New York: Macmillan, 1968.

Lenczowski, George. *Russia and the West in Iran, 1918–1948.* Ithaca, N.Y.: Cornell University Press, 1949.

Lewin, Ronald. *Ultra Goes to War.* London: Hutchinson, 1978.

McCann, Thomas P. *An American Company: The Tragedy of United Fruit.* New York: Crown, 1976.

McDermott, Louis. "Guatemala, 1954: Intervention or Aggression?" *Rocky Mountain Social Science Journal,* Vol. 9 (January 1972).

Macmillan, Harold. *The Blast of War.* New York: Harper & Row, 1968.

Marchetti, Victor, and Marks, John. *The CIA and the Cult of Intelligence.* New York: Knopf, 1964.

Masterman. J. C. *The Double-Cross System in the War of 1939–1945.* New Haven: Yale University Press, 1972.

May, Stacy, and Plaza, G. *The United Fruit Company in Latin America.* Washington: National Planning Association, 1958.

Mazo, Earl. "Ike Speaks Out: Bay of Pigs was all JFK's." *Newsday,* September 10, 1965.

Melville, Thomas and Marjorie. *Guatemala: The Politics of Land Ownership.* New York: Free Press, 1971.

Miller, Francis P. *Man From the Valley.* Chapel Hill: University of North Carolina Press, 1971.

Minott, Rodney G. *The Fortress That Never Was.* New York: Holt, Rinehart & Winston, 1966.

Monroe, Keith. "Guatemala, What the Reds Left Behind." *Harper's Magazine,* Vol. 211 (July 1955).

Montagu, Ewen. *The Man Who Never Was.* London: Lippincott, 1954.

Mosley, Leonard. *Dulles: A Biography of Eleanor, Allen and John Foster Dulles and Their Family Network.* New York: Dial Press, 1978.

———. *Power Play.* Baltimore: Penguin Books, 1974.

Murphy, Robert. *Diplomat Among Warriors.* Garden City, N.Y.: Doubleday, 1964.

Nathan, James A. "A Fragile Détente: The U-2 Incident Re-examined." *Military Affairs,* Vol. XXXIX (October 1975).

Pahlavi, Mohammed Reza Shah. *Mission For My Country.* London: Hutchinson, 1961.

Parmet, Herbert. *Eisenhower and the American Crusades.* New York: Macmillan, 1972.

Payne, Walter. "The Guatemalan Revolution, 1944–1954." *Pacific Historian,* Vol. 17 (Spring 1973).

Pentagon Papers (12 volumes). Washington: Government Printing Office, 1971.

Pentagon Papers, as published by the New York *Times.* Toronto: Quadrangle Books, 1971.

Phillips, David. *Night Watch: Twenty Years of Peculiar Service.* New York: Atheneum, 1977.

Pogue, Forrest C. *The Supreme Command.* Washington: Department of the Army, 1954.

Powers, Francis Gary. *Operation Overflight.* New York: Holt, Rinehart & Winston, 1970.

Powers, Thomas. *The Man Who Kept the Secrets: Richard Helms and the CIA.* New York: Knopf, 1979.

Report by the Supreme Commander to the CCS on Operations in Europe of the Allied Expeditionary Force. London, 1946.

Roosevelt, Kermit. *Countercoup: The Struggle for Control of Iran.* New York: McGraw-Hill, 1979.

Rosengarten, Adolph G., Jr. "With Ultra from Omaha Beach to Weimar Germany—A Personal View." *Military Affairs,* Vol. XLII (October 1978).

Rosfelder, Roger. *Today in France,* No. 99 (January 1972).

Rositzke, Harry. *The CIA's Secret Operations: Espionage, Counterespionage, and Covert Action.* New York: Reader's Digest Press, 1977.

Ryan, Cornelius. *A Bridge Too Far.* New York: Simon & Schuster, 1977.

———. *The Last Battle.* New York: Simon & Schuster, 1966.

Schlesinger, Stephen. "How Dulles Worked the Coup d'Etat." *The Nation,* Vol. 227 (October 28, 1978).

Severeid, Eric. "CBS Reports: The Hot and Cold Wars of Allen Dulles." CBS-TV, April 26, 1962.

Smith, Richard Harris. *OSS: The Secret History of America's First Central Intelligence Agency.* Berkeley: University of California Press, 1972.

Stagg, J. M. *Forecast for Overlord.* New York: Norton, 1971.

Stern, S. and Radosh, R. "The Hidden Rosenberg Case." New Republic, Vol. 180 (June 23, 1979).

Strauss, Lewis. *Men and Decisions.* Garden City, N.Y.: Doubleday, 1962.

Strong, Sir Kenneth. *Intelligence at the Top: The Recollections of an Intelligence Officer.* London: Cassell, 1968.

Taylor, Edmond. *Awakening From History.* Boston: Gambit, 1969.

Tedder, Arthur W. *With Prejudice: The War Memoirs of Marshall of the Royal Air Force, Lord Tedder.* London: Cassell, 1966.

Tompkins, Peter. *The Murder of Admiral Darlan: A Study in Conspiracy.* New York: Simon & Schuster, 1965.

Tully, Andrew. *The CIA: The Inside Story.* New York: Morrow, 1962.

United States Department of State. *American Foreign Policy, 1950–1955, Basic Documents, I.* Washington: Government Printing Office, 1957.

———. *Foreign Relations of the United States.* Washington: Government Printing Office, 1970.

———. *Tenth Inter-American Conference.* Washington: Government Printing Office, 1954.

United States House of Representatives, Committee on Foreign Affairs, 92d Congress, 2d Session (October 10, 1972). *Inter-American Affairs.* Washington: Government Printing Office, 1972.

———. Subcommittee on Latin America of the Select Committee on Communist Aggression. *Ninth Interim Report, Communist Aggression in Latin America.* Washington: Government Printing Office, 1954.

United States Military Academy, Department of Military Art and Engineering. *West Point Atlas of American Wars,* Vol. II. New York: 1959.

United States Senate. *Final Report of the Select Committee to Study Governmental Operations with Respect to Intelligence Activities* (Church Committee Report), Senate Report 94-755, 94th Congress, 2nd Session. Washington: Government Printing Office, 1974.

———. *Hearing Before the Committee on Armed Services on Francis Gary Powers,* 87th Congress, 2d Session, March 6, 1962. Washington: Government Printing Office, 1962.

Unna, Warren. "CIA: Who Watches the Watchman?" *Harper's Magazine,* Vol. 216 (April 1, 1958).

Walters, Vernon. *Silent Missions.* Garden City, N.Y.: Doubleday, 1978.

Warlimont, Walter. *Inside Hitler's Headquarters.* New York: Praeger, 1964.

Winterbotham, F. W. *The Ultra Secret.* New York: Harper & Row, 1975.

Wise, David, and Ross, Thomas. *The Invisible Government.* New York: Random House, 1964.

Wyden, Peter. *Bay of Pigs: The Untold Story.* New York: Simon & Schuster, 1979.

Ydígoras Fuentes, Miguel. *My War With Communism.* Englewood Cliffs, N.J.: Prentice-Hall, 1965.

Ziemke, Karl. "Operation Kreml: Deception, Strategy, and the Fortunes of War." *Parameters; Journal of the U. S. Army War College,* Vol. IX (March 1979).

Zonis, Marvin. *The Political Elite of Iran.* Princeton, N.J.: Princeton University Press, 1971.

ACKNOWLEDGMENTS

SAM VAUGHAN of Doubleday had the idea for this book. He and his assistant, Betty Heller, provided guidance, counsel, sympathy, and understanding as the work proceeded. I cannot thank them enough.

The staff of the University of New Orleans library provided me with expert, professional help at every turn. I am also grateful for assistance from the Eisenhower Library in Abilene, Kansas, the New York Public Library, and the Library of Congress. The staff at the Modern Military Branch of the National Archives in Washington, D.C., was superb. Without the aid of that staff, the World War II sections of this book could not have been written. I am especially in the debt of Mr. John Taylor of the Archives.

When I was just beginning to write the World War II section, I had the great good luck to meet Dr. Richard Immerman of Princeton University. Immerman had just finished his dissertation on the CIA in Guatemala in 1954. He was working with Professor Fred Greenstein at Princeton on a major project to reassess the Eisenhower presidency. On a beautiful Fourth of July, 1979, at Princeton, I discovered in a six-hour nonstop conversation with Immerman that here was a brilliant young historian who knew the sources for the Eisenhower era as well as anyone in the country.

I asked Immerman if I could use his Guatemala material, especially the Howard Hunt interviews. He readily agreed. A few days later, back home in New Orleans, I realized that I had dozens of questions for Immerman. I therefore asked him if he would collaborate with me. To the great benefit of the book, he agreed.

Immerman was the first researcher to go through, in a systematic and professional manner, the recently opened Eisenhower papers in Abilene, covering the presidential and retirement years. The fruits of his hundreds of hours of research include, among other items (all printed here for the first time), the quotations from Eisenhower's private diary, the notes of the meetings of the National Security Council, the summaries of telephone conversations, General Goodpaster's notes on various informal meetings in the White House, and Ike's private correspondence with his closest friends.

Immerman made an equally valuable and essential contribution through his interviews. He had previously interviewed Richard Bissell and Howard Hunt on Guatemala; he returned, as my collaborator, tape recorder in hand. He interviewed a number of others; as all the subjects can testify, he is an intelligent and probing interviewer who is adept at getting his subjects to relax and tell the full story.

Some might say my writing habits are a bit extreme. When writing a book, I normally get up at 3 A.M. and write until 8 A.M. I go to bed immediately after dinner. Such a schedule disrupts the household regime, to say the least, especially with five teen-agers in the house and a wife finishing her M.A. and beginning her teaching career.

Moira and the children were models of patience and understanding. Without their support, I couldn't do the work. Without their love, it wouldn't be worth doing.

STEPHEN E. AMBROSE
New Orleans
December 19, 1979

INDEX

ALSO BY STEPHEN E. AMBROSE

CRAZY HORSE AND CUSTER
The Parallel Lives of Two American Warriors

On the sparkling morning of June 25, 1876, 611 U.S. Army soldiers rode toward the banks of the Little Bighorn in the Montana Territory, where 3,000 Indians stood waiting to battle. The lives of two great warriors would soon be forever linked throughout history: Crazy Horse, leader of the Oglala Sioux, and General George Armstrong Custer of the Seventh Cavalry. Both were men of aggression and supreme courage. Both had become leaders in their societies at very early ages; both had been stripped of power, and in disgrace had worked to earn back the respect of their people. And to both of them, the unspoiled grandeur of the Great Plains of North America was an irresistible challenge. Their parallel lives would pave the way, in a manner unknown to either, for an inevitable clash between two nations fighting for possession of the open prairie.

American Studies/History

ALSO AVAILABLE
The Supreme Commander, Biography/History

ANCHOR BOOKS
Available wherever books are sold.
www.randomhouse.com